Henri Troyat was born a Russian (Lev Trassov), but was educated in France. He is a member of the French Academy and in 1938 he won the Prix Goncourt. He has written many other works: biographies, an epic series of novels about Russia, short stories, historical essays and travel books.

Also by Henri Troyat

Gogol: The Biography of a Divided Soul
Pushkin: A Biography
Tolstoy

Fiction
Daily Life in Russia under the Last Czar
La Neige en Deuil
La Tête sur les Epaules

Henri Troyat

of the French Academy

Catherine the Great

Translated by Emily Read

A PANTHER BOOK

GRANADA

London Toronto Sydney New York

Published by Granada Publishing Limited in 1981

ISBN 0 586 05301 8

First published in Great Britain by
Aidan Ellis Publishing Limited 1979
Copyright © Flammarion 1977
English translation copyright © Aidan Ellis 1978

Granada Publishing Limited
Frogmore, St Albans, Herts AL2 2NF
and
3 Upper James Street, London W1R 4BP
866 United Nations Plaza, New York, NY 10017, USA
117 York Street, Sydney, NSW 2000, Australia
100 Skyway Avenue, Rexdale, Ontario, M9W 3A6, Canada
PO Box 84165, Greenside, 2034 Johannesburg, South Africa
61 Beach Road, Auckland, New Zealand

Printed and bound in Great Britain by
Richard Clay (The Chaucer Press) Ltd, Bungay, Suffolk
Set in Plantin
Phototypesetting by Georgia Origination, Liverpool

Granada®
Granada Publishing®

The majority of the text – letters, reports,
memoirs – quoted in this work were written by Russian authors
in French, the common language during Catherine's
time. I have reproduced them without correcting
the errors in style and syntax in order to keep the
feeling of another time, the harshness of the style,
the piquancy and the authenticity.

H.T.

Contents

CHAPTER I

Figchen

They had hoped for a boy but it was a girl. The future Catherine II of Russia was born on 21 April, 1729, at Stettin in Pomerania and was given the names Sophia Frederica Augusta. Her young mother, Johanna-Elisabeth, was sorry not to have been able to give birth to a boy and did not take to the baby. She was anyway convinced that with her beauty and worldly wisdom she could have attained a higher position in life. Born Holstein Gottorp, was she not related after all to the ducal house of Holstein whose senior branch could make claims to the Swedish crown?[1] But instead of the brilliant future she had dreamed of, she had been obliged to settle for a more modest match. Her family had arranged it without consulting her, and at the age of fifteen she was married to Prince Christian-Augustus of Anhalt-Zerbst – a man twenty-seven years older than she was. He was, undeniably, an unimportant figure – one of those obscure, impoverished princes who swarmed over the fragmented Germany of the Eighteenth Century. Then a major-general in the Prussian Army, and a pillar of order, economy and religion, this worthy man overwhelmed Johanna with affection, but for her it was not enough. She loved worldly intrigue, and fumed at her low place in society. Garrison life in the depths of the provinces seemed to her humiliatingly monotonous. Luckily, soon after Sophia's birth, the family were able to move into the fortress at Stettin. It was a sort of promotion. Another auspicious event took place in the following year when Johanna at last gave birth to a boy. God had heard her prayers. She felt for the new baby all the affection and pride which she had

---

[1] Some historians maintain that Sophie, the future Catherine II, was in fact the illegitimate daughter of Frederic II of Prussia, who, at the time, was only heir presumptive and a mere sixteen-years old! Others, no less ingenious, have given her Count Ivan Betsky for a father. These assertions are not backed by any authoritative documents and arise from the naïve view that a person as exceptional as Catherine II could not have come from ordinary parentage.

denied her daughter. Sophia, still very small, suffered bitterly at seeing her younger brother preferred to herself [1].

Entrusted at first to wet nurses, the children soon passed into the hands of governesses. There might not have been enough sheets at the castle but one's position in society came first. The family was surrounded by tutors, dancing masters, music masters, ladies-in-waiting, gentlemen of the bedchamber and a variety of servants with ill-defined duties. Because the Anhalt-Zerbsts were princes it was important that the youngest members of the family should, despite their poverty and obscurity, be initiated into the customs of the European courts. As soon as they were able to move without becoming entangled in their finery, they were taught to curtsey and to kiss devoutly the edge of a grandee's robes. Very early on Johanna made Sophie absorb the atmosphere of the drawing-room. She dragged her to the balls, banquets and masquerades which were given from time to time by important local families. Dressed as a woman despite her age, as fashion then demanded, 'Figchen' as Sophie was nicknamed, already astonished her entourage by the quickness of her repartee. In a panelled dress, with an open neckline over a flat chest, her angular arms sticking out of lace sleeves and her hair powdered, she once found herself at a reception in front of Frederick William the First of Prussia: quite unabashed, she refused to kiss the edge of the royal coat. 'His coat is so short that I can't reach it,' she cried to explain her behaviour. The king remarked severely: 'An impertinent child.' She was then four years old. Johanna concluded from this incident that her daughter was an arrogant rebel, and that nothing would ever intimidate her. It was, she thought, a characteristic which would have to be fought in this child since her future must lie in marriage – or in other words in submission to a husband. She became therefore more and more strict with her daughter and affectionate towards her son. 'For my part,' Catherine was to write in her *Memoirs*, 'my existence was only tolerated: often, and sometimes unjustly, I was violently told off.' And again, 'My father whom I saw less often, thought me an angel; my mother did not care much about me.' [2]

Her mother's coldness and her father's aloofness (he seemed so

---

[1] Her first brother, Wilhelm-Christian-Frederic, born in 1730, died in 1742; her second brother, Frederic-Auguste, born in 1734, died in 1793; her sister, Elisabeth-Augusta-Christine, born in 1742, died in 1745.

[2] Catherine started writing the first version of the *Memoirs*, in French, on 21st April 1771, when she was forty-two years old. Other versions followed. The writing broke off abruptly during the events of 1759. The complete *Memoirs* were published in 1953, painstakingly edited by Mme Dominique Maroger with a preface by Pierre Audiat.

dignified, austere and preoccupied) only increased her thirst for love. This need for affection and adulation was made stronger by her belief that she was ugly. In her early childhood she had suffered from impetigo, and her hair had had to be cut off several times in order to remove the scabs. At seven she nearly died of pleurisy. When she was in a fit state to get up, they noticed that her spine was crooked. 'My right shoulder had become higher than the left one, the spine went in a zig-zag, and there was a hollow in my left side.' The doctors declared themselves baffled by this mysterious deformation, so they called in a bone-setter who turned out to be none other than the Stettin executioner. Without hesitation this terrifying man ordered that every morning before six a girl with an empty stomach should come and rub the child's back and shoulders with her saliva. Then he made her a corset which she was not allowed to remove by day or by night except to change her linen. This torture lasted for almost four years. At last, when the little girl was eleven, her back straightened, her health improved, and happiness and strength returned.

However, although her constitution was stronger, she was still plain. She had a long nose, a pointed chin, and was as thin as a flayed cat; and she knew already that these physical imperfections would handicap her in the marriage stakes. But equally she had noticed that she could charm people with her sparkling look and quick wit – more perhaps than somebody with perfect features. This discovery made her concentrate upon reading and studying. Her governess Elisabeth (or Babet) Cardel was a crucial influence in this respect. She was French, the daughter of a Huguenot who had taken refuge in Germany after the repeal of the Edict of Nantes, and according to the child 'she knew practically everything without having learnt it'. Sophie does not stint her praise in the *Memoirs*. 'A model of virtue and wisdom; her soul was naturally elevated, her mind cultivated, her heart excellent; she was patient, gentle, gay, just, steadfast . . . ' Her enthusiasm for Babet was to remain so lively that even in her old age, writing to Voltaire, she was to pride herself on the title of 'pupil of Mlle. Cardel'.

In fact Mlle. Cardel's teaching covered everything: between two dictations she would advise Sophie to always hold in her chin: 'She found it excessively sharp and said that if I let it stick out I would hit whomever I met.' Mlle. Cardel broadened her mind simply by making her read Corneille, Racine, Molière and La Fontaine. She communicated to Sophie her love of the French language, at that time a prerequisite for the educated upper-classes; with this the child developed a taste for wit and speed both in writing and in conversation, so much so that, by contrast, she began to hate Herr Wagner, her heavy and pedantic German teacher. She felt at times, that her mother-tongue originated not in Berlin, but in Paris. Of course she had many other tutors, amongst them a Lutheran pastor named Dowe who gave her her first insights into religion and theology. The child, instead of simply accepting what she was told, wanted to understand and asked embarrassing questions. Why were good men such as Marcus Aurelius or Titus doomed for mere ignorance of the revelation? What was original chaos? What was circumcision? How could one reconcile the infinite goodness of God with the terrible ordeal of the Last Judgment? The pastor became angry, refused to answer and threatened his pupil with the cane: Babet Cardel had to intervene to calm the storm. What worried the pastor most were the little girl's efforts to seek for rational explanations to the holy dogmas. He saw in this a manifestation of the sin of pride. He had to admit, however, that apart from this, his pupil was well-behaved, conscientious and gifted with both an exceptional memory and a readiness to absorb learning in bulk. Of all the tutors who took part in Figchen's education, only the music teacher was disappointed: she had no ear and the sweetest of harmonies were lost on her. This distaste was to remain with her throughout her life. 'Rarely has music been anything other than noise to my ears,' she was to say.

After a day's work with Mlle. Cardel, Sophie desperately needed to work off her excess energy. She hated playing with dolls, unlike other girls of her age: she was bored by the idea of simpering around a painted wooden baby, and was not disposed to play the little mother around a miniature cradle. She was only interested in action and movement. Her parents, in spite of their princely position, allowed her to invite the children of the local bourgeoisie into the grim castle of Stettin: the courtyard echoed with laughter and squeals. Sometimes the whole gang would spill into the street. Figchen loved violent games and even shot birds; this wild and inventive tomboy eagerly took command of the little group around her, and they in turn readily acknowledged her leadership.

But she preferred travelling to these childish entertainments, and her mother was so bored at Stettin, and starved of worldly pleasures that any pretext was a good one if it enabled her to escape with her husband and children. There were so many families in Germany related either to the Anhalt-Zerbsts or the Holstein Gottorps that invitations flooded in: they went from castle to castle, to Zerbst, Hamburg, Brunswick, Entin, Kiel and even Berlin. Everywhere they found friendly relations, very little comfort, and an atmosphere filled with court gossip: by listening to these conversations Figchen learnt the genealogy of all the kings and princes of Europe, and she felt that she was part of a vast brotherhood where blood ties transcended frontiers. Thus a little German princess was closer to an unknown Swedish prince than to a neighbouring German commoner. She felt instinctively before having had the slightest hint of her fate, that she belonged with those who rule rather than those who obey; her vocation came long before its fulfilment. In 1739, her parents took her to Kiel to attend a party given by her mother's cousin, Adolphe Frederick of Holstein Gottorp[1]. Johanna, who was proud of belonging to one of the greatest families in Germany, particularly regretted her mediocre marriage when she found herself among them; and her stubborn, superficial heart would flutter whenever her ten year old daughter was seen exchanging a few words with the possible heir to the thrones of Sweden or Russia – Peter Ulrick of Holstein.

This boy, who was a year older than Figchen, was small, sickly and deformed; his conversation was disappointing – he had not read anything and was only interested in military manoeuvres. But he was Peter the Great's grandson. This fact gave him a sort of halo, and mothers of marriageable daughters – amongst them Johanna – ogled him with deferential greed. Figchen overheard conspiratorial whisperings as these women calculated, on the sly, the chances of a union between the two children – after all were they not third cousins through the Holsteins? Figchen began to daydream: according to the family code, her birth forbade her to marry a young man, no matter how charming, whose quarterings were insufficient. Her poverty and plainness might repel serious suitors, and there was a large choice of European princesses, certainly enough to satisfy all tastes and political leanings. With detachment, Figchen saw that she held very few trump cards in this silent contest for thrones. And yet she believed in her luck and felt that, with a strong character, one only needed to want something badly enough to get it in the end. Even physical grace – one could become beautiful by sheer will-power. When she left Peter Ulrick, she felt regenerated. Indeed the reflection she saw in the mirror appeared more and more agreeable, and sometimes even surprised her with actual beauty. 'The extreme ugliness I had possessed was disappearing,' she was to write. At thirteen she was slim and well proportioned. Her dark eyes sparkled so that she forgot the long nose and the pointed chin. One day she heard her father's steward saying about the marriage of Princess Augusta of Saxe-Gotha to the Prince of Wales: 'Well, really, that princess had a much worse upbringing than ours; she isn't beautiful either and yet there she is destined to be Queen

[1] Future king of Sweden.

of England, who knows what ours will become?' Another time at Brunswick, at the dowager duchess' home, a visionary canon who practised palmistry asserted that he saw three crowns in Figchen's palm. The child took the prediction very seriously. 'Child that I was,' she was to write, 'the title of queen delighted me. From then on my companions teased me about him (the young Peter Ulrick of Holstein) and little by little I became used to thinking of myself as destined for him.'

Thus, as the months passed, the thought of Russia came to the minds of both mother and daughter. This parallel dream was based on the blood link which connected the Russian Imperial family to the house of Holstein, of which Johanna proclaimed herself a part. Peter the Great's eldest daughter, Anne, had married Duke Charles-Frederick of Holstein Gottorp and had had as a son, the Peter Ulrick whom Figchen met at Kiel. His second daughter, Elisabeth, had been engaged to one of Johanna's brothers, the young and charming Charles-Augustus of Holstein Gottorp. He died of smallpox shortly after the engagement and it was said that this premature death had left Elisabeth inconsolable. Indeed her sexually licentious behaviour since had only been a way of forgetting him. Deprived of the young prince to whom she had wished to devote her life she never married and continued to keep up affectionate relations with the dead man's family.

Suddenly on the 6th of December, 1741, there was a thunderbolt: the inconsolable fiancée of Charles-Augustus had, by one of Russia's frequent palace revolutions, put an end to the reign of the little Ivan of Brunswick, and to his mother's regency. Elisabeth I, daughter of Peter the Great, was on the throne of Russia. Johanna thought rapturously that, but for the cursed smallpox which had brought down her brother, she would now be sister-in-law of an empress. She immediately wrote to the Tsarina to congratulate her and to assure her of her devotion, and received a friendly reply. The following month, there was another surprise: the Empress brought the young Peter Ulrick from Kiel to St Petersburg and proclaimed him as her heir. Now at last Russia seemed closer to Stettin: Holstein blood, the blood of Figchen's own mother, was a part of the general triumph. Figchen herself took a lively interest in these faraway events. It sometimes seemed to her that occult powers were gathering behind her.

In July 1742 King Frederick of Prussia elevated Figchen's father to the rank of field-marshal – was it a coincidence or the result of a mysterious promotion on the European chessboard? In September Figchen's mother received, from a secretary at the Russian embassy, a portrait of the Tsarina in a diamond-encrusted frame. At the end of the year Figchen was taken by her mother to Berlin to pose for the excellent French painter Antoine Pesne. The artist's brief was to obtain a likeness, at the same time imparting as much gracefulness as possible. This sweetly ingratiating portrait was intended to give the Empress Elisabeth some clues as to the young girl's physical attributes. It went on its way to St Petersburg, and the model returned to Stettin. Meanwhile General Korf and another gentleman from the Russian court, Count Sievers, had asked to see the little princess in order to make their report in high places. They took a second portrait away in their luggage. All these upheavals upset Figchen very much: more and more she felt herself merely a weak stake in some vast diplomatic game: 'It worried me and in my own mind I determined to marry him (Peter Ulrick) because he was the most considerable match of all those suggested.' In order to be patient she told herself that no doubt she had many rivals and that zealous ambassadors were sending to St Petersburg portraits of all the noblest marriageable young ladies of Europe. She imagined the Empress frowning, hesitating before a gallery of fifty smiling beauties, each vying with the other on canvas. But in her dreams the canon's prediction always overcame these gloomy thoughts. As if to encourage her optimistic forecasts, the elder branch of the Anhalts died out and her father and uncle became joint reigning princes. This strengthened the family in the race for the crown. Although Figchen thought about this crown by night and by day, she never worried about what was beneath it – it did not matter to her that Peter Ulrick was graceless and stupid; love had no bearing on her calculations for the future. She was interested in the throne, and not the bed.

And yet at thirteen she already showed signs of robust sensuality. Neither Babet Cardel, nor her mother, nor any of those around her had enlightened her on the subject of physical relationships. Yet she often felt sudden blazes of desire, vague feelings of tenderness, and a need for carnal contact which she could not explain. At night expecially she was seized with frenzy. Then she would get astride her pillow, and, as she was to write later, would 'gallop' in her bed 'until (her) strength was exhausted'. These nocturnal rides would calm her agitated nerves. When the excitement had passed she became once again a good child who thought not of love but of her career. She deserved credit for this as one of her uncles, Georges Louis, was captivated by the bloom of this adolescent, who was hardly more than a child, and had begun to court her. He was ten years older than her, and he stunned her with his passionate declarations, dragging her far from her parents to steal light kisses. She was flattered and allowed him to do this – surely this was proof that she could attract a man other than her father! Peter Ulrick should not be harder to please than her uncle Georges Louis. But the weeks passed and the Russian court remained silent. Georges Louis, for his part, driven mad by the young girl's reticence and without any thought, asked her to marry him. Their kinship was not a problem as brides of this sort were common amongst the high European aristocracy, but Figchen was reluctant to abandon her Russian dream in favour of the German reality. 'My father and mother won't allow it,' she said. Then she pretended to accept 'on the condition that my parents have no objection'. The uncle's kisses now became more passionate. But she was to assert, 'give or take a few embraces, everything remained quite innocent.' Georges Louis restrained himself in the hope that time would work in his favour, and Figchen allowed these childish games thinking that they wouldn't last and that the longed-for call from the north would soon arrive.

On the 1st January 1744 the whole family were gathered at Zerbst around the table celebrating the New Year, when a courier arrived from Berlin and presented Prince Christian-Augustus with a packet of letters. The prince sorted through it and held out to his wife an envelope with the following address on it: 'Personal! Very urgent! To the high-ranking and well-born Princess Johanna-Elisabeth of Anhalt-Zerbst in her castle at Zerbst.'

Johanna broke the seals, began to read and was overcome by happy agitation. The letter was written by Brümmer, the Grand Marshal, at the court of Grand Duke Peter Ulrick at St Petersburg. 'By the special and express order of Her Imperial Majesty the Empress Elisabeth Petrovna, I have to inform you, Madam, that this August Sovereign wishes that Your Highness, accompanied by the Princess, your eldest daughter, should journey as soon as possible and without losing time to this country, to whichever town the Imperial Court is residing in... Your Highness is too enlightened not to understand the true eagerness with which Her Majesty awaits you here, as well as the Princess of whom she had heard such fine things...'

This very long letter specified that under no circumstances could Johanna be accompanied by her husband, and that her entourage should only consist of one lady-in-waiting, two lady's maids, one officer, one cook and three or four footmen. She was also ordered to keep their destination a secret. The expenses of the journey would of course be met by the Empress: a draft of ten thousand roubles on a Berlin bank was affixed to the letter. It was not a lot, but it was important said Brümmer not to make the expedition too splendid, in order to avoid attention from ill-disposed people. Once in Russia of course, the

Princess and her daughter would be treated with all the consideration due to their rank.

Johanna's agitation as she read the letter was such that Figchen, sitting next to her, was able to glance stealthily at the letter. The words 'accompanied by the Princess your eldest daughter,' leapt up. She understood immediately that her destiny was taking its course. But Johanna had no intention of taking her daughter into her confidence. She left the table and retired with her husband for a private conversation. Not two hours later a second courier galloped up bringing this time a letter from King Frederick of Prussia. If Brümmer had not made clear the reason for the imperial invitation, then Frederick revealed it.

'I will not conceal the fact that since I have an especially high esteem for you and the Princess your daughter, I have always hoped to arrange for her an especially high fortune. Thus I have often wondered whether it would not be possible to marry her to her third cousin, the Grand Duke of Russia...'

Johanna re-read this sentence ten times in order to fully take in its importance. Her heart beat with inordinate pride and yet she was worried. After all, for the moment, it was only a wish of Frederick's. The Empress had not sent an official proposal of marriage, only an invitation to come and see her. Figchen was requested at the Court of Russia in order to be tried out. If the trial was not conclusive she would be sent back to Germany and the shame of this failed match would rebound on her whole family. Figchen's father was even more apprehensive: if Figchen was accepted, she would no doubt, in order to marry the Grand Duke, have to convert to the Russian Orthodox faith. And that Christian-Augustus, as a convinced Lutheran, could not allow. And even if, by some extraordinary exception, she were allowed to keep her faith, what would her life be like in that faraway and barbarous country? How could one trust the Empress Elisabeth, when she had just imprisoned a German princess, Anne of Brunswick, and her son, the little Tsar Ivan? By becoming the daughter-in-law of this omnipotent, violent and profligate sovereign, Figchen was surely embarking on a tragic career. What one heard about the morals of the Russian court was enough, thought Christian-Augustus, to make the most ambitious parent draw back in horror. Johanna agreed that there was food for thought there. But surely, she retorted, when one was a princess of Anhalt-Zerbst, one had no right to refuse a marriage that served the interests of the country? Once she was the mother-in-law of the Grand Duke, she could work behind the scenes for better relations between Russia and Prussia. She saw a political future for herself, using the fragile personality of a girl of fourteen. She had suffered so much from her obscure life in this provincial backwater – now at last she would be able to give full rein to her diplomatic skills. King Frederick of Prussia had implied it in his letter. He had written to her, not Christian-Augustus, so he obviously considered her to be the real head of the family. Thus, tossed between fear and enthusiasm, Figchen's parents talked endlessly and fruitlessly. Held apart from these discussions, and suspecting their content, the girl resented not being consulted in something that concerned her so closely. For three days she observed the general agitation, overheard whispers, and watched faces to try and find out which way the wind was blowing. Then when her patience was exhausted she went to her mother and said that all the mystery surrounding this famous letter was absurd as she knew perfectly well what it was about. 'Well, miss,' said her mother, 'since you're so knowledgeable, why don't you guess what the rest of this twelve-page business letter contains?' That afternoon Figchen gave her mother a piece of paper on which she had written in large letters:

>   *All an omen*
>   *That Peter III will be your husband!*

Taken by surprise, Johanna regarded her daughter with admiration mingled with fear and, to relieve her conscience, told her about the unruly customs of the Russians. Nothing was certain there, the most important person might find himself from one day to the next, in prison or in Siberia, and political life went from *coup d'état* to *coup d'état*, from one pool of blood to another. Figchen replied firmly that she was not afraid of chaos, and that God would help her in this move. When she had fixed her mind on something, a thunderbolt would not have made her turn back. 'My heart tells me that everything will turn out well,' she concluded. Her mother then murmured, embarrassed, 'but what will my brother Georges say?' So she knew about the romance between Figchen and her uncle! It was the first time she had alluded to it to her daughter. Unmasked, Figchen blushed and answered: 'He can only wish for my future and my happiness!' She had never for a second considered weighing the 'bashful suitor' against the Grand Duke Peter. The prospect of one day reigning over twenty million subjects was easily worth the sacrifice of a childish flirtation. She coldly told her mother this; the latter, shaken, asked her to keep their conversation secret.

It remained to them to convince Christian-Augustus, who obstinately refused any thought of his child changing her faith. Johanna led this battle: she argued so well that in the end her husband gave in. However he kept for himself the right to give Figchen precise instructions on how to conduct herself in Russia in both court and religious matters. Having torn her husband's consent from him, Johanna forced him then and there to write a letter of acceptance in the proper form which she handed to the courier to take, post-haste, to Berlin. Then she began the preparations. It was put about in the castle and the neighbourhood that there was a simple pleasure trip being prepared. But the servants' curiosity was aroused by the coming and going of messengers, the serious expressions on the masters' faces and the importance given to the luggage. A marriage was in the air. Would the beloved Mlle. Cardel be a part of the entourage? No. She would remain at Zerbst. The only people going were M. de Lattdorf, Mlle. de Kayn, four maids, a footman, a cook and several orderlies. Babet Cardel was miserable and begged her pupil to at least tell her the object of the expedition. Figchen remained immovable despite her beloved governess' tears. It seemed to her that the future wife of a Grand Duke should be able to hold her tongue under any circumstances. By remaining silent before Babet Cardel, she felt that she was already learning to guard State secrets. When the governess, after crying, became angry and accused her of not trusting her, and even of not loving her, Figchen replied with dignity that she had given her word, and that, for her, principles would always be stronger than sentiment.

On the 10th of January, nine days after the invitation had reached the castle, Prince Christian-Augustus, Johanna and Figchen set out on their way. The prince's fatherly pride had been mortified at his not being invited to Russia and he insisted at least on accompanying them as far as Berlin. There, to comply with the King of Prussia's wishes, they made a short stop. As an organizer of matrimonial transactions, Frederick II wanted to see the Grand Duke's future fiancée, so as to form his own opinion as to her chances of pleasing him, and her mother so as to give her instructions on the secret role she was to play at the Russian Court. Johanna was enchanted with the prospect of being able, one day, with the help of her beauty and her skill, to pull the strings of European politics – so much so indeed that she almost considered herself the most important member of the trio. Her main worry, for the moment however, was the matter of the wardrobe. Christian-Augustus with his usual meanness had refused to embark on any expenditure. In any case there wasn't time to assemble a trousseau suitable for the two travellers. Johanna only possessed two court dresses – a mockery! As for Figchen she was setting out for the future of her dreams without a single ceremonial outfit in the luggage. 'Two or three dresses, a dozen shirts, and as many stockings and handkerchiefs' made up the entire wardrobe of the Grand Duke's future fiancée. It was true that the Empress was, they said, very generous. At St Petersburg the mother and daughter would lack for nothing. But how to appear in Berlin without losing face? Christian-Augustus was sunk in gloom oblivious of these coquettish preoccupations. His daughter was reaching for the stars, whilst he pondered on his humiliations and worries. Before they got into the coach he solemnly handed Figchen Heineccius' treatise denouncing the errors of the Greek Orthodox religion, and an exercise book filled by his own hand, and inscribed *'Pro Memoria'*. In this text, hurriedly written for the daughter who might be leaving him for ever, he wondered whether it would not be possible 'by some arrangement' for her to marry the Grand Duke without abandoning the Lutheran faith. He advised her as well to be respectful and compliant towards influential people in her own country, never to thwart the Prince's wishes, never to confide in 'any lady' of the entourage, and never to become involved in government affairs 'so as not to embitter the Senate'. He had already given this advice several times out loud to her, and Figchen at the time had acknowledged its wisdom. Would she put it into practice once she was there? She didn't know, nor did she want to think about it. Everything that was happening to her seemed like a fairy-tale. Shut up in the carriage between her elated mother and her gloomy father, she could hardly believe that she had really left behind Babet Cardel, her exercise books, her playmates, her whole childhood, and that she was travelling, very bumpily, towards that future of intrigue, glory and power that she had dreamed of for so long.

CHAPTER II

On the Way

King Frederick II of Prussia had come to the throne four years earlier at
the death of his father, Frederick William I, the terrifying 'Sergeant-
King' and reorganizer of the army. The new ruler, who was thirty-two
years old, quickly gained the esteem of the German princes through his
enlightened spirit, great culture, energy and political judgment. He was
conscious of the threats that Russia to the north and Austria to the east
represented to his country and accordingly searched unremittingly for an
accord with Russia. The Empress Elisabeth, however, under the
influence of Chancellor Bestuzhev, had declared herself to be anti-
Prussian. When the subject of finding a fiancée for the Grand Duke
Peter Ulrick arose, the Tsarina's entourage was in an uproar. The
Bestuzhev clique insisted that the Empress should choose a Saxon
princess, Mariana, second daughter of the King of Poland; this would
have united Russia, Saxony, Austria, England and Holland, in other
words three-quarters of Europe, against Prussia and France. The
opposing French faction directed from a distance by Frederick of
Prussia tried to make this match fail. Obviously Frederick could have
suggested his own sister, Princess Ulrica, as most suitable a match, but
he refused to make such a sacrifice. 'Nothing could have been more
unnatural,' he was to write, 'than to sacrifice a royal princess of Prussia
simply in order to oust a Saxon.' On the other hand, the little princess
Sophie of Anhalt-Zerbst seemed like a good candidate to him. She was
neither too perceptive nor too dim; her parents wouldn't get in the way:
he launched her on the market. Brümmer, the Grand Duke's German
tutor, and the French Lestocq took it upon themselves to impress the
Tsarina with the advantage of this solution.

Elisabeth agreed that Sophie, coming from a minor family, would no
doubt be more compliant than someone of higher birth. Antoine
Pesne's portrait revealed a healthy and attractive girl. And finally she
was descended from the Holstein line, so dear to the Empress since the
death of her fiancé Charles-Augustus. If it had not been for that tragic
loss, Sophie would now be her niece. Peter Ulrick was her nephew – it
was all a family affair. So she ordered Brümmer to convey an invitation

to Johanna and her daughter. Frederick II had won the first round, but that did not mean that the matter was settled. Would this little Sophie be a worthy bearer of all Russia's hopes? As soon as the travellers arrived, the King asked to see the child. Johanna, in a panic, sent word that Sophie was ill. This happened again on the second and third days. The King became impatient and refused to believe the excuse. Why was his 'candidate' being kept from him? Was she ugly? Lacking in spirit? When pressed, Johanna finally admitted that there was one major obstacle to her presenting her daughter: she had no court dress. The King immediately had one of his sister's dresses sent round. Figchen, trembling, got dressed and rushed to the palace where the guests were already assembled, awaiting her arrival. She was used to drawing-rooms, but here the stakes were so high that she could hardly control her heart-beat. Frederick II came to meet her in the antechamber and his face lit up at the sight of this slender child with shining eyes. She curtseyed to him, very shyly, and this shyness only added to her grace. After a few words with her Frederick decided that he had made the right choice. The meal went on for a long time. When they rose, Prince Ferdinand of Brunswick, the Queen's brother, told Sophie that she was invited to sup at the King's table that very evening. She immediately told her mother who said crossly, 'That is very strange as I have been invited to the Queen's table!' Johanna could not understand that, at this juncture, the King was more interested in her daughter than in herself. She was, after all, the brain, whereas Figchen was merely a pawn on the chess board. Her surprise turned to amazement that evening at supper when she saw that not only was Figchen at the King's table but she was also next to the King himself. At first paralysed by this intimidating proximity, Figchen soon became bolder and kept up the conversation with liveliness and tact. To put her at her ease Frederick asked a lot of questions. 'He asked me a thousand things, talked of the opera, the theatre, poetry, ballet, goodness knows what, anyway a thousand things one could talk about to a fourteen year old ... The rest of the company was amazed to see His Majesty deep in conversation with a child.' Blooming in her lovely borrowed dress, with pink cheeks and a beating heart, Figchen felt that all eyes were upon her. As if to consecrate her triumph, the King asked her to pass a dish of preserves to a gentleman standing behind his chair, and said to him in a loud voice! 'Receive this gift from the hands of Love and Grace.' This compliment, spoken in public by the King of Prussia, thrilled Figchen. She was to remember it, word for word, thirty years later. She really felt that she was living the story of Cinderella, taken from obscurity, cast into the bright lights of the ball, and capturing all hearts, beginning with the Prince's. She would have to give back the dress the next day. But she felt sure that other celebrations awaited her beyond the frontiers.

A few days later they left Berlin. At Schwedt, on the Oder, Figchen said goodbye to her father who had to return to Stettin, failing his invitation to Russia. Despite the excitement of the journey she was shattered by this separation. She felt that she would never see this good and simple man again, and she was right. As for him, he was overcome by emotion and could only repeat, sobbing: 'Remain faithful to your religion, my child! Don't forget to read my instructions!' Through floods of tears, she promised him all that he wished. Only Johanna remained cold.

In order to thwart the intrigues of the opposing faction in Russia, it had been agreed that the two princesses should travel under a false name. Johanna's papers were entitled 'Countess of Reinbeck'. She found that this secrecy added spice to the expedition. The four heavy carriages which bore mother, daughter, servants and luggage were uncomfortable with inadequate suspension. It was also a bad moment to be travelling. It was not snowing yet but it was extremely cold, despite the little braziers inside the carriages. Muffled in furs, with their faces masked to protect their noses and cheeks against the cold, the women sank into apathetic drowsiness. Sometimes a sudden bump would jolt their spines; they moaned: the coach had tipped into a muddy hollow. The coachman swore – a stop in the icy wind. And then off again. The stages were long, monotonous and exhausting. And in a Prussian posthouse there was no hope of comfort or good food. 'As the rooms were not heated,' Johanna was to write, 'we had to take shelter in the inn-keeper's own room, which was no better than a pig-sty: husband, wife, guard dog, hens and children slept all over the place in cradles, beds, behind stoves, on mattresses...' Figchen had indigestion from drinking too much beer. After Memel the journey got worse. They had cursed the posthouses: now there weren't any, and they missed them! They were forced to hire fresh horses from the peasants. Twenty-four were needed for the convoy, and this meant arguments and haggling every time, which infuriated Johanna. They attached sledges to the backs of the carriages in case of snow.

The exhausted travellers at last arrived at Mitau where they found a Russian garrison. The commander, Colonol Voyeykov, presented himself politely to Johanna, did her the honours of the town, and said that he was to accompany her to Riga. The next day when they were close to Riga, Figchen and her mother started as they heard a series of explosions. Voyeykov explained that the garrison was firing a salute in their honour. The convoy stopped. Prince Simon Kiryllovitch

Naryshkin, Grand Marshal at the Court and former ambassador in London, and Prince Dolgorouki, the Deputy Governor, appeared before the two German princesses. They bowed very low, presented them with sable cloaks from the Empress and begged them to climb into the state sledge, which took them rapidly to the castle. There, footmen in livery led them in slow procession to their apartments.

Still stunned by the sudden change of surroundings, Johanna and Figchen changed and joined the bedecked company which awaited them in the drawing-rooms. Johanna felt at the peak of glory in front of all these bowed heads. After the coarseness of the inn-keepers, and all her exhaustion, she felt rewarded by the signs of respect which now surrounded her. 'When I went to the table,' she was to write, 'all the trumpets in the palace, and the drums, flutes and oboes of the outer guard pealed out . . . it never occurred to me that all this was for poor me, for whom in other places they hardly beat a drum, and elsewhere, nothing at all.' Figchen, for her part, was eagerly absorbing this new world. All around her they spoke French and German, and yet she was in Russia, the Russia of Peter the Great which, one day, might be her country too. At last it was beginning. From now on, every step counted. She must not stumble on a single pebble.

After their visit to Riga the travellers, accompanied by Naryshkin, set off once again. They were going to St Petersburg where, according to the Empress's orders, they would rest and replenish their wardrobes before joining the Court which was at that time residing in Moscow. Johanna was pleased with the composition of the convoy: she was now accompanied by several officers, an equerry, a major-domo, a few cooks, a cellar-man and his assistant, an official in charge of coffee and one in charge of preserves, eight footmen, two grenadiers and two quartermasters. A troop of cuirassiers led the way, and a detachment from the Livonian regiment galloped around the principal sledge. This sledge, which the Empress had put at her guests' disposal, was extremely spacious. It was hung with red cloth braided with silver, and had a feather bed with damask cushions and coverlets of satin and precious furs. The snow, the sun, the jingling bells all induced an agreeable sensation of unreality in the two princesses. Soon after Riga, this luxurious procession passed some miserable black sledges, with curtains drawn, accompanied by soldiers. Sophie wanted to know who the invisible travellers were. Naryshkin was embarrassed and answered evasively that it was probably the family of the Duke Antoine Ulrick of Brunswick. Sophie learnt later that the little dethroned Tsar Ivan VI and his mother the ex-regent Anne, had in fact been taken that day to Riga, to be locked up in a fortress at Oranienburg. Thus, whilst she had dreamt of the generous Tsarina who awaited her in Moscow, and who would perhaps raise her fortunes, the innocent victims of this same woman had been two steps away from her, on the snowy road, inside a sledge surrounded by soldiers. Thus the path of glory had crossed the path of downfall. The fates had revealed the tragedy of those they had destroyed to the one they were raising.

On the 3rd/14th February (one must now use the Julian calendar, eleven days behind the Gregorian one used in the rest of Europe) the convoy arrived in St Petersburg, and stopped at the steps of the Winter Palace[1]. It was midday. With the sun and the frost everything sparkled from the frozen Neva to the cupolas of the churches. When the princesses, who had been travelling for more than a month, stepped out, a salvo of guns rang out from the Peter and Paul fortress on the other side of the river. At the foot of the staircase were crowded those courtiers and diplomats who had not followed the court to Moscow. Four ladies-in-waiting surrounded Sophie. 'When I arrived in my apartment,' Johanna wrote to her husband, 'I was introduced to a thousand people. My mouth was dry with cold. I dined alone with the ladies and gentlemen supplied by her Imperial Majesty! I was served like a queen.'

Straight away she plunged herself delightedly into the intrigues of the Court. The French ambassador, the Marquis de la Chétardie, who had stayed behind in St Petersburg, had been the Empress's lover and had, behind the scenes, led the French party which favoured a marriage with the little Sophie of Anhalt-Zerbst. He stunned Johanna by his compliments and assured her that she would be called on to play a vital part in the conclusion of the alliance with Austria. In order to do this, they should quickly take advantage of the arrival in Russia of the Grand Duke's future fiancée. The 10th February was his birthday and if they didn't spare the horses they could reach Moscow by that date. The Empress would appreciate this eagerness. It was too bad if they were tired! Johanna was galvanized and begged Naryshkin to speed up the preparations for their departure. In the midst of this adventure she hardly thought of Figchen, although she did write to her husband in her strange German-French jargon, *Figchen southeniert die fatige besser als ich* (Figchen supports fatigue better than I do). And, to King Frederick II: 'My daughter supports fatigue admirably; like a young soldier who scorns danger, ignoring what it is, she rejoices in the splendour

---

[1] It is not the Winter Palace which can be seen today and which was commissioned by Elisabeth and built by Rastrelli, but Peter 1st's Winter Palace which stands on the site of the present Hermitage Museum.

surrounding her.' Her main concern was that Figchen should overcome all these trials without falling ill, since the slightest indisposition of the Grand Duke's fiancée could be used against her by enemies of the Prussian cause. The Empress would never accept a delicate daughter-in-law. So she had to both hurry and remain healthy.

Before packing again, Sophie had time to visit the city with her ladies-in-waiting. It was in full carnival, and a slow and happy crowd milled around the fair-stalls. But the young girl was not attracted either by the multi-coloured swings, or by the trained bears. She was moved most by the sight of the Guards barracks, that historic place from whence, three years earlier, Elisabeth had set out to seize the throne. She saw the fierce grenadiers of the Preobrajenski regiment, who had accompanied the Tsarina on that night of the 5th December, 1741. They showed her the route they had followed to the Winter Palace, to cries of 'long live our little mother Elisabeth'. The story of this *coup d'état* filled her with premonitory excitement, and she was sorry to have to return to the demands of the present. Her mother was becoming impatient. Everything was ready for the departure, and they set out at night. At dawn the white road melted into the white sky. Once again Sophie was struck by the immensity of the Russian plain. In this country everything was immoderate, the distances, the cold, the political passions. Johanna complained feebly. She was beginning to feel her eyes freezing and her nostrils bristling with icicles. Luckily the sight of the Russian escort galloping beside the sledges reminded her that she was the mother of the Grand Duke's future fiancée, aunt to the heir to the Russian throne, secret agent of King Frederick of Prussia, confidante and ally of the French ambassador . . .

The sledges flew on the untouched snow. They travelled by day and by night. At seventy versts from Moscow, sixteen horses were harnessed to the two princesses' sledge. Coming through a hamlet, the sledge, going hell for leather hit the corner of a hovel. A great iron bar fell off the roof and hit Johanna on the head and shoulder. She screamed and thought that her plans were ruined. How could she contend with Bestuzhev with a bump on her head and a pain in her side? Sophie reassured her – there was nothing, not even a bruise. On the other hand, two grenadiers from the Preobrajenski regiment lay with their heads bleeding. They had been on the front of the sledge and had broken the force of the blow. The peasants gathered around the sledge whispered, 'It's the Grand Duke's intended.' Voyeykov ordered them to take care of the wounded and the coach-man whipped his horses.

The procession of thirty sledges arrived at last in Moscow towards eight o'clock on the evening of 9th/20th February, and drew up at the wooden steps of the Kremlin, where the Empress lived. It had been fifty days since Johanna had received, at Zerbst, the invitation from Elisabeth of Russia. Now she was about to meet the woman who made an empire quake. At the last stop she and Figchen had put on the court dresses given to them by the Empress. 'I remember that I wore a tight-fitting dress, without hoops, made of pink and silver moiré,' Catherine was to write in her *Memoirs*. The two princesses were led into their apartments by the Prince of Hesse-Homburg, and had hardly had time to refresh themselves when Grand Duke Peter Ulrick appeared. Figchen's heart sank when she saw his degenerate appearance – the long face, the bulging eyes, the flabby mouth. She had not remembered him being so sickly and plain as that. Had he changed since their meeting, or had she subconsciously idealized him in her dreams? Anyway he was delighted to greet his aunt and cousin, and having welcomed them in German, he invited them to come into the presence of Her Imperial Majesty.

The procession moved through a suite of rooms, each one crammed with dignitaries in brilliant uniforms and court ladies whose dresses, which were as elegant as those at Versailles, made Johanna cross-eyed. She was walking on air, on Grand Duke Peter's arm. Figchen followed on the arm of the Prince of Hesse-Homburg. As the front of the procession reached the Empress's audience chamber, the double doors opposite swung open and Elisabeth of Russia appeared. She was a tall and beautiful woman of thirty-five with a rosy complexion, and an ample and sturdy figure crammed into a hooped dress of silver watered silk with gold trimmings. It was said that she was very vain and that she possessed fifteen thousand French-style costumes and five thousand pairs of shoes. 'On the side of her head she had a straight black feather and her hair was studded with diamonds,' Sophie noted. The girl came close to fainting at the sight of this goddess decorated like some holy shrine. But she soon regained her composure, sustained by the thought of the part she had to play. She bent forward and made a deep curtsey, in the French manner. Johanna, next to her, was dazzled, and stammered out compliments, thanking the Empress for her kindnesses and kissing her hand. Although she was used to this sort of tribute, Elisabeth too was nonetheless very much moved. She saw in Johanna's face the features of her dead fiancé. And, looking at Sophie, she was struck by her fresh, submissive and intelligent look. At first sight she seemed an excellent choice. That idiot Peter would have a prize morsel in his bed. Would he be capable of making the child happy? It didn't matter. During the long interview which took place first in the audience chamber, and then in the Empress's bedroom, Sophie felt she was being examined from every aspect, undressed, fingered and weighed as if by a careful housewife at the market. She had expected this: it was part of life for a marriageable princess. The courtiers and diplomats watched the scene. The apparent satisfaction on Elisabeth's proud face strengthened the hopes of the Franco-Prussian clan, the Prussian Ambassador, Mardefeldt, the Marquis de la Chétardie, and her Majesty's physician, Lestocq. The Vice-Chancellor, Bestuzhev, who supported Austria, England and Saxony, hid his chagrin with a forced smile.

The next day, the 10th/21st February was the Grand Duke's birthday and the Empress appeared before her crowd of courtiers wearing, this time, a brown costume edged in silver, with 'her head, neck and torso' covered in jewels. The Count Alexis Razumovsky followed her bearing the insignia of the Order of Saint Catherine on a gold plate. He was, and had been for several years the Empress's official lover, and was nicknamed 'the night emperor'. 'He was one of the handsomest men I have ever seen,' Catherine wrote in the *Memoirs*. This 'handsome man' was in fact a Ukrainian peasant with a beautiful voice whom Elisabeth had engaged as cantor in her private chapel before luring him into her bedroom. The cantor's nocturnal services had been rewarded by every kind of honour and title, including that of Count. It was even rumoured that he had secretly married the Empress. Amazingly he never used his influence over her for political purposes. Figchen stared at this important person with astonished respect! He was mature, with regular features, a coaxing expression, and a powdered wig. Without knowing exactly what the favourite's duties were, she saw in him a mysterious fulfiller of the Queen's desires, a sort of walking delicacy. He must have been possessed with supernatural, sublime virtues to be so much to the Queen's taste. She was prepared to accept everything about this fascinating Court, and it didn't occur to her yet to criticize it. She was trying to learn. The Empress, that day, seemed in an excellent mood. She advanced towards Figchen and her mother, solemn yet smiling, and conferred on them the order of Saint Catherine. Madames Choglokov and Vorontsov, both 'portrait ladies' to the Empress[1], pinned the star-shaped brooch on to the breasts of the German princesses. Everyone around them appeared to be moved. 'My daughter and I are living like queens,' Johanna was to write to her husband. Already, in her mind, she could see Figchen married to the Grand Duke, with herself advising the Empress towards the greater good of Prussia, and Bestuzhev overthrown.

[1] 'Portrait ladies' are those who, either through their kinship with the Imperial family or by exceptional merit, were authorized to wear, on their court clothes, a miniature of Her Majesty, in a diamond frame.

CHAPTER III

The Steps of the Throne

The Empress continued to shower the princesses with favours. Johanna could not get over having a chamberlain, ladies-in-waiting and pages attached to her person. Life in Moscow consisted of a succession of parties, balls and dinners which dazzled her with their magnificence. Sophie, on the other hand, kept her head amid this throng of faces and names; after a moment of dizziness she began to observe and make inquiries. She would try to guess what each person's estate and rank amounted to. She already saw that she would have to understand court customs if she ever wanted to move freely in these brilliant and sophisticated circles. At Stettin, she had stood dreaming before the portrait of the Empress, so resplendent in her court dress, with her buxom chest and dark blue eyes. Her mother, to prepare her for a possible 'Russian destiny', had taught her to respect this powerful and magnanimous sovereign. The truth about her, however, was quite different and Sophie came to learn it little by little, by listening to the secret whispers of the court. Who was the real Elisabeth of Russia? She was beautiful, greedy, lazy and sensuous; in her youth she had been in love with her fiancé (Johanna's brother) and, after his death, had embarked on a series of squalid affairs. Lovers followed each other in her bed: court officials, ambassadors, coachmen, footmen, guards officers, anyone would do. In 1730, when Peter the Great's grandson, Peter II, died, she could have taken the throne, being the Emperor's direct descendant since her sister Anne's death. But she was too preoccupied with her sex life and preferred to step down in favour of another Anne, Peter the Great's niece[1], widow of the Duc de Courland. She in turn, not having any children, wanted to make her great-nephew her heir; he was the son of the third Anne, the Duchess of Mecklenburg. In 1740, when the Empress Anne died, the 'heir', only a few months old, was proclaimed Emperor under the name of Ivan VI, and his young mother, Anne of Mecklenburg, took on the regency. At

[1] The daughter of Ivan, eldest brother of Peter the Great.

the Court, the Russian party, strongly supported by French representatives, was indignant that a great-great-nephew of Peter the Great should become Emperor, whilst Elisabeth, who was Peter the Great and Catherine I's own daughter, remained in the background. The Marquis de la Chétardie, who was French ambassador and the doctor, Lestocq, both Elisabeth's lovers, persuaded her that if she did not act very quickly the regent, Anne of Mecklenburg, would have her arrested and thrown into a convent. Elisabeth, alarmed, at last agreed to put herself forward. The officers of the Preobrajenski guard were secured for her, and in a trice the little Tsar Ivan VI, Anne of Mecklenburg and her husband, the Duke of Brunswick, were seized and incarcerated in a fortress.

Once she had become Empress, Elisabeth appeared, in her new role, as a strange mixture of laziness and obstinacy, vanity and cruelty, and devoutness and profligacy. Her amorous excesses, her taste for orgies and her manic passion for clothes (she never wore the same costume twice) did not prevent her from fearing God and worshipping icons. She dyed her hair and her eyebrows black, covered herself in jewels and would not tolerate any other woman trying to appear dazzling next to her. Although she spoke fluent French, Italian and German, she was uneducated and badly brought up. On her accession to the throne she abolished capital punishment, out of soft-heartedness, but inflicted simulated executions on several courtiers before sending them to Siberia, and in 1743, the Countess Lopoukhin and Countess Bestuzhev had their tongues cut out when they were exposed in a plot. 'Her Majesty has a marked taste for strong drinks,' wrote the Chevalier D'Eon, Louis XV's secret agent. 'Sometimes they affect her to the point of fainting. Then her dress and corsets have to be cut open. She beats her servants and women.' She was vain, touchy and vindictive, and took part only intermittently in political affairs, when the fancy struck her. All the same, her ministers trembled before her, as they knew that she was perfectly capable of sending them, in a moment of temper, straight from their office into a fortress. In two years of reign her authoritarian yet unstable nature had established itself to such an extent that foreign diplomats regarded her as the most difficult person to understand and circumvent. Despite the laxity in her private life, she never doubted for a moment the quasi-divine legitimacy of her power over the Russian people. It therefore appeared vital to her to ensure her succession. Without a child, and unable to have any, she thought of her nephew, Charles-Peter Ulrick of Holstein, son of her dead sister Anne, and grandson of Peter the Great. This sickly and quasi-retarded boy had been brought up at Kiel by German officers. He was militarily trained and drilled, from the age of seven, with a small gun and sword, learning to stand guard and speak the language of the barrack-room. At nine years old he was promoted to sergeant, and would stand at arms by the door of the room in which his father feasted with his friends. He could hardly hold back covetous tears at the sight of the delicious dishes being carried past him. At the second sitting his father relieved him from his post, publicly conferred on him the rank of Lieutenant and ordered him to sit down amongst the guests. The child was so overcome with happiness that he lost his appetite and was unable to swallow anything. He said later that that was *the happiest day of his life*. In 1739, after his father's death, the Holsteinian Brümmer, Grand Marshal at the ducal court became his chief tutor. He was a limited and brutish maniac, a 'horse trainer'. Disregarding his pupil's delicate health, he would punish him by depriving him of food or by making him kneel on dried peas, so that, according to his other tutor Stehlin, 'his knees became red and swollen'. One day Stehlin had to intervene to prevent Brümmer from punching the little prince with his fists. Peter Ulrick was terrified and called the guard to help him. Sometimes the child would vomit bile when threatened by Brümmer. Under this régime, he became timorous, cunning, shifty and secretive. When the Empress Elisabeth brought him to Moscow, in February 1742, she was disappointed by the morally and physically deformed fourteen-year old produced by Brümmer. She, who loved full-blooded men, wondered desperately whether this pathetic human scrap would even be capable of sitting straight on the throne. He spoke only German properly; he was Lutheran; he had not the slightest aptitude for governing a country. Too bad. One had to use what was at hand. The main thing was to assure the future of the Romanov dynasty. The Empress's nephew was baptized Peter Fedorovich, according to the Orthodox custom, and was proclaimed Grand Duke and successor to the Russian throne. But he despised his new religion, laughed at the Orthodox priests, balked at learning Russian and pined for his home country. It was strange that Elisabeth, having swept the Mecklenburgs out of her way, who in the eyes of the people represented German influence, should adopt as her heir another German. And now she was offering him a German fiancée!

The fiancée, despite her youth, had sound judgment. Whilst appreciating the joyful welcome and friendliness that she received from Grand Duke Peter, she found his conversation childish and his reactions unpredictable. What delighted him about her arrival was the fact that at last he had a friend of his own age to chat with. 'In this short space of time,' Catherine wrote in her *Memoirs,* 'I saw and understood that he set little value on the nation he was destined to rule, that he clung to Lutheranism, that he disliked his surroundings, and that he was extremely childish.'

Sophie's polite interest in his conversation made him more confident and he confessed to her that, although he found her very nice as a cousin, he loved another, a Miss Lopoukhin, who had unfortunately been banished from the court after her mother, convicted of political intriguing, had had her tongue cut out and been sent to Siberia. He added naively that although he would have liked to marry that young lady, he was resigned to marrying her, Sophie, 'because his aunt wished it'. 'I listened, blushing to his talk of relationships, and thanked him for his untimely confidence in me,' Catherine wrote, 'but I was secretly astonished by his rashness and lack of judgment in so many things.' So there it was, settled. She could not expect any pleasant surprise in matters of the heart. She had had a foreboding of this on setting out for Russia. However, she had not made the journey for the sake of a great love affair, but in order to fulfil a political purpose. She was not yet fifteen, and yet, instead of following her mother into the flurry of worldly intrigue, she remained in the background, preparing her future with studious determination. From the beginning, she understood that, if she wished to please the Empress, impress the courtiers and gain the sympathy of both great and small, she would have to become as Russian as if she had been born in the country itself. Whilst her imbecile cousin, Grand Duke Peter, upset his entourage by continually affecting German customs, she set herself to work on a crash study of the Russian language and the Orthodox religion. Her religious instructor was Simeon Todorski, a refined, cultured and broadminded priest. He spoke fluent German and explained to Sophie that the gap between the Orthodox and Lutheran faiths was not as great as was thought, and that she would not betray her promise to her father by passing from one to the other. The girl hardly needed convincing. God, she thought, would not blame her for changing her faith, when the Russian Empire was at stake in the change. In order to prepare the ground, she wrote to her father that there was no doctrinal antimony between the two religions. Only the 'outer forms of worship' were different. These 'outer forms' clearly disturbed her a little with their oriental splendour. Brought up with Lutheran austerity, she saw in this world of gilt, incense, icons, candles, genuflexions and mystical chants, a necessary background to what she called 'the brutality of the people'. But surely what was important was the uplifting of the soul and not the ritual surrounding this exaltation. Christian-Augustus, surprised by the speed of his daughter's change of heart, wrote in vain that she must 'consider this trial with gravity'– she had already chosen her camp.

Her desire for 'Russianisation' was such that her Russian teacher, Adodurov, was full of praise for his pupil's enthusiasm. She begged him to prolong her lessons beyond their set time. To perfect her knowledge of the language, she would get up in the night, barefoot in her nightshirt, and set herself in front of her books to learn lists of words by heart. As a result she caught a chill. At first her mother accused her of 'pampering herself' and made her conceal her illness from a Court which watched for the slightest weakness on the part of the Grand Duke's fiancée. She obeyed, but her temperature rose, she fainted and the doctors diagnosed acute pneumonia. The Princess's life was in danger. Immediately Bestuzhev's anti-French clique took heart again. If Sophie died, another candidate could be put forward, this time someone favourable to the Anglo-Austrian cause. But the Empress repeated that, whatever happened, she did not want a Saxon princess. And Brümmer confided to La Chétardie that 'in the sad extremity that we must envisage' he had taken precautions by sounding out for the Grand Duke a princess from Darmstadt 'with a charming face' whom the King of Prussia had suggested 'in case the princess from Zerbst should not succeed'.

Whilst a replacement was thus being found for her, Sophie shivered in her bed, poured with sweat, complained of a pain in her side, and put up with her mother railing and arguing with the doctors. They wanted to bleed the patient but Johanna was against it. Her brother, she said, the Empress's fiancé, had died as a result of being bled. They decided to ask Elisabeth who was praying at the Convent at Troitska. Five days later, she arrived with her factotum Lestocq, scolded Johanna for daring to contradict the men of science, and ordered the bleeding. When the blood started to flow, Sophie lost consciousness. She came to in the arms of the Empress. Despite her extreme weakness she thought of her chances. Suddenly she had a mother – and it was Elisabeth of Russia! To reward her for her courage Elisabeth gave her a diamond necklace and a pair of earrings. Johanna estimated that they were worth twenty thousand roubles. But in her haste to see the young girl cured, the Empress ordered more and more blood-letting – more than sixteen sessions in twenty-seven days. Johanna protested. The Empress confined her to her apartments.

Meanwhile at the Court, everybody knew by now that the little princess had become ill by spending her nights learning Russian. In a few days she had gained the devotion of all who were disheartened by the Grand Duke's Teutonic habits. When her condition did not improve, her mother wanted to bring a Lutheran pastor to the patient's bedside. Although she was consumed by fever and exhausted by the bleeding and fasting, Sophie with an extraordinary effort of will murmured: 'What is the use? Rather bring Simeon Todorski. I would certainly talk to him.' And Simeon Todorski did indeed bring solace from the Orthodox faith to the Grand Duke's gentle Lutheran fiancée. The Empress was moved to tears. Sophie's words were repeated throughout the town.

Whilst the young girl thus gained ground in the hearts of those around her, her mother made more and more enemies by her tactlessness. She asked her dying child to give her a piece of pale blue material with silver flowers, a gift from her uncle Charles Louis. Sophie unwillingly gave it to her. Seeing her so compliant, everybody was outraged by Johanna's selfishness. In order to console the girl, the Empress had sent to her a parcel of much richer materials than the one she had had to part with. These marks of affection convinced Sophie that, if she recovered, she would not return to Zerbst. Despite her extreme weakness she continued tenaciously to take advantage of everything she saw and heard. Often she would close her eyes and pretend to sleep so as to overhear conversations between the court ladies charged by the Empress to sit with her. 'They spoke of everything on their minds, and thus I learnt many things.'

Little by little, despite the potions and bleeding, Sophie's strength returned. The danger was at last averted. She could return to the breach. On the 21st April, 1744, her fifteenth birthday, she re-appeared in public. 'I had become as thin as a skeleton,' she wrote, 'I was taller but my face and features had become elongated; my hair was falling out, and I was deathly pale. I found myself terrifyingly ugly and could hardly recognize myself. That day the Empress sent me a pot of rouge and ordered me to put some on.'

A few days later, still moving stubbornly towards her intended goal, she wrote to her father to tell him that she intended soon to adopt the Orthodox faith:

'As I can see practically no difference between the Greek religion and the Lutheran religion, I have resolved (having taken note of your Highness's gracious instructions) to convert, and will send him my profession of faith at the earliest opportunity. I flatter myself that your Highness will be pleased.'

As she wrote these ceremonial phrases, she knew perfectly well that her father would be deeply upset when he read them. But Zerbst was now so far away that her German past seemed to belong to someone else; she had completely turned towards her new family and her new country. So long as her mother did not spoil everything with her busy plots and intrigues! Johanna now received in her drawing-room Vice-Chancellor Bestuzhev's worst enemies: Lestocq, La Chétardie,

Mardefeldt, Brümmer...she was more excitable and talkative than ever. She thought she had political flair, but failed to notice that the Empress had, for some time, been very cold towards her.

In May 1744, Elisabeth and her Court went again to the convent at Troitska. Sophie, Johanna and Grand Duke Peter were ordered to join Her Majesty there. They had hardly arrived when the Empress summoned Johanna to her apartment. Lestocq followed. Whilst the trio talked behind closed doors Sophie and Peter sat on a window-sill, elbow to elbow, with their legs dangling, chattering happily. More grown up since her illness, Sophie felt even closer now to the adult world than to her cousin's childish universe of lead soldiers and tittle-tattle. This badly brought up, foul-mouthed and unloved brat did not think of her as his fiancée, or even as a girl, and showed not the slightest politeness towards her. And yet he sought her company. As she laughed at the silly things he said, the door opened: Lestocq, the Empress's counsellor and doctor, burst in with a tragic expression, and said harshly to Sophie: 'This happiness will stop immediately! Pack your bags! You are returning straight home!' Rendered speechless by this insolent attack Sophie remained silent whilst the Grand Duke asked for explanations. 'You'll soon find out,' said Lestocq, and went away with a self-important look on his face. Sophie immediately assumed that her mother had made a blunder. 'But even if your mother is in the wrong, you are not,' said the Grand Duke. 'My duty is to follow my mother and to do as she orders,' she replied. In her heart of hearts, she hoped that the Grand Duke might beg her to stay. But it never occurred to him. Her, somebody else... 'I could see clearly that he would have abandoned me with no regrets,' she wrote in her *Memoirs*. 'And seeing how he felt, I was indifferent to him, but not to the Russian crown.' Was her dream collapsing? Would she have to return to Zerbst in disgrace? Racked with anguish, Sophie guessed that her future was being decided at that very moment behind the doors which enclosed her mother and the Empress. At last the Tsarina emerged from her room. She was red in the face, and looked angry and spiteful. Behind her trotted Johanna, overcome, 'her eyes red and tear-stained'. Instinctively, the two young people jumped down from their high window-sill. Their haste seemed to disarm the Empress's fury. She smiled at their childish movement and kissed them. Hope sprang again in Sophie's heart. All was not lost, since Elisabeth obviously made a distinction between the guilty mother and the innocent daughter.

After the Tsarina had gone out Sophie at last found out from her weeping mother the reason for this outburst. Whilst Johanna had been plotting with other friends of France and Prussia to overthrow the Vice-

Chancellor Bestuzhev, he in turn had had La Chétardie's secret correspondence intercepted and deciphered (although officially on leave, he still had ambassadorial privileges). In his extremely disrespectful letters, La Chétardie had criticized the Empress's laziness, frivolity and unbridled passion for clothes, using Johanna's opinion to support these comments, and mentioning her as an agent of King Frederick. When he had assembled enough evidence against his enemies, Bestuzhev showed these documents to the Tsarina. Blind with rage, she ordered La Chétardie to leave Russia within twenty-four hours, then summoned Johanna and poured on her a stream of abuse. The Princess of Anhalt-Zerbst's standing at court was in ruins, brought down by her intrigues. She was now shunned by everyone – nobody dared to frequent her drawing-room. And yet she was not escorted back to the frontier, but, out of regard for her daughter, simply allowed to vegetate in her apartments. She fumed at the thought of her enemy Bestuzhev's victory – he was now Chancellor. Full of resentment, she turned on Sophie, whose equanimity enraged her, and blamed her for their joint humiliation, heaping sarcasm and abuse upon her. Sophie stoically took up the web that Johanna had so clumsily destroyed, and began to mend the thread, buy back mistakes, and regain sympathy. Left to herself in this foreign court, in the heart of a country whose customs and language she did not understand, burdened with a vain and tiresome mother, deprived of friends and help, surrounded by traps, she nonetheless never lost sight of the path she had chosen to follow. She must seduce the Empress, since there was no question of seducing Peter, and make Bestuzhev relent, since there was no question of over-throwing him. In fact, it seemed to her, after the first moment of panic, that she might emerge advantageously from this crisis which had destroyed Johanna. The girl's ingenuousness would appear even more touching to the Empress when compared with the mother's sly schemings. She was certain, this time, that she was on the right track, and she redoubled her enthusiastic study of the Russian language and the Orthodox religion. The storm passed. Talk of the engagement and the conversion resumed. Dates were put forward. The different stages of the two ceremonies were solemnly discussed. Sophie did her utmost to look tenderly upon the miserable Peter with his pale skin, grim look and hollow chest. Would there ever be a spark between them? No, the Grand Duke prepared for marriage with as much indifference as if he were changing his clothes. 'My heart predicted nothing agreeable,' she was to write in her *Memoirs*, 'only ambition sustained me. I had in my heart a strange certainty that one day I should, by my own efforts, become Empress of Russia.'

CHAPTER IV

The Engagement

By order of the Empress the 28th of June 1744 was at last fixed as the date for Sophie's conversion to the Orthodox faith. On the next day, the 29th of June, feast day of St Peter and St Paul, the engagement between the young convert and Grand Duke Peter would be celebrated. As the two ceremonies drew closer, Sophie felt a mixture of excitement and terror. On the point of fulfilment, she suddenly wondered whether she had done the right thing. What trials would this surfeit of honours bring in its wake? However, she did not allow her anxiety to show. 'She slept well for the whole night,' wrote her mother, 'a sure sign of an untroubled soul.'

A large crowd squeezed into the Imperial chapel, and Sophie appeared in an 'adrienne' dress, similar to that of the Empress, in red Tours cloth braided with silver, with a white ribbon holding back her unpowdered hair. 'I must admit she looked beautiful,' her mother noted. The whole gathering was struck by the elegance of this small dark girl, with her pale skin, blue eyes and her noble yet unassuming bearing. She read out in Russian with a strong German accent 'fifty quarto sheets of paper' and recited, in a firm voice without stumbling on the words, the creed of her new faith. The Empress was moved to tears – the courtiers could not do less and joined in with her sobs. In the midst of the general emotion Sophie endeavoured to appear strong, happy and serene: 'For my part I held firm and was praised for it.' She changed her name that day. She could easily have been baptized into the Orthodox church under the name of Sophie, a common name in her new country, but the Empress was against it, obsessed as she was by the memory of her aunt, the formidable regent Sophie who had had to be thrown into a convent to put an end to her thirst for power. Catherine, on the other hand, was her own mother's name – could there be a better choice? But in Russia everybody bore their father's name as well as their own Christian name. The new Catherine's name was Christian-Augustus. Catherine Christianovna or Catherine Augustovna would sound strange, and annoyingly reminiscent of the regent Anne Leopoldovna, mother of little Ivan VI whom Elisabeth had ousted. The

Grand Duke's prospective bride would therefore be called Catherine Alexayevna, in other words Catherine daughter of Alexei, which ought to please all Slavic hearts. Thus Sophie's father, who was not invited to the celebrations, did not even appear by name at his daughter's confirmation. Debaptized, rebaptized, uprooted, transplanted and Russianized, she had undergone a metamorphosis, outwardly at least. She knew that really there was no fundamental difference between yesterday's Sophie and today's Catherine. She had simply covered another stage of the journey she had set out on. As she came out of the church, she received a diamond necklace and brooch from the Empress. But she was exhausted by the ceremony and begged permission not to appear at the meal. She must at all cost recover her strength for the following day's festivities.

The next morning, the day of the engagement celebrations, she received, almost as soon as she awoke, a portrait of the Empress and one of the Grand Duke, both framed in diamonds. Once she was dressed she went to Elisabeth who received her with her crown on her head and her imperial cloak over her shoulders. The procession was organized: first came the Empress walking beneath a massive silver canopy supported by eight major-generals; she was followed by Catherine and the Grand Duke. Behind them came Johanna, the Princess of Homburg and the court ladies 'in order of rank'. The procession slowly descended the main staircase of the palace, the *krasnoye kriltso,* passed between two rows of guards regiments and after crossing the square, entered the cathedral where a bearded, gilded and deferential clergy awaited its sovereign. Elisabeth led the two young people to a velvet covered platform in the middle of the church. Archbishop Ambrose of Novgorod conducted the ceremony which lasted for four hours, during which everybody remained standing. Catherine's legs became numb and she swayed with exhaustion. At last they exchanged rings. 'The one he gave me was worth twelve thousand roubles,' she wrote, 'and the one he received from me, fourteen thousand.' After this the cannons were fired and the bells of Moscow rang out. The little Princess from Anhalt-Zerbst had become a 'Grand Duchess of Russia' an 'Imperial Highness'. She received the elevation with calm smiles and dignified modesty. Johanna, on the other hand, boiled with indignation. Once again it seemed that she was not being treated with all the respect due to the mother of the 'heiress' to the throne. At the engagement dinner she demanded that she should sit with the Grand Ducal couple, next to the Tsarina; her place, she said, was not with the other court ladies. The Empress was offended by this pretension; Catherine suffered in silence from her mother's latest blunder; the master of ceremonies did not

know where to turn. At last a separate table was put up for Johanna in a
room with a glass bay facing the throne. She dined there 'as it were,
incognito'.

She made up for it that evening at the ball. She was allowed to dance
on the carpet in front of the throne, which in theory only the Empress
and the Princess of Hesse were allowed to tread on in the course of a
minuet. These ladies' partners were Grand Duke Peter, the British,
Danish and Holsteinian ambassadors and the Prince of Hesse. The
other courtiers had to revolve around this sacred area. The ball took
place in the *Granovitaya palata*, or the faceted saloon whose carved
walls were like the inside of a pomegranate. An enormous pillar
supported the low ceiling. Footmen in French livery with powdered
wigs and white stockings guarded the doors. The music was deafening.
Everybody was bowing and kissing hands. Johanna remarked that at the
end her hand bore 'a red mark the size of a German florin' as a result of
all the kisses it had received. Catherine, for her part wrote, 'One was
practically stifled by the heat and the crowds.'

After the festivities, presents from the Empress poured in. Catherine
received gifts not only of jewellery and precious materials, but also
thirty thousand roubles for the new Grand Duchess's minor expenses[1].
Catherine was dazzled by the size of the sum. She had never received
any pocket money whatsoever. She immediately sent her father some
money to help him look after her younger brother who was ill. She now
had her own court, carefully chosen by the Empress to keep her happy:
the chamberlains, gentlemen of the bedchamber and ladies-in-waiting
were all young and high-spirited. And none of them belonged to
Johanna's former clique. Indeed Chancellor Bestuzhev's own son was
one of them. From now on, the Princess of Anhalt-Zerbst had to be
announced if she wished to see her daughter, and a chamberlain would
often attend the audience. Johanna was now forced by etiquette to
behave deferentially towards someone whom, previously, she would
have slapped, without hesitation, for some misbehaviour. She was
humiliated by this reversal in the hierarchy and complained about
everything particularly the little court surrounding Catherine which
was too merry and frivolous for her taste. In the Grand Duke's and the
Grand Duchess's apartments anything was an excuse for fun: they
played blind-man's buff, they jumped, they danced, they ran – they

---

[1] A gold rouble was worth five tournament pounds at the time, according to Castéra.
Equally, although it is very difficult to determine an equivalent between the currency of a
former period and our own, it is estimated, based on the current value of a Napoleon, that
a tournament pound is the equivalent of twelve new francs. Therefore, a golden rouble
from the time of Catherine would be worth sixty new francs.

even took a clavichord to pieces so that they could make a slide out of the lid. By joining in these childish games Catherine was trying to gain the affection of her future husband. The Empress understood this and encouraged the enterprise. Brümmer, however, thought differently. He asked Catherine to help him to 'reclaim' his pupil's character. She refused. 'I told him that it was impossible, and that if I did he would begin to find me as hateful as everybody else.' She understood instinctively that, to win Peter over, she must take the opposite side to that of his tutors. If he found in her a governess rather than a friend everything would be lost. While she tried thus to prepare for a happiness she could not believe in, Johanna was tirelessly making new friends. But once again she chose badly. The Empress did not like the people surrounding her. She was infatuated with the Chamberlain, Ivan Betsky[1], whom she had known for a long time, and was seen everywhere with him to such an extent that malicious rumours of an affair began to spread through the court. Catherine was told, but was unable to reason with Johanna, for whom withdrawal and moderation were concepts unworthy of a woman of quality.

Having had her fill of parties, balls and banquets the Empress prepared to set out for the holy city of Kiev. For her the exercise of piety had always gone well with her taste for pagan distractions. Pleasure led to prayer, and prayer made her long for pleasure. Of course the Grand Duke, the Grand Duchess and Johanna were to come too. At the prospect, Catherine was torn between excitement at the novelty and fear lest her mother, by another blunder, should sink even lower in the Tsarina's estimation.

Kiev was about a thousand versts from Moscow. The enormous train, made up of carriages for the travellers and carts for the luggage, dragged along the dry July roads. Days passed, village followed village, the horizon went on retreating and still they were in Russia. It seemed that Elisabeth's empire had no limit. In her carriage, with her mother and fiancé, Catherine stared eagerly through the doorway at the landscape, and was overwhelmed by an impression of strength and immensity. There could be nothing greater in the world than this country which was, from now on, hers. The Empress followed, a few days behind. Apparently she was in a nasty temper and had exiled several members of her entourage. At each stop, eight hundred horses awaited the convoy. At the relay at Koseletz, Grand Duke Peter accidentally broke the lid of Johanna's money-box. 'He was jumping around in order to make me laugh,' Catherine wrote. Johanna was exasperated and called him 'a badly brought up little boy'. He replied that she was behaving like a

[1] Ivan Betsky was the Prince of Hesse's brother-in-law.

shrew. Catherine tried to calm her mother and received such a brutal rebuff that she burst into tears. 'From that moment, the Grand Duke took a dislike to my mother,' she wrote 'and he never forgot the quarrel; she also kept a grudge against him. I tried very hard to mollify them, but I only succeeded intermittently, they each always had some sarcasm ready to sting the other with; my position thus became more and more thorny.' But despite her lack of interest in her fiancé, Catherine felt closer to him than to her mother. After all her future lay with him and the gigantic Russian Empire, not with Johanna and the minute principality of Anhalt-Zerbst.

At last the Empress herself arrived at Koseletz and the festivities started again: they played cards and danced until they were out of breath. On some evenings, up to fifty thousand roubles were at stake on the various tables. The ladies rivalled each other with the lavishness of their costumes but lived in cramped surroundings. Catherine and her mother had to share a room and their followers were heaped in a jumble in the hall.

Then the whole court moved, in great pomp, to Kiev. There, even more than in Moscow, Catherine was struck by the solemn beauty of the religious ceremonies, and also by the fervour of the humble people kneeling on the ground as the processions passed by. The gilt of the icons and chasubles: the greyness of the ragged peasants, the fanatic pilgrims, and the psalm-singing beggars! The little German Princess was astonished by the contrast between the wealth of the church and the poverty of the worshippers, accustomed as she was to the strict arrangements in Lutheran chapels. A new world appeared before her, revealing unknown depths. Suddenly she discovered behind the double splendour of the cross and the throne, the stupendous misery of this countless, enslaved and obscure nation. As she walked slowly beside the Grand Duke, behind the holy banners, she looked sharply at the crowd and felt the terrible contrast between such magnificence and such abasement. It was still only simple curiosity, such as one might feel at the sight of wild animals, but with it went a feeling of unease. Without her realizing it, her first real Russian lesson was taking place here in Kiev. But she was soon caught up again in the whirl of court life. Once the drawing-room doors had closed behind her, it seemed that she had only imagined this plunge into the darkness and density of the country. After a grand ball for her feast day, the Empress suddenly could not hold still. Everything bored her. She wanted a change of scene. Enough of Kiev and its churches, convents, priests and catacombs. Her Majesty could not wait to get back to Moscow, persuading herself that she had now purified her soul by this pilgrimage.

Back in Moscow, Catherine found once again scandal-mongering, talk of precedence, intrigues, frivolity, smoke-screens, and traps. 'I counted as a child,' she wrote in her *Memoirs*, 'I was afraid of displeasing people and did my best to win over those with whom I was to spend my life. My respect for and gratitude towards the Empress were extreme, I thought of her as a faultless divinity, she said that she loved me almost more than the Grand Duke.' And the Empress did indeed appreciate the new Grand Duchess's mixture of gravity and high-spirits, of strong will and obedience. Catherine, at that time, whilst learning her job as a public figure, nonetheless adored dancing. Every day at seven o'clock in the morning the French ballet master Landé would come, with his pocket violin, and teach her the latest steps from France. He would come back at four o'clock in the afternoon. And in the evening Catherine would amaze the court with the elegance of her movements in the balls and masquerades.

Some of these masquerades were in doubtful taste. The Empress decided that, every Tuesday, the men should dress up as women and the women as men. The men, looking clumsy and grotesque in their great panelled dresses, silently cursed their sovereign's whim, whilst the women bemoaned having to appear at a disadvantage in tight male clothes. But Her Majesty was delighted: she knew that this sort of disguise suited her perfectly. 'The only person who looked right was the Empress herself,' wrote Catherine, 'since men's costumes suited her perfectly. She looked very beautiful in such an outfit.' The masquerades were really an excuse for jostling and mincing so that the dancers, embroiled in their borrowed costumes, would fall on top of each other. One evening, Catherine's childish laughter caused general merriment when she was knocked over in the course of a dance, and found herself on all fours, underneath Chamberlain Sievers' hooped dress.

However, a few days later, she suddenly felt the chill wind of imperial displeasure. During an interval at the theatre Elisabeth had an interview with her advisor Lestocq, looking angrily and repeatedly towards the box where Catherine, Johanna and the Grand Duke sat. Soon afterwards, Lestocq came to see Catherine and announced drily that the Empress was furious with her because she had become heavily in debt. At the time when Her Majesty was only a princess she had had to be economical since 'she knew that nobody else would pay for her,' said the emissary in a peevish tone of voice. Catherine choked and could not stop herself from crying. Instead of consoling her Peter took the Tsarina's side, and Johanna exclaimed that this was all the result of giving a girl of fifteen too much freedom.

The next day, Catherine asked for her accounts and discovered that, indeed, she owed seventeen thousand roubles. She had innocently assumed that the Empress's previous allowance would be continued, and without limits. She had certainly been a spendthrift, but could she have done otherwise? When she arrived she only had four dresses in her trunk, whilst at court they changed three times a day. At first she had used her mother's sheets without complaining. But as soon as she had the means, she had wanted to set up her own household. Also she had very soon understood that in this hostile and strange society, small gifts helped gain the friendship of influential people. She had therefore heaped gifts upon those around her. Not forgetting her mother, whose sour temper needed sweetening! Nor the Grand Duke, who must be made more attached to her! She saw in this accusation of waste one of Bestuzhev's cruel manoeuvres since he would invent anything to lower her in the Empress's opinion. Even yesterday she had thought of herself as Elisabeth's 'favourite', almost her spiritual daughter, and here she was now receiving attacks from her protector which wounded her honour and threatened her future. She felt naively surprised that such a great sovereign could take such pleasure in humiliating her. The two sides of the Empress, one charming and one terrifying, were now revealed to her and she understood the distress of ministers and courtiers whose fortunes depended upon a whim from on high. Day after day, by careful diplomatic behaviour, she attempted to get back in favour with the Empress. The latter, after an outburst of fury, mellowed and eventually forgot the whole incident.

The next thing that happened was that the Grand Duke caught measles. 'This illness,' wrote Catherine, 'made him grow considerably taller, but his mind remained very childish.' During his convalescence he made his footmen, his dwarfs and even Catherine, on whom he had bestowed a rank in his personal army, perform military exercises at the end of his bed. When his tutors scolded him for his absurdity, he simply insulted them and sent them away. He was becoming more and more touchy, and conscious now of the privileges of his rank and age (he was sixteen!) he refused to take any more orders. 'I was the recipient of his childish confidences, and it was not my business to correct him; I simply let him talk and act.' Peter was disarmed by her great gentleness, and without feeling the slightest bit attracted to her, he felt at ease in her company. It was perhaps only with her that he dared to speak freely. And whilst she judged him with pitiless lucidity, she recognized that it was with him that she felt safest in the midst of this foreign court. They had so much in common! Both the same age, both German speaking, both slightly lost in this country they knew so little of, and both having to do their apprenticeship for power under the god-like shadow of the Empress.

As soon as the Grand Duke was up, the court left Moscow for St Petersburg. It had snowed heavily. It was very cold. They travelled by sledge. At Khotilovo, the Grand Duke began to shiver. His temperature rose rapidly and blotches appeared on his face. Brümmer forbade the Princess to come into his room, as the patient was already showing all the symptoms of smallpox which at that time was a terrible scourge. Johanna's own brother, the Empress's fiancé, had died of it. To remove Catherine from the danger of infection, her mother decided to continue the journey with her, leaving the Grand Duke in the care of his personal court. At the same time she had a messenger sent to the Empress; she had already arrived in St Petersburg but set off immediately back to Khotilovo. The Princesses met her sledge on the snowy track in the middle of the night. After asking for news of her nephew, Elisabeth pressed on. This woman who, in so many cases, appeared frivolous, cruel and selfish was not afraid this time of exposing herself to a mortal danger out of a simple sense of duty. As soon as she arrived at Khotilovo, she installed herself at the patient's bedside and set about looking after him herself. Her determination could not be shaken by the protests of her entourage. Although she was so proud of her beauty, even the threat of disfigurement could not turn her away from the bed in which Peter shook with fever. She was to stay beside him for six weeks.

When she heard about the Empress's courage, Catherine slightly regretted having, out of daughterly obedience, agreed to go with her mother rather than stay at Khotilovo. In St Petersburg it seemed to her that some of the courtiers were already turning away from her, in anticipation of the Grand Duke's death. And, indeed, if Peter did die she was finished. Her future was being decided far away in a stifling room, amongst the phials of medicine. Being unable to influence the course of her fate, she resorted to prayer and sent the Empress tender and respectful letters asking after her fiancé's health. She wrote these letters in Russian, or rather, she copied out the conventional and turgid text drawn up by her Russian teacher, Adoduroy. No doubt the Empress was not taken in by this subterfuge, but she was touched by the attentions of a child who could put such energy into forgetting that she was German.

The Court, back in the capital without the Tsarina, was humming with plots. Johanna foresaw the end of her hopes and quarrelled with her daughter on the slightest pretext. While she waited for something to happen, Catherine calmed her nerves by listening to wise advice from Count Gyllenborg, the court of Sweden's official envoy[1]. She had

---

[1] He came to Russia to announce the marriage of the heir to the Swedish throne, Adolph Fréderick, Catherine's uncle, to Princess Ulrica of Prussia.

already met him in Hamburg, and the young diplomat (he was only thirty-two) had been charmed in a few minutes by the girl's intelligence. He reproached her for her taste for luxury and pleasure: 'You only think about social arrangements,' he said, 'allow your mind to follow its natural inclination. Your spirit is destined for great things and yet you occupy yourself with inanities. I could bet that you have not read a book since arriving in Russia!' And he advised her to read, as soon as possible, the life of Cicero, Plutarch, and the *Considerations on the causes of the greatness of the Romans, and of their decline,* by Montesquieu. She threw herself wholeheartedly into the ultra-serious prose, and inspired by this contact with great minds decided to produce a literary essay on herself, entitled *Portrait of a fifteen year old philosopher*. Count Gyllenborg read this text, was delighted, and returned it to its author with twelve pages of commentary and advice, intended to elevate and strengthen the young girl's soul[1]. In the midst of her loneliness and confusion, she was very happy to find such a kind mentor. She read and re-read his precepts, steeping herself in them, as she had once done with her father's words of advice. So, even at a time when she did not know whether the Grand Duke would recover or not, she was dreaming of astonishing the world with her culture and her liberality.

Anyway, the Grand Duke did recover. Elisabeth wrote, in Russian, to Catherine: 'Your Highness, my dearest niece, I am infinitely grateful to Your Highness for her kind messages. I have until now delayed my reply as I was unable to reassure you on the subject of His Highness the Grand Duke's health. However, today I am able to assure you that he is, to our joy and by God's grace, restored to us.'

At the end of January 1745, the Empress left Khotilovo, with her nephew, and returned to St Petersburg. Absence, distance and worry had transformed Peter's image in Catherine's memory. Of course he was weak and bony, his eyelids heavy and his smile alternately sly and inane, but all the same she was fond of him and was impatient to see him again. As soon as the travellers arrived at the Winter Palace, between four and five in the afternoon, she appeared in a big room where her fiancé awaited her. She saw, in the dusk, a terrifying scarecrow. Peter had grown a lot and his face had been ravaged by the smallpox. His eyes were deeply sunk into their sockets, and he looked like a skull. 'All his features were enlarged,' wrote Catherine, 'and his face was still swollen; one could tell that without doubt he would remain badly scarred; as his hair had been cut off, he was wearing an

---

[1] The subject of this portrait has not survived to the present day. Catherine asserts that she burnt it in 1758, with other documents, when she feared a search of her apartments.

enormous wig which disfigured him even more. He came up to me and asked if I was able to recognize him. I stammered out my congratulations on his recovery, but in fact he had become hideous.'

Overcome by this brief interview, Catherine escaped back to her apartment where she fainted in her mother's arms.

On the 10th February, the Grand Duke's birthday (he was beginning his seventeenth year), the Empress decided not to show him in public since he was so disfigured by smallpox, and invited Catherine to dine alone with her 'on the throne'. Fearing that the young girl might turn away in disgust from this unsightly companion, and on an impulse break off the engagement, she became doubly tender towards her. She went into ecstasies over the Russian letters that Catherine had written her, made her speak the language, praised her pronunciation, exclaimed at her beauty which, she said, had become even more pronounced in the last few weeks. The Court, which had lately been keeping its distance from Catherine, observed the warmth of relations between the Grand Duchess and the Tsarina at this dinner, and immediately followed suit. Catherine was once again surrounded, admired and adulated. She was very happy: she had never for a moment considered retracting her promise despite the repugnance she felt for Peter. She was marrying a country, not a face. 'My aim was to please those with whom I had to live,' she wrote in her *Memoirs*, 'so I adopted their habits and ways of doing things; I wanted to be Russian so as to gain the Russians' affection!' And again: 'I showed no preference for either side, I minded my own business, I always looked serene, and showed attention and politeness towards everybody ... I displayed great respect towards my mother, limitless obedience towards the Empress, special consideration for the Grand Duke, and I sought public esteem with the greatest care.'

The Grand Duke meanwhile suffered from being physically degraded in the sight of his fiancée. The more beautiful, impulsive and loveable she appeared the more aware he became of his own ugliness. At times he almost took a perverse pleasure in causing her disgust. Her friendliness towards him seemed to be motivated by simple convenience, or possibly even deliberate calculation. He held her feminine bloom against her, as his own masculinity appeared so feeble beside it. While she worked at learning Russian, or attended Orthodox services, and generally tried to forget her German origins, he obstinately remained both German and Lutheran. He only felt at ease amongst his footmen, with whom he talked in a coarse language. Romberg, a Swedish ex-dragoon, told him that a wife must always keep quiet and tremble at her husband's decisions. 'Subtle, like a cannon shot,' was Catherine's expression, when the Grand Duke repeated these remarks to her. On that occasion, he also let her know that later he would rule her with a rod of iron. She was neither surprised nor offended, and let him talk. Her main pleasure now was riding: she was learning at the Ismailovsky regiment's barracks. And to strengthen herself, she drank milk and soda-water every morning on the doctor's advice.

Using a change of household as his excuse – the Empress and her nephew had moved to the Summer Palace – Peter sent word to Catherine via a servant that he now lived too far away to be able to visit her very often. 'The Grand Duke's attentions towards me now ended,' she wrote. 'I saw perfectly well how unenthusiastic he was and how little he felt for me; my vanity and self-esteem were wounded but I was too proud to complain. I should have felt debased if the only attention I received was as a result of pity. When I was alone, I shed some tears, then wiped them away, and went to play with my companions.'

Suspecting the dislike growing up between the engaged pair, the Empress decided to speed up the marriage celebrations. The main object for her was to ensure the succession. The Court doctors respectfully advised her to wait. According to them, the Grand Duke was not mature enough to take a wife; as he was, he was incapable of reproducing; he must be given time to become a man in the full sense of the word. The Empress was not convinced. Peter was only indifferent to his fiancée's charms because he drank too much. Deprive him of alcohol and he would turn into a proper rooster. The doctors bowed before the Empress's superior knowledge. They looked at the calendar and discussed the date of the ceremony.

Catherine now contemplated with horror the event she had previously longed for with all her heart. It was a year and a half since she had arrived in Russia. 'The closer my wedding-date came,' she wrote, 'the sadder I became, and I would often find myself crying without really knowing why.' The thought of spending her life with this great oaf, who was as ugly as he was stupid, suddenly filled her with disgust. With revulsion she pictured the nocturnal contacts, the familiarities to which she would have to submit, out of respect for the religious sacraments. Her innocence was such that, on the eve of her marriage, she did not know exactly what the difference was between the sexes, or what it was a man did with a woman in a bed. Worried, she consulted her ladies-in-waiting; but although they knew about all the amorous intrigues at court, they were unable to inform the Grand Duchess about this physical act which apparently took place after some impulse of the soul. They sat around Catherine's bed and discussed the subject in a naive and excited manner, each advancing a theory, offering an explanation, or, with a blush, passing on an elder sister's confidences. Faced with these incoherent offerings, Catherine decided to consult her mother, so that she could then enlighten her companions. But at the first question Johanna was shocked, refused to answer and scolded her daughter for her lewd curiosity.

The Grand Duke also tried to find out what he would have to do once he was married. His usual cronies, the footmen, gave him a crude mechanical description of the sexual act. They talked to him as if he were a gay dog; but he was only a retarded child. He was paralysed instead of being aroused and although he sniggered as he listened to them, he was in fact terrified.

Around these two confused people, the Court busied itself preparing for the celebrations. Catherine was disappointed by her mother's sharpness and her futile neurotic state, and she hoped against hope that her father might be invited to the wedding. She thought that he at least with his rough simplicity would be able to advise and support her. He had written over and over again, for months, begging Johanna to obtain from the Empress the invitation he was so obviously entitled to. But the Empress feared that this narrow-minded Lutheran would be disgusted by the spectacle of an Orthodox wedding ceremony, and preferred to keep him away. Prince Christian-Augustus would remain at Zerbst. Anyway even Johanna, now that she had incurred the sovereign's displeasure, was only just tolerated as part of her daughter's entourage. She was lucky not to be sent home before the great day, like a serving-maid fired for insolence!

It was the first time the Russians had had to prepare for a ceremony of this kind. The Empress did not have a precedent, and wished to make her nephew's wedding an occasion of international splendour, so she consulted the French Court whose Dauphin had just been married, and the court at Dresden, where Augustus III of Saxony, son of the Polish king, had also been married. Those who specialized in ceremonials had a field day. Memos from embassies, minute descriptions, samples of velvet and braid, sketches of details of the French and Saxon ceremonies, all poured into St Petersburg. Elisabeth examined them, made calculations, imitated some things, and added new ideas. She wanted to surpass all Russia's rivals by the subtlety of the etiquette and the splendour of the garments. As soon as the ice on the Neva had been broken, English, German and French ships arrived in St Petersburg and unloaded carriages, materials, furniture, livery and valuable china, ordered from all four corners of Europe. Christian-Augustus, although not invited to his daughter's wedding, sent precious materials from Zerbst. England distinguished herself by sending Elisabeth's favourite silk, which had a pattern of gold and silver branches on a pale background.

Postponed again and again, the wedding was at last fixed for the 21st August, 1745. From the 15th to the 18th August heralds in coats of mail went through the streets with a detachment of mounted guards and dragoons, accouncing the date of the ceremony to the sound of kettle-drums. Crowds herded into the Admiralty Square to watch the installation of fountains of wine and benches and tables for the popular feast, and to the Kazan cathedral whose interior was being decorated by hundreds of workmen. On the 19th August a squadron of galleys dropped anchor in front of the Winter Palace. On the 20th, the city shook with the sound of gunshot and bells ringing. That evening, Johanna was suddenly seized with panic and guilt. She went to Catherine and spoke to her in vague terms of the ordeal that awaited her, of her 'future duties', and in the middle of all this, burst into tears. But why exactly was she crying? Was it for the failure of her diplomatic hopes in the Russian court, or was it for her daughter's uncertain fate, destined as she was to either the greatest glory or the greatest danger? 'We cried a little,' Catherine noted in the *Memoirs*, 'and then we separated very affectionately.'

CHAPTER V

The Wedding

On the 21st August 1745, Catherine rose at six o'clock in the morning: while she was in her bath, naked and unmade-up, the Empress appeared to inspect this girl who henceforth was to perpetuate the Russian dynasty. The examination was satisfactorily concluded. Catherine was passed for service and handed back to her maids. While she was being dressed with slow solemnity, an argument arose between the Empress and the hairdresser as to whether the bride should have a flat or curly wig on the top of her head. They finally chose a curly wig, hoping that it would not unbalance the crown. The ceremonial dress was made of silver brocade with a wide skirt, a tight bodice and short sleeves; the seams, edges and train were embroidered with silver roses; she had a cape of silver lace over her shoulders; the whole outfit was so heavy that, once she was dressed, Catherine could hardly move. All the jewels from the Imperial treasure were laid out before her. On the Tsarina's instructions, she harnessed herself with bracelets, pendant, ear-rings, brooches, rings and buckles in order to dazzle the crowds as she passed. When she looked at herself in the mirror she saw a living constellation, and her heart froze with dread. She was so pale that they applied some rouge. 'Her complexion has never been more beautiful than it is now,' her mother remarked. 'Her hair is dark but very shiny, which accent-uates her youthful look and adds to the advantages of a brunette, whilst preserving the softness of a blonde.' At last the Empress placed the Grand Duchess's crown on the dark and slightly curly hair. It was heavy and Catherine had to stiffen herself to keep her head straight. At midday the Grand Duke arrived, also dressed in silver cloth and covered with jewels: this sumptuous apparel only accentuated his simian appearance.

At three o'clock, the procession of a hundred and twenty carriages set off to accompany the young couple to the Kazan cathedral. The people fell to their knees as soon as the fabulous carriage appeared containing the Empress and the two young people; it was gilded and carved and drawn by eight white horses. The team was led at a walk by grooms, preceded by the Grand Master of ceremonies and the Grand Marshal of the Court in an open barouche, and surrounded by important dignitaries on horseback. 'You could never hope to see anything grander or more magnificent,' wrote the French chargé d'affaires, d'Allion.

During the sermon which preceded the nuptial blessing, one of the court ladies, Countess Tchernychev, who was behind the young couple, whispered in the Grand Duke's ear that he must not take his eyes off the priest, since there was a superstition that the first of the bridal couple to turn away would be the first to die. Peter shrugged and muttered, 'What rubbish', and passed it on to Catherine. She took no notice, gathering all her strength to maintain her statuesque bearing in the midst of a twilight of gold, candle-light and massed faces.

After the religious ceremony, which lasted for several hours, came dinner and a ball. Catherine was exhausted. Her crown bore down on her forehead, and she asked if she could take it off for a few minutes but was told that it would bring bad luck. In the end the Empress did allow her to remove the heavy diadem for a moment, but she had to replace it almost immediately to join in a series of polonaises. Luckily the evening was cut short by the Empress who was impatient to get the young couple to bed.

At nine o'clock, Her Imperial Majesty, accompanied by the highest dignitaries of the court, her ladies-in-waiting, a few other privileged people, and Johanna, escorted Catherine and Peter to the nuptial suite. There the couple separated; Peter retired to change his clothes in a nearby room, whilst the women helped the young girl to undress. The Tsarina took off her crown, the Princess of Hesse helped her into her nightgown, the mistress of the bedchamber put on her dressing-gown. 'Apart from this ceremony,' wrote Johanna, 'there is much less involved in the undressing of the couple than there is at home. No man dares come in once the bridegroom has gone in to dress for the night. They don't dance around them here, and they don't hand out garters.' Now that she had got rid of her heavy apparel Catherine could, with freed movements but a tight heart, contemplate this state bedroom where the sacrifice was to be performed. Walls stretched with red velvet patterned in silver. A bed surmounted by a crown and covered with red velvet patterned in gold. Here and there, lighted candelabras. And herself, Catherine, with all eyes upon her – some curious or amused, some depraved, mocking or sympathetic. At last everybody went out, leaving her alone in bed with her fears. She felt like a goat tethered for bait. Her mother had given her vague warnings, *in extremis,* and, in her pink nightgown from Paris, she awaited the impact, the onrush, the tearing and the revelation. She kept her eyes fixed on the door through which would appear this formidable and unavoidable figure: her husband. Time passed and the door remained closed. After two hours she began to worry. 'Should I get up?' she wrote. 'Should I stay in bed? I had no idea what to do.' Towards midnight, Mme Kruse, the new chamber-maid came, 'very merrily,' to tell her that the Grand Duke was having supper. Whilst she had been counting the minutes, he had been carousing with his favourite servants. At last, after he had eaten and drunk his fill this cantankerous, drunken joker appeared and declared: 'The servants would be amused to see us in bed together.' Then he fell into bed and into a brutish sleep next to his young wife, who lay with her eyes wide open in the dark, wondering whether to be relieved or worried by such neglect.

The following nights brought Catherine no more surprises, and she resigned herself to remaining a virgin with this indifferent and inexperienced husband. During this private defeat, the public jollity continued, brilliantly orchestrated by the Empress, and a succession of balls, masquerades, fireworks and entertainments took place in the bedecked capital.

On the 30th August, the Tsarina went to the Alexander Nevsky convent where Peter the Great's famous boat, built with his own hands, the 'Diedouchka', 'ancestor of the Russian Fleet', was kept in dry dock in a shed. The wormeaten bark, which could no longer stay afloat, was hoisted on to a barge. A portrait of the Tsar who had created modern Russia was pinned to the mast. Elisabeth, wearing the uniform of a naval officer (still this taste for male costume!), went on board and, to the sound of gunshot, kissed her father's portrait. The procession set off down the Neva, behind the 'ancestor of the Russian Fleet', a procession of lavishly decorated vessels bore the courtiers whose hairstyles were being ruined by the wind and ears numbed by the sound of trumpets and drums. Once again, Peter the Great led by his beloved daughter was moving around this city that he had built through sheer will-power, on a swamp. A brand new city, half on earth and half on water, criss-crossed with canals with their banks shored up with rows of posts, a few stone houses and many wooden ones, a few paved streets and a lot of waste land. 'The only stone buildings,' wrote Catherine, 'were on the Millionaya, the Lougovaya, and the English quay, which formed as it were a curtain concealing the nastiest wooden huts you could imagine. The only house decorated with damask was that of the Princess of Hesse; all the others had either whitewashed walls or bad wallpaper or painted cloth.' Never mind, Elisabeth was proud of her capital. And by organizing this waterborne procession, led by Peter the Great, she was emphasizing for all to see, the fact that she had inherited her father's masculine virtues. Johanna was highly impressed by the arrangement and the lavishness of the procession (she described it in detail in her letters); Catherine, on the other hand, began to grow tired of this succession of parties. The balls were especially disappointing, since young people were more or less excluded from them. She had to dance endless quadrilles with sixty-year-old partners, 'mostly lame, gout-ridden, or senile'. She would like to have become closer to the Grand Duke, but, she said, 'My dear husband took no notice whatsoever of me, and spent all his time with his footmen, playing military games, drilling them in his room, making them change uniforms twenty times a day; I either yawned and was bored, with no one to talk to, or else I was on parade as well.' Madame Kruse terrorized the young waiting-maids whose chatter sometimes distracted Catherine from her boredom. They were forbidden to whisper to the Grand Duchess and to 'play' with her.

The end of the festivities also represented the end of Johanna's stay in Russia. In twenty months she had managed to both marry her daughter and lose her reputation in the eyes of the Empress. First her political schemings and then her amorous liaison with Count Ivan Betsky had been frowned upon by the court. It was whispered that thanks to this gentleman, she was pregnant and that the Grand Duchess was soon to have a little brother or sister. Catherine could not ignore these rumours, and her pride suffered. But, whilst she disapproved of her mother's frivolity, she could not help feeling sorry for her being so much snubbed and humiliated, and dared not reproach her. Although she had decided to send the intriguer away, the Empress wished to appear magnanimous and gave her sixty thousand roubles with which to settle her accounts. However once the main debtors had been paid off with this money, Johanna realized that she still owed seventy thousand roubles. Catherine was horrified by the size of this debt, but promised to pay it off, bit by bit, by cutting down on her own personal allowance of thirty thousand roubles a year.

When she had packed her trunks, Johanna asked for an audience with the Empress, and fell at her feet begging forgiveness for any displeasure she might have caused her. Unmoved by this repentance Elisabeth only replied that it was too late to discuss the matter but that, 'if the princess had always been as humble as this, it would have been better for everybody.' In describing this farewell scene Johanna emphasized the 'kindness' of the Empress. This euphemism was intended for Christian-Augustus and failed to conceal the extent of her disgrace. D'Allion, the French chargé d'affaires hinted that she had actually been sent home because of her continuing secret correspondence with Frederick II, which was regularly intercepted and deciphered by the secret service.

To avoid giving too much pain to her daughter, Johanna left Tsarskoe Selo at dawn without saying goodbye to her. When she arrived in Berlin, she received a message from Elisabeth asking her to tell Frederick II to recall his ambassador, Mardefeldt, who had become unwelcome at the Russian Court. She was in fact forcing the miserable Johanna to reveal herself, in front of the King of Prussia, the failure of the secret dealings he had entrusted her with.

Meanwhile at Tsarskoe Selo, Catherine burst into tears when she found the apartment empty after her mother's departure. She suddenly missed the woman she had criticized so often. Despite all her faults, she was the best friend Catherine had. Now that she had gone the atmosphere at court became stifling: Catherine had never felt more alone. Ever since he had acquired the right to approach her, Peter avoided ever being alone with her. Was he afraid of her? Did he find her ugly? She didn't understand. 'I could easily have loved my new husband if he had shown the slightest wish or capacity to be loved,' she wrote in her *Memoirs*, 'but I made a cruel observation about him during the very first days of our marriage. I told myself: "If you love this man you will become the most unfortunate creature on earth; being the sort of person you are, you will expect some response; but that man does not even look at you, he more or less talks only about dolls, and pays more attention to any other woman than you; you are too proud to make a fuss; so rein yourself in, please, when it comes to showing affection towards this gentleman; think of yourself, madam." This first imprint in a waxen heart remained with me, and these thoughts stayed in my mind.'

The lack of communication between Catherine and Peter grew rapidly. He disappointed her by night, and exasperated her by day. Because his physical development had been retarded by his many childhood illnesses, the Grand Duke suffered mentally at being unable to satisfy his young wife, and took his revenge by pretending to be drawn to other women. Catherine, with complete innocence, assumed that her husband was finding elsewhere the pleasures that she was incapable of providing and because of her pride, pretended to ignore the princely infidelities. His effrontery increased in the face of indifference, and she, embittered by his coarseness, distanced herself even more from this man who, it seemed, preferred any woman to his own wife. Did she not realize that he was a virgin?

The Empress had at first been touched by this childish couple, but now they were beginning to irritate her. She had not rested until the young people were married and could ensure the future of the dynasty, but now that they were installed with all the privileges of heirs to the throne, she regarded them with mistrust, hostility almost. Imbued as she was with a sense of total power she found it hard to bear the constant sight of a 'successor', as though it were unthinkable that the people should be able to worship anyone else after worshipping her. Peter and Catherine, whom she had thought of as her own children, now appeared suddenly as rivals whose machinations were to be feared. Would they start to plot against her, with their friends, and try to gain power prematurely? Every sign of favour towards the Grand Duke and the Grand Duchess became an insult to the Tsarina. She decided to curb this youth, and a period of harassment now succeeded the period of favour. To begin with, the Empress banished from the court a chambermaid of Catherine's, whose only crime was her total devotion to her mistress. A little later, Catherine's chief chamberlain, Zahar Tchernychev, was forced to leave her to go on a diplomatic mission to Ratisbon. Reason: 'We're afraid he's falling in love with the Grand Duchess. He's always staring at her.' Other courtiers suspected of being friendly towards Catherine were sent away under different pretexts. Her Majesty only wanted those she felt sure of, her own people, around the Grand Ducal couple. 'She was giving pain freely and capriciously, without the slightest reason,' wrote Catherine.

Despite the increased severity towards her, Catherine continued to behave like a genuine Grand Duchess, learning Russian and observing Orthodox rites. She had felt from her first moments in Russia that her salvation could only lie in constant efforts to naturalize and acclimatize herself, and identify herself with political and religious life. Once she had chosen a line of behaviour, nothing would turn her away from it. The Grand Duke teased her about this obstinacy. Why didn't she avoid all that mystical mumbo-jumbo as he did? His passion at the moment was puppet theatres. He had one built for his personal use in a room next to the Empress's apartments. One day he heard a noise behind the partition and made several holes with a brace in the panel of a disused door. With his eye glued to the hole he saw Elisabeth's private dining-room. The Empress was seated with her official lover, Razumovsky, who was wearing a brocade dressing-gown and a dozen intimate friends. Peter was thrilled to have caught his aunt in such loose company. He assembled all his friends, arranging benches and chairs in front of the holes, and ran to fetch Catherine to come and enjoy the entertainment. Terrified by his rashness, Catherine cried that he must be mad, that he had brought 'at least twenty people into the secret', and that this fooling might cost them dear.

Soon afterwards, the Empress, as one might have expected, found out what had happened, saw the holes in the door, rushed to Catherine's room and summoned her nephew, who appeared in his dressing-gown, holding his night-cap. Choking with rage, Elisabeth lambasted the idiot. She screamed that he had forgotten 'all that he owed her', that she could only think of him as 'an ungrateful brute', that her own father, Peter the Great, had also had an ungrateful son, Alexis, and that he had punished him 'by disinheriting him', that she herself under the Empress Anne had never deviated from 'the respect due to a crowned head', that in other times such *lèse-majesté* would have been punished by incarceration! The most worrying part of this diatribe, for the two young people, was the reference to the Tsarevich Alexis, whom Peter the Great had in fact not only 'disinherited', but had actually had tortured to death. When the Grand Duke tried to defend himself, Elisabeth ordered him to be quiet and 'poured out insults and shocking things, showing as much contempt as rage'. Catherine could not prevent herself from crying at this violent outburst. The Empress comforted her. 'I am not saying these things to you,' she muttered. 'I know that you took no part in what he did, and that you neither looked, nor wished to look through that door.'

All the same it was Catherine who, some time later, received the thunderbolt. Nine months had gone by since the wedding and she was still not pregnant. The Empress took this infertility as a personal insult. She thought that the Grand Duchess must be entirely to blame, for not arousing desire in her husband. She summoned Catherine and brutally said this to her face. 'She said . . . that if I didn't love the Grand Duke, it wasn't her fault, she would never have made me marry against my will, that she knew perfectly well that I loved another; anyway a thousand awful things – I've forgotten half of them.' Now, carried along by a tide of fury, the Empress passed from conjugal to political grievances. Catherine understood, as soon as she began, that the Tsarina, urged on by Bestuzhev, the enemy of the Franco-Prussian faction, now suspected her of sharing her mother's views. This was madness as Catherine had, from her arrival at the court, made an absolute rule for herself not to get involved in state affairs. Nothing could have been found in her correspondence (opened by the Chancery) to justify these accusations. But that didn't matter to the Tsarina! Everything connected with Johanna seemed polluted to her, and she took it out on the daughter, now that she had got rid of the mother. 'She began slandering me,' Catherine wrote, 'asking me if I behaved as I did on instructions from my mother, saying that I was betraying her for the sake of the King of Prussia, and that she knew all about my guile and cunning tricks . . . '

This time Catherine's tears failed to appease the imperial virago. Elisabeth's face was crimson, her eyes shone, she yelled and shook and raised her fists. 'I could see that she was about to hit me ... I knew that she beat her women, her entourage, sometimes even her lovers during rages; I could not avoid her by escaping as I had my back to the door and she was right in front of me.'

The Grand Duke's unexpected arrival caused a diversion. Elisabeth clenched her teeth and turned away. Catherine who was half dead with terror returned to her apartments, had herself bled, went to bed and cried until the evening.

From that day onwards the Empress, on Bestuzhev's advice, decided to make life hard for the two young people. It was a matter of reining them in, by politically isolating and neutralizing them. Bestuzhev personally drew up in the Tsarina's name a list of instructions for 'the two distinguished people' who would be placed close to their Imperial Highnesses as master and mistress of the court. The 'distinguished person' in charge of the Grand Duke would, according to the document, 'correct some of his Highness's unseemly habits, such as that, for instance, of pouring the contents of his glass over the servants at table; or of shouting rude remarks and coarse jokes at those who had the honour of approaching him; or of disfiguring himself in public with grimaces and continual contortions of all parts of his body.' The 'distinguished person' allocated to the Grand Duchess should, for her part, encourage her in the practice of the Orthodox faith, prevent her from meddling in the affairs of the Empire, and forbid her any familiarity with the young lords, gentlemen of the bedchamber, pages or footmen. Also the new duenna would urge the Grand Duchess to show more enthusiasm for conjugal love-play. 'Her Imperial Highness, chosen to be the worthy wife of our beloved nephew, his Imperial Highness the Grand Duke, heir to the Empire, has been elevated to her present position as Imperial Highness for this sole purpose: that her Imperial Highness (Catherine) should, by her measured behaviour, her intelligence and her virtue arouse His Imperial Highness's (the Grand Duke) sincere devotion, and by capturing his heart, produce a descendant for our great family and much-desired heir for the Empire.'[1] A final point: Catherine was henceforth forbidden to write to anybody without going through the Foreign Office. Thus her letters to her father and mother would have to be copied, word for word, from a form established by the Chancery. She was not even allowed to tell the scribe what she wished to say to her parents, since the Foreign Office, of course, knew better than she did. Little by little the palace was becoming her prison. Although she was not, properly speaking, a

---

[1] Quotation from *History of Catherine II* Tome 1, chapter XIX by Bilbassov.

captive, her margin of freedom had been reduced practically to nothing.

But, more than ever, she wanted to enjoy herself. Amongst the Grand Duke's friends were three handsome, elegant and high-spirited boys – two brothers and a cousin – the Tchernychevs. André, the eldest, was Peter's favourite and soon became Catherine's as well. Even during her engagement, she had engaged in a sort of flirtatious duel with him, which had kept them both amused. Peter, who loved ambiguous situations, had encouraged his fiancée in this unhealthy game. Talking to André about Catherine he used to jokingly call her 'your intended'. After the marriage the Grand Duchess chose to call her follower *synok* (sonny), whilst he gave her the name *matouchka* (little mother). This slightly flirtatious friendship did not go unnoticed by the other courtiers. Fearing a scandal, Catherine's faithful footman, Timothy Evreinov, begged her to be careful. When she protested her innocence and spoke of simple goodness and pure friendship, he retorted: 'What you call goodness and friendship because he is faithful and serves you, others around you call love!'[1] Struck by this judgment she looked into her heart and realized, with a mixture of fear and gratitude, that very tender feelings had grown up in her, without her realizing. So as not to compromise the Grand Duchess, André Tchernychev pretended to be ill and asked for leave of absence. A few weeks later in April 1746, he reappeared at court. During a concert at the Summer Palace Catherine, bored by the music, left her chair and tiptoed out. Nobody followed her. Her husband was playing the violin in the orchestra. The Empress was away. The ladies-in-waiting were busy elsewhere. She went to her room. This room gave onto the great saloon where painters, perched on scaffolding, were repainting the ceiling. Suddenly her heart missed a beat: she saw André Tchernychev at the other end of the saloon. Unable to prevent herself she beckoned him. He begged her to let him come into her room. Although she longed to give in she refused and went on talking to him in a low voice through the open door. In the middle of their conversation, she heard a slight noise, turned, and saw at the other door of the room the chamberlain, Count Devier spying on her. 'The Grand Duke is asking for you, Madam,' he said, bowing.

The next day the three Tchernychevs were sent as lieutenants to regiments billeted near Orenburg. And on the same afternoon the 'distinguished person' charged with watching over Catherine's conduct took up her duties, on Bestuzhev's orders. Her name was Maria Semenovna Choglokov, and she was the Empress's first cousin. She was twenty-four-years old, possessed a pretty face, a dull mind, armour-clad

[1] Catherine II *Memoirs.*

respectability, and a sense of duty which stiffened her from head to toe. She adored her husband, who was on a mission to Vienna at that time, she had children, she was pious, she swore by Bestuzhev and the Empress; in other words she would be, they thought, a living example to the Grand Duchess, who was so much in need of guidance. Catherine received this spy with terror. She found her 'extremely stupid, nasty, capricious and very self-seeking'. At the slightest light-hearted remark, Choglokov would cry out: 'Her Majesty would not like such talk!' or 'The Empress could not possibly approve of such a thing!' The Grand Duke also found his whole entourage changed. Prince Basil Repnin was allocated to him as tutor. Finally the young couple were ordered to go and confess to Simeon Todorski, now bishop of Pskov, who interrogated them separately on their relations with the Tchernychevs. When they swore their innocence, the priest cried: 'But how is it that the Empress has been told the opposite?' Although the holy man, ignoring the secrecy of the confessional, made a favourable report to Her Majesty, the surveillance around Catherine and Peter was not relaxed. They could not move a step outside their room without asking for permission. Every day brought fresh humiliations. At times it seemed to Catherine as though she had become, without knowing how or why, the Empress's sworn enemy.

CHAPTER VI

The Virgin Wife

Just as Catherine had, little by little, discovered the terrible side of Elisabeth which hid behind the idealized image of the great-hearted Tsarina, so also did she find out, as the days went by, the true barbaric, cruel and miserable nature of Russia, behind the civilized façade. Everything here was an illusion. Peter the Great's attempts to 'Europeanize' his country had only superficially succeeded. Since the 'Builders', people wore wigs instead of beards, dressed in French clothes, took snuff, danced as they did in Vienna or at Versailles, proclaimed progressive ideas, and yet knew nothing of genuine Western culture. The Emperor, by condemning Russian traditions — archaic forms of worship and a rough patriarchal morality – had thrown the aristocracy into confusion. Since they were expected to ape the West, the courtiers plunged into debauchery. The licentious behaviour of Elisabeth's entourage only reflected the Tsarina's own escapades. And this profligacy was not accompanied, as it was in other European courts, by an intellectual refinement. Here the ladies-in-waiting competed fiercely in terms of elegance, but most of them could not read. They were only interested in intrigues, dancing and coquetry. They were coarse with their servants and coy with their partners. The men, whether they were guards officers or high officials, did not show any more interest in books. Their favourite pastimes were flirtations, gambling and drink. A man was a man when he had a bottle or a pack of cards before him, not a desk or a printed page. It was difficult to obtain French or German works in St Petersburg, despite the country now being open to the west. As for works in Russian, they hardly existed. A national literature was still in its infancy. Nobody was interested despite the feeble efforts of the new Academy of Fine Arts. Also, the nobles surrounding Elisabeth were of a humble origin! Peter the First had replaced the old families with a meritocracy. No more boyars – only functionaries now. From now on the 'Table of Ranks' established once and for all the position of each member of the immense structure of the Russian administration. The most zealous servants of the Empire received the titles of count, baron, even prince. Count Alexis

Razumovsky was a simple Ukrainian peasant, and Biron, a stable-boy, became Duke of Courland. These rich, arrogant newcomers were looked upon with scorn by the great families of the ancient nobility, the Trubetskoys, the Volkonskys, the Repnines, the Galitzines, the Obolenskys or the Dolgoroukys. Catherine herself, who was used to the old German aristocracy, was shocked by the coarseness of the Empress's friends. Beneath the superficial veneer the wood was unsanded and unplaned. 'There seem to be two types,' wrote a perceptive contemporary, the Chevalier de Corberon, 'two different nations on the same soil. You are simultaneously in the fourteenth and the eighteenth centuries. But even the civilized part is only civilized on the surface. It is a nation of clothed savages, people . . . who have beautiful cuffs but no sleeves, of green fruit that has rotted from over-forcing. Form takes precedence over content: everybody loves appearances, and nobody considers what is essential or important.' And indeed although great splendour was the rule at court receptions, although Elisabeth's suite was the most brilliant and numerous in Europe, although foreign visitors were dazzled by the gildings, mirrors and murals in the state chambers, the actual living rooms had no comforts whatsoever. In these hastily-built palaces, the doors didn't shut properly, the windows let in draughts, the stairs were rickety, the walls oozed water and the fires smoked. In winter the air was unbreathable because of the sour smell of soot. There was a permanent fire hazard because the stoves were so badly maintained. As the houses were nearly all made of wood, they could burn down in a matter of hours. The Russians were used to this type of catastrophe – as far as they were concerned roofs were never permanent. After the flames had died down they swept away the ashes and started to rebuild. Elisabeth's palace in Moscow had in this way been wiped out by flames in three hours. She ordered that it should be rebuilt in six weeks. During the rebuilding, Catherine camped in the 'bishop's house' which itself caught fire three times. 'There has never been a worse year for fires,' she wrote, 'at times I have seen two, three, four, even five fires burning simultaneously in different parts of Moscow.' She was hardly ever comfortable in the apartments allocated to her. At St Petersburg, in the Summer Palace, her windows gave onto the Fontanka on one side, then no more than a foetid mud pond, and on the other, onto a tiny courtyard. In Moscow everything crawled with vermin and water dripped from the panelling. The Grand Duchess's seventeen ladies and maids-in-waiting slept in the same room, next door to her own, which was also her bathroom. When they were travelling, the post-houses were kept for the Empress, and Catherine often had to sleep in the pantry or in a tent. 'I remember,' she wrote, 'getting dressed one day in front of the oven where they had just cooked the bread, and another time there were two inches of water in the tent where they had put up my bed.' Furniture was sparse, and not being an integral part of any dwelling, would travel with the Court. Everything went with them, as if they were nomads moving camp. Carpets, mirrors, beds, tables, chairs, sofas, crockery were loaded onto carts when the Empress moved from the Winter Palace to the Summer Palace, or from Peterhof to Moscow. 'A lot were smashed and broken on the journeys,' wrote Catherine, 'and were then handed back to us in pieces, so that we could hardly use them any more.' Thus valuable pieces of French cabinet work were mishandled, dismembered, left in the rain, and ended up totally ignored in the great freezing palaces. The courtiers aching from the journey would put on their best clothes, and dine off gold plate in the enormous dining-rooms, off wobbly tables with logs wedged beneath them. They might be powdered and be-wigged, the men might be scented, the women might have devastating beauty-spots by their lips, but that night most of them would be sleeping on pallets for lack of proper bedding.

This mixture of luxury and penury seemed to Catherine to be an essential characteristic of Russian society. 'It is not unusual,' she wrote, 'to see emerging from an enormous courtyard, deep in sludge and horrors of every sort, beside a rotten wooden shack, a superbly dressed woman covered in jewels, in a magnificent carriage drawn by six miserable nags in filthy harnesses, unkempt footmen ruining their beautiful livery by their awkward bearing... There is a stronger disposition towards tyranny here than in any other part of the inhabited world; it is inculcated at an early age into children who see the cruelty with which their parents behave towards their servants, as no house is without iron collars, chains, whips and other such instruments used to torture, for the slightest fault, those whom nature has placed in this unfortunate class, which they cannot escape from without committing a crime.' She was not intimate with these shadowy inhabitants of the servants' hall and the countryside, but she could guess at their misery. They were the same people she had so often seen prostrate on either side of the imperial processions. She knew that, for them, nothing had changed for centuries. And that the serfs' conditions had in fact worsened since Peter the Great's reforms. They were the live strength of the country, everything rested on their backs, nothing could be done without them and yet they had no control over either their destiny or their bodies. At best their master, part of whose wealth they formed, would treat them like cattle. And it never occurred to anybody to be surprised at this. How many were there? Impossible to count. A real ant-heap. Some said that the peasants formed ninety-five per cent of the total population. One would have thought that crowds were a totally Russian phenomenon. Catherine realized at last that, contrary to appearances, she was not in Europe but in Asia, and she had arrived there after going back two centuries in time. She began to panic, and pined for Stettin, her German family, her friends and Babet Cardel.

Her thoughts had reached this stage when she heard of her father's death at Zerbst. Never did she curse so much the imperial decision preventing her from corresponding freely with her parents. Longing to pour out her grief in an intimate, warm and personal letter, she was forced to countersign insipid condolences from the Chancellery. Reeling from the shock, she shut herself up in her room and cried. After eight days, Madame Choglokov came to tell her, on the Empress's behalf, that she must stop crying, as her father 'wasn't a king'. 'I answered that it was true that he wasn't a king but that he was her father. At that she replied that it was most unsuitable for a Grand Duchess to mourn a father who wasn't a king.'[1] At last, the Empress allowed Catherine as a pittance, the right to wear mourning for six weeks.

After this, life at Court resumed its absurd and monotonous round of journeys, banquets, masquerades, naval reviews and religious services. To numb her mind, Catherine played Faro for high stakes, and to please the Empress she said her prayers; she also rode, read, gossiped and complained about the boredom of the social events. 'The ball was very meagre and badly organized, the men were harassed and bad-tempered,' she wrote. And again, 'At the Court ... there was no conversation, everybody cordially hated everybody else, slander was substituted for wit, and the slightest mention of work was treated as *lèse-majesté*. People were careful not to talk of art or sciences, because they were ignorant about them. One could bet that half the company could not read, and I am not sure whether even a third could write.'

Sometimes one of the Empress's whims would shake up this vain and obsequious little world. She would suddenly decide on a journey that would upset everybody from the lowest servant to the highest dignitary, or else she would change the mealtimes, or, as she suffered from insomnia she would force her entourage, who were dropping with exhaustion, to keep her company through the night. One winter's day, in 1747, she ordered that all the ladies of the court should have their heads shaved, and sent them 'black uncombed wigs' to wear until their hair grew again. Young and old sacrificed their hair in deference to the imperial will. There was a concert of moans in every room as the

[1] Catherine II *Memoirs*.

hairdressers proceeded with the shearing. As for the ladies of the town, although they did not have to be shaved, they were not allowed to appear in drawing-rooms without the same black wigs on top of their hair. This double-decker hair-style made them appear 'even dowdier than the court ladies'. The reason for this new capillary rule: the Empress, unable to remove the powder from her hair, had chosen to blacken it; then as the dye could not be removed, she had had to shave her head. How could she, in these circumstances, accept in her wake all these women with their proud locks! No, the right behaviour for all good subjects was to imitate their sovereign in all things. However, Elisabeth made Catherine an exception, since she had lost all her hair after an illness, and had only just begun to have a hairstyle again. Her Majesty was not always so magnanimous. A few months later, on Saint Alexander's day, when Catherine appeared at court in a white dress 'embroidered on the seams with large gold Spanish stitch' the Empress had her instructed to remove immediately this garment which was too similar to those of the Knights of the Order of Alexander Nevsky. In fact, there was no resemblance at all between the two garments. 'It is possible,' wrote Catherine, 'that the Empress found my costume prettier than her own, and that was the real reason why she had me ordered to remove mine. My dear aunt was very susceptible to such little jealousies, not only towards myself, but towards all the other ladies, and those younger than herself were particular targets.' And she cited the case of the beautiful Madame Naryshkin, whose elegance and grand manner irritated the Empress so much that, one evening at a reception, she rushed on the unfortunate lady with a pair of scissors and cut a 'charming decoration of ribbons' off the top of her head. Another time she picked on two of her maids-in-waiting, too pretty for her taste, and savagely chopped their curly hair. 'The young ladies,' wrote Catherine, 'said that Her Majesty had removed skin as well as hair.'

Keeping to her plan, the Empress continued to deprive Catherine and Peter of anyone whose friendship might relieve their loneliness. Three pages whom the Grand Duke was fond of, were arrested and taken to the fortress. His uncle the Bishop of Lübeck was sent away. All the Holsteinian gentlemen of his entourage were, equally, removed. His steward Kramer, 'a gentle and orderly man, who had been attached to the prince since his birth' was dismissed. Another valet, Rombach, was sent to prison. For her part, Catherine had to be separated, on the Empress's orders, from a little Kalmouk whom she was fond of and who did her hair every morning, and from several other servants, including the faithful Evreinov. These endlessly repeated blows made Catherine write that she led 'a life which would have driven ten others mad, and made twenty others die of grief.'

In fact the Empress's persecutions drew the young people together in their unhappiness. Peter was an incurable gossip, and he knew that he could hold forth without fear that his words would be repeated to the Empress. So, waving his arms, he would carry on a monologue about trivialities. And she would listen with a mixture of dejection and pity. 'Often I would become very bored by his visits, which lasted for several hours,' she wrote, 'and also tired, as he never sat down one always had to walk with him up and down the room... He walked very fast, with large steps, and it was hard work to keep up with him and sustain a conversation about minute military details, which he loved, but never finished once he had started.' There was nothing in common between these two people yoked to the same chain. 'Never did two minds resemble each other less than ours,' Catherine wrote. If she tried to tell him about what she had been reading, his eyes would open wide. The only books that interested him were 'stories about highwaymen'. 'There were, however, moments when he did listen to me,' added Catherine, 'but they were always moments of distress, as he was very cowardly and his mind was feeble.' Yes, when fear gripped his heart, Peter would seek Catherine's advice. He was terrified of his aunt, and was haunted at night by the thought of the fortress: he could not forget the Tsarevich Alexis who had been killed by his father, and the little Tsar Ivan VI incarcerated by Elisabeth. He saw plots everywhere, he imagined tortures, he saw blood under his feet, he shook with fear, and Catherine would try to reassure him. Suppressing her own worry, she would tell him that the Empress was not a monster, despite a certain roughness of character, that she would never lay a finger on her nephew, and that the most he need expect were angry words. Calming down as quickly as he had become upset, the Grand Duke would return to his infantile amusements. At eighteen, he remained untouched by fleshly attractions, and continued as he had done from his earliest infancy to play with wooden soldiers, miniature cannons and toy fortresses. Madame Kruse, the chief chambermaid, procured for him as many as he wanted, behind Madame Choglokov's back. But after supper when the couple were in bed, Madame Kruse would shut the door and the fun would begin. Installed in bed next to his fresh and smiling young wife in her nightgown – still a virgin – Peter with shining eyes and blazing cheeks would make his regiments of wooden soldiers manoeuvre on the bedcover, imitating the sound of the cannon, shouting orders and inviting Catherine to join in the battles. This game would continue until two in the morning. 'I often laughed, but more often I became fed up and uncomfortable,' wrote Catherine, 'as the whole bed was covered and filled with quite heavy dolls and toys. One night Madame Choglokov, intrigued by the noises she could hear from outside, knocked on the bedroom door. Before opening it the Grand Duke and the Grand Duchess hurriedly pushed the toys under the cover. The duenna came in, inspected the room with a suspicious eye, declared that Her Majesty would be displeased to hear that the young people were not yet asleep and withdrew. 'Once she had gone,' Catherine wrote, 'the Grand Duke continued his game until he wanted to go to sleep.'

It was no doubt hard for her to accept that her young husband found her less attractive in bed than a collection of toy soldiers. However she did not let her impatience show. Chastity was not yet a hardship for her. Peter, for his part, had been told that a slight physical imperfection was preventing him from assuming his proper role as a husband. He would need a very simple operation to free him from this problem. But he was afraid of the lancet. All things considered, he preferred to remain a child, away from the world, in the midst of his toys and his dreams. 'The Grand Duke,' wrote Champeaux in a memo drawn up for the cabinet at Versailles in 1758, 'was incapable of having children owing to an obstacle which, amongst eastern people, was remedied by circumcision, but which he thought was insurmountable.' And Castéra, another diplomat, also wrote; 'Such was the shame which his misfortune brought upon him, that he (the Grand Duke) did not even have the courage to reveal it, and the Princess, who now received his advances with repugnance and was then no more experienced than himself, sought neither to console him nor to make him find means which would draw him back into her arms.'

Peter was seized by a new passion: he wanted to rear spaniels for the hunt. Soon about ten animals were assembled in the bedroom. They slept in a heap in the alcove, behind a wooden screen. Their continual barking and their smell disturbed Catherine. 'We both had to sleep in the midst of this stench,' she said. Despite her protests the Grand Duke refused to be separated from his pack. He became drunk with the total power he had over his dogs. On the pretext of teaching them to obey, he would stun them with guttural orders, and beat them with whips and sticks. One day Catherine found him hitting, as hard as he could, a tiny King Charles spaniel that one of his servants was holding up by the tail. She cried and begged him to stop 'but that only made him hit harder'. 'In general,' she observed, 'tears and cries instead of making the Grand Duke feel pity, sent him into a rage, pity was to him painful, even unbearable.' When he had had enough of tormenting his dogs, he seized his violin and walked around the room for hours vigorously scraping the strings with his bow. 'He did not know a single note,' wrote Catherine, 'but he had a strong ear and made the beauty of the music depend on the violence with which he drew the sound from his instrument.' Having said that, she still preferred the squeaks of the fiddle to the Grand Duke's invective after he had drunk too much with his servants. A few years later, she remarked: 'He had already begun to smell all the time of wine and tobacco, which was unbearable for those who came near him.' For one whole winter, Peter talked to Catherine about a new whim: to build a country-seat like a Capuchin convent, dress the courtiers up as monks, and give them each a donkey to go about their business on. He choked with laughter as he elaborated the details of this project. His wife, to humour him, had to draw hundreds of plans of this imaginary establishment. She was exasperated. 'When he went out,' she said, 'the most boring book would appear delightfully amusing.'

Scorned by her husband, she had to reason with herself so as not to lose faith in her powers of seduction. She was eighteen. The image she saw in the mirror, which she consulted more and more often, was on the whole satisfactory. 'I was becoming more and more beautiful,' she wrote, 'I was tall and had a fine figure;[1] I only needed a bit more shape as I was quite thin. I liked to go without powder, as my hair was a fine brown colour, thick and luxuriant.' Anyway she did not lack for male admiration at the Court. Cyril Razumovsky, brother of the Empress's lover, whispered compliments which she dared not interpret as declarations of love. The Swedish ambassador found her so beautiful that he bade Madame Lestocq tell her so. Catherine was flattered but, 'either through modesty or coquetry', it made her 'awkward in her bearing' each time she met the diplomat.

These drawing-room flirtations could not be enough to appease the demands of a lively temperament. Married and yet deprived of a man, Catherine tried to relax her nerves by physical exercise. In summer, she would rise at dawn, put on a masculine outfit and, followed by an old servant, go and shoot ducks 'in the reeds near the sea, on either side of the Oranienbaum canal'. But riding, even more than shooting, helped her to forget her sad state. In a headlong gallop, she enjoyed the rough pleasures of togetherness with a horse, mastery of speed and freedom through effort. She sometimes rode for thirteen hours a day. 'The more violent the exercise the more I liked it, so that if the horse happened to run away, I would chase it and bring it back,' she wrote. Her natural leaning towards virility made her ride like a man on a flat saddle. The

---

[1] Although Catherine said she was 'tall', it appears from some of her dresses, which have been preserved, that she was only one metre and sixty centimetres high.

Empress saw in this a possible reason for the Grand Duchess's sterility. So Catherine secretly had modified saddles made. 'They had,' she explained, 'an English hook, and one could put one's leg over so as to be seated like a man; as well as that the hook could be unscrewed and another stirrup could be raised or lowered according to how I wanted it.' This ingenious device permitted the Grand Duchess to ride side-saddle in front of Elisabeth, and astride again as soon as she was no longer being watched. A divided skirt helped these changes of position. She had lessons with a German equerry, an instructor for the cadet corps, and her rapid progress earned her silver 'spurs of honour'. A second victory, this time at dancing; one evening at a ball, she challenged Madame Arnheim, the wife of the Minister of Saxony, to see who could whirl around longest without losing her breath. She won and was very proud of it. At another reception, the Chevalier Sacrosomo, who had just arrived at St Petersburg, approached her, kissed her hand and slipped her a note saying: 'This is from your mother'. Terrified at the thought that someone might have seen them, Catherine hid the note in her glove. Later, in the safety of her room, she read the message from her mother which seemed to come from another world, read it again, became moved, cried and decided to answer by the same route, at the risk of being found out. Sacrosomo's instructions were that she was to give the letter to a cellist, during the next concert. On the appointed day she went round the orchestra, found the man and stopped behind his chair. At once he pretended to look for a handkerchief and opened his pocket wide. She dropped the paper in. Nobody had seen her. She could breathe freely. For how many more years would she have to fear the Empress's spies? In vain she bent to anything to please this woman, all she received in return was hatred, scorn or suspicion. Impulsive and inconsistent as she was, Elisabeth could easily send her back to Germany the very next day, having got the Church to annul the unconsummated marriage. Should Catherine dread or hope for this extreme solution? She no longer really knew. The Chamberlain Afzin took her aside and passed on to her a view that the Empress had just expressed at her table, to whit that the Grand Duchess was 'overloading herself with debts', that everything she did 'was stamped with stupidity', that she thought she was clever but 'fooled nobody', that one must keep an eye on her, that she was dangerous ... he added that he had been ordered to repeat this speech, word for word to the person concerned. Catherine swallowed down her misery and, resigned, waited for the next blow.

Gyllenborg had, in the past, given her a taste for reading. More than ever she sought consolation and instruction from books. She began with

novels by La Calprenède and Mlle de Scudéry, *l'Astrée* by Honoré
d'Urfé, *Clovis* by Desmarets. But she soon became bored with these
stories, idealized as they were to the point of dullness. She turned to the
works of Brantôme which she found amusing, if extremely light.
Madame de Sévigné's letters were her great delight. She longed to be
able to write like her, with such a sharp pen, combining observation
with irony, intelligence with elegance. Throughout her life, when faced
with a blank sheet of paper, she would remember this unapproachable
stylist. She also read, with laudable efforts, *The General History of
Germany* by Father Basse, at the rate of one volume every week, and
The History of Henry the Great by Father Peréfixe. She was filled with
admiration for the noble figure of Henry IV. If she was to reign one day,
she would use him as her model, she thought. But really she believed
less and less in such a splendid eventuality. A little later she discovered
Voltaire and was in raptures. Then she plunged into the four volumes
of Bayle's Dictionary, greedily devouring the generous ideas of this
precursor of the encyclopedists.

After the delights of a stroll in this garden of great minds, the
awakening, to face the Empress, Peter and the Choglokovs was a
painful one. The excellent Prince Repnin had been relieved of his
duties as tutor to the Grand Duke and replaced by Madame
Choglokov's own husband, whilst she remained the Grand Duchess's
guardian. Still convinced that the Choglokovs were an exemplary
couple, the Empress was counting on their influence to persuade the
young people to love each other and have children. From the beginning,
Catherine took against Choglokov. 'He was blond and conceited, very
fat, and his mind was as thick as his body,' she wrote. 'He was hated like
a toad by everybody, and was not in the least bit lovable; his wife's
jealousy and her nastiness and spite were also things to be avoided,
especially by me, since I had no support in the world except myself and
my abilities, if I had any.' Then this puffed-up fool, this so-called
paragon of conjugal virtue, seduced in a trice, and made pregnant one of
the Empress's maids of honour, a Miss Kosheleva. Rage from the
Tsarina who spoke of hounding the seducer out of the Court. Tears
from the wife who, whilst condemning her husband's behaviour, had
agreed to wipe the slate clean. The Empress made a surprising decision:
the Choglokovs would remain with the Grand Duke and Grand
Duchess, but the lady-in-waiting would have to go. All the same the two
guardians did lose some of their arrogance after this mishap. Choglokov
softened to such an extent that he began daring to make eyes at
Catherine. Did he hope that she, like Mademoiselle Kosheleva, would
give in to him? Indignant as she was at his attentions, she avoided a

public clash. Madame Choglokov, who kept a careful eye on the seducer's activities, was grateful to Catherine for discouraging him so discreetly. She, anyway, was about to give him a dose of his own medicine by merrily having an affair herself.

Catherine, in the midst of this tangle of scandals, tried to remain balanced and clear-minded. She knew that the sort of licence tolerated in others would be roundly condemned in her, should she be weak enough to fall. It seemed that everybody at court was engaged in extra-marital affairs. Except herself. The Empress, with her official lovers, set the example for debauchery, but watched jealously over the Grand Duchess's behaviour. As soon as Catherine had finally got used to her first maid, Madame Kruse, she was briskly removed and replaced by Brascovia Vladislavova. For once Catherine did well by the exchange. Madame Kruse was German, Madame Vladislavova passionately Russian. She was intelligent, high-spirited, and cultured, and was a living chronicle of the old days. She knew everything about the great families surrounding the throne: kinships, connections, fortunes, antecedents, mental troubles, hidden vices. Listening to her, Catherine felt as though she were breaking into the most heavily guarded of dwellings. But Madame Vladislavova was very pious. The Grand Duke could not forgive her for that. He mocked her for venerating icons. He felt more and more repugnance towards anything Slav. His nostalgia for his home country was such that he said he preferred the town of Kiel to the whole Russian Empire. Despite pressure from the Tsarina, Bestuzhev and some foreign diplomats, he always refused to exchange the miserable little duchy he had inherited from his father for the counties of Oldenburg and Dalmenhorst. Holstein was under his skin. He could not emulate Catherine's efforts at Russianization. His idol was Frederick II of Prussia whom he had never met, but who, for him, was the incarnation of German nobility, science and severity. He suffered from the fact that Elisabeth and Bestuzhev considered this great king to be their enemy. In their place he would have subscribed to any Prussian demand, and he proclaimed this to anyone who would listen.

For her part Catherine did not forget all that she owed to Frederick II. She kept a fond memory of the meeting in Berlin. But she was careful not to express her opinions openly for fear of reprisals. On the 11th November 1748, at a lively gathering in Her Majesty's apartments, she found herself placed next to Lestocq, who was the Empress's doctor and intimate adviser, a crafty man who had often been less than polite to her. When she spoke to him, he looked terrified and stammered: 'Don't come near me . . . leave me in peace, I tell you!' She thought that he had been drinking and went away. The day after next, she heard that

Lestocq had been taken to the fortress, accused of carrying on a coded correspondence with the Prussian ambassador, against Russia's interests. A special commission, consisting of Count Bestuzhev himself, General Apraxin and Count Alexander Shuvalov, investigated the case. It was whispered that in some of the letters, the question had arisen of the Grand Duchess's Russian sympathies. Put to the torture Lestocq admitted nothing, betrayed no one, and bravely accepted to be condemned with no evidence to exile and the confiscation of his possessions. 'The Empress had not enough strength to give justice to an innocent man,' Catherine observed, 'she would have feared the revenge of such a person, and that is why, since her reign began, nobody innocent or guilty, has emerged from the fortress without at least being exiled.'

Amazingly, Catherine was not directly implicated in this accusation of high treason. But she had felt the chill of the dungeon pass over her shoulders. Henceforth she was to live in fear of a plot which could remove the small amount of freedom she still enjoyed.

In the following year, 1749, there was a new alert: in the midst of the carnival, the Empress was struck down by a violent attack of 'constipation colic'. The strength of her pain made people fear for her life. Confined to their apartments, which they were not allowed to leave without permission, Catherine and Peter learned through their servants and Madame Vladislavova, that Count Bestuzhev, General Apraxin and several other dignitaries known to be hostile to the couple, were holding frequent 'top secret meetings behind closed doors'.[1] Perhaps, foreseeing the Empress's death they were preparing a coup, which would remove Peter from the succession and put back on the throne Ivan VI, the fallen Tsar, who was at present languishing in the fortress of Schlüsselburg. The threat of exile and prison brought Peter out in a cold sweat, and Catherine, although very worried herself, tried to reassure him by saying that if there was any danger she would organize his escape: 'The ground-floor windows of our apartments were low enough to jump into the street, if necessary'.[1]

The Empress recovered, but the Grand Duke continued to be obsessed by the fear of a palace revolution. During a hunting party, Lieutenant Baturin, of the Boutovsky regiment, took advantage of a moment alone with Peter to get off his horse, kneel down and swear that he recognized no other master but Peter, and that he would do anything to serve his cause. Terrified by this oath the Grand Duke spurred his horse and, leaving his worshipper prostrate in the clearing, galloped off to ask Catherine's advice. A little later, Baturin was arrested, brought

[1] Catherine II *Memoirs*.

before the secret police, tortured and found guilty of having plotted to 'kill the Empress, set fire to the palace, and, by this outrage and the ensuing fight, bring the Grand Duke to the throne'. As for the Grand Duke, after first being afraid, he took solace in the fact that the secret police did not even call him as a witness in this affair. Catherine suspected him of being secretly flattered at having such devoted partisans as Baturin in the army. Although he was far too pusillanimous to take on the responsibility of being head of a group, he was nonetheless affected by any gathering of sympathy towards his person. 'Since that time,' Catherine observed, 'I saw the thirst for power growing in the Grand Duke's mind, he was dying to reign, but did nothing to make himself worthy of it.' On any occasion, he would try to prove his independence. In 1750, towards the end of the carnival, as Catherine was getting ready to take a bath, Madame Choglokov came to tell the Grand Duke, on the part of the Empress, that he too must have a bath. Now, of all Russian customs, bathing was the one he hated most. This passage through the sweating-rooms, which he had hitherto avoided appeared 'contrary to his nature'. He cried that he did not wish to 'die' in order to obey his aunt's fantasies, that his life was 'dearer to him than anything', and that anyway he was not afraid of punishment. 'We'll see what she can do to me,' he ended, 'I'm not a child.' Madame Choglokov threatened him with the fortress. He cried and pranced with rage, but did not give in. When Madame Choglokov returned, the argument changed tack. She no longer mentioned the bath, now it was a question of child-bearing. The Empress, she said, was very angry that the Grand Ducal couple were still childless; she wanted to know 'whose fault it was', and she was going to send a midwife to Catherine, and a doctor to Peter. The Grand Duke exploded, Catherine bowed her head, Madame Choglokov went away and the Empress forgot about her warning. As in the past, Peter only came to Catherine's bed to play soldiers or to sleep. And, as in the past, he covered his deficiencies by boasting to her of his success with other women. 'He, as it were, paid court to all women,' she noted, 'only the one who bore the name of his own wife was excluded from his attentions.'

In fact, he hopped from one to the other, without ever touching them. This asexual seducer was happy, at the age of twenty-three, with illusions of conquest. But he named names, and gave details, and Catherine's pride suffered. At the moment everything was calm in her own heart. Certainly she sometimes thought about the handsome André Tchernychev, who had been removed because she found him too attractive, and whose retreat she had discovered. He corresponded with her through the intermediary of a 'Finnish wardrobe girl'. This girl could only talk freely to the Grand Duchess when the latter was sitting on her commode. Catherine would slip her admirer's letters into her pocket, her stocking, or her garter. She would reply secretly, using her rare moments of solitude. They were only tender messages of friendship. In order to write them, Catherine used a silver pen which she had specially bought.

Later another Tchernychev, called Zahar, came to disturb her somewhat. Count Zahar Tchernychev, also exiled for the crime of sympathy towards the Grand Duchess, reappeared at court in 1751. Back in Catherine's presence, he was dazzled by her transformation. He had left an angular sixteen-year-old adolescent, and found on his return a blooming young woman of twenty-one. Overcome, he dared murmur to her that he found her 'very much more beautiful'. 'It was the first time in my life that anyone had said anything like that to me,' she wrote, 'I didn't find it at all bad. Indeed, I had the good nature to believe that he was telling the truth.' At each ball, Zahar and Catherine would now exchange 'slips', little pieces of paper on which elegiac verses were printed, some confectioner's inspiration. Then handwritten notes succeeded the ready-made slips. They passed them to each other surreptitiously, between minuets. Catherine was delighted with this secret correspondence, but it was not enough for Zahar. During a masquerade, he begged her to allow him an 'audience' in her room. If necessary he would disguise himself as a servant in order to reach her! Touched by his insistence, she nonetheless declined the adventure. Regretfully the two young people went back to written declarations. And at the end of the carnival, Zahar Tchernychev returned to his regiment. 'One must admit that flirtations were rife at court then,' Catherine wrote. Miraculously the Empress had not noticed, or had not wished to notice, the Grand Duchess's taste for a pleasing face. She even, intermittently, showed a certain gentleness towards this young woman, whose main fault in her eyes was that she had not yet provided an heir to the throne. At one of the notorious balls where men were dressed as women and women as men, Catherine obsequiously complimented the Tsarina on how much masculine clothes suited her, adding that if she were really of the opposite sex, she would turn many a head. Flattered, Elisabeth replied that if she had been a man Catherine would have been the one she would have given the apple to. 'I bowed down to kiss her hand, at such an unexpected compliment,' wrote Catherine.

At another ball, she decided to astonish the court ladies, who she knew would be superbly dressed, by appearing in a simple white dress 'on a very small hoop'. 'I had a very small waist then,' she said. In her hair which was tied in a foxtail 'a single rose with a bud and leaves, which looked totally real'. Another rose at her breast. A gauze ruff around her neck. Sleeves and apron of the same gauze. Seeing her, the Empress cried, 'Good God, what simplicity! What? Not even a beauty spot?' And she dexterously brought out of a little box a small beauty spot, which she put on the young girl's face.

Catherine proudly showed off the imperial beauty spot to the courtiers who immediately surrounded her. 'I cannot remember ever in my life receiving so much praise as I did on that day. They said I was as beautiful as the day, and quite sparkling; to tell the truth, I never thought myself extremely beautiful but I was attractive, and that was my strong point.'[1]

[1] Catherine II *Memoirs.*

CHAPTER VII

Love and Motherhood

'He was as handsome as the day, and certainly nobody could equal him at the main Court, and even less at ours. He lacked neither wit nor that combination of knowledge, manners and habits learned in the great world, and particularly at Court. He was twenty-six years old; all in all he was both by birth and by his other qualities a distinguished gentleman; he knew how to conceal his faults; the greatest of these was a taste for intrigue, and lack of principles; these were not yet apparent to me.'

This was the portrait that Catherine in middle age drew of the man who had affected her so much in her youth. He was called Serge Saltykov, and he was, with his brother Peter, one of the chamberlains at the young Grand Ducal court. The Saltykov family was one of the most ancient and noble ones in Russia. Serge's father was the Tsarina's *aide-de-camp;* his mother, whose maiden name was Princess Golitzvin, was famous for her moral levity. According to the Princess of Anhalt 'her lovers were Her Majesty Elisabeth's three hundred grenadiers'.[1] When Catherine picked out Serge Saltykov in 1752, he had been married for two years to one of the Empress's ladies-in-waiting, Matriona Pavlovna Balk, whom he had fallen in love with when he saw her on a swing. This passion died down as quickly as it had arisen and Serge Saltykov soon turned towards other ventures. Without being quite as handsome or brilliant as Catherine described him, he was charming, good-humoured and glib. He was very dark, of medium height, agile and well-proportioned, attractive to women and aware of it. Nothing interested him more than the hunt for women, the siege and the ensuing conquest of virtue. Catherine's loneliness gave him the courage to approach her. He was stimulated by the surveillance she lived under. 'He would have risked Siberia for an intrigue,' wrote Monsieur de Champeaux (son) to Paris. First of all Serge Saltykov set himself to allay the suspicions of the two 'Cerberuses'. Having gained the Choglokovs' sympathy, he came to visit them with his friend the court buffoon, the

[1] Letter from Princess d'Anhalt to M de Pouilly, 1st September 1758.

'born Harlequin', Leo Naryshkin, and met Catherine and her friend Princess Gagarin. Madame Choglokov, 'pregnant and often unwell', was less vigilant than usual. Anyway since her conjugal mishaps she had lost a lot of her arrogance, and remained grateful to the Grand Duchess for the dignity she had maintained throughout the affair. As for Choglokov, who was himself infatuated with Catherine, the young people soon found a way to get rid of him. Serge Saltykov persuaded him that he had great talent as a poet, urged him to write, supplied him with themes for his songs, and the delighted fellow retired to a corner 'near the stove' to compose. As soon as he had finished, Leo Naryshkin grabbed the manuscript, put the words to music and sang the piece with the author. 'And meanwhile,' wrote Catherine, 'the conversation in the room carried on and one could say what one wanted.' At last, during one of these musical interludes, Serge dared to whisper to Catherine that he was madly in love with her. She was moved and did not discourage him but as he insisted, she murmured, 'What about your wife, whom you married out of passion two years ago, and whom you are meant to be in love with, what will she say to all this?' He dashed aside this objection. He didn't love his wife any more. She was a dead weight in his life. He added that 'all that glitters is not gold' and that 'he was paying dearly for a moment of blindness'.[1] Catherine so much wanted to be convinced that she began to feel sorry for this handsome and unhappily married young man, sighing after an inaccessible Grand Duchess. She saw him 'practically every day' and listened to him with growing pleasure. Sometimes however she tried to fight the dizziness that was overcoming her. In order to escape him, she cried feebly: 'What do you know of me? Perhaps my heart is spoken for elsewhere.' Far from being put off he was urged by this inexperienced girl's remark to push forward his advantage. Neither of them worried about the Grand Duke whose indifference was known to everybody. Serge, like a good strategist, patiently awaited the moment of victory.

During a hunting party organized by the Choglokovs on an island in the Neva, Serge, leaving the others to chase hares, dragged Catherine aside and spoke to her again of his passion, of the happiness which awaited them if only she would give in, and begged her to tell him if he was really 'the favourite'. She laughingly prevaricated, to cover her weakness and, after an hour and a half of very tender conversation, ordered him to go so as not to compromise her. But he refused to leave her, unless she would say, there and then, that she liked him. 'Yes, yes,' she said, 'but go away!' He jumped onto his horse and spurred it away.

---

[1] Catherine II *Memoirs*.

And, as he disappeared, she shouted jokingly: 'No, no!' 'Yes, yes!' he replied, galloping away.

That same evening, the whole company met at the house which the Choglokovs owned on the island. During supper the wind got up and the waters of the Neva rose rapidly, covering the steps and beating against the walls. There was no question of getting back into the boats to cross the river, which was very wide at this point. The laws of precedence no longer existed when the wind was about to tear off the roof. The guests piled themselves in a jumble in the twilight lit only here and there by the trembling flames of the candelabras. Catherine found herself next to her admirer. 'Serge Saltykov said that the heavens themselves were favourable to him that day, because they were making him enjoy her company for longer, and a whole lot of things like that.'[1] She was frightened both by the storm and by the man. He urged her, and she defended herself more and more weakly. She was 'displeased' with herself. 'I had thought that I was able to govern and control his head and mine, and I realized that both were difficult, if not impossible.' At last at three o'clock in the morning, the wind dropped, the waves calmed down and the numb and stiff guests made a disorderly embarkation. Catherine was no longer the same. She had decided to give in, even if she had not yet done so. The matter would be settled.

She was twenty-three. After eight years of virginity within marriage, she discovered bodily delights with amazement. Her first lover entirely satisfied her. She did not feel the slightest guilt when she was in his arms. Compared with the pathetic Grand Duke, he possessed for her every possible quality: energy, courage, grace. But she was afraid that their secret might be discovered. Bressau, the Grand Duke's French valet, repeated to Serge disturbing remarks of His Highness's: 'Serge Saltykov and my wife are deceiving Choglokov, they make him believe anything they want, and then laugh at him.' No jealousy in his speech. Peter did not take Catherine's infatuation with Serge Saltykov seriously. He saw in it a mere worldly flirtation. Was he not himself madly in love with Martha Chafirov, the Grand Duchesss maid of honour, without there being anything between them except a few saucy smiles and a few suggestive puns? All the same Serge, 'a demon for intrigue' according to Catherine, saw very well the danger of being the lover of a woman whose husband was famously a virgin. If she were to become pregnant, who would be suspected? To ward off this danger, the young chamberlain summoned up his courage to speak to the Empress about the physical obstacle which was standing in the way of 'the Grand

[1] Catherine II *Memoirs.*

Duke's happiness'. He would take it upon himself, he said, to persuade His Highness to consent to the operation. The Tsarina, very interested, approved and encouraged him. During a merry supper where the Grand Duke had laughed and drunk a great deal, his comrades turned the conversation to the pleasures of love-making. 'The Prince,' wrote the diplomat Castéra, 'let slip his regret at not being able to enjoy them. Then all the guests dropped to their knees and begged him to take Saltykov's advice. The Grand Duke seemed overcome. They took a few stammered words as a consent. Everything had been prepared. They brought in the famous doctor Boerhave and a skilled surgeon. There was no way he could escape and the operation passed off very successfully.'[1]

To make sure that the Grand Duke, after his operation, was in working order the Empress told Madame Choglokov to find him a woman who would initiate him. Madame Choglokov put on 'a lot of bustle' in order to obey the Empress's orders and, thanks to the valet Bressau, found a certain Madame Groot 'the pretty widow of a painter', who agreed to teach the young man. 'She (Madame Choglokov) expected great rewards for her troubles, but she was mistaken on this point, and she got nothing: however, she proclaimed that the Empire was in debt to her.'[2]

Thus Peter was freed from his impediment. When Catherine saw this triumphant male coming to her, she regretted the time when she had not had to fear his caresses. In love with another man, she was forced to submit to this repulsive contact, in order to ensure the safety of their affair. Her first experiences with her husband were pathetic gymnastic exercises compared with the intoxication she felt with Serge. Anyway he neither loved nor desired her, and was only fulfilling a duty by sleeping with her. The day after this belated wedding night, he sent to the Empress, on Serge Saltykov's advice, a sealed box containing the evidence of the Grand Duchess's so-called virginity. 'Elisabeth,' wrote J. Castéra, 'seemed convinced of its authenticity. No doubt some people laughed to themselves, but out loud everybody congratulated the Prince on his happiness.'

As for Serge Saltykov, he gave a sigh of relief. Catherine was already, at the time, pregnant by him. It was certainly time for the husband to appear on the scene and assume at least an appearance of being the possible father of the child. In fact she was less worried by the approaching birth than by Serge's strange attitude towards her. Hunting parties still brought them together at Peterhof. Everything seemed unreal, even the costumes, as Elisabeth made everybody wear

[1] J. Castéra *The Life of Catherine II.*
[2] Catherine II *Memoirs.*

the same clothes: 'grey jacket, and the vest blue with a black velvet collar'. Thus couples could go off together without being identified from a distance. These delightful *tête-à-tête*s were the last moments of a declining happiness.

Either through boredom or prudence, Serge showed himself to be less and less assiduous. 'He became,' Catherine wrote, 'conceited, arrogant and dissipated and made me angry.' Suddenly Serge and his companion, Leo Naryshkin, decided to go to the country. A necessary separation, he said, so as to allay suspicion. But perhaps he just wanted to escape, for a time, from this overpowering mistress? She was in despair. The court was moving to Moscow and Serge still had not returned. The Grand Ducal couple set off on the 14th December 1752. During the journey, Catherine was seized with 'violent gripes'. A miscarriage. Thank God. Having got rid of her burden, she awaited Serge's return from voluntary exile with mounting impatience. When she saw him again, she was so moved that she declared herself ready for anything that would keep them together. He, on the other hand, appeared more and more distant and reticent. He said to Catherine that he feared that some spy might inform the Empress of their relationship. So she decided to approach her sworn enemy, Bestuzhev, in order to gain from him a friendly, or at least a neutral attitude. A certain Bremse who was a 'familiar' both of the 'little court' and the chancellor's house, went to see the latter to tell him from the Grand Duchess that she was 'less distant from him than she used to be'. The Chancellor was delighted with this act of allegiance, and felt sure that he now held all the cards. He received Serge Saltykov the following day with a great show of friendship. 'He spoke to him about myself and my situation as if he had been living in my bedroom,' wrote Catherine. Since Bestuzhev was not horrified by this adulterous affair, about which he seemed to know all the details, it must be, she thought, that he was inclined in favour of the relationship between her and Serge. In a flight of generosity, the Chancellor even went so far as to say: 'She (Catherine) will see that I am not the werewolf they had led her to believe I was!' Serge repeated this remark to Catherine who congratulated herself on having such a powerful ally up her sleeve 'without a living soul knowing anything about it'. All the same she could not quite understand the motives of this man, who had hitherto been so careful to have the Grand Duchess's virtue guarded by the two watch-dogs, in now encouraging her lover's activities with 'several wise and useful pieces of advice'.

A few days later, the watch-dogs themselves changed their attitude. They turned from guards into go-betweens. Madame Choglokov who, said Catherine, 'was still obsessed with her favourite project – that of ensuring the succession', engaged the Grand Duchess in a curious conversation. With a serious expression, she explained to her in a low voice that although, in ordinary life, women were expected to remain faithful to their husbands, there were cases where reasons of State could justify departures from normal conduct, for example when it was necessary to guarantee the succession to the throne. Catherine was disconcerted at first, and let her carry on 'not knowing what she was getting at, and whether she was laying a trap or speaking sincerely'. It was obviously one of two things: either Bestuzhev and the Empress were so worried about the Grand Duke being sterile that they were looking for another sire as quickly as possible, or they had decided to unmask and destroy Catherine for betraying her duties. Catherine cautiously pretended not to understand Madame Choglokov's mysterious whispers. So the latter changed the subject, saying: 'You'll see how much I love my country and how sincere I am. I have no doubt that you have a preference for somebody. I'll let you choose between Serge Saltykov and Leo Naryshkin. If I'm not mistaken, it's the latter.' Catherine cried, 'No, no, not at all!' So Madame Choglokov observed triumphantly: 'Well! If it's not him, it must be the other, obviously!' And she added, 'You'll see, I won't put any difficulties in your way.' 'I acted the fool,' wrote Catherine, 'to the point where she scolded me several times in the town and in the country.'[1] Bestuzhev, for his part, lectured Serge Saltykov now he was about to detach himself from the Grand Duchess. He was looking elsewhere. She clumsily reproached him for his inconstancy. He defended himself with specious arguments. She sadly let herself be convinced. 'He gave me such excellent and valid reasons that as soon as I had seen and spoken to him, my own reflections on the subject melted away.' Now she used all the flirtatious devices she could to entice him, from time to time, to her bed. She did this of course only for pleasure. But Madame Choglokov, Bestuzhev, and in the background the Empress all hoped that the lover would make her pregnant.

In May 1753, she noticed 'more signs of pregnancy'. Despite her exhaustion she followed the court in all its displacements, and took part from a carriage in the hunts and other expeditions, sleeping in a tent. Back in Moscow, after a ball and a dinner, she had a second miscarriage, this time very painful. 'I was in great danger for thirteen days, because they suspected that part of the afterbirth had not come away ... At last on the thirteenth day, it came out by itself ... They made me spend six weeks of unbearable heat in my room after this accident.'

---

[1] Catherine II *Memoirs*. The account of Catherine's conversation with Mme Choglokov was thought so compromising by the St Petersburg Academy of Sciences, that it was omitted from the 1907 edition of the Complete Works of the Empress.

The Empress came to see her and seemed 'very affected'. She had good reason to be! She had put such faith into an arrangement which gave an appearance of legitimacy to Catherine's bastard! Serge Saltykov thought to himself that, thanks to this mishap, he would be forced to remain in service with a woman he no longer loved. As long as he had not done his duty as a stallion, he would not be free to roam. And the Grand Duke? Had he seriously believed that he was to be a father? One might doubt it. Beside the fact that his rare moments of intimacy with his wife had been most disappointing, he knew too well that she was in love with Serge Saltykov not to suspect that it was he who had impregnated her. He was condemned to play the part of the *mari complaisant*, and could not complain about it to anyone, since the Empress herself was covering up the plot. He hated his wife and yet did not mind her deceiving him. He raged and sniggered at the same time. He wanted to escape from this adult world and, as usual, took refuge in gambling and drink in order to forget it. His favourite valet, a Ukrainian, supplied him with strong drink. He got drunk with his servants, and when, under the influence of alcohol, they forgot the respect due to a Grand Duke, he would hit them with a stick, or the flat of his sword. One day Catherine came into his room and found a large rat hanging 'with all the instruments of torture'. When asked for the reason for this capital punishment, the Grand Duke replied that the rat was guilty, according to military law, of having eaten two soldiers made of starch, and that he had been hanged after having his kidneys broken by a dog, and that he would remain exposed to the public eye 'for three days, to set an example'. Catherine thought he was joking and burst out laughing; Peter's face darkened. If his wife could no longer join in his games, what use was she to him?

The business of the hanged rat made a strong impression on Catherine. When she was writing about these faraway times, other rats came into her mind. Those she had seen when the Annenhof Palace in Moscow had burnt down at the beginning of the winter. 'I saw then a strange thing,' she wrote, 'an extraordinary quantity of rats and mice coming down the stairs in a line, not hurrying very much.' All the Empress's dresses – four thousand of them! – disappeared in the flames. But Catherine's books were miraculously spared. She was delighted at this as they represented in Russia a far more irreplaceable treasure than a wardrobe. The Grand Ducal couple, without a roof over their heads, took refuge in the Choglokovs' house. 'The wind whistled in every direction, the windows and doors were half rotten, the floor had three or four inch gaps in it; it was also overrun with vermin.'

In February 1754, seven months after her second miscarriage,

Catherine realized that she was pregnant again. This time the Empress hoped very much that the pregnancy would come to full term. Serge Saltykov hoped so too because, as an amateur of light-hearted affairs, he was finding this long quasi-official liaison somewhat wearisome. Catherine read his mind and was saddened. 'Boredom, sickness and the physical and mental discomfort of my situation made me into a hypochondriac,' she wrote. Uncomfortably lodged with the Choglokovs, she shivered in the draughts, and awaited visits from a lover who was entertaining himself elsewhere. Sitting opposite her, Madam Choglokov also complained because her husband was dining out with friends. 'See how we are abandoned!' she sighed. 'All this put me in a filthy temper.' Anyway, soon afterwards, Madame Choglokov, so upset by her husband's absences, conceived a passion for Prince Repnin, and showed Catherine the torrid letters she received from her lover. While this was going on, Choglokov died of 'a dry colic'. The Empress, considering that a widow could not decently appear in society, immediately relieved Madame Choglokov of her duties with the Grand Duchess. Catherine was miserable since Madame Choglokov, having once been her enemy, had now become her accomplice. Her vexation turned to terror when she discovered the name of the man who would now be watching over her; Count Shuvalov, the uncle of Elisabeth's favourite, and Chief of the State Inquisition, in other words, the secret police. This formidable person suffered from a 'convulsive movement' which from time to time twisted the right side of his face from the eye to the chin. 'It was amazing,' wrote Catherine, 'that they had chosen this man with his hideous grimace, to be continually at the side of the pregnant woman. If I had given birth to a child with this unfortunate tic, I don't suppose the Empress would have been very pleased.'

At last at the beginning of May 1754, the whole Court prepared to leave Moscow for St Petersburg. With the prospect of a twenty-nine day journey, Catherine was 'dying of fear' in her own words, that Serge Saltykov would not be on the journey. Now that he had made her pregnant, he was of no more interest to the noble figures surrounding the throne. Luckily the Empress was on hand. The lover was allowed to be a part of the train, no doubt out of consideration for the future mother's nerves. It was true that he could not come near her 'because of the constraint of the continual presence of the Shuvalov couple'. 'I was bored to death in the carriage and cried the whole time,' wrote Catherine.

At St Petersburg, the Grand Ducal couple was once again installed in the Summer Palace. There Peter organized concerts and exerted himself by playing the violin in the orchestra. Catherine, now heavy with child, took advantage of these musical sessions to escape from the room and exchange a few tender words with her lover between the doors. As the date of the confinement approached, she persuaded herself that there was a plot against her happiness being organized in high places. 'I always had tears in my eyes and a thousand worries went through my head; I could not get away from the idea that everything was leading up to a separation from Serge Saltykov.' Thus, on the verge of motherhood, her thoughts were not for the child about to be born but for the man who had given her a taste for pleasure. When Alexander Shuvalov showed her the apartment specially prepared for the labour, right next to Her Majesty's personal apartments, she felt as though she had received 'an almost mortal blow'. Living within talking distance of the Empress, she would no longer be able to receive Serge as she wished. She would be isolated, cloistered 'as miserable as a stone'. She despondently inspected the two sparsely furnished rooms stretched with crimson damask, the decor for the birth of the heir to the Russian throne. And supposing it was not an heir but an heiress? How would the Empress take such a disappointment? Would she take her revenge by finally expelling Serge from the court, or would she keep him for another try?

During the night of the 19th and 20th September 1754, nine years after her marriage, Catherine was seized by violent pains. The midwife alerted the Grand Duke, Count Alexander Shuvalov and the Empress who rushed to the scene of labour. At midday on the 20th September, the midwife held up in her bloody hands a screaming bundle of flesh; it was a boy; Paul Petrovich. The Empress was overjoyed. As soon as the baby had been washed, swaddled and baptized by a priest, she had him taken to her apartments by the midwife. He would stay there under her guard for as long as she deemed it necessary. By giving birth to her child, Catherine had lost all rights over him. She was now only a stomach emptied of its contents. Nobody was interested in her anymore. Suddenly her room was empty. The bed was between a door and two large windows which did not shut properly. An icy wind blew through the room.

'I had sweated a great deal; I begged Madame Vladislavova to change my linen and put me to bed; she said she did not have to do so. She sent for the midwife several times but she did not come; I asked for a drink, but got the same reply. At last after three hours, Countess Shuvalov appeared, beautifully dressed up. When she saw me still lying where she had left me she cried out that it would kill me. This was a great consolation to me: I had been in tears since the birth, particularly at being abandoned as I was, extremely uncomfortable after a rough and painful birth, nobody daring to put me into my own bed two steps away, and lacking the strength to drag myself there. Madame Shuvalov went off straight away and I think she sent for the midwife, as the latter appeared half-an-hour later and told us that the Empress was so pre-occupied with the child that she had not once let it go. Nobody thought of me ... All this time I felt that I was dying of exhaustion and thirst. At last they put me into my bed and I did not see a living soul for the rest of the day, nor did anyone send to enquire about me. The Grand Duke was drinking with anyone he could find, and the Empress was busy with the child.'[1]

None of the contemporaries considered the child to be the son of the heir to the throne. Paul as he grew up certainly bore a slight resemblance to Peter – he was as ugly. And yet when one compares portraits of them as adults the differences spring to the eye. Paul's face, flattened like that of a bull-dog, has nothing in common with the long moon-like appearance of Catherine's husband. As for their characters although they were both unbalanced, cruel and cowardly, these similar faults could be traced to the upbringing they both received under Elisabeth's oppressive shadow. Catherine anyhow, in her *Memoirs*, lets it be clearly understood that Serge Saltykov was the father of the child. And the Empress's behaviour in removing the child at birth and looking after him herself, made it quite clear that if she had no consideration for the mother, she had none for the father either. Her interest in the child was so passionate that some of those around her went further in their speculations. She had taken Paul's cradle into her own room. 'As soon as he cried, she ran to him herself, and he was literally stifled by attention.' The Marquis de l'Hôpital, a French diplomat, echoed in his dispatches to the French court the strange rumours circulating in St Petersburg society. 'This child,' he wrote, 'is the Empress's own – she has exchanged the Grand Duchess's son for hers.' Idle talk, perhaps, but it showed enough that for many people at the time little Paul's consanguinity was a far from settled matter.[2]

Catherine, abandoned in her bed, and a prey to fever and despair, nonetheless did not complain. 'I was too proud, the idea of being unhappy was unbearable to me.' Thus she avoided asking for news of her son, who remained invisible to her. Such curiosity might have been taken as casting doubt on the Empress's care of the child and 'would have been very badly received,' she said. A strange scruple on the part

[1] Catherine II *Memoirs*.
[2] According to another equally unlikely theory, Catherine had purposely let it be believed that Paul was Saltykov's son so that she could not be accused, after Peter III's murder, of having let the father of her child be assassinated.

of a young mother brutally deprived of the child she had just given birth to. Could a matter of etiquette stifle natural maternal instincts to such a point? In fact Catherine was more concerned with her own future at court than with the future of her child. However she did see him one day, for a moment, and was worried. 'He was kept in an extremely hot room,' she wrote, 'wrapped in flannel, in a cradle lined with black fox fur. I saw him covered like this several times; his face and body were pouring with sweat, so that the slightest breeze that reached him chilled him and made him ill. As well as this, he was surrounded by old matrons who, by their ill-considered care and lack of common sense, did him far more physical and mental harm than good.'

On the day of the baptism, as soon as the ceremony was over, the Empress brought Catherine an order for a hundred thousand roubles and a few jewels in a case, on a gold platter. This was the wage a Grand Duchess received for giving birth. The money was welcome as, by her own admission, Catherine 'had not a penny' and she was 'riddled with debt'. But the jewels were disappointing. 'There was,' she said, 'a miserable necklace with some earrings and two pathetic rings I would have been ashamed to give to my chambermaids. In the whole case there was not a single stone worth a hundred roubles.' Five days later, while she was planning the use of the money, Baron Cherkassov, the Empress's cabinet secretary, came to beg her to renounce it as Her Majesty's chests were empty. Catherine sent back the money – it was given back to her three months later – and soon afterwards learnt that the hundred thousand roubles she had returned had been given to her husband. Peter had demanded a present of at least equal value to his wife's as a reward for this birth, for which he was probably not even responsible. Perhaps he saw in it a compensation for the notoriety of his humiliation?

From the depths of her alcove, Catherine heard echoes of parties, banquets and fireworks celebrating the happiness of the nation. Seventeen days after the birth she was struck at the heart by some terrible news: Serge Saltykov had been chosen by the Empress to bear the official announcement of Paul Petrovich's birth to the Swedish court. Thus the generally accepted illegitimate father of the child would receive congratulations destined for the legitimate father. The mission had all the appearance of humiliation. He swallowed his pride and set off, leaving Catherine in despair. 'I pretended that my leg was hurting again, and that I could not rise; but the truth was that I could not, and would not see anyone, because I was so unhappy.'[1]

---

[1] Catherine II *Memoirs*.

On the fortieth day, for the churching ceremony, the Empress at last allowed her to see her child. 'I found him beautiful and the sight of him cheered me somewhat,' she wrote. She was allowed to look at him from afar, for the time it took to say the prayers, and then he was immediately removed again.

On the 1st November 1754 there was a great commotion: the valets hastily installed a few beautiful pieces of furniture in the room next to her bedroom. In an inkling, this gloomy place was full of warmth and light. It was like a theatre five minutes before the curtain. When the decor was ready, Madame Vladislavova made the Grand Duchess sit on a bed of rose-coloured velvet, embroidered with silver, and all the courtiers filed past her, offering their congratulations. After that, the furniture was removed and the heroine of the day was left forgotten in her corner.

To console herself, she immersed herself in books. Passionately she devoured Tacitus' *Annals* 'which caused a strange upheaval in my mind', Voltaire's *Essay on the customs and spirit of nations,* and Montesquieu's *Spirit of the Laws.* With Montesquieu, she learnt about liberalism, she worried about the excess of personal power, she dreamt of a good, equitable and intelligent régime. Voltaire taught her the advantage of reason in the conduct of public affairs, and what the chances of success for despotism were, no matter how 'enlightened'. Tacitus showed her how to analyse historical events as a cold, pitiless onlooker. She also read 'all the available Russian books'. Not to find any enriching thoughts, but to become more familiar with her country's language. Because, despite her humiliations, her loneliness and her fear of the future, she still believed that her destiny lay on this inhospitable soil. The road back to Germany was forever blocked to her. Whatever happened, she must go forwards.

It was cold and damp in her little room, with its windows overlooking the Neva. Next door, she could hear the Grand Duke and his friends, night and day, drinking, arguing, laughing and carrying on as if in a barrack-room. The indirect pieces of news that she received from Sweden were rare and worrying. The Empress, they said, had already decided Serge Saltykov's fate. As soon as he returned from Stockholm she would send him to Hamburg as the resident Minister from Russia. And that would be a definitive separation. He reappeared at St Petersburg towards the end of the carnival and, trembling with hope, Catherine made a rendezvous in her bedroom. She waited until three o'clock in the morning 'in mortal fear'. In vain. The next day he sent a message through his friend Leo Naryshkin that he had been delayed, later than expected, at a masonic lodge. But Catherine was not fooled. 'I saw as clear as daylight that he had failed to come out of lack of enthusiasm for me, without the slightest feeling for what I had been suffering for so long, out of attachment to him . . . To tell the truth, I was extremely offended.'

She wrote him a reproachful letter and this time he came. Falling under his spell, she melted as she had done in the early days of their affair. 'It was not difficult for him to appease me, as I was already inclined to forgive him,' she wrote ingenuously. However she very soon guessed that he was only seeing her out of pity. Instead of talking about love, he advised her to distract herself, to go out into the world, in other words to forget him. He could not have been more explicit – he was gently breaking off the relationship. Thrown at first, she conquered her feelings with a surge of pride. The blow, far from crushing her, brought her to life. She refused to go on suffering for the sake of a man, even one as seductive as Serge. 'I resolved to show those who had caused me so many different sorts of suffering, that it was no longer possible to offend me with impunity,' she wrote. The first manifestation of this juvenile revolt took place on the 10th February. She decided to reappear at Court not as a victim but as conqueror, and had made for herself for that day a magnificent dress of blue velvet embroidered with gold. Her appearance in the drawing-rooms caused a stir of admiring curiosity. Motherhood had made her even more beautiful. The ill-feeling that she sensed here and there made her stiffen her bearing and sharpen her sarcastic tongue. She passed between the groups of courtiers with a lively look and a mocking smile, throwing out an acid remark from time to time. The Shuvalovs were her favourite target. Her sayings were repeated and commented on. Everyone was amazed. Where was the docile, naive, Grand Duchess of yesteryear, whose love-life was such a subject for pleasantry? A new Catherine had emerged, perhaps with the birth of her son. A hard, resolute and distrustful Catherine. 'I held myself straight,' she wrote, 'I walked with my head high, more like the head of a powerful faction than like a humiliated and oppressed person.' And she added that, when they saw her thus transformed, Alexander Shuvalov and his friends 'did not know, for a moment, which foot to stand on'.[1]

Here she was deluding herself. Despite her superior manner, she could not yet intimidate the great beasts of the Palace. At the most, they told themselves that Her Highness was resilient and that, from now on, she must be taken into consideration in the balance of political combinations. In the spring of 1755, Serge Saltykov set off to take up his post at

[1] Catherine II *Memoirs.*

Hamburg. His disappearance left a frightful vacuum in Catherine's life. But she fiercely refused to allow herself to miss this man who had grown tired of her. She never saw him again.[1]

[1] When she became Empress, Catherine made Serge Saltykov ambassador to Paris. A few years later Count Panin suggested sending him to Dresden. Catherine wrote in the margin of the report, 'Has he not committed enough follies as it is? If you will be his guarantor, send him to Dresden, but he will never be more than the fifth wheel of the carriage.' Serge Salykov's diplomatic career ended in obscurity.

CHAPTER VIII

The First Political Moves

The Grand Duke was not the last to notice the transformation that had taken place in Catherine. At dinner in her room he told her that she was becoming 'insupportably proud', that she lacked respect for the Shuvalovs, that she held herself 'very stiff', and *that* he could not tolerate. 'I asked him if I would have to hunch my back in order to please him, like the slaves of the Great Master,' wrote Catherine. 'He became angry and said that he would make me see reason.' And to back up his threat he half pulled his sword out of its scabbard. Catherine was quite unmoved, and took this gesture as a joke, and he pushed back the sword muttering that she was really 'horribly wicked'.

In any case he too was keen to assert himself, faced with a Court which did not take him seriously. But he chose a way of doing so dramatically opposed to Catherine's. As he grew older his passion for the Duchy of Holstein, which he administered, had grown as well. He was so desperate for a German military atmosphere that he promised Alexander Shuvalov all sorts of favours, if the latter would, for the moment, turn a blind eye on the arrival in Russia of a contingent of Holsteinian soldiers. Shuvalov, seeing this only as the whim of a bored young man, persuaded the Empress, who was normally hostile to any German influence, to give in to her nephew's innocent request. And the detachment set off from Kiel and installed itself at Oranienbaum. Wild with joy, Peter wore the uniform of the Holsteinian regiment to receive his 'compatriots'. 'I shuddered at the terrible effect this move of the Grand Duke's would have on the Russian public, and even on the Empress whose views I knew well,' wrote Catherine. She was not mistaken. The officers of the guard stationed at Oranienbaum murmured, 'These damned Germans are all in the pay of the King of Prussia; they have brought traitors into Russia.' The soldiers groaned they were treated like 'valets' by the newcomers. The Court livery complained that they were having to wait on 'a pack of peasants'. And Catherine said that Peter, by his childishness, had foolishly alienated the sympathy of a part of the Russian army. Whilst he, in his enthusiasm for 'his troop', went and established himself in a camp near the Palace, she took pains to make it clear that she disapproved of his conduct. Her views were repeated in tents and barrack-rooms, and around the bivouac fires. Next to her husband, who was considered a traitor to Russia, she appeared as the incarnation of the national tradition. Foreign diplomats watched this manoeuvre carefully and reported back to their respective governments.

In 1755 England, wishing to renew its treaty of alliance with Russia since there was now the inevitable prospect of a break with France, sent a new ambassador to St Petersburg – Sir Charles Hanbury-Williams. He was courteous, charming and very good company, and he tried in vain, between minuets, to embark on a serious political conversation with the Tsarina; in the end he thought that it would be more skilful to win over the Grand Duchess, who was said to have been in Bestuzhev's favour. Was it not also said that Her Highness had a weakness for handsome men? Her amorous adventures with Saltykov had given her the reputation of being a great lover. And she was reeling from the break with Saltykov. All the more so as she had just heard that Serge had, in Sweden, 'told all the ladies he met about it'.[1]

'My misfortune is that my heart cannot be happy, even for an hour, without love,' she wrote. Now Sir Charles had with him exactly what was needed to satisfy this insatiable heart. Too old to seduce the Grand Duchess himself (he was forty-six), he put forward one of his suite, a charming young man called Count Stanislaus-Augustus Poniatowski. Stanislaus belonged, through his mother, to one of the grandest families in Poland, the Czartoryskys. At twenty-three he had read a great deal, spoke several languages, had a smattering of philosophy, had visited all the courts in Europe, had been introduced into the most refined drawing-rooms; in Paris he had gained the esteem of Madame Geoffrin whom he called 'mother'; he felt at home everywhere – in short he was a cosmopolitan gentleman of the first water. Certainly, this Parisian Pole although agreeable looking did not have Serge Saltykov's rough beauty, but Catherine, as soon as she saw and heard him, was enchanted. In her eyes, he personified that elegance of mind which she had been separated from at the Russian court, and which she could only rediscover sometimes in her room by reading Voltaire or Madame de Sévigné. What she did not yet know but was soon to find out, was that this brilliant gentleman was in reality a shy and romantic boy for whom women were beings of a superior order, and feelings of love manifestations of the divine will. Despite all his travelling he had managed, he said, to keep himself free from 'all dissolute contacts' as if he had wished to save himself 'especially for she who has since controlled my

[1] Catherine II *Memoirs*.

fate'.[1] A neophyte in love, he trembled with ecstasy before the woman who would henceforth be the only passion in his life.

'She was twenty-five,' he wrote, 'and had only just risen from her first experience of childbirth; she was at that moment when beautiful women are at their height. Her skin was white against her black hair, her eyelashes were black and very long, her nose was Greek; her mouth seemed to beg to be kissed, her arms and hands were perfect, her figure slender and tall rather than small, her movements lively and yet very noble, the sound of her voice agreeable and her laughter as merry as her disposition.'[2] However Stanislaus hesitated before making the first move. What he had heard about the sad fate reserved for the discarded lovers of Empresses and Grand Duchesses in Russia, reinforced his natural shyness. It was the high-spirited Leo Naryshkin, who had also advanced Catherine's affair with Serge Saltykov, who encouraged the young Pole to go ahead. He was a born go-between, and his main pre-occupations in life were laughter and licentiousness. Had he himself ever been Catherine's lover? Possibly once or twice, in passing, on an empty evening, as a distraction from boredom. In any case he knew all the young woman's secrets and interpreted all her wishes. Urged on by him, Stanislaus 'forgot there was such a place as Siberia'.

Catherine, amused, let herself be easily carried away. The first kisses were exchanged in her own room, into which Leo Naryshkin had pushed the nervous suitor. 'I cannot deny myself the pleasure,' wrote Stanislaus, 'of recalling the very clothes she was wearing that day: she was in a little white satin dress; a light lace shawl mixed with pink ribbons was the only ornament.' Catherine taught the boy the joys of physical love. 'By a curious singularity,' he added, 'I was able, although twenty-three years old, to offer her something that nobody else had.' From that day onwards, nocturnal escapades took place at the rate of two or three a week. As soon as Madame Vladislavova had put the young woman to bed and the Grand Duke had retired to his room (they had slept apart since the birth), Leo Naryshkin would creep into the apartments and miaow like a cat outside the Grand Duchess's door. That was the signal. She leapt up, did her hair, dressed up like a man and met her visitor in the dark hall. A carriage bore them through the silent town to Naryshkin's house where Anna (Naryshkin's sister-in-law) and Stanislaus awaited them. 'The evening would pass in the maddest way imaginable,' observed Catherine. Sometimes Stanislaus

---

[1] *Memoirs* Stanislaus Poniatowski.

[2] *Memoirs* by Stanislaus Poniatokwski. Two errors in this portrait: Catherine at the time, was entering her twenty-seventy year. And she was 'small rather than tall.'

would come and fetch her in a sledge. Coming out of the servants'
entrance of the Palace, she would rush towards him gasping with fear
and impatience. Standing in the snow, in the moonlight, he would
embrace the slender young woman in her male costume, with her hair
hidden by a large hat. 'One day when I was awaiting her like this,' he
wrote, 'a junior officer came and walked around me, and even asked me
a few questions. My head was wrapped in a large hat and my body in a
large fur coat. I pretended to sleep like a servant waiting for his master.
I must admit I felt hot despite the terrible cold. At last my questioner
went away and the Princess appeared. But it was a night for adventures.
The sledge hit a stone so hard that she was thrown out of it, face down.
She did not move, I thought she was dead; I ran to pick her up; she was
all right apart from a few bruises, but when she came back she found
that her wardrobe-maid had, by some oversight, shut the bedroom door.
She was in great danger until at last a happy chance made somebody
else open the door.' To avoid a repetition of such incidents, from then
on her lover came to her own room, right next to the Grand Duke's
apartments. 'We took particular pleasure in these furtive meetings,' she
confided. These 'furtive meetings' became so frequent that the snarling
little dog she now possessed treated Stanislaus like an old friend, which
aroused ironic suspicions in another visitor, the Swede Horn.
Stanislaus' luck went to his head. He had everything he could wish for.
'My entire existence was devoted to her (Catherine), far more sincerely
than that of most people in similar situations.'

Catherine was certainly moved by this juvenile passion, but she
responded with moderation, almost condescendingly. Her recent
adventure with Serge Saltykov had brought her to her senses. She was
very willing to be involved with a man for the pleasure he could give
her, but she would no longer make him the centre of her universe. As
she had been naive and vulnerable with her first lover, so she was
worldly and lucid with the second. Her romantic disillusionment had,
in a sense, made her virile. She now took on the male role in the couple.
'I was an honest and loyal knight,' she wrote, 'with a far more
masculine than feminine spirit, but all the same I was not the least bit
mannish and I had, along with the spirit and character of a man, all the
allurements of a woman.'[1] She was disillusioned, mistrustful and
cynical and she dominated the weak Stanislaus who was, anyway, three
years younger than herself.

Sir Charles was, nonetheless, very satisfied with his *protégé*'s progress
in the Grand Duchess's affections. He hoped, through him, to advance

---

[1] Catherine II *Memoirs*.

England's cause. Also to reinforce this advantage he offered the young woman ready money, as well as an agreeable lover. Now Catherine was careless and happily extravagant (her losses at gambling in 1756 amounted to seventeen thousand roubles); she had a taste for luxury; she would ruin herself for the sake of one dress; she could not count and refused to try; so she accepted the offer. The 'loans' that she secretly received from England came to a large total. Thus on the 21st July 1756, she wrote to Baron de Wolff, the banker and English consul: 'It is with difficulty that I bring myself to address you once more; please could you add to the debts that I already owe you another thousand gold ducats.' And four months later, on the 11th November 1756: 'Received from the Baron de Wolff, the sum of forty four thousand roubles which I will return on demand either to himself or on his order.' The Grand Duke also accepted this English manna. Why shouldn't he? England was allied with Prussia, and he was 'a Prussian at root'. The maintenance of his Holstein regiment preoccupied him more and more. When he was in his Oranienbaum residence, he reviewed the troops ten times a day. When he was in St Petersburg, lacking flesh and blood soldiers, he would, with the same seriousness, manoeuvre soldiers made of wood, lead, starch or wax. He no longer hid them under his bed, as he had done in his youth, but ostentatiously arranged them on long tables in the middle of his room. These tables were equipped with strips of brass which, when they were shaken in a certain way, sounded like 'a rolling burst of gunfire'. Each day at a particular hour, the 'changing of the guard' took place as he passed from one table to the next. 'He would take part in this parade in full uniform, boots, spurs, holster and scarf,' wrote Catherine, 'and those of his servants admitted to this fine exercise had to take part in it as well.'

These childish entertainments did not prevent him from drinking like a fish and chasing women. Inconsequential romances with ladies-in-waiting were a thing of the past. Liberated from his impediment, Peter now had mistresses. He would invite not only singers and dancers to his intimate suppers but also, according to Catherine, 'townswomen from very ill-famed circles were brought to him from St Petersburg'. Although completely indifferent to his wife, he kept her informed about his escapades and even asked for her advice. He called her 'Madam Resourceful'. 'However cross or sulky he felt towards me, if he was in any sort of trouble, he would come rushing to me, as was his habit, for my advice and, as soon as he had got it, would rush off as quickly as he could.'[1] Thus he consulted Catherine on how best to decorate his room

[1] Catherine II *Memoirs*.

to receive Madame Teplov whom he was in love with. 'In order to please the lady,' wrote Catherine, 'he had filled the room with guns, grenadiers' hats, swords and bandoliers, so that it looked like an arsenal. I let him get on with it and went away.' Another time, he rushed to Catherine, pushed a letter from Madame Teplov under her nose, shouting furiously: 'Can you imagine, she has written me a letter of four whole pages and she thinks I must read it, and, what is more, answer it, when I've got to go and drill (he had brought the troops from Holstein once again), then dine, then shoot, then go and see the rehearsal of an opera and a ballet the cadets are dancing in. I'm going to tell her straight out that I haven't got time, and if she gets cross I'll quarrel with her until winter.' Catherine agreed with him and he went away happily. Madame Teplov was anyway only an intermediary for him. Recently Elisabeth Vorontsova had become the real passion of his life. Why had he chosen her? True, she was from a good family, being the niece of the Vice-Chancellor Michael Vorontsov, Bestuzhev's rival in the Empress's political circle, but she limped, squinted and was marked by smallpox. These physical shortcomings were accompanied by a fiery temperament. She was always prepared to drink, sing, sprawl on the bed, or scream abuse, and the coarseness of her manners endeared her to the Grand Duke. He did not feel inferior when he was with her, and was not ashamed of being ugly, uneducated and foul-mouthed. Catherine froze him with her elegance and intelligence, whereas Elisabeth Vorontsova's stupidity and coarseness excited him. His passion for his mistress made him even more tolerant of his wife's infidelities. After a short absence, Stanislaus Poniatowski had returned to St Petersburg as the King of Poland's envoy, thus consolidating his position at Court. But one day at dawn, as he was slipping away from the castle of Oranienbaum where he had spent the night with Catherine, he was seized by some soldiers from the Grand Duke's guard. He was disguised with a blond wig and a large coat. When brought before Peter, he refused to explain his presence near the castle at such a curious hour. The Grand Duke sarcastically asked if he was his wife's lover. Stanislaus swore that he was not. Then Peter, who understood exactly what was going on, pretended to believe that there must be a plot against his person. For several days after this he spoke of throwing into prison this foreign spy caught in his garden. Catherine, fearing a scandal, took it upon herself to approach her husband's mistress. The latter, delighted to have her influence thus recognized, made Peter receive Stanislaus Poniatowski in his room. As soon as his wife's lover appeared, Peter cried, roaring with laughter: 'Aren't you a fool not to have let me into the secret earlier! If you had done so this row would never have taken place!' And he explained that he was not the least bit jealous, that the guard around the house was only for his personal security and that he was happy that this misunderstanding was over. 'As we're such good friends now, we need one more person here!' he ended. 'Upon this,' wrote Stanislaus Poniatowski, 'he went into his wife's room, pulled her out of bed and without giving her time to put on her stockings, shoes, dress or petticoat, brought her to me in this state saying, "Well! Here you are! I hope you're pleased with me!"'[1]

The two couples dined merrily together and did not separate until four o'clock in the morning. This bizarre *ménage à quatre* met frequently in the ensuing weeks. 'I often went to Oranienbaum,' wrote Stanislaus Poniatowski again, 'I would arrive in the evening and go up to the Grand Duchess's apartment by a hidden staircase; there I would find the Grand Duke and his mistress; we would sup together; after which the Grand Duke would take his mistress saying, "Now my children, you won't be needing me any more, I think!" and I would stay for as long as I wished.'

Stanislaus was at first shocked by the Grand Duke's coarseness, and he described him as 'a guzzler', 'a milksop', and 'a clown', but gradually he began to feel sorry for him. Peter, loose-tongued as he was, was eager to confide his state of mind to Stanislaus. 'You see how unhappy I am,' he would say. 'I was about to go into the service of the King of Prussia; I would have served him zealously and to the limits of my capability; by now, I am quite confident that I would have had my own regiment and the rank of lieutenant-general or even major-general. But not at all: all that happened was that I was brought here and made Grand Duke in this blasted country!'[1] When he was not complaining to his wife's lover, he was doing so to his wife. 'He would repeat yet again,' she wrote, 'that he felt that he was not born for Russia, that he did not suit the Russians, nor they him, and that he would perish in Russia. When he said that I told him that he should not dwell on such a gloomy idea, but should do his best to make himself loved by everybody in Russia.'[2]

Catherine, whilst she encouraged him to take seriously his duties as heir to the throne, was becoming more and more doubtful about their futures. The child she had given birth to, which remained firmly hidden from her, represented a threat. They spoke secretly at Court of the possibility that the Empress might remove her unworthy nephew from the succession and make little Paul Petrovich her heir. What

[1] Stanislaus Poniatowski *Memoirs.*
[2] Stanislaus Poniatowski *Memoirs.*

would Catherine's role be then? Would she be sent back to Holstein with her husband? Would she be given a derisory place on the Council of Regents? In any case the grandiose hopes she had been nurturing for thirteen years would be in ruins. To have received so many insults for nothing! She refused to envisage the possibility. All was not lost. Chancellor Bestuzhev was sincerely devoted to her. She had gained the friendship of Field-Marshal Apraxin. The diplomats had all observed that there were two courts in Russia: the Empress's one, and that of the Grand Duke and Grand Duchess, known as the 'young court'. Catherine decided to give the 'young court' a sparkle, a meaning that would attract progressive spirits towards her. She wished to appear to the ambassadors and the nobility as the personification of movement, imagination and enlightenment. She said to the Marquis de l'Hôpital: 'There is no woman braver than myself. My boldness is quite unbridled.' General Lieven cried as he saw her pass: 'There's a woman for whom a man would willingly suffer a few blows from a knout!'[1] And the Chevalier D'Eon, a secret agent and a wise observer, described her thus; 'The Grand Duchess is romantic, ardent and passionate. She has a bright glassy hypnotic look like that of a wild animal. She has a high forehead and unless I am mistaken, a long and terrifying future marked upon it. She is thoughtful and friendly and yet, when she approaches me I automatically back away. She frightens me.' The young woman was thrilled by the complex game of politics. After a very long wait, she guessed that the end was in sight. The Tsarina's health, flourishing until now, was rapidly declining. So far there had only been small alerts, the occasional dizziness, but nothing escaped Catherine. She was ready and awaited her moment. As payment for future diplomatic help, she continued to receive subsidies from Sir Charles Hanbury-Williams. But in 1756 Russia reversed its alliances and sided with France and Austria against England and Prussia. Sir Charles, having failed in his mission, was recalled to England. Catherine was miserable and wrote him a letter which was, to say the least, compromising.

'I have resolved to write to you as I was unable to see you to bid you farewell. May the most sincere regrets accompany one whom I regard as one of my best friends. In order to reward you in a manner suitable to the nobility of your feelings I will tell you what I wish to do; I shall seize every possible opportunity of bringing Russia round to what I know to be her best interests, that is to say, to be closely linked with England, to give her all the help it is in human power to give, and the dominance she must have, for the good of Europe, and especially for

[1] Catherine II *Memoirs.*

that of Russia, over France, their common enemy, whose greatness is
Russia's shame.'

Sir Charles, delighted, wrote back: 'You were born to command and
to reign.' She believed this so strongly that she secretly confided her
plans to him. 'Here is my dream. When I have been informed of her
death (Elisabeth), and have assured myself that there is no mistake
about it, I shall go straight to my son's room. I shall also send a trustworthy person to alert five guards officers, each one of whom will, I
know, bring me fifty soldiers... I shall send orders to Apraxin and
Lieven to come to me and, in the meantime I shall go to the death-
chamber where I shall call the captain of the guard, make him swear the
oath of loyalty and keep him with me. It seems to me that it would be
wiser and safer if the two Grand Dukes (Peter and Paul) were together
rather than with me; equally that the gathering of supporters should be
in my antechamber. If I see the slightest sign of trouble, I shall secure
myself either with the help of my own people or of the captain of the
guard, as well as the Shuvalovs and the aide-de-camp on duty. Anyway
the subalterns and the bodyguards are trustworthy... May God give
me a clear head! The novelty of this business and the haste with which I
am communicating it to you have necessitated on my part a great effort
of imagination.'

Thus, well before Elisabeth's death, Catherine had made a plan. Not
a very clear one, certainly. When she says that she wished to keep 'the
two Grand Dukes together' she does not specify with what intention she
would do so. Certainly not to help Peter onto the throne. More likely in
order to prevent him from declaring himself emperor. The palace
revolution must go in *her* favour and take place thanks to *her*
'supporters'. Conscious of having gone too far in her confidences to Sir
Charles, she added, 'You must understand that all this bears on the
future, after the Empress's death.'

Meanwhile, far from the diplomatic marshes of St Petersburg,
cannons were sounding, flags unfurling and men falling. King
Frederick II had marched with his army into Saxony. War at last![1]
Russian military men rejoiced: they had been champing the bit since
Peter the Great. But supplies were lacking. The soldiers were badly
equipped. The Marquis d l'Hôpital, the new French ambassador,
claimed that they had neither shoes nor guns, and that there were
amongst them Kalmuks who still fought with bows and arrows. The old
Field-Marshal Apraxin was worried at the thought of confronting such
a great strategist as Frederick II. He was winning victory upon victory,

---

[1] It was the beginning of the Seven Years War.

overturning the Saxons at Pirna, devastating Bohemia, beating the Austrians at Prague. The 'young court' at St Petersburg was passionately in favour of this genial sovereign who could keep such an alliance of nations in awe of him. The Marquis de l'Hôpital immediately saw that, despite Russia's alliance with France, the sympathies of this small and juvenile côterie were for Prussia. Catherine was extremely embarrassed by her predicament. Sir Charles' generosity had enfeoffed her to England and, consequently, to Prussia. But her recent friendship with Chancellor Bestuzhev obliged her to support his anti-British and anti-Prussian policies. In order to survive, she was forced to manoeuvre, invent and conceal, and she became quite intoxicated by this risky apprenticeship.

Since Apraxin still could not make up his mind to do what the whole of Russia was waiting for, and unleash a wholesale offensive, Bestuzhev asked Catherine to use her influence with the Field-Marshal and persuade him to act. He was so fond of her! She must write, therefore, without the Empress knowing. She complied, less out of personal conviction than in order to show her good will. Bestuzhev was satisfied and gave her a secret memorandum drawn up thanks to him and intended to regulate the succession to the throne. According to this document, on the Empress's death Peter would be declared Emperor but would have to share all his powers with Catherine, who would govern jointly with him. Beside the new imperial couple, Bestuzhev had reserved for himself the lion's share of appointments: the command of the guard, and the foreign, war and naval ministries. Although she was flattered by the Chancellor's trust in her, Catherine nonetheless perceived the danger of making dynastic speculations whilst the Tsarina was still alive. She did not completely reject the plan, but observed to its author that she thought it would be difficult to carry out. Bestuzhev promised to reshape it. 'To tell the truth,' she wrote, 'I regarded his project as a sort of old man's rambling, à bait to gain himself more and more of my affection.' Despite her great ambition, she never took wishes for reality. Even in her wildest enterprises, good sense restrained her galloping imagination. She was astonishingly practical in her extravagance. She liked to feel solid earth beneath her feet. She was fanatically reasonable; clear-sighted rather than visionary.

Bestuzhev's collusion with the Grand Duchess was sniffed out by the foreign diplomats, despite their precautions. The Empress also guessed at the bargaining going on behind her back. At forty-seven, exhausted by a life of debauchery, she was subject to hallucinations and fits of terror; she never slept two nights running in the same room and conversed in a whisper with images of saints: she dreaded the approach of death. Sometimes too she would suffer from convulsions which left her for a long time dazed and lethargic. 'At such times, one could not speak to her or tell her about anything,' wrote Catherine. When the Tsarina came round, the Grand Duke and Grand Duchess seemed to her like two birds of prey perched at the end of her bed. They seemed to be waiting for the moment when her eyes closed to fall upon her. There were only two cures for her haunted and feeble state: drink and sex. Although she was tired, heavy and gasping, she needed a man in her bed more than ever. 'She had moved unknowingly from moderate pleasures to debauchery, and her taste for prayer had grown with that for sensation,' wrote J. Castéra. 'She often drank too much, and then, too aroused and impatient she would not allow herself to be undressed. Her women would simply cut away with scissors the dress she had put on in the morning and then carry her to bed where she would try to regain her strength in the arms of some new athlete.' There was one favourite amongst all these 'athletes': Ivan Shuvalov, Razumovsky's replacement. He was eighteen years younger than the Empress, and had a handsome baby-face with a dimpled chin and a long nose over a sensual mouth. He wore a lace jabot and a white wig, and bore the title of President of the Academy of Fine Arts. Elisabeth could now only see through his eyes. But he was Bestuzhev's sworn enemy.

Suddenly the whole Court thrilled with excitement: after months of equivocation, Apraxin decided at last to take vigorous action against the Prussians. In July 1757, Russian troops took Memel, and in August of the same year crushed the enemy at Gross-Jaegersdorf. The victory was celebrated with a *Te Deum*. Catherine, to demonstrate her patriotism, gave a great party in the gardens of Oranienbaum. Peter could scarcely conceal his chagrin in the face of the general gaiety. 'He was upset to see Prussian troops being beaten when he had thought of them as invincible,' wrote Catherine. The Grand Duke's disappointment, however, was short-lived. Whilst people in St Petersburg were already crying 'To Berlin! To Berlin!', Apraxin suddenly beat a retreat, abandoning the equipment and spiking the guns. The Russians greeted this inexplicable evasion with a chorus of indignation. Bestuzhev hurriedly asked Catherine to write to the Field-Marshal once again 'as his friend' and beg him to stop the rout and face the enemy. The letter was sent at once, but not answered. Around the Tsarina, people spoke openly of plots and treason. Some said that the Field-Marshal, knowing that the Empress had a serious illness, and thinking that she was dying, had ordered the retreat in order to comply with the heir's well-known Germanophile views. Others, including the Marquis de l'Hôpital, accused Catherine and Bestuzhev directly of having been paid by

England, Prussia's ally, to urge Apraxin to retreat despite his victories over Frederick II. 'This was carried on before Her Majesty's eyes,' wrote the Marquis de l'Hôpital; 'but as her health at the time was most uncertain, she was completely preoccupied with that, whilst the whole Court bent to the wishes of the Grand Duke, and to those particularly of the Grand Duchess, who had been seduced and won over by the charm of Knight Williams and his English gold.'

On the Empress's orders, the Field-Marshal was dismissed and sent to his estates to await trial. His second in command, the German, Fermor, succeeded him at the head of the army. After a brief inquiry he stated that the Russian withdrawal had been made on purely military grounds: the soldiers had not been paid, they had lacked arms and ammunition, and had been dying of hunger as the supply wagons had not been able to keep up with the rapid progress of the troops. These excellent reasons did not shake Elisabeth's conviction. As far as she was concerned, Apraxin had obviously acted on the instigation of some highly placed person. And quite naturally suspicion fell on Catherine. Ever since that little busybody had got it into her head to take an interest in politics, the young court had been in a turmoil. That little hen-run needed a good sweep-out.

Unfortunately nothing could be done against the Grand Duchess for the moment: she was once again pregnant. By whom? It didn't matter. Her pregnancy was a matter of State. She was protected by her large stomach. Meanwhile gossip was rife in the drawing-rooms. The real father's name was on everybody's lips: Stanislaus Poniatowski. Although the Grand Duke was very broad-minded when it came to his honour as a husband, he was heard to say in front of witnesses: 'God knows where my wife gets her pregnancies from: I am not at all sure whether it is my child, and whether I should be responsible for it!'[1] This insulting remark was immediately repeated to Catherine, and she was worried by it: was it a veiled threat to disown the child? She took the initiative and said to Leo Naryshkin: 'Make him (Peter) swear that he has not slept with his wife, and tell him that if he swears this, you will immediately tell Alexander Shuvalov, the Grand Inquisitor of the Empire.' Peter, up against the wall, refused to swear. Was it because he had in fact got into Catherine's bed between two visits to Elisabeth Vorontsova or, more likely, did not wish to make a scandal out of something as unimportant as this? 'Go to the devil and don't bother me about that any more,' he said to Leo Naryshkin.

Catherine was relieved and decided that from now on she would take

---

[1] Catherine II *Memoirs*.

'a separate path,' that is to say, she would no longer link her destiny with Peter's. 'It was a case,' she wrote, 'of either dying with or because of him, or of rescuing myself, my children and possibly even the State from the shipwreck towards which this Prince's moral and physical faculties were leading us.'

The hostility she sensed all around her only increased her pugnacity. When Vice-Chancellor Vorontsov and the favourite Ivan Shuvalov arranged that Stanislaus Poniatowski should be recalled to Poland, she asked Bestuzhev to delay this measure. Surely they weren't going to deprive her once again of her lover just when she was about to give birth! She felt the first pains during the night of the 8th and 9th December 1758. The Grand Duke was told immediately and rushed into her room. He was wearing the Holstein uniform, booted and spurred, with a sash around his body and 'an enormous sword at his side'. He staggered about with wandering eyes and a pasty mouth, announcing to Catherine that he had come to defend her against all her enemies, like a brave Holsteinian soldier. 'I saw immediately that he was drunk,' she wrote, 'and I advised him to go to bed so that the Empress, when she arrived, would not have the double annoyance of seeing him drunk and armed from head to foot with the Holsteinian uniform, which I knew she loathed.'

A few hours later, the Empress and the Grand Duke, who had meanwhile changed his costume, took up their places by the 'bed of pain' to witness the last phases of labour. This time Catherine gave birth to a girl. She wanted to call the child Elisabeth, to please the Tsarina. The Empress, unmoved by this gesture, chose the name Anne, which was that of her elder sister, the Grand Duke's mother. After which she had this second child baptized and took her, as she had done with the first, back to her apartment. Catherine did not protest. It was the rule. Once again she received a gift from the Empress (sixty thousand roubles) and once again she was abandoned, without care, in her room. However, on the pretext of preventing draughts, she this time installed large screens around her alcove, forming a private corner. Here, without the Empress knowing, she received her closest friends, and particularly Stanislaus Poniatowski. He would arrive, wearing a blond wig, which made him unrecognizable, and when a guard called out 'Who goes there?' he would reply imperturbably, 'One of the Grand Duke's musicians!' If a stranger to the little group came into the room and asked what the screens beside the bed were hiding, Catherine would say, 'The commode.' Thus Count Shuvalov would come from the Empress to find Catherine in bed, apparently sad and alone, whilst two steps away, behind the screens, the friends 'were doubled up with giggles at the absurdity of the scene'.[1]

The laughter and games did not prevent Catherine from anxiously following Apraxin's trial. The old Field-Marshal died of 'an apoplectic stroke' after the first interrogation but the inquiry continued. And, as the days passed, it became more and more clear that Chancellor Bestuzhev would be implicated in the affair. His rival, Vice-Chancellor Vorontsov, impatient to take his place did not hesitate to denounce him as a traitor to the Empress. The Shuvalov brothers, uncles of Elisabeth's lover, openly supported the accusation. According to them, this hard and powerful man who had been for fifteen years the master of Russia's foreign policy was no more than an ungrateful intriguer. Instead of continuing to blindly serve the Empress he had secretly drawn close to the young court, espousing the interests of the Grand Duchess, and had taken a sacrilegious bet on Her Majesty's approaching death. The Austrian and French ambassadors, Count Esterhazy and the Marquis de l'Hôpital, supported the slanderous campaign by Vorontsov and the Shuvalovs.

One Sunday in February, as the young court was preparing to celebrate a double wedding (Leo Naryshkin and Count Buturlin), Catherine received a note from Stanislaus Poniatowski informing her that Bestuzhev had been arrested the night before, as well as the jeweller Bernardi whom she had frequently used as a go-between for her correspondence, her old Russian teacher Adodurov and an old friend, Elagin. She immediately took measure of the dangers which threatened her. Obviously Bestuzhev's enemies would point her out as his main accomplice. The disgraced Minister's papers would be searched. Letters she had written to Apraxin and Bestuzhev, and the plans for the succession to the throne would be enough to condemn her. Were these her last hours of freedom? With 'a knife in her heart' she went first to church. There nobody spoke to her about what had happened. But there were worried faces. Only the Grand Duke, who had never liked Bestuzhev, appeared happy. He publicly stood apart from his wife, as if to show that he had nothing to do with the crimes she was suspected of.

That evening after the double nuptial ceremony, Catherine had to appear at the feast and then the ball as if nothing had happened. But she could not bear to remain in this uncertainty any longer. With chilling bravery she approached Prince Nikita Trubetskoy, one of the commissioners in charge of the inquiry, and asked him: 'Have you found more crimes than criminals, or more criminals than crimes?' Surprised by such audacity he stammered: 'We've done what we were

[1] Catherine II *Memoirs*.

ordered to do, but, as for crimes, we're still looking for them. Up to now there have been no fortunate discoveries.' Then she asked the same question of another commissioner, Marshal Buturlin, who sighed: 'Bestuzhev has been arrested but at the moment we're trying to find a reason for it.'[1]

The next day, the Holsteinian Minister Stambke passed on to Catherine a reassuring note from the arrested Chancellor: he had had time 'to throw everything on the fire'. She quickly followed his example. In one night she too 'burned everything', papers, account books, old letters, various scribbles. A clean sweep. If they arrested her they would find no proof of her so-called political machinations. But meanwhile, the inquisitors had found a few lines from Poniatowski to Bestuzhev. That was enough for the Empress and she sent a formal demand for Stanislaus' recall to the King of Poland. The young man, in dismay, pretended he was ill and dug himself in. 'During the day he hid in his house, and by night he went secretly to the Grand Duchess,' wrote J. Castéra. Catherine begged Stanislaus to space his visits. Faced with the Empress's relentless pursuit of her friends, she dared not ask anyone to come and see her. She was isolated as if she was pest-stricken, and it was whispered that she would not remain sheltered for long against the imperial thunderbolts. At best she could expect disgrace and exile back to Germany; at worst, torture, prison and death.

[1] Catherine II *Memoirs*.

CHAPTER IX

The Great Confrontation

On the last day of the carnival of 1759, the Court theatre was getting ready to perform a Russian comedy. Stanislaus Poniatowski immediately begged Catherine to attend this gala performance, so as to put an end to rumours that she was being confined to her apartments on the Empress's orders. So she ordered the carriages for herself and her suite; but Count Alexander Shuvalov, his face twitching, announced that the Grand Duke was opposed to the outing. She immediately guessed the reason for this abrupt forbiddal: if she went to the play, her maids of honour would have to accompany her, amongst them Peter's 'favourite sultaness' Elisabeth Vorontsova, with whom he had planned to spend the evening. As she insisted on going, Peter appeared 'screeching like an eagle'. She stood up to him and to Alexander Shuvalov – she would go to the theatre, she said, on foot and alone if necessary. But before doing so, she would write to the Empress, tell her about the way her husband treated her, and ask for permission to leave the Court and return to her family in Germany. The Grand Duke retired, rather shame-faced, followed by Alexander Shuvalov, and Catherine immediately took up her pen. 'I started to write my letter to the Empress in Russian, making it as moving as I could,' she says in her *Memoirs*. 'I began by thanking her for the goodness and favours she had showered upon me since my arrival in Russia, and said that, unfortunately, events had shown that I had not deserved them, since I had only succeeded in attracting the Grand Duke's hatred, and Her Majesty's marked disfavour; that, seeing my unhappiness and that I was dying of boredom in my room, not being allowed the most innocent distractions, I begged her to end my misfortunes straight away by sending me back to my relations, by any means that she judged suitable; that, as far as my children were concerned, since I never saw them, even though we lived in the same house, it made little difference to me whether I was in the same place, or hundreds of miles from them; that I knew that the care they received from her far surpassed anything my own feeble capacities could provide, and I begged her to continue with it; that, confident of this, I would spend the rest of my life with my family praying to God for her, the Grand Duke, my children and all those who had done me both good and harm, but that my health had been reduced by unhappiness to such a state that I must endeavour at least to save my life; and that to this effect I begged her to allow me to go to take waters and thence return to my family.'

Catherine had, no doubt, been composing this letter in her mind for a long time. The moment had come, she thought, to gamble everything. Under threat herself, she issued a threat. She bluffed with terrifying coolness. What she appeared to seek – departure from Russia – was in fact the thing she dreaded most. Where, anyway, would she go, if by some awful chance the Empress did grant her request? To Germany? Her father was dead, her only brother had quarrelled with the King of Prussia and was fighting with the Austrians; her mother, deprived by Frederick of the revenues of the duchy of Zerbst, had taken refuge in Paris under the name of Countess of Oldenburg, and there, crippled with debts and caught up in endless amorous and political intrigues, she lived a miserable emigrée's life, cursing her enemies and dreaming of being admitted to Versailles. The Empress wished to hear nothing more of this tiresome 'cousin'. And the Grand Duchess was unable to respond, out of her own purse, to all her mother's demands for money. In 1759, Johanna was practically ruined. She said that her daughter only ever sent her 'a few pounds of tea and rhubarb'. In fact, Catherine would have liked to forget her entire past and family. She embodied an extreme case of voluntary alienation. Most people, as adults, remain refreshed by the clear waters of their childhood and are held by a thousand sensitive threads to the deep soil of their country. Not Catherine. She had decided once and for all that her place was in Russia. Of all feelings self-doubt was the one furthest from her nature. She hated backward turns, second thoughts, hesitation or evasion. She had lived, from her earliest youth, purely in order to fight and succeed. Now she hoped that the Tsarina would, when put on the spot, back away from this spectacular disavowal. Still, it was with some trepidation that she gave the letter to Alexander Shuvalov, asking him to carry it straight to Her Majesty. He promised to do so and, softening suddenly, told her 'with a wink' that the carriages she had ordered were ready. Catherine swept out triumphantly, and found the Grand Duke and Elisabeth Vorontsova in the antechamber, playing cards. 'He got up as soon as he saw me, which he never usually did, and so did she. I made a deep curtsey and proceeded on my way.'[1]

In her box at the theatre she faced a hundred malevolent looks in her

---

[1] Catherine II *Memoirs*.

direction with a straight head and a clear eye. The Empress had not come. 'I think my letter stopped her,' Catherine reported with satisfaction. She thought the letter could not remain unanswered. But the days passed and the Tsarina remained silent and distant. A wall of indifference. Had Alexander Shuvalov even passed on the letter? Catherine wondered why the Empress was so hard towards her, when she had no great sin on her conscience, and so indulgent towards Peter, continuing as he did to flaunt his base Prussianism. No doubt it was because she was the daughter-in-law, the outsider, and Elisabeth, anyway, disliked young women: also because Her Majesty saw that Catherine had a dominating nature, whereas the Grand Duke was nothing more than a fool. It was the beginning of Lent. Catherine decided, calculating her every move, to make long daily appearances in public at church 'so that my attachment to the Greek Orthodox faith could be seen by all'.[1] It was a waste of time. The Empress continued to refuse to see her. What was worse, in the third week of Lent the faithful Madame Vladislavova was suddenly removed from the Grand Duchess's service, on the Empress's orders. Torn between fury and despair, Catherine burst into tears, announcing that anyone who replaced Madame Vladislavova could only expect from her 'every possible form of bad treatment, even blows.' In the end, surrounded by weeping women, she said she was ill and took to her bed. Alexander Shuvalov called doctors who, one by one, took the Grand Duchess's pulse, said she was weak and offered remedies: she sent them all away and demanded a confessor. But not any confessor – only the Empress's would do. It so happened that this priest, Father Dubyansky, was the uncle of one of Catherine's chambermaids. By calling him to her bedside she hoped to procure a smooth mediator between herself and the terrifying Elisabeth. She was not mistaken. When he had heard her confession, the old almoner 'less of a fool than they said' said that she was completely in the right, condemned the wickedness of her enemies, and encouraged her to continue, from her bed, to claim that she wished to return to Germany, since according to him Her Majesty would never consent to her departure. Anyway, he said, he was going to go straight to the Tsarina to persuade her to receive the unhappy child. He kept his word. Alexander Shuvalov announced to Catherine that the Empress would grant her an audience 'the following night'. Indeed, it was true, Elisabeth slept more and more during the day and was wide awake when others slept.

On the 13th April 1759 at ten o'clock at night, Catherine got out of

[1] Catherine II *Memoirs*.

bed, had herself dressed, her hair done, and prepared for the confrontation. Her nerves were at snapping point. Alexander Shuvalov had promised to come and fetch her at midnight. She waited. Nobody came. To remain calm she told herself: 'Fortune and misfortune are within each person's heart and soul; if you sense approaching misfortune, rise above it, so that your happiness does not depend on any particular event.'[1] Despite these brave thoughts, she was so exhausted and worried that she let herself collapse on a sofa and fell asleep. At about half-past one in the morning she was woken up. Alexander Shuvalov led her to the Empress's apartments but did not withdraw once he had introduced her into Her Majesty's presence. The Grand Duke was there as well. This was not the *tête-à-tête* Catherine had hoped for, but more an appearance before a tribunal of hostile judges. Her husband had not visited her once during her so-called illness and she had learnt, incidentally, that that same morning, he had sworn to marry Elisabeth Vorontsova as soon as he was a widower: 'They both rejoiced a great deal at my state.'

Her Majesty received the accused in a vast, icy room lit only by a few well-spaced candelabras. The gold basins used for the Empress's toilet glimmered between two windows. In one of these basins, Catherine saw a bundle of papers. Were those her letters to Apraxin and Bestuzhev? Yes, they were! Pieces of evidence for the trial. She was caught in a trap. She could hear breathing and guessed that there were people hidden behind the large screens in front of the casements. She learnt later that Elisabeth's lover Ivan Shuvalov and his cousin, Count Peter, had hidden there in order to hear her defence. The public was ready; the play could begin. Instinctively Catherine chose to play the part of the vague, effusive broken woman. The huge Empress, heavily made up, with her buxom chest and large hips, considered her with a cold eye. She fell to her knees at the feet of this censorious statue and reeled off her list of complaints: she was at the end of her tether, nobody loved her, she must be allowed to return to her native country. The naturally tearful Empress was shaken, and, secretly wiping her eyes, she begged Catherine to rise. Catherine refused.

'How can I send you away?' said the Empress. 'Remember that you have children!'

'My children are in your hands, and could not be better placed,' replied Catherine, still on her knees. 'I hope that you will not abandon them.'

'But what reason could I give the public for your return?'

[1] Catherine II *Memoirs*.

'Your Majesty will say what she thinks fit, and give the reasons for which I have incurred your disapproval and the Grand Duke's hatred.'

'And what will you live off with your parents? ... Your mother has fled; she has been obliged to leave her home and go to Paris.'

'I know it,' sighed Catherine. 'She was thought to be excessively attached to Russia's interests, and the King of Prussia hounded her out!'[1]

Thus Johanna and consequently her daughter now appeared as Martyrs to the Russian cause. Elisabeth, who had not expected this explanation, thought a little; then, softening, held her hand out to the young woman slumped before her in her pretty dress, and made her rise, murmuring:

'God is the witness of how much I cried when you were so ill that you nearly died on your arrival in Russia, and if I did not love you I would not have kept you here.'

And, whilst Catherine poured out her thanks for past kindnesses, which only made her present disgrace more painful, the Empress approached her and continued, with her face close to Catherine's:

'You are extremely proud. Do you remember one day at the Summer Palace, I approached you and asked if your neck was hurting, as you had hardly bowed to me – it was only pride that stopped you from bending your head.'

Catherine protested her humility and her faithful adoration but the Empress cut her off:

'You think that nobody has more spirit than yourself.'

'Nothing would cure me of that thought better than my present state, and this very conversation,' moaned Catherine, 'since I see that, because of my stupidity, I have only now understood what it pleased you to say to me four years ago.'

The Grand Duke was disappointed by the turn this conversation was taking, away from political matters and towards those of wounded pride; he whispered, in his corner, to Alexander Shuvalov and then, raising his voice said:

'She is terribly wicked and very headstrong!'

'If you are referring to me,' cried Catherine, 'I am quite happy to tell you, in front of Her Majesty, that I am truly only wicked towards those who advise you to carry out injustices, and that I have only become headstrong since finding that compliance only brought down your enmity upon me!'

She was gaining confidence by the minute. Perhaps she would escape

[1] Catherine II *Memoirs*.

with a simple reprimand, a mere brush between aunt and niece. In any case, the Empress appeared to have forgotten the main accusation, that of treason. She strode up and down the room, rustling her enormous dress. And suddenly, she launched a frontal attack – the final assault after the preliminary skirmishes.

'You meddle in things that don't concern you,' said the Tsarina, with a withering look. 'I would never have dared to do such things in the Empress Anne's time. How, for instance, did you dare to send orders to Marshal Apraxin?'

Catherine jumped:

'Me! It never occurred to me to send him any!'

'How can you deny that you wrote to him? Your letters are there, in that basin!'

She showed her the papers in the gold basin and added:

'You are forbidden to write!'

'It is true that I transgressed that rule and I beg your pardon for it,' said Catherine without being put out. 'But since my letters are there, they will prove to Your Majesty that I never sent him (Apraxin) any orders, and only that in one I said that his conduct was being talked about... The two others only contain congratulations, in one, for the birth of his child, and in the other, good wishes for the new year.'

'Bestuzhev said that there were many others.' Catherine held the Empress's stare, and answered in a calm voice:

'If Bestuzhev says that, he is lying.'

'Well,' cried Elisabeth, 'if he is lying about you, I will have him tortured!'

Catherine did not flinch. Such a crude threat could almost have made her smile. She now felt sure that all the evidence gathered against her was so much nonsense. The Empress's rage was punctured, and she slowly calmed down. The Grand Duke chose this moment to burst into clumsy curses against his wife. He saw that she was about to win the day and wanted to reverse the situation. 'One could clearly see,' Catherine wrote, 'that he was aiming to push me out, so as to put his current mistress in my place, if he could.' Deafened by her nephew's railings, the Empress began to show signs of fatigue. In this domestic dispute, where the husband bawled and gesticulated, whereas the wife maintained a dignified silence, her sympathies were decidedly with the wife. She went up to Catherine and, giving a significant look in her nephew's direction, said in a low voice:

'I have many more things to say to you but I don't wish to sow any more discord between you!'

This expression of trust, coming at the end of a hard confrontation gave Catherine the measure of her victory. 'I became all heart,' she wrote. And she whispered in the Empress's ear:

'I too cannot speak, although my heart and soul are bursting to open to you.'

Again the Empress's eyes filled with tears. To hide her confusion, she sent Catherine and the Grand Duke away, keeping only Alexander Shuvalov with her. It was three o'clock in the morning. Radiant and exhausted, Catherine was being undressed by her chambermaids when Alexander Shuvalov knocked on her door. He came on behalf of the Empress who sent 'her compliments' to the Grand Duchess, begged her not to be upset any more, and promised to have a second conversation, this time alone, with her. Catherine went to sleep on a cloud that night. The next day a remark of Her Majesty's to a courtier was reported to her: 'She (the Grand Duchess) loves truth and justice; she is a woman with a great deal of spirit, but my nephew is just an animal.'[1]

Despite these flattering words, Catherine went on waiting for the promised 'second conversation'. Might the Empress, lazy and fickle as she was, have suddenly changed her mind? Anyway, Peter had lost none of his insolence, and Vorontsova was so certain that he would marry her that she now did the honours of the Grand Ducal apartments quite as though she was already installed there as a legitimate wife. Fearing that, as the weeks passed she might lose the advantages she had gained in the nocturnal battle, Catherine began to talk again about departure. Once again the ruse succeeded. One of her worst enemies, the Vice-Chancellor, Count Michael Vorontsov, who was an ally of the Grand Duke's, begged her, sobbing and puffing (he had 'some sort of goitre') to give up this plan which was upsetting the Empress so much! She held out against him. She spoke of how her children were kept from her. She said that everything was organized so that she would have no wish to stay. A few days later she was told that she could see her son and daughter that very afternoon at three o'clock and that Her Majesty would receive her after the visit.

When she arrived punctually for the appointment, she found herself before two little strangers who looked at her with cold bewilderment: Paul was five years old, Anne only a few months. Catherine played with them in the midst of a circle of nurses and governesses, who looked on with reproving eyes. She was not, in fact, particularly moved. She had given birth to these two beings for somebody else's benefit. She had resigned herself to a sort of abstract motherhood, and was more preoccupied with her forthcoming interview with the Empress than with

[1] Catherine II *Memoirs*.

these fresh faces dancing in front of her. She was almost impatient to leave them and go straight to the person who ruled her destiny. At last, Alexander Shuvalov announced that the Empress was available. She rushed forward. The door opened, then closed. They were alone together. Not even the smallest screen to hide witnesses. Straight away the Empress made a condition: 'I demand that you tell the truth about everything I ask you.' Catherine swore, 'to open her heart without the slightest restriction.' They spoke again of the letters to Apraxin, Bestuzhev's betrayal, the Grand Duke's misconduct ... No doubt as well – but Catherine is silent on this matter in her *Memoirs* – the Tsarina wished to know more about her niece's liaisons with Serge Saltykov and Stanislaus Poniatowski, about the chill in her relationship with Peter, about Paul and Anne's true ancestry.

Whatever happened, after this meeting behind closed doors, a sort of *modus vivendi* established itself between the two women. It was a lukewarm and respectable peace, built on concessions, resignation, and constant surveillance. Catherine reappeared at Court and no longer spoke of leaving Russia. 'The Empress received her very well, and was more welcoming than usual,' wrote the Marquis de l'Hôpital. She obtained the unhoped-for right to see her children once a week. They were brought up in the Imperial Palace of Peterhof, whilst she lived in the palace of Oranienbaum, twenty versts away. She was no longer touched by political currents. Anyway, the Bestuzhev affair had fizzled out. The threat to execute this disloyal minister had been set aside, and he was simply exiled to his estates. His 'accomplices', Bernardi, Elagin and Adodurov suffered the same sort of fate. Stanislaus Poniatowski had finally been expelled from Russia. Catherine received this blow with bitter serenity. She had been expecting it for such a long time! But in April 1759 a few weeks after her lover's departure, she lost the daughter she had had by him, the little princess Anne. And this sudden death plunged her once again into tears. It was lucky, however, that the child had died far away from her – otherwise she would have been accused of neglect! The following year her mother died in Paris. The French put Johanna's correspondence under seal. Catherine feared that some of her secret letters to her now dead mother might return to Russia and fall into the Tsarina's hands. But the Duc de Choiseul saw to it that the compromising documents were burned. As for the furniture, the 'Countess of Oldenburg's' numerous creditors seized and threatened to auction it. The Empress grudgingly agreed to pay a few hundred thousand pounds in order to avoid a scandal. Catherine was relieved, but, still, felt a great emptiness around her. Even politically, she was isolated. When Bestuzhev had been running the nation's affairs, she had known that he would support her to the end. Now that he had been removed, she had only herself to rely on in the daily struggle for the throne. This did not frighten her. Her best trump was, she thought, the Grand Duke's unpopularity: the more he amazed the Court with his follies, the better her chances were of supplanting him. Already the Empress no longer counted. She was going to die. The question of the succession was more or less open. Catherine was thirty; and she had a giant's appetite for power and love. It sometimes seemed to her that she had not yet begun to live.

CHAPTER X

Love, Darkness, Betrayal

While Catherine was trying to raise support in the drawing-rooms, the war continued far away, violent, bloody and unresolved. The Russians, under Fermor's command, occupied Koenigsberg by January 1758 and, on the 15th August in the same year, fought a battle at Zorndorf which was so deadly and yet indecisive that both sides celebrated it as a victory and sang *Te Deums*. In the following year, Frederick was beaten by the Russians at Kuenersdorf and the Austrians occupied Saxony. He quickly recovered and in August 1760 won the battle of Liegnitz. True, two months later Austrians and Russians entered Berlin, but they had to evacuate the city soon afterwards. There was another Prussian victory at Torgau. These successes, coming from an enemy thought to be on his knees, aroused a mixture of vexation and admiration in the Empress's entourage. How could one not admire the pugnacious spirit of a king who refused to bow down before this coalition of three great powers? However, a very different state of mind from that at the Palace reigned amongst the medium ranks of the army, drawn mostly from the nobility and imbued with patriotic traditions. The Court, with its diplomats, foreign visitors and family alliances which straddled frontiers, was open to outside influences. There, it was thought good to listen to reports from Europe. One took pride in an open mind. But as in the ranks of the army one was Russian before anything else. Many officers did not conceal their indignation at the fact that eminent people were, in a war, openly expressing sympathy for the Prussian cause. Some went so far as to insinuate that the Grand Duke, whose passion for Frederick was well-known, was betraying Russia and giving information to the one he called 'my King, my master'. And, indeed, Peter, his mind clouded by his idol, had only one wish: to pass on to him all that was said at the secret sessions of the Empress's war council. The new ambassador from England, Keith, received the information and passed it on as quickly as possible to Frederick. Thus the King of Prussia knew of movements planned for Russian troops even before they themselves had been informed of them. The Grand Duke received some money for his services of course, but there is no doubt that he would have done the same merely for the beauty of the gesture. In the summer of 1759, he took up the cause of a Prussian officer who had been taken prisoner at the battle of Zorndorf. This was Count Schwerin, the King of Prussia's *aide-de-camp*. This eminent captive was treated by the Russians as if he were a distinguished traveller passing through the capital. It was considered an honour for all to receive and entertain him. 'If I were emperor, you would never be a prisoner of war!' said Peter, carried away with enthusiasm. And he installed him in St Petersburg in a house close to the Imperial Palace.

Two Russian officers were placed with this splendid prisoner, more for company than surveillance. One of these was a young lieutenant, Gregory Orlov, who had behaved heroically at the same battle of Zorndorf. Wounded three times, he continued to fight more bravely than ever at the head of his men. To reward him and let him rest, his superiors sent him to St Petersburg as bodyguard to Count Schwerin. Gregory Orlov found 'rest' mainly in gaming rooms, drinking parlours and prostitutes' beds. And he did not spurn smarter ladies. Thus he seduced and carried off the beautiful Helena Kurakina, mistress of his superior, General Peter Shuvalov.[1] The risks he took there, either through passion or bravado, made women's hearts beat faster. His amorous prowess only enhanced his martial reputation. He was treated as a madman and much admired. Everybody expected Peter Shuvalov to destroy this pushing young man's career. But he was born under a lucky star: the General died suddenly, without having avenged his honour. Women said that it was a miracle, men scowled. For the former, Gregory Orlov was a force of nature; for the latter he was a dissipated swashbuckler whose conduct deserved an exemplary punishment. Catherine, in her semi-retreat, followed the capers of this fiery colt with some amusement.

There were five Orlov brothers in the Guards regiments: Ivan, Gregory, Alexis, Fyodor and Vladimir. Of the five, the second, Gregory was certainly the most attractive. He was very tall, built like an athlete, with regular features and a proud bearing. The softness and refinement of his face contrasted strangely with the sense of power emanating from his body. This formidable colossus had a velvety look and an almost feminine smile. He was certainly more handsome than Stanislaus Poniatowski whose departure had upset Catherine somewhat, and more handsome too than Serge Saltykov. But he was only moderately intelligent and had hardly been educated. His background was humble. His grandfather, a simple archer, had been compromised in 1689

---

[1] Peter Shuvalov was the cousin of the Empress's lover Ivan Shuvalov.

during the revolt of the *Streltsi*. Condemned to death and taken to the place of execution, he had calmly kicked aside the bleeding head of a decapitated companion and advanced to the block. Peter the Great, impressed by such offhandedness, had decided to reprieve him. Taken into the regular army, the guilty man had served the Tsar faithfully and become an officer. His son, Gregory Ivanovich, who became governor of Novgorod, had married, at the age of fifty-three, a noble young lady by the name of Zinoviev, and had had nine sons from her, of whom five had survived. These five, 'of heroic stature', were the five Orlov brothers, whose exploits entertained the Court and the town. As close to each other as the fingers on a hand, they formed a happy group, held together by mutual help and trust. Their intelligence was limited and their health strong; they had in common a sense of honour, love for their regiment and a taste for drink, cards and women. Their men loved them for their almost mindless bravery and for the freedom of their ways. They were the kings of the barracks. And, at Court, many eyes were turned towards them.

One evening Gregory Orlov, who had accompanied his 'prisoner' Schwerin to a reception at the Grand Duke's, was on guard at the Palace. Catherine, who had just been through a painful scene with her husband, rushed in tears to the window and saw below her a giant with an angel's head. He looked up at her with respectful admiration. She melted on the spot and determined to strike up a relationship with this Heaven-sent consoler.[1] He was clearly not of grand enough extraction to be admitted to the Court and into the Grand Duchess's circle, as had been Serge Saltykov, Stanislaus Poniatowski and even Zahar Tchernychev. Catherine knew too well how determined her enemies were to blacken her, to introduce a follower with such a dubious reputation into her circle. She asked her friend, Prascovia Bruce, to arrange meetings for them 'elsewhere', in a small house on an island in the Neva, the Vassily Ostrov. They seemed to get on perfectly from the start. How was it that this subtle-minded woman, this passionate reader of Voltaire and Montesquieu, should take such pleasure in the company of a man with a splendid forehead and the brain of a child? She was thirty, which at that time was the height of maturity for a woman, and he was twenty-five. She could not have had those half-intellectual, half-romantic conversations with him which she normally enjoyed so much. But there was, to hold her, the warmth of his skin and the strength of

[1] Neither Catherine nor Gregory Orlov, nor anyone close to them, has borne witness to the beginning of this relationship. This episode, passed on by word of mouth, is related particularly by Helbig: *Russian Favourite*.

his loins. Catherine, with her simple and healthy sensuality, greedily appreciated Gregory Orlov's caresses; back at the Palace she secretly wrote very tender letters to Stanislaus Poniatowski, the inconsolable exile, familiar with great spirits, the only one who could understand all the subtleties of her state of mind. Ah, if only she could have them both with her. Another, purely political, consideration, drew Catherine to the handsome Gregory. For her, he and his brothers represented the Russian army. By letting herself go on her lover's chest she was leaning on the guards barracks. How could she forget that the present Empress had risen to the throne thanks to the soldiers' enthusiastic support? It was even said that she had got them drunk in order to win them to her cause! Catherine would not go as far as that. But she understood very quickly that it would be better for her to count on the devotion of the fundamentally Russian subalterns, than to seek help from the high command, caught up as it was in the machinations of the court. Thus, by sleeping with Gregory Orlov, she was satisfying herself as well as preparing for an eventual *coup d'état*. Good sense and pleasure, in equal proportions, justified her affair. As for Gregory Orlov, he was living in a dream. Princess Helena Kurakina was immediately supplanted. It was true, Catherine was no longer as fresh as she might have been, but she seemed to be illuminated by her proximity to the throne. Her rank made her younger, more beautiful, more desirable. The insults she suffered from a husband sold to Germany made it a duty for any honourable man to protect her. She had a hundred times expressed her love for Russia, her attachment to the Orthodox faith and her respect for the traditions of the army. The whole Orlov clan was proud that one amongst them had been chosen by her. All five brothers were ready to be at her service. Meanwhile they raised support for her amongst their brother officers.

Alexis, the third Orlov, seemed even more resolved than Gregory to overcome the Grand Duchess's enemies. Alexis was less handsome than his brother, and was nicknamed 'the Scarface' because of an enormous scar from his mouth to his ear, the result of a sword slash received during a brawl in a tavern. He bore himself proudly all the same. Capable of stunning a bull with his fist, he was intelligent, cynical and ambitious as well as strong. He was made of harder metal than Gregory. But Catherine was a little afraid of this man's excesses: he was more interested in action than politics. In order to succeed she had to be able to count on strength (the Orlovs and the army) and on subterfuge (the court alliances). She had lost a lot of ground with Bestuzhev's downfall. The old statesman, now cut off from public affairs, had been a wise adviser to her. Luckily, a friend of the fallen Chancellor had remained in favour with the Empress: this was Count Nikita Panin. As Bestuzhev's political pupil, Panin was cultured, had fine manners, a liberal outlook, and a taste for good food and female company. Ten years beforehand, Bestuzhev had even thought of his occupying the position of the Empress's lover. But Panin, instead of bursting into the sovereign's room at the right moment as a triumphant lover, had fallen asleep outside the door. Sent on missions to Copenhagen and Stockholm, he was recalled to St Petersburg by Elisabeth in 1760. The Tsarina, old and disappointed, now no longer thought of him as a replacement for the tireless Ivan Shuvalov. However, she made him tutor to the Tsarevich Paul. Catherine immediately drew closer to Panin. Their political views coincided in some respects. Like her, he was opposed to the Grand Duke's Prussian leanings. Like her, he believed that Peter would have to go after the Empress's death. But he envisaged placing little Paul on the throne, with the help of a regency council presided over by her, whereas she could see no reason why her son should be Emperor when she was prepared to exercise power totally and personally.

Whilst they were thus secretly deliberating, the Vorontsovs, on their side, planned that Peter should take the crown, immediately divorce Catherine, announce little Paul's illegitimacy, and marry their cousin Elisabeth Vorontsova. The Grand Duke was entirely in favour of this plan. His two obsessions were, firstly, an immediate end to the war with Prussia, and, secondly, marriage to his mistress. Catherine and the bastard would of course have to be removed from sight first. Already the hunch-backed and squinting mistress, mockingly called the Pompadour' by Catherine, was behaving like a lawful wife. She moved in the Grand Duchess's own rooms as if in conquered territory. The walls and furniture belonged to her. Some people sought her help in the prospect of future upheavals. Convinced that he was at last loved for himself, Peter found his mistress's ugliness and vulgarity extra incentives for him to cherish her and advance her cause. And the more tied he felt to her by bodily and other interests, the more he hated the one who, by her very existence, represented an obstacle to their happiness.

But in order for him to get rid of Catherine, the Empress had to die first. And at fifty, although she was worn-out and weakened, Elisabeth clung to life desperately. Puffed up with fat, her legs swollen, short of breath, she refused to take care of herself, and ate and drank until she almost burst, and spent hours praying. Sometimes she was shaken by news of the war, and would swear to carry it on until victory; and to remain loyal to her allies. Then she would fall into a stupor and it would be impossible to make her sign anything. Important telegrams would lie unattended on her table; she sat shivering; the caresses of her young lover were no longer enough to warm her up. Anyway Ivan Shuvalov, feeling that his privileges as her lover would shortly be coming to an end, was already looking around for a new protectress. And, spontaneously, having previously fought with Catherine, he began to court her. Clearly the prospect of moving from the Empress's bed to that of the Grand Duchess did not displease him: he knew that, from the point of view of pleasure, he would be gaining from the exchange, but also, unlike the Vorontsovs, he thought that when Her Majesty died, the young woman would become if not Tsarina, then regent at least. And for a long time, since Paul was only six years old. And it was Ivan Shuvalov's nature to need to be close to the sun. Catherine saw his game, was amused by it, and did not discourage him. Together with the Orlovs and Panin, this new ally could only reinforce her position against the Grand Duke.

She suddenly acquired yet another supporter, if anything an even more surprising one than Ivan Shuvalov. She was Catherine Dashkova, *née* Vorontsova, the actual sister of the Grand Duke's mistress. Recently married to Prince Dashkov, this very young woman, only seventeen, had openly quarrelled with her family and fallen under Catherine's spell. The more her sister, father and uncles criticized Catherine, the more she admired her. She was enormously cultured, spoke only French, was passionate about art, literature and philosophy and made up for her unfortunate appearance by her great liveliness of spirit. Diderot, who met her several years later and was dazzled by the brilliance of her conversation, described her thus: 'She is small; her forehead is large and high, her cheeks puffed out, eyes neither big nor small, a bit sunken in their sockets, hair and eyebrows black, flattened nose, large mouth, thick lips, bad teeth, round straight neck, typical Russian figure, concave chest, no waist, rapid movements, no grace, no nobility . . . '

During the summer of 1761, Catherine would, every Sunday, after having visited her son at Peterhof, stop on the way back at Princess Dashkova's house. They would set off together for Oranienbaum and spend the rest of the day at the Palace, discussing serious scientific, artistic, or social problems. This girl, who was later to exasperate Catherine by her self-satisfaction, muddle-headedness and endless demands, was at present a marvellous interlocutress, full of a jumble of literary knowledge, quick to defend good causes with a great affinity to her both in mind and heart. Since it was impossible to have an interesting conversation with Gregory Orlov, she made up for it with this child. But, curiously enough, the athletic lover and the sickly friend had this in common: the same fiery spirit, the same taste for storms, chances and leaps in the dark. Catherine, who never lost her bearings, had to preach moderation to both of them in order to prevent them from compromising her.

One night in December 1761, Princess Dashkova, hearing that the Empress was worse, left her bed, although suffering from a bad cold herself, and feverishly decided to wrap herself in furs and set off to the wooden Palace on the Moika where the imperial family dwelt; there, she ran through the snow and into the hall, and wandered blindly through the dark corridors, and unknown rooms. Just as she was despairing of finding her way, she met a chambermaid who agreed to take her to the Grand Duchess. Catherine, who was in bed, scolded her visitor for such rashness, and making her climb into her bed to get warm, wrapped her in blankets and held her in her arms. 'Madam,' whispered the shivering princess, 'in the present state of things, when the Empress has only a few days, or perhaps even hours to live, I can no longer bear the uncertainty in which the approaching event will place your interests. Have you made a plan, or safeguarded yourself? I beg you to give me your orders and directions.'

Moved by such devotion, Catherine blinked, sighed, pressed her friend's burning hand to her bosom and begged her not to raise her head. She who, for years, had been weighing up all the possibilities and who, more recently still, had exposed her plan of action in writing to Williams, now pretended to be impartial and submitted to fate. 'My beloved Princess,' she said sadly, 'I am more grateful to you than I can possibly say. But I have formed no kind of plan, I will not embark on anything, and I believe the only thing there remains for me to do is to bravely accept events as they happen. Thus I am placing myself in the hands of the Almighty, and my only hope is for His protection.' 'So, Madam,' cried the princess, 'it will be up to your friends to act for you! For myself I have enough enthusiasm to excite them all!' Catherine, consummate actress that she was, persisted in her holy obstinacy, murmuring as she kissed her wild supporter: 'In the name of God, Princess, do not think of exposing yourself to danger, at the risk of causing irremediable harm.'[1]

Princess Dashkova was disappointed by these wise words. She accused Catherine of flagging only two steps from her goal. But it was not weakness of character that was preventing Catherine from acting. She was at that moment pregnant by Gregory Orlov, and was afraid lest

---

[1] Princess Dashkova *Memoirs.*

the Grand Duke, discovering her state, should take it as a reason for officially repudiating her. Nobody would defend her, in the face of such a scandal. She would be definitely and ignominiously moved away from the throne. All because of a stupid foetus in her stomach. She was in her fifth month of pregnancy, and wore loose dresses to hide her shape; she would say she was tired, stay in her room, and receive very few people. And then this young scatter-brain came and called her to battle! No, she would have to wait for a better moment. After the birth, which would have to be a secret one. If only the Empress could hold on until then!

At Court everybody was plotting – Russians and foreigners alike. The Tsarina's death was at the centre of all calculations. Ambassadors poured out coded messages to their governments. Everybody had his own prediction about who would reign. Peter, Paul, Catherine? Would there be a palace revolution, like the one which brought Elisabeth to the throne? Baron de Breteuil, the French ambassador wrote: 'When I see the hatred of the country for the Grand Duke, and this prince's errors, I am tempted to foresee the most total revolution (on the Empress's death); but when I observe the pusillanimous and base nature of those in a position to throw off the mask, I can see fear and servile obedience coming to the fore with the same ease as at the time of the Empress's (Elisabeth) usurpation.'

On the 23rd December 1761, the Empress had an attack and, utterly exhausted, received extreme unction in the presence of the Grand Duke and the Grand Duchess. After she had twice whispered the prayer for the dying, she begged the forgiveness of those around her for any offences and wickedness she had been guilty of. The candles were lit, the priests gathered in their funerary garb, the monks in their tall black head-dresses; Catherine, in the midst of this sinister display, with the funeral chants and the sighs of courtiers and dames of honour, remained kneeling, crying for this enigmatic woman, still wondering whether she had been her enemy or her friend. The Grand Duke was like marble. As for the main dignitaries, each one was secretly wondering what repercussions this death would have on his own life.

Two days later on the 25th December, Christmas Day, at four o'clock in the afternoon,[1] Nikita Trubetskoy came out of the Empress's room and, with a solemn face, his voice trembling, declared to the assembled group that Her Majesty Elisabeth 'had ordered them to live a long time'. This was the sanctioned expression for announcing a death in Russia, whether of a prince or peasant. Then as sobbing broke out,

---

[1] The 25th December 1761, according to the Julian Calendar, or the 5th January 1762, according to the Gregorian.

Nikita Trubetskoy proclaimed the accession of Emperor Peter III. At once despair turned to gaiety. The courtiers rushed forward, bowed down and kissed their new master's hands. Catherine was forgotten. Perhaps she had even lost the fight. Baron de Breteuil had been right. Despite the aversion he inspired, Peter could rest assured of the total submission of a nation and a court that had been trained with the whiphand of his grandfather, Peter the Great.

CHAPTER XI

The Reign of Peter III

Embalmed, made up, enormous, with her body bundled into a silver dress, a gold crown on her head, her hands joined, the impassive death-mask of Empress Elisabeth remained exposed for six weeks in a room in the Winter Palace, watched over by ladies of the court and officers of the guard. Then she was taken for ten days to the cathedral of Our Lady of Kazan. The populace, in tears, filed past the monumental catafalque. To the humble people, she was the daughter of Peter the Great – they knew nothing of her extravagance, violence, lewdness and incompetence. There was so much gold, so many jewels and candles around her coffin, it must mean that she was a powerful sovereign. A real Russian. And it was said that her successor was a German!

According to custom, the nobility, the clergy, the army, and representatives of the middle-classes and the trade guilds had sworn an oath of loyalty to the new Emperor. Peter III had nothing but contempt for the nation he had been put at the head of. He did not conceal his hatred for the dead Empress, nor the sacrilegious joy he took in being rid of her surveillance. Suddenly, for this man held so long in leash, everything was permitted. He staggered, drunk with new found freedom. Mocking the grief of the very country he now embodied, he refused to hold a vigil beside the body, and when he happened to approach the coffin it was with the deliberate intention of shocking the attendants: he would talk in a loud voice, make jokes, make faces, tease the priests. The courtiers who wanted to please him had to take part in dinners and shows which he organized in his apartments, without the slightest regard for Russia's mourning. At these gatherings, black was forbidden. Everybody had to wear party clothes, and drink, laugh and sing. Catherine herself was sometimes forced to attend these gatherings, in ball costume. She made up for this by showing exemplary piety the rest of the time. For the ten days that the Empress's body lay exposed in the nave, she would go regularly to the cathedral and there, kneeling at the foot of the catafalque, draped from head to toe in black veils, she would engulf herself for hours on end in prayers and tears. She imposed this hardship upon herself less out of love for the departed, than out of concern for her own public image. The crowds which filed past, drawn from every class, bourgeois, workers, peasants, merchants, soldiers, priests, beggars, to salute the dead Empress, also saw the living Empress, broken with grief, without crown or jewels, amidst the candles and the icons. In their eyes this religious display conferred on Catherine a sort of Russian authenticity. Her signs of the cross and her genuflections made her one of them. If she had opened her mouth they would have been very surprised to hear her German accent. Catherine felt this human river flowing around her in the semi-darkness, and could sense almost physically, the sympathy this posture engendered amongst the people.

'The Empress is gaining ground in most minds,' wrote Baron de Breteuil, the plenipotentiary minister from France. 'Nobody is more assiduous than herself in rendering to the deceased Empress the accustomed duties, which in the Greek faith are many and full of superstition – no doubt she secretly mocks them, but the clergy and the people believe her to be very much moved by them and are grateful to her for that. She observes – with an assiduity surprising to those who know her well – the feast-days, fasts, days of abstinence, all things that the Emperor treats lightly, but which certainly matter in this country. She is not the woman to either forget or forgive the threat that the Emperor often made when he was Grand Duke, namely that he would have her shaved and locked up, as Peter the First did to his first wife. All that, together with the daily humiliation she suffers must be fermenting in her brain and only waiting for the right opportunity to burst out.'

On the day of the burial, Peter capped his insolence by contorting himself behind the coffin. The dignitaries holding up the long train of his funeral robe, saw him running away from time to time and had to let go. Panels of black material floated in the wind behind him and he thought this very funny. Then he would stop, the old courtiers would catch up with him and he would mark time so as to disrupt the procession. During the funeral service he several times burst out laughing, stuck his tongue out, and talked in a loud voice, interrupting the priests. It seemed that he could not think of enough ways of arousing the hatred of his subjects. Was his mind clouded by the idea of total power? Or by the memory of Peter the Great's and Elisabeth's excesses? Or again, more likely perhaps, was it the pull the man at the edge of a chasm feels towards the gulf? Yes, a sort of inner fatality urged him a bit nearer each day to the doom which would engulf him. Every word he spoke, every gesture he made, now drew him closer to the end.

The very night after his accession, he sent messengers to all divisions of the army with orders to cease hostilities. The troops operating with the Austrians left them straight away; those occupying Eastern Prussia, Pomerania and Brandenburg evacuated these territories; the newly conquered town of Colberg was handed back. At the same time, Peter sent a personal letter to Frederick to assure him of his admiration and friendship. The King of Prussia, who had been losing the war, was exultant – an unhoped-for rescue for himself and his army. A madman had handed him victory on a plate. Violating the agreement made by the Senate not to conclude a separate peace, the Russian Emperor signed, on the 24th April/5th May 1762, a treaty with Frederick, whereby he would not only restore to him all the occupied territories, but would also send his troops to join the Prussians against the Austrians, his recent allies. He had, mounted in a ring on his finger, a portrait of his idol, which he would kiss passionately and repeatedly. He wore a single medal: the ribbon of the Prussian Black Eagle. 'Befuddled with wine, able neither to support himself or articulate,' he mumbled in drunken tones to the Prussian minister: 'Let's drink the health of your king, our master. He has done me the honour of entrusting me with one of his regiments. I hope he doesn't send me on leave. You may assure him that if he ordered it I would take my whole empire to fight in Hell for him!'[1] The English ambassador reported in a coded message to his government: 'The friendship, or rather the passion of His Imperial Majesty for the King of Prussia is beyond all expression.'[2]

Not content with having alienated the army by this shameful *volte-face*, which appeared very much like treachery, Peter now sought to impose Prussian discipline upon it, and even the Prussian uniform. Now, although the officers at that time would consent readily to change enemies for political reasons, they had a very strong *esprit de corps*, and even more respect for military traditions. By dressing his soldiers up as Germans, the Emperor insulted them. By submitting them to the 'Frederick Code' he disrupted their lives. Under the previous rule, they would accept to be flogged for a peccadillo, and would return to the ranks with flayed backs, but with robust good humour. Now they complained at being made to perform an exercise over and over again on the pretext that it had not been executed with the precision of a company of automatons. Carried away by his Germanophilia, Peter dissolved the regiment of bodyguards and replaced it with a Holsteinian regiment. He made Prince George of Holstein commander of the Russian armies, and put him at the head of the horse guard, an élite unit

[1] Despatch from Baron de Breteuil, 29th June, 1762.
[2] Coded message of the 8th March, 1762.

which had hitherto only had the sovereign himself as colonel. To create the illusion of being permanently at war, he ordered artillery salvos all the time. From morning to night, St Petersburg shook to the sound of gun-fire. It made heads ache, and nerves jangle. 'It sounded like a siege in this peaceful capital,' wrote Rulhière. 'One day he ordered that a hundred cannons should be fired simultaneously; to prevent this fantasy from taking place they had to explain to him that the city would collapse. He would often rise from table and kneel, with a glass in his hand, before the portrait of the King of Prussia. He would cry, "My brother, together we shall conquer the universe!" He had taken a special liking to this prince's envoy. He wanted him to have all the young ladies of the court. He would shut him up with them and stand on guard by the door with his sword unsheathed.'

After he had shaken up the army, Peter turned to the Church. Although he had been baptized Orthodox for the sake of the cause, he remained at heart a Lutheran. The faith held by his subjects appeared to him as a jumble of stupid stories and barbaric superstitions. As a European, he would have to sweep all that away. Despite Frederick's urging, he had not yet been consecrated Emperor in Moscow and consequently was not officially head of the Church, but he would see to it nonetheless that this mitred rabble did not hold out against him. Inspired by a desire for progress, he planned to remove all sacred images from places of prayer, except for those of Christ and the Virgin Mary, to replace the priests' cassocks with pastors' frock-coats, and to force the holy men to shave off their beards; he had a Lutheran chapel erected in the Palace and personally attended ceremonies there; he proclaimed equality of rights between the two faiths, and decreed tolerance towards the Russian 'heretics', notably the Old Believers; last and not least, he dared to order the confiscation of church possessions. Here he was attacking the holiest of holies. The Russian Church was very rich and very powerful. It owned vast estates, where dwelt possibly the most ill-treated serfs in the Empire, and it did not pay any taxes to the State. Its influence on the people was so great that hitherto no sovereign had dared to oppose it. Whoever thwarted it thwarted God. Whoever touched its riches was stealing from God. Faced with the order to secularize a part of the convents' riches, bishops became indignant, and priests cursed; the new Emperor was a heretic, a Lutheran, the personification of the Anti-Christ! Riots broke out in the countryside. 'There was a public cry of discontent,' observed the Baron de Breteuil in a despatch of the 18th June, 1762.

There were, however, amidst this avalanche of decrees, some which were well received. Thus Peter, with a stroke of his pen, abolished the office of the secret police or 'private Chancellery' of which Keith wrote in his report of the 5th February, 1762: 'This abominable Council has shown itself to be more cruel and tyrannical than the Spanish Inquisition.' Many people close to the throne heaved sighs of relief. But the aristocracy in particular was pleased by the Tsar's proclamation of the 'Manifesto on the freedom of the nobility', exempting them from military service, except in times of war, allowing them to travel abroad, and strengthening their power over the serfs.

However, the happiness of the great Russian families did not last long. Peter recalled from Siberia the dignitaries exiled under Elisabeth: Biron, Munnich, Lestocq and the Ostermanns. Once again he was surrounded by German-born advisers. Most of them urged him to execute 'his declared enemies'. He hesitated. He did not have in him the cruel decisiveness of the true autocrat, for whom torture and execution are the necessary adjuncts to any political decision. If he was a sadist it was with regard to small matters. He loved to upset, humiliate and wound, not to kill. One day, he seriously thought of forcing all the courtiers to divorce, so that he could re-marry them to women of his choice. Then another idea came into his head and he forgot this ridiculous plan. Dazzled by the King of Prussia's example, he now wished to distinguish himself as well on the field of battle. After so many miniature battles on tables with starch soldiers, he wanted real ones, with real soldiers, on real ground. No sooner had he proclaimed his 'wish for general peace', than he decided to declare war on Denmark, so as to reconquer his hereditary province of Schleswig, although Russia had no need for it. Frederick was worried by this whim and tried to discourage him. In vain. Although treasury funds were very low, and the soldiers angry at having been deprived of a certain victory over Prussia, Peter ordered the army and the fleet to prepare.

Whilst he was thus enthusing over his new dream, Catherine continued to affect grief, piety and resignation. She had a good reason for leading such a quiet life; her pregnancy, which she continued to hide from all, particularly her husband. Thinking that he was humiliating her, he confined her to apartments at one end of the Winter Palace, whilst he was installed at the other with Elisabeth Vorontsova. However, this arrangement gave Catherine the freedom of movement that she needed. Elisabeth Vorontsova glowed, as did the rest of the Vorontsov clan. Peter had proclaimed her 'to begin with' Grand Mistress of the Court. This new distinction did not enhance either her charm or his dignity. 'She has no wit,' wrote Baron de Breteuil in January 1762. 'As for her appearance, it is as bad as it could be. She resembles in every point, an ugly tavern-maid.' The German Scherer, gave an even harsher appraisal: 'She swore like a trooper, squinted, stank and spat as she spoke.' It was also said that she hit the Emperor and got drunk with him, and that he very much enjoyed this violence and intemperance. 'If he succeeded in having a male child from his mistress many people thought that he would make her his wife, and the child his successor,' wrote Baron de Breteuil, on the 15th February, 1762. 'But the way Mademoiselle Vorontsova described him publicly in the course of their argument was most reassuring on that subject.' In everybody's opinion, Peter was sterile without being impotent. In any case he never missed an opportunity to scoff at Catherine in front of the one who he thought would soon be replacing her as Empress. On the 18th January, 1762, the same Baron de Breteuil had written to the Duc de Choiseul: 'The Empress is in the most miserable state and is treated with the most obvious contempt. I told you, my lord, that she was attempting to remain philosophical, and also how little this suited her character. I have found out since, and cannot doubt it, how impatiently she bears the Emperor's behaviour towards her and the arrogance of Mademoiselle Vorontsova. It seems clear to me that this Princess, whose courage and violent nature I know well, will eventually be driven to extreme behaviour. I know she has friends who try to appease her but who would risk everything for her if she wished.'

On the 10th/21st February, during his birthday festivities, Peter ordered his wife to hand over to his mistress the insignia of the Order of Saint Catherine, which was reserved for Tsarinas and the wives of heirs to the throne. Catherine herself had only received this honour after being officially designated as fiancée of the Grand Duke. It was clear that Peter wished by this gesture to publicly show his intention of repudiating the actual Empress and giving Russia another Empress in the form of Elisabeth Vorontsova. Catherine, with her stomach held in to hide her condition, blanched, controlled herself and then obeyed without a murmur. For her, this was the only possible conduct as the child, already moving inside her, forced her to be on the defensive. The calmness and nobility of her attitude gained her the sympathy of those who ignored the real reasons for them. Her main worry now was how to give birth at the Palace without awakening the courtiers' suspicions, eager as they always were to destroy a reputation. Frequent comings and goings, a cry of pain, the wails of a new-born baby, a servant's gossip and all would be lost. As the fateful day approached, Catherine faked a sprain and kept to her room. She received visitors there, in bed or in her dressing-gown, with her foot bandaged, her face marked with exhaustion. One experienced and trustworthy chambermaid took care of her. But she could also trust her valet, Chkurin, who was prepared to die for her. When he learnt of the affair, he devised a bold plan with which to distract the Emperor. When Catherine was on the point of giving birth he would rush to his little house, which was some distance from the Palace, and set fire to it. The Emperor, a great fire enthusiast, would rush over there with his mistress as he always did. And they would be kept watching the blaze for as long as necessary. Catherine agreed to this plan, and on the evening of the 11th/22nd April, as soon as she felt the first pains, Chkurin set fire to his house. The fire spread rapidly from his shack to the whole neighbourhood. Informed of this exceptional event, Peter and Elisabeth Vorontsova, who were preparing to go to bed, got dressed quickly and went to the spot to enjoy the scene, followed by a crowd of courtiers. While the Emperor enjoyed himself handing out orders, insults and blows with a cudgel, Catherine, helped by her servant, gave birth to a son. The newborn baby, as soon as he had been washed and swaddled, was taken away from his mother by Chkurin, wrapped in a beaver coverlet, and entrusted to a foster-mother.[1]

Once again Catherine had scarcely seen the child she had just given birth to. But she had avoided a scandal, and the enormous relief she felt consoled her for the slight disappointment. She was very quickly on her feet again. Her 'sprain' was cured. Diplomats congratulated her on her happy recovery. Ruhlière, then attached to the French embassy was dazzled. 'Her figure is noble and pleasing,' he wrote, 'her bearing is proud; her appearance and manner extremely graceful. She has the look of a queen. She has a wide forehead, and a fresh mouth with fine teeth. Brown eyes, very gentle, in which the light makes blue reflections. Pride is the real key to her physiognomy. What pleases is her strong desire to please and attract people.' Mercy d'Argenteau wrote, for his part, to Maria-Theresa: 'One can hardly believe that she is not concealing some secret enterprise beneath her calm exterior.' When he complimented Catherine on her sparkling look, she replied with a mysterious smile: 'You cannot imagine, sir, what it costs a woman to be beautiful.'

Peter, however, did not give up the quarrel. He seized every possible opportunity to undermine the prestige of the woman he could not forgive for being his wife. On the 9th June, 1762, he gave a dinner for four hundred people to celebrate the ratification of the peace treaty with Prussia. For this occasion he wore Prussian uniform and the ribbon of the Black Eagle. Whether they wanted to or not, the Russian officers

[1] This illegitimate child, baptized Alexis, became Count Bobrinsky and was the founder of one of the most important families in Russia. The name Bobrinsky came from the Russian word *bobre* – beaver.

would have to drink to the glory of Frederick II. But before proposing this toast, Peter proposed one to the health of the Imperial family. All the guests stood up, pushing back their chairs. At the other end of the table Catherine remained seated, as was fitting. She had hardly put down her glass when the Emperor, through his *aide-de-camp*, Gudovitch, asked why she had not risen like the others. She replied that she did not have to rise because she was herself a member of the Imperial family. Irritated at being corrected, Peter sent the officer back to the Empress to tell her that she was a fool. Then fearing no doubt that Gudovitch might tone down the insult out of respect for Her Majesty, he yelled, 'Fool!' (*Doura*) across the table, looking at his wife with hatred. The word rang out like a blow in the general silence. Everybody had heard. Peter added straight away that the only members of the Imperial family whose presence he recognized in the room were himself and his uncles, the two Princes of Holstein. It was the first step towards repudiation. A public proclamation to the effect that Catherine had ceased in his eyes to be either wife or Empress. Before the shock of this mad insult Catherine could not keep back her tears, and turning to her neighbour, Count Stroganov, begged him to tell her a funny story. Razumovsky and the Baron de Breteuil joined in the conversation and tried, by their animated talk, to relieve the Empress's misery. After a moment of amazement the rest of the company joined in. Affectionate looks were turned towards the unjustly outraged Tsarina. Peter, thinking that he was crushing her, had unwittingly served her cause. That very evening, out of chagrin, he exiled Count Stroganov to his estates, guilty of having been too eager to comfort his Imperial neighbour. Four days later, he ordered that Catherine should be locked up in the Schlusselburg fortress. His uncle, Prince George of Holstein, begged him to abandon such an extreme measure which, he said, might alienate the army and a part of the nobility. Peter gave in half-heartedly. But Catherine had already been warned of the plan. She knew now that her future was only a matter of heads or tails: her or him, prison or the throne. Or possibly death. 'Peter III's insane and barbaric ferociousness made his threats to crush his wife quite believable,' wrote Bérenger, the French chargé d'affaires.

As the danger became more clearly defined, Catherine's friends contemplated more seriously the possibility of a palace revolution. Princess Dashkova, 'very prudent although courageous' according to Bérenger, took it upon herself to win round some of the drawing-room officers. The five Orlov brothers recruited supporters amongst the young guards officers. Gregory, who had been made paymaster for the artillery corps, dug into the coffers and managed to bribe hundreds of soldiers. In the Preobrajensky Regiment, the officers Passek and Bredikin now only swore by Catherine. Of the Ismailovsky Regiment one could count on Roslavlev and Lassuasky. There was always of course Cyril Razumovsky, the wise Panin and a few other birds of a lesser feather. Would they be enough to overturn an Emperor who was the grandson of Peter the Great, in favour of a princess who had not a single drop of Russian blood in her veins? They needed more money to buy more people. Catherine secretly asked for money from Louis XV's ambassador, the Baron de Breteuil. This young and brilliant diplomat had been sent to St Petersburg not long ago in the hope that his fine bearing would win him Catherine's favours. But, when he appeared, the position was filled. Also the Duc de Choiseul had unwisely allowed him to take his wife, who was pretty and had no intention of being deceived, even for political reasons. Breteuil's relationship with the Empress thus never went beyond the limits of courtesy. But she appreciated his wit and his manners, and felt that he was sympathetic towards her. It was therefore from him that she begged an immediate loan of sixty thousand roubles. Following the Duc de Choiseul's instructions, Breteuil avoided the issue. In order not to compromise France, he did not give a definite answer and left St Petersburg for Warsaw, then Vienna, leaving his chargé d'affaires Bérenger to unravel the situation. A few days later, Catherine, disappointed and indignant at the diplomat's obtuseness, sent Bérenger the following note: 'The purchase will soon be made but more cheaply; thus we do not need any more funds.' Bérenger was delighted. A thorn had been removed from his flesh. He did not believe that this plot, hatched by hotheads, stood any chance of success. The 'buttresses' of the conspiracy appeared very weak to him. But Catherine, meanwhile, had turned towards England to finance the 'purchase'. A hundred thousand roubles were advanced by an English trader. She was now more than ever England's ally and France's enemy. The cabinet at Versailles soon realized that they had committed a political error. 'The sovereign will never forgive you for abandoning her at such a crucial moment,' wrote Monsieur de Broglie to Breteuil. In fact, despite their excitement Catherine's friends had no precise plan, and no idea of how, at the right moment, they would place her on the throne. With them it was all smoke, fever and last-minute improvisation.

Peter, oblivious to all this, had left St Petersburg on the 12th June 1762 to go to his summer residence at Oranienbaum. He wanted to rest there for a few days before joining his army in Pomerania so as to demolish the Danes and reconquer the precious Duchy of Schleswig. Unfortunately the Russian fleet was in no fit state to set sail. An epidemic had severely reduced the number of sailors. Never mind: Peter signed an order to the sick men to recover without delay. Meanwhile he caroused with his mistress and reviewed his troops. In vain did his closest advisers point out the dangers of deserting his capital and his empire, leaving in St Petersburg a group bent on removing him – he took no notice. He did not pay any more attention to Frederick II when he advised, through his envoys Baron de Goltz and Count Schwerin, that Peter should first be crowned in Moscow, that the Russians were too much bound by custom to respect a ruler who had not yet been consecrated by the Church, that a wise monarch never went to war without leaving solid ground behind him. The only precaution Peter agreed to take was to do with where Catherine resided. He ordered her to leave St Petersburg and install herself at Peterhof, near Oranienbaum on the gulf of Finland. Catherine's friends sensed a trap. She herself was worried. But she did not wish to go backwards. She simply decided to go alone, leaving her son Paul in Panin's care.

When she arrived in Peterhof on the 19th June, she did not install herself in the actual Palace, but a little distance away in a pavilion called 'Mon Plaisir' beside the water. There she remained expectantly, prepared equally to welcome Orlov's emissaries or to flee from her husband's *sbirros*. Peter had word sent that he would come to Peterhof on the 29th June to celebrate his name-day (St Peter and St Paul), and that she must be prepared to receive him. Was he going to use the banquet as another opportunity of insulting her, or, better still, have her thrown into the fortress, as he had threatened a hundred times before? Hearing of this dangerous meeting, Catherine's friends gathered, indecisively and anxiously. And then on the 27th June one of them, Captain Passek, was arrested. He had drunkenly insulted the Tsar in front of witnesses. He might say more under torture. This was the moment. They could not wait any longer. They must attack immediately and at all costs. Fyodor Orlov, Gregory's younger brother, rushed in the dead of night to the house of Cyril Razumovsky, a dedicated supporter of Catherine's. He was President of the Academy of Sciences and went to wake up Taubert, director of typography at the Academy, asking him to print immediately a manifesto proclaiming the fall of Emperor Peter III and the accession to the throne of Catherine II. This was madness as not a single soldier had yet marched in support of the Empress. Taubert, terrified, argued and equivocated. But Razumovsky cried, 'You already know too much! Now your head, like mine, is at risk!' And Taubert, defeated, gave the order to compose the text. It only remained to tell Catherine. Alexis Orlov took charge of that.

CHAPTER XII

The Coup d'Etat

Alexis Orlov arrived at Peterhof on the 28th June/9th July, 1762, in a carriage at dawn. The park was bathed in the milky light of the summer's morning. Silhouettes of a few Holstein guards floated like ghosts in the half-light. Alexis avoided them, and crept stealthily between the bushes until he reached a side door of 'Mon Plaisir'. As he went through the dressing-room he noticed the court dress which the Empress was to wear to receive her husband. A minute later the chambermaid, Chargorodskaya, was waking Catherine, who had been in a deep sleep. Alexis Orlov was there, she said, and urgently wished to speak to Her Majesty. Catherine quickly gathered her wits. She received Alexis sitting up in bed, in her night clothes. He looked ready for a fight.

'It is time to rise,' he said. 'Everything is ready for you to be declared Empress.'

And he added:

'Passek has been arrested. We must go!'

This time Catherine did not hesitate an instant. She had an almost animal-like flair for the right moment. She knew instinctively when to retreat and when to spring forwards. She was already up and dressed 'without washing'. The trembling Chargorodskaya helped her and the last button had hardly been done up before they were following Alexis out to the carriage. Catherine jumped in, her maid beside her; the faithful valet Chkurin, whom they had awakened as they went past, climbed up behind with Lieutenant Bibikov, Alexis got up next to the coachman, and the team set off at a gallop on the road to St Petersburg. From time to time, Alexis looked back to see if they were being followed. The unexpectedness of this dawn flight, the bumps, the cool air, the shouts of the coachman, fear of being caught, hopes of success, all mingled in Catherine to produce a sort of happy excitement. She suddenly burst out laughing, when she noticed that her maid had lost a shoe and that she herself was still wearing her lace night-cap. On the way, they met Michel, Her Majesty's French hairdresser, who was on his way, as every morning, to take up his duties. They took him on board, and he combed the Empress's hair as they went along. The horses, which had already travelled thirty versts on the way out, were beginning to flag. One of them tripped and fell, and got up with some difficulty. Would they last? In his hurry, Alexis Orlov had forgotten to prepare any relays. He raged at the thought that such a marvellous project might turn to catastrophe thanks to him. Then a peasant appeared driving a cart. Alexis and Chkurin stopped and asked him to exchange his fresh horses for their exhausted ones. The peasant agreed and they galloped off. A few versts from St Petersburg, Prince Bariatinsky awaited them in an open carriage. She quickly changed vehicles. Gregory was also there, on horseback. He had come to meet the fugitive. Catherine was exultant at the sight of her handsome and resolute lover. He capered along beside her for a while, proud to be escorting her on the path of glory, then he spurred his horse and galloped on to announce the Empress's arrival to the Ismailovsky Regiment.

The carriage drew up alongside the barracks a little after seven o'clock in the morning. Drums were beating. Catherine, with a tight heart, stepped forwards, frail and upright in her mourning dress, towards this mass of men on whom her future depended. Standing in his stirrups, the splendid Gregory Orlov saluted her with his sword. She had nothing to fear: the soldiers were white-hot with enthusiasm. Anyway they had been promised an issue of vodka. As soon as she appeared before them, the lines broke and a great cry rose from the rough faces, 'Hurrah! Our little mother Catherine!' The chaplain of the regiment raised a cross. The officers surrounded this unfortunate Empress who needed their courage to protect her. They knelt and kissed the hem of her cloak. Count Cyril Razumovsky, the Commander of the regiment, knelt in turn before her. Then he stood up and called for silence. But the troops' cheers only redoubled. When at last he managed to dominate this happy chaos, Cyril Razumovsky proclaimed her Majesty the Empress Catherine sole and absolute ruler of all the Russias, and in the name of his soldiers swore the oath of loyalty.

Then they were off to the barracks of the Semeonovsky Regiment! The priest in his sacerdotal robes led the march with his cross held high. Around the Empress's open carriage rode Gregory Orlov, Cyril Razumovsky and countless other officers, their faces red with excitement. Behind them, a horde of untidy and hilarious soldiers shouting: 'Long live our little mother Catherine! We'll go to our death for her!' The Semeonovsky Regiment in its enthusiasm joined the Ismailovskys, and the great wave now rolled towards the other barracks. Everywhere they melted together in an overflow of joy. Except when it came to the Preobrajensky Regiment, whose conspirators had been unable to circumvent the officers. Simon Vorontsov, brother of the Emperor's mistress, was a captain in this elite unit. The cause of the Empire was, to him, the same as the cause of his sister. With the help of Major Voyeykov, he harangued his men, ordering them to respect the oath they had sworn to the Tsar, and marched with them towards the mutineers. The two groups came face to face in front of the Kazan cathedral. Catherine's partisans were vastly in the majority. But they were a disorderly, confused rabble, mostly unarmed, whereas opposite them the Preobrajensky Regiment, smartly equipped from head to foot, surrounded by its officers, appeared as a formidable array of disciplined men ready to fight. Simon Vorontsov categorically rejected Gregory Orlov's exhortations. Rifles were lowered. This was the fateful moment. If the loyal regiment were to open fire there would be instant panic amongst the rabble surrounding Catherine, followed by a stampede, pursuit, arrest, prison and execution. Suddenly Menchikov, a major in the Preobrajensky Regiment cried, 'Hurrah! Long live the Empress!' After a second's hesitation the cry was taken up in chorus by his men. They broke ranks, rushed towards their comrades, embraced them, fell on their knees before Catherine, accusing their officers of having deceived them. Voyeykov and Simon Vorontsov broke their swords. They were arrested.[1]

It was a clear summer morning, cool and cloudless. The crowd on the Nevsky Prospekt was such that the wide avenue was completely blocked. Citizens, appearing from all sides, mingled with the soldiers to cheer the heroine of the day. The carriage was surrounded by a sea of happy faces. Sabres and guns waved above their heads. A thousand voices yelled one name: 'Catherine! Our little mother Catherine!' With difficulty, the horses pushed a way through to the Kazan cathedral. Three hours after she had been hauled out of bed by Alexis Orlov, Catherine advanced with firm steps towards the high clergy awaiting her. Once inside the church she saw how well her public piety had paid off. The Archbishop of Novgorod, surrounded by officiating priests, received her as an autocratic sovereign and blessed her and her absent son, the heir to the throne, Tsarevich Paul Petrovich.

After this short ceremony Catherine went, still in the carriage, and surrounded by the Orlov brothers and Cyril Razumovsky, to the Winter Palace. Six regiments and the whole artillery were massed on the quay in front of the building and behind it, so that it looked like an enormous

---

[1] Catherine later pardoned them, but Vorontsov had to leave the army and, made ambassador in London, lived there 'in a sort of honourable exile'.

entrenched camp. Priests presented the cross to soldiers who knelt with their heads bowed. As soon as she arrived in her apartments, Catherine called for her son, the Tsarevich. Count Panin brought him to her at once. The child, who had just woken up, was in his nightshirt and cotton night-cap. She took him in her arms and appeared with him at a window. The crowd roared with joy when it saw them. Little Paul, who was eight, was frightened and clung spasmodically to his mother. For the moment, this frail child with fair curls was helping her to legitimize her conduct before her subjects. However, he must not be allowed to supplant her in the public's favour. She intended to rule not only whilst her son was a minor but for as long as her strength held out. The present ambiguity, if her plan succeeded, would not be held to in the future. She let the others believe what they wanted, and continued to follow inflexibly the line she had prepared for herself for so long. Princess Dashkova arrived next, her hair in disarray, and rushed into the arms of 'her' sovereign. The two women hugged each other happily. 'God be praised!' cried Catherine. At her order, the doors of the Palace were opened wide: everyone, today, could approach the Empress. Members of the Holy Synod, senators, important officials, court dignitaries, ambassadors, townspeople, merchants all crowded into the drawing-rooms and jostled each other in order to be able to kneel before Her Majesty and congratulate her on her success. Catherine, smiling and serene, spent hours receiving compliments from high and low. Meanwhile, outside, the manifesto printed in the night was being distributed and read, the text of which had probably been inspired by her and drawn up by Cyril Razumovsky:

'We Catherine II,
The loyal children of our Russian nation have clearly perceived the supreme danger to which the Russian State has been exposed in the course of recent events. Indeed our Greek Orthodox Church has received such a blow that she has been exposed to the greatest danger of all, that of the substitution of a heterodox faith for our ancient orthodoxy. Secondly the glory of Russia, elevated so high by its victories and spilt blood, has been effectively ground under foot by the conclusion of peace with our most mortal enemy (Frederick II), and the nation abandoned to total subjection, whilst the internal order, on which depends the unity of our entire nation, has been completely overturned. For these reasons we have felt ourselves obliged, with God's help, and on the clear and sincere wishes of our subjects, to take the throne as sole and absolute sovereign, to which effect our faithful subjects have solemnly sworn the oath of obedience.'

The foreign diplomats took note of this document, and half of them rejoiced at it. What a turnabout, on the very first day! There was no doubt that, having castigated Frederick II in her manifesto, Catherine would break the alliance with Prussia and return to the one with France and Austria. The Austrian ambassador, Mercy d'Argenteau, expressed his satisfaction to the Empress, but she listened expressionless, and spoke of other things. It was impossible to read the thoughts of this calm strong woman, as she chatted amiably with her admirers even at the height of the tense wait. From time to time she gave orders in a low voice to the Orlov brothers, to Cyril Razumovsky, or to Panin: they must watch the public houses to avoid any excess of drink, close the gates of the city and forbid any travel on the road from St Petersburg to Oranienbaum so that the Emperor should hear about the *coup d'état* as late as possible . . .

And indeed despite the first spectacular success, nothing was yet settled. Whereas Catherine had at her disposal a few hastily rallied regiments, Peter could count on all the troops gathered in Livonia for the war against Denmark, and on the fleet at anchor before the island fortress of Kronstadt. If St Petersburg was attacked from land and sea, it could not resist an energetic attack for more than two hours. Therefore the Emperor must be caught as soon as possible, and the co-operation of the navy ensured. Admiral Taluizin was immediately sent to Kronstadt with a note giving him full powers in the name of the Empress.

That afternoon, Peter, who as yet knew nothing, left Oranienbaum to go to Peterhof where he expected to celebrate the feast of St Peter and St Paul the next day, as he had told Catherine. He was accompanied by his mistress, Elisabeth Vorontsova, General Munnich, whom he had recalled from twenty-three years of exile in Siberia, the Prussian ambassador, Baron Goltz, Prince Trubetskoy, Chancellor Michael Vorontsov, the Senator Roman Vorontsov, and seventeen court ladies in full dress. The carriages drew up in front of 'Mon Plaisir'. Everything was silent. Doors and windows were shut. They searched in vain for a servant. At last one of the officers at the guard post stepped forward and stammered out, 'The Empress went away at dawn. The house is empty.' Seized with fury, Peter pushed aside the officer, rushed into the pavilion, shouting, 'Catherine! Catherine!' as if he refused to believe that she was not there. His weak legs took him from the winter garden to the Chinese room, from the audience chamber to the music room. Suddenly he heard footsteps. She was there. She was hiding. She had played a trick on him. As she used to do during their childish engagement period. He rushed forward and found himself face to face with Chancellor Michael Vorontsov. When questioned, the Minister mumbled that he had just received, through a secret messenger, the news that Catherine had been proclaimed Empress at St Petersburg. Peter immediately lost all his pride. He hung around Michael Vorontsov's neck, not moving, panting and sobbing, whilst the other man tried to make him stand up; 'Courage, your Majesty! Courage! One word from you, one domineering look, and the people will fall to their knees before the Tsar! The men of Holstein are ready! We will march on St Petersburg within the hour!' But Peter refused such a confrontation. He searched for other solutions, ran in all directions, fainted, came to, drank large glasses of burgundy, dictated a list of people to be imprisoned for conspiracy, drew up two manifestos condemning Catherine, had them copied out several times by the courtiers, begged Michael Vorontsov to go to St Petersburg instead of himself and order the mutinous regiments to submit to him; then he changed his mind, called for the Holsteinian regiments which had remained at Oranienbaum, and when they arrived declared that he did not need them, and, at last, giving in to Munnich's entreaties, agreed to embark for Kronstadt, where the fleet and garrison would support his cause. But he refused to be separated from the women on this expedition. He was drunk, and staggered and cried; they had to hold him up to get him onto a schooner at ten o'clock in the evening. The whole weeping horde of women led by Elisabeth Vorontsova followed him up the gangplank.

At one o'clock in the morning on an almost unreal, silvery night, the schooner arrived at Kronstadt. When the fortress was within calling distance of the boat, Munnich announced the Emperor's arrival.

'There is no longer an Emperor!' replied the officer on guard. 'Pass along!'

Munnich insisted. Then the officer shouted to him that the fleet and the garrison had already sworn the oath to the Empress. If the boat did not pass on immediately, a salvo would send it to the bottom. Thus Taluizin, Catherine's emissary, had beaten the Emperor to it. Despite this warning, Munnich would not admit defeat and begged Peter to disembark. They would not dare shoot at him. As soon as he was on solid ground these Kronstadt lunatics would repent and throw down their arms. But Peter rushed down to the bottom of the hold. He was sweating with terror and his teeth were chattering. He had only ever dealt with wooden soldiers. Why couldn't they leave him with his dreams? He sobbed great hiccuping sobs. The women around him gave piercing screams. It was such a pitiful sight that Munnich burst out laughing and made the boat go about.

At dawn on the 29th June, the boat drew up alongside the Summer

Palace at Oranienbaum. Munnich suggested transporting the Tsar immediately on another boat to Reval. From there he could rejoin the main body of Russian troops destined for the campaign against Denmark. With them it would be easy to reconquer the throne. 'Do this, sire, and six weeks later St Petersburg and Russia will once more be at your feet. I'll stake my head on it!' These words only exhausted Peter. He had had enough of taking decisions. What he wanted to do was sleep for a few hours, watched over by Elisabeth Vorontsova. He sent everybody except her away and collapsed on his bed.

Whilst Peter was sailing towards Kronstadt, Catherine had put on a uniform borrowed from an officer of the Semeonovsky Regiment. For man's work, you needed a man's outfit. On a corner of the table, she scribbled a short note for the Senate: 'Gentlemen, I am leaving the city at the head of the army to ensure peace and security for the throne. I leave my supreme power, with complete trust, in the hands of the Senate, along with my country, people and my son.' She left the Palace, came down the great outside staircase and, before the assembled troops, easily swung astride the grey thoroughbred that had been brought for her. Suddenly she noticed that she did not have a pennant on her sword. A non-commissioned guards officer rushed forwards and gave her his own, tearing it off the handle of his sword. Catherine took it and smiled at this handsome ecstatic face. The young man's name? Gregory Potemkin. She would remember him.

As she left the town, she reviewed her regiments. Most of the soldiers had stripped off the German uniforms that Peter had made them wear, and put on old ones from the time of Peter the Great, dug out of the stores. With her naked sword in her hand, Catherine mastered her horse, which shied impatiently. A crown of oak leaves encircled her sable-lined hood. Her long chestnut hair flew in the wind. All eyes were turned admiringly towards this woman in military costume, who appeared to symbolize both strength and grace, fragility and determination. Cheers drowned the rhythmic beat of fifes and drums. Beside the Tsarina, Princess Dashkova was also in uniform and on horseback. By the time the last company had gone past it was ten o'clock at night, but still broad daylight. They were on their way!

It was a dream-like ride in the unreal glow of the northern light. The men marched without knowing exactly where they were going, nor what they were going to do, but their enthusiasm was totally engaged in this mad adventure, mingling as it did light and shade, duty and revolution, truth and illusion. At the head of the slow procession, a woman, perhaps the goddess of war. Behind her, the Orlov brothers and many officers, all of whom seemed to be in love with her. The military band played stirring tunes. And when it stopped, the soldiers struck up old marching songs, broken by happy shouts and whistles. Always the same cry: 'Long live our little mother Catherine!' Each time she heard her name yelled by these rough throats, she quivered with almost sexual joy. That was what she needed: a people which would be for her like a many-shaped lover, always ardent and always submissive.

At three o'clock in the morning the Tsarina and her general staff halted at Krasni-Kabak, in a miserable inn. The men, who had been on their feet since dawn, needed rest. Not her. Urged by her followers, she agreed to lie down, however, beside Princess Dashkova, on a narrow, hard straw mattress. But she did not sleep. She was thinking. What was Peter doing? Had he assembled his troops to march towards the insurgents? Had he installed himself at Kronstadt before Admiral Taluizin had been able to reach the garrison? She tossed and turned, worrying about the lack of food and ammunition. At five o'clock in the morning a truce-bearer was announced: Chancellor Vorontsov himself. He came, with the Emperor's mandate, to offer the Empress a power-sharing arrangement. As soon as he had begun to speak, Catherine understood that she had won the battle. Her reply was to burst out laughing. Vorontsov did not insist, but knelt down and swore the oath of loyalty. How could he hesitate between the debilitated puppet he had just left and this calm, self-assured woman, who already behaved like a queen? Other messengers arrived, bringing similar propositions, and all, impressed by Catherine's authority, arranged themselves, like Vorontsov, at her side. Towards six o'clock in the morning, Admiral Taluizin appeared, exultant, at Krasni-Kabak: 'Kronstadt belongs to the Empress! The garrison has refused entry to the Tsar!' Catherine's heart was bursting with joy, but her face remained impassive – as if she had foreseen all this. Now, she must exploit her advantage without wasting time on celebrations. Her troops were already on the march – would they clash with the Holsteinians? Catherine was in the saddle, and galloped in one stretch all the way to Peterhof. There she found her soldiers camped peacefully around the castle. Giving up the idea of a fight, Peter III had withdrawn the main body of his forces, and the few remaining sentinels had been easily disarmed. Not a drop of blood had been shed. It was more than a victory. It was a miracle. Installed at 'Mon Plaisir' Catherine dictated the Act of Abdication which the Emperor was to sign:

'During the short time of my absolute reign over the Russian Empire, I have realized that my strength was not sufficient to bear such a burden... That is why, after careful consideration, I declare, solemnly and under no constraint, to all of Russia, and to the entire world, that I renounce for life the government of the said Empire.'

Gregory Orlov and General Ismailov immediately set off to take the document to Oranienbaum, where the Emperor was virtually a prisoner. When they had gone, Catherine, who was now very hungry, boldly took her place at table amongst her officers for a meal. She drank moderately, as was her habit. Half a glass of wine. And she urged the others to do the same. The day was not over. Amidst the hubbub of raucous male conversation she continued her calculations tirelessly. What would she do if her husband refused to abdicate and let himself be taken as a captive to Peterhof? And if he did come, what to do with him there?

Meanwhile, at Oranienbaum Peter, in a collapsed state, copied out and signed the document which Catherine's envoys had brought. 'Like a child being sent to bed,' said Frederick II later. He was put in a carriage with his mistress and the Adjutant General, Godovich. When he arrived at Peterhof, he asked to be taken to the Empress. Perhaps he hoped to make her relent by reminding her of all that still linked them together? But she refused to receive him. Officers removed all his decorations, his sword and his uniform and gave him a civilian costume. He let them do it, crying all the time. Nikita Panin informed him that by order of the Empress he was henceforth a prisoner of the State and that he would be guarded in a villa at Ropscha,[1] not far from St Petersburg, awaiting a decision on where he would eventually reside. This definitive residence, Peter knew, could only be the terrible fortress of Schlusselburg, where the ex-Tsar Ivan had been mouldering for so many years! He was horrified and his cries and tears redoubled; he fell on his knees before his son's tutor, kissed his hands and implored him at least not to separate him from his mistress. 'I consider it as one of the great misfortunes of my life that I had to see Peter at that moment,' Panin was to write. With pain and repugnance, Panin announced to him that the Empress could not allow Elisabeth Vorontsova to follow the prisoner to his retreat. It would amount to legitimizing adultery. The mistress would be sent to Moscow. Anyway the whole Vorontsov family had already turned its back on her and rallied to Catherine. Then Elisabeth Vorontsova mingled her own hysterical cries with her lover's sobs. Both dragged themselves at Panin's feet, but he remained unswerving.[2] Peter, now worn out, asked if he could take with him to

[1] Ropscha was 27 versts from St Petersburg.

[2] Elisabeth Vorontsova was placed in a guarded house in Moscow. But later Catherine pardoned her and even found her a husband in the form of Senator Poliansky.

Ropscha his violin, his negro Narcissus and his favourite dog Mopsy. They replied that the Empress would consider this request in her own good time. In the event, Catherine did allow this triple favour. She even authorized that the prisoner should be served by his usual valet, Bressau. But for the moment he must obey. He had wanted to flout and humiliate her. Now she was taking her revenge. Did she have a single sentimental thought for their childhood engagement, their silly games long ago behind Empress Elisabeth's back? No, the man and woman that they had become had nothing to do with the charming ghosts of their youth. As the days had gone by, mortal hatred had grown up between them.

As evening fell, Alexis Orlov heaved a dislocated puppet, green with terror, into a Berlin coach with drawn curtains. It set off for Ropscha.

The next day, Sunday the 30th June, 1762, Catherine made a triumphal entry into St Petersburg, greeted by ringing bells, gunfire and wild cheers. The troops' rapture, stoked by distributions of vodka, was such that, on the night after her return, the soldiers of the Ismailovsky Regiment demanded to see the Tsarina to make sure that she had not been either assassinated or kidnapped. She had, whether she liked it or not, to drag herself from her bed, put on her uniform, and show herself to her men in order to reassure them. 'My situation is such,' she wrote later to Poniatowski, 'that the lowest soldier on guard, when he sees me, can say to himself "That is my creation".'[1] Thus, succeeding the Empress Catherine I, Empress Anne Ivanovna, the regent Anne Leopoldovna and Empress Elisabeth, a fifth woman, Catherine II, after two brief male interludes, took the country's destiny into her hands. After thirty-seven years, the Russians had become accustomed to being governed by skirts – this newcomer was continuing a sort of national tradition. Her first act was to reward the makers of her fortune. In a few months the bill for 'presents' amounted to nearly 800,000 roubles. Gregory Orlov, Princess Dashkova, skilful advisers, officers of all sorts, all were showered with gold. It was said that 41,000 roubles was spent merely on vodka for the regiments. Catherine was generous by nature, and did not want any numerical limit set on her gratitude. At the same time, she worried about her husband's fate. He wrote pitiful notes from Ropscha, in French, full of mistakes and almost unreadable.

'I beg Your Majesty to be truly sure of me and to have the goodness to remove the guards of the second chamber, because the chamber I am

---

[1] The best sources for the details of the *coup d'état* are Catherine's own accounts (letters to Poniatowski), those of Princess Dashkova, Panin and also Bilbassov.

in is so small that hardly can I move, and, as she knows that I always walk about my room, it will make my legs swell up. And I beg you not to order the officers to stay in the same room; as I have personal needs, that is impossible. Moreover, I beg Your Majesty not to treat me like the greatest miscreant, as I am not aware of having ever offended her. I beg for her magnanimity and that she should allow me as soon as possible to depart with the said person (Elisabeth Vorontsova) to Germany. God will surely repay her and I am your very humble valet, Peter. PS Your Majesty may be sure of me, I will never think nor do anything against her person or her reign.'

And again: 'Your Majesty, if you do not wish to kill absolutely a man who is already unhappy enough, have pity on me and allow me my only consolation which is Elisabeth Romanovna (Elisabeth Vorontsova). You would be performing one of the greatest charitable acts of your reign. Also if Your Majesty would see me for a moment, my cup would be full.'

Catherine took care not to reply. But as Peter was said to be ill, she sent a doctor to him at Ropscha. He was better. She did not know whether to rejoice or be sad at this. As long as he lived, the possibility of a *coup d'état* would hang over her, fomented by discontented officers or a few courtiers longing for intrigue. Even fallen and imprisoned, he represented a permanent threat to the throne. After all, he was descended from Peter the Great, she was not. She must quickly consolidate her position as Head of State. On the 6th July she published a second manifesto announcing both her accession and Peter III's abdication. In this document, which was read before the Senate, she declared her intention of deserving the love of her people, 'in whose interest we realize we were brought to the throne'.

That very evening a message from Alexis Orlov was brought to her at the Palace. It was a crumpled piece of paper, a pencilled scribble which she could hardly read: 'Our little mother, merciful Empress! How to explain, how to describe what has happened? You will not believe your devoted servant, but, before God, I am telling you the truth. Little mother, I am prepared to die, but I do not know myself how the misfortune happened. We are lost if you do not forgive us. Little mother, he is no longer. But none of us wished it – how could we have dared to lay hands on the Emperor? And yet, Majesty, the tragedy happened. He had begun to argue with Prince Fyodor (Baryatinsky) during the meal, and before we could separate them he was no longer! We cannot even remember what we did, but every one of us down to the last man is entirely guilty and deserves to be sentenced to death. Have pity on me, even just out of love for my brother! I have confessed my fault and there is no more to say. Pardon us or have us quickly executed. The light of day is awful to me. We have offended you and are eternally damned for it.'[1]

Catherine was thunderstruck. It was obviously an assassination performed by her friends to serve her cause. She was free from the pitiful Peter. But her reputation was for ever sullied. Would it not have been better to live in fear of a plot, than in the certainty of public repudiation? Was it not absurd to sacrifice the future renown of a reign to immediate political advantage? It was a choice of two evils. Catherine, according to some intimate witnesses, fell into a faint, came to, and sighed, 'My glory is finished! Posterity will never forgive me this involuntary crime!'[2] And also, 'This death causes me inexpressible horror! I am flattened by this blow!' Princess Dashkova, hearing her, replied: 'Madame, this death is too sudden for your glory and for mine.'[3] Other witnesses, on the other hand, emphasized the serenity affected by Her Majesty at Court that evening. The two testimonials are not contradictory: Catherine had always been able to control herself at crucial moments. Whatever her inner turmoil, she refused to make a spectacle of herself before the clique of diplomats and courtiers. This death which she had wished for without ordering, this death which both suited and embarrassed her, represented an affair of state, not an affair of the heart. And affairs of state had to be treated coldly in private. It would be thus in this case. Catherine felt no remorse, only worries. Even the rage she felt against the guilty ones was tempered by sympathy, even tenderness. They had thought they were doing the right thing, indeed their very clumsiness demonstrated their good faith. The next day, the 7th July, she published a third manifesto, thus:

'On the seventh day of our accession to the throne of Russia, we have been advised that the ex-Tsar Peter III suffered another of his habitual haemorrhoidal attacks, together with a violent colic. Aware of our duty as a Christian, we immediately gave the order to supply him with all necessary care. But to our great sadness we received, last night, the news that God's will had put an end to his life. We have ordered that his mortal remains should be taken to the Nevsky Convent and be buried there. As Empress and Mother of the Empire, we invite all our faithful subjects, without any resentment for the past, to bid farewell to his

---

[1] According to Princess Dashkova, this letter was found by Paul I in 1796 in a box containing his mother's papers. The original had been destroyed. A copy was published in the Vorontsov archives.

[2] Countess Golovin *Memoirs*.

[3] Princess Dashkova *Memoirs*.

body and to raise to God fervent prayers for the salvation of his soul, whilst at the same time attributing the unexpected blow of his death to a decree of Providence, which directs the destiny of our country along paths known only to its own sacred will.'

Amongst the people, the announcement of this death and its official explanation brought no reaction. In the midst of joy at the new accession, the good folk refused to let themselves be distracted by insulting assumptions about the little mother. At court they pretended to believe the unbelievable. But really, for all those close to the Empress, the fact of the assassination was obvious. Although there were few who said that she had actually ordered it, many held her indirectly responsible. Whether she wished it or not, she was the one who gained from the crime. She had blood on her hands. 'One does not know for certain what part the Empress played in this event,' wrote Rulhière. And the Chevalier de Corberon: 'What appears certain is that the Orlovs alone struck the blow.' And Bérenger: 'What a spectacle for the nation and what *sangfroid* one needed to observe it! On the one hand the grandson of Tsar Ivan languishing in irons, whilst a Princess of Anhalt usurps the crown of their ancestors, with a regicide as prelude to gaining the throne... I do not suspect the Princess (Catherine) of having such a vile soul as to have been involved in the Tsar's death... But the suspicion and the odium will remain on the Empress's account.'[1] And the Baron de Breteuil, back at last in St Petersburg: 'I have known for a long time, and it has been confirmed since my return that her maxims (Catherine's) are that one must be firm in one's resolves, that it is better to do badly than to change one's mind, and most of all, that it is only fools who are indecisive.'

As for the circumstances of the murder, there are different versions. Some spoke of poison in the wine, some of strangulation with a gun sling, some of suffocation under a mattress. According to most people it was Alexis Orlov who had organized the ambush. On his return to the capital he had that evening an expression 'hideous to see', because of 'the conscience of his baseness and inhumanity, and the remorse which was tormenting him'– according to Helbig, a secretary at the Saxon Embassy. And Ruhlière confirms that, according to trustworthy witnesses, Alexis Orlov was 'dishevelled, covered with sweat and dust, his clothes torn', and he had 'an agitated expression, full of horror and panic'.

What is certain is that Alexis Orlov's action was not, as he said in his letter, the result of a banal argument between two slightly drunken

[1] Dispatch of the 12/23 July, 1762.

guests. He and his friends had certainly premeditated it. When they heard that Peter was to be transferred to Schlusselburg, they feared that they would not be able to get near him in the fortress and rushed to visit him at Ropscha. As a preliminary, they had Peter's valet Bressau seized by soldiers and removed from the area. By ridding the Tsarina of a burdensome husband, Alexis Orlov thought that he was opening the way to the throne for his brother Gregory. And indeed, once she was a widow why should Catherine not marry the man of her choice? Thus she would be doubly fulfilled both as a woman and as an empress.

Thanks to Alexis Orlov, Catherine was now no longer guilty of dreams but of action.

It would have been easy for her to immediately hand over the murderers to the law, since they were all known to her. She would have cleared herself by blackening them. But could she, a few days after her accession, send Alexis Orlov and his accomplices to the rack and the scaffold – the very men to whom she owed her crown? These men's devotion obliged her to protect them. She was linked to them by a sort of tacit acceptance, if not of their criminal plan, at least of its result. Only weak souls would punish inferiors in order to justify themselves. Catherine was of another metal. By upholding the official story of death through illness, she was saving her supporters, and taking any suspicions upon herself. Two days after the Tsar's assassination she reappeared in public and, with Olympian calm, faced the obsequious and evil-minded curiosity of the Court.

Following the orders she had given, the dead Peter III was taken to the Alexander Nevsky Convent. But the pomp stopped there. The dead man, although he was Peter the Great's grandson, was only a fallen Emperor. His body lay without any decorations in a plain open coffin. He had been dressed, for his last sleep, in the pale blue uniform of the Holstein Dragoons. Was this out of respect for the dead man's taste in clothing, or was it to remind the crowds that he had always been a declared enemy of Russia? Those who filed past his coffin were struck by his tragic appearance. His face was almost black, and his neck was wrapped in a military scarf, no doubt to hide the marks of strangulation; gloves covered the hands which normally should have been bare. However nobody, either amongst the people or the courtiers, raised their voice to question the official story of natural death. It was easier and safer to keep quiet. At least for the moment. Catherine did not watch by the body, nor attend the funeral. The Senate had respectfully begged her to keep away from this sad ceremony 'so that Her Imperial Majesty should save her health out of love for the Russian nation, and for her truly loyal subjects'.

CHAPTER XIII

Apprenticeship for Power

The Empress's seizure of power had been so sudden that the foreign diplomats did not yet believe her to be definitively installed. Baron de Breteuil saw Catherine as 'a young adventuress' who could not hold on for long against the squalls of political life. Sir Robert Keith saw her as witty and likeable, but superficial and unable to govern with the necessary authority. The Prussian Solms predicted a revolution: 'It would only need one hot-head ... people are saying such free, dangerous and unguarded things against the Empress ... it is clear that Empress Catherine's reign, like that of the Emperor, her husband, is destined only to make a short appearance in the history of the world.'

And indeed, after a few days of euphoria, the army pulled itself together. Some officers deplored the fact that the soldiers had broken their oath to the Tsar 'for a barrel of beer', according to Bérenger (the French chargé d'affaires). It was murmured that the unfortunate Ivan VI should be released from his prison and given back the crown. Foreign courts advised their ambassadors to be extremely cautious towards somebody who, in their eyes, was no more than a usurper. Louis XV instructed the Baron de Breteuil thus: 'The reigning Empress, Catherine's, capacity for dissimulation and her courage at the moment of executing her project show her to be a princess capable of conceiving and carrying out great things ... But the Empress, who in no way belongs to Russia ... will need unfailing strength to keep herself upon a throne which she owes neither to the love of her subjects nor to their respect for the memory of her father ... you know already, and I will repeat it clearly here, that my policy towards Russia is to keep it as separate as possible from European affairs. Thanks to the discord which is sure to reign in this court, she will be less able than she might have been to accept attitudes suggested by other courts.'

Later the Duc de Choiseul wrote to his ambassador in St Petersburg:
'We are aware of the animosity of the Russian court towards France. The King (Louis XV) so profoundly despises the Princess who reigns over that country, with regard to both her feelings and her conduct, that our intention is not to take a single step towards changing them. The

King feels that Catherine's hatred is greatly to be preferred to her friendship.'

Conscious of the delicacy of her position, Catherine wanted to make the ground firm under her feet as quickly as possible. She wisely kept in charge of public affairs the same men who had been there in the time of Elisabeth and Peter III. Thus Count Michael Vorontsov, although he had always been antagonistic towards his present sovereign, remained in the position of Chancellor. Nikita Panin, on the other hand, to whom she had given the Ministry of Foreign Affairs, was sincerely devoted to her cause, despite a few differences of opinion. Unlike Peter III who, either out of thoughtlessness or contempt, had for months not bothered to get himself consecrated as Emperor by the Church, she decided that her coronation should take place on the 22nd September in Moscow, with great splendour, to impress both the Russian people and the foreign ministers. She made her intention public on the 7th July, the very same day that she announced the death of her husband due to 'Haemorrhoidal colic'. Two and a half months was the minimum time needed to prepare for a ceremony of such importance. Between now and then she must conciliate the army. Therefore war would not be declared on Denmark, but nor would an alliance be signed with Prussia. However, a seven-year war against the latter would certainly not begin again. There would be nothing but smiles for France and Austria. Equally for England. As for the Church, affected as it had been by Peter III's anti-Orthodox activities, she did it the honour of suppressing the order confiscating the riches of the clergy. (She could always bring back this measure once she was firmly on the throne.)

As regards the government of the Empire, Catherine wished to hold to certain principles inspired by her reading and which she had intelligently written down, before she ever attained power:

'I want and hope only for the good of this country which God has brought me to . . . the glory of the country is my own glory.'

'To join the Caspian to the Black Sea and both to the North seas; to make trade with China and the East Indies pass through Tartary; this would elevate this Empire (Russian) to a degree of power above all the other Empires of Asia and Europe: And who can resist the unlimited power of an absolute monarch ruling over a war-like population?'

But, although Catherine preached the 'absolute power' of the monarch and Russia's domination over other states, she did intend to reign above all for the good of the people. As a good pupil of the philosophers, she condemned serfdom: 'It is against the Christian religion and human justice to make men born free into slaves . . .'

'Freedom, at the heart of everything, without you all is dead. I want people to obey laws but not to be slaves.'

This proclamation of liberal beliefs did not prevent her, on her accession, from handing out to the main architects of the *coup d'état* (the Orlovs, the Razumovskys, Panin...) eighteen thousand peasants attached to the crown lands. In any case she did not think it was possible to free the serfs: 'To perform such a dramatic stroke (freeing the serfs) would not endear me to the landowners...' At best, since this evil existed in Russia, one could try to ameliorate conditions: 'Go to a village, ask a peasant how many children he has had. He will reply, as common, ten, twelve, often even twenty. How many are still alive? He will say one, two, four... We must lower this mortality rate, consult doctors, see to the needs of small children... They run about stark naked and in the snow and ice. The one who survives is tough, but nineteen die, and what a loss that is for the State.'

Now it was a matter of moving from theory to practice. When Catherine first called together the Senate at the Summer Palace she was horrified by the picture they drew of the country's social and financial position. Years later she still remembered with agony this brutal contact with reality.

'The main body of the army was abroad and had not been paid for eight months,' she wrote. 'The fleet was abandoned, the army in disarray, the fortresses were collapsing in ruins. The budget owed seventeen million roubles, with a hundred million in circulation. Nobody in the whole Empire knew what the revenues of the Treasury were. The State budget was not fixed precisely. Nearly all branches of commerce were under individual monopolies. About 200,000 peasants belonging to mine works and monasteries were in a state of open revolt. In many areas the peasants refused to obey and pay various dues to their landlords. Justice was sold at auction. Minds were embittered by the fact that cruel tortures and punishments were meted out for trifles as much as for serious crimes. Everywhere the people complained of corruption, extortion and every sort of malpractice and injustice.'

Coldly, Catherine decided to first attack the deficit in the budget. To fill the State coffers. But how? The worthy senators despaired of finding a solution. She firmly imposed one: she suppressed some of the 'monopolies', those shares in big industries which some of the greatest families such as the Shuvalovs regularly drew on. And, to forestall any discontent from those who were losing part of their incomes, she solemnly gave up, in front of the whole Senate, the 'Chamber funds', which formed the Tsar's personal allowance. This amounted to a thirteenth of the total budget of the Empire. The senators, amazed by such generosity, cheered and sobbed with gratitude. But it would need more than that to float the ship. Especially as Catherine had every intention of reigning opulently, whilst at the same time channelling new money into the Treasury. She quickly took other measures: she borrowed, created new taxes and increased existing ones, notably the one on the moujiks' beards. This tax had been set up by Peter the Great – every bearded man had to pay it upon entering the capital city. Obviously the peasants could have escaped it by shaving, but they feared a thunderbolt from the Church since, according to the dispositions of a council in 1551, 'There is no heretical custom which is more damnable than that of shaving off the beard... to shave your beard in order to please men is to make yourself the enemy of God who created us in His image.'

However, the most important measure was obviously the foundation of a bank of issue which would print assignats according to the demands of the Imperial Treasury. Throughout the whole of her reign, Catherine was thus to print enormous quantities of rouble assignats. In any other country such a policy would have brought inflation and bankruptcy. But Russia was protected from that type of catastrophe: this was because the security for these assignats, the only guarantee for this public credit, was not the backing of gold, but an imperishable moral one. And this moral cover was the infinite respect felt by the nation towards Her Majesty's own person. The confidence thus established at home gradually spread abroad. Foreign money was attracted by the blind confidence of the Russians in their own financial destiny. An eighteenth century philosopher, Possochkov, wrote on this subject. 'What makes the value of a piece of money is not the gold, silver or brass, the more or less precious metal used to make it..., but the image of the sovereign struck onto this metal; it is the will of the sovereign, as expressed by this image, to attribute to this piece of metal a power such that one will accept without hesitation things in return which have a real value... And, from that time onwards, the metal from which the coin is struck matters little. If the sovereign wished to attribute the same value to a piece of leather, *or a piece of paper,* that would suffice to make it so.'

Thus Catherine, by churning out assignats, was splendidly ignoring conditions ruling economic life everywhere else. What, in France, had brought about the collapse of assignats and Louis' bankruptcy was the shaking of public confidence. In Russia confidence was unshakeable. The subjects' obedience served as a basis for the issue of paper money. It was a conjuring trick, alchemy, turning air into gold. 'Coming here,' wrote the Comte de Ségur a few years after Possochkov, 'one must forget all the ideas about financial dealings that one had learnt in other countries. In other European States, the sovereign can rule over men's actions, but not over their opinions; here opinion is also a subject, and the mass of banknotes, the knowledge that there are no reserves to back them, the debasement of the coinage, which leaves gold and silver coins only half their value, in a word everything which, in another state would bring with it bankruptcy and dire revolution, here produces not only not the slightest shock, but not even the slightest loss of confidence, and I am convinced that the Empress could make leather acceptable as money if she were to order it.'[1]

Those around Catherine were astonished that this young woman, unused as she was to the exercise of political power, should show such a desire to see and understand everything, and to control and decide everything herself. She was not in the least intimidated by her ignorance of public affairs – indeed it seemed to stimulate her. She never doubted for a second her ability to run a country which, on top of everything, was not even her own. It seemed as though she had been preparing for it all her life. Whether it was a question of international relations or of home problems she immediately knew how things stood. In any case, she was such that she, the beginner, was right and the old-timers wrong. She had the fresh conviction of the self-taught person. And absolutely no feeling of inferiority before the gigantic tasks ahead of her. There was nothing troubled, nothing involuntary, nothing unconscious about her daily behaviour. She had a healthy and simple attitude towards politics, as towards love. Hers was a natural vigorous and open attitude to life. Unlike Empress Elisabeth, she was less interested in the brilliant outer trappings of power than in its secret workings. The office work appeared to her, as it had to Peter the Great whom she wished to emulate, the hidden but vital part of a sovereign's job. Never tiring, she pored over reports, memos, national accounts and diplomatic correspondence. Having been kept away from 'serious matters' for eighteen years, she fell on them like a starving person. She presided over all the Ministerial Councils, all the meetings of the Senate, confusing the high officials with merciless questions and repeated appeals to their devotion to civic duty. She dared to suggest to these men, who had long ago arranged for themselves an easy life in the incoherent routine of the administration, that they should get up earlier and continue their sessions into the afternoon. She herself was up at five in the morning and worked for twelve or fourteen hours a day. She hardly took any time off to eat and in the evening, around nine, after a

[1] Waliszewski *The Story of an Empress* and Brian-Chaninov *Catherine II.*

short dinner with her close friends, she would collapse, exhausted, into bed. Her plans were drawn up with such speed that the copyists were amazed and, indeed, shocked. One day, when the Senate had just announced that every town in the Empire would henceforth have its *'voyevod'* or military governor, she asked: so how many towns are there in Russia? Consternation. Nobody had the slightest idea. Never mind: they could count them on a map, she said. Yes, but there was no map of Russia in the Senate archives. Catherine, smiling, gave five roubles to a young official and told him to go to the Academy of Sciences and purchase Kirilov's *Atlas*. The senators, caught without information, fawned on her. There were hundreds more occasions on which she had to call them to order. Her mind had been trained from an early age by reading Montesquieu and Voltaire and she found it easy to dominate the lazy dignitaries. She pushed them around and forced their pace. Despite her long apprenticeship in Russia she could not get used to the incredible chaos of the nation's administration. Here, rules contradicted one another, everything was based on custom – justice was meted out haphazardly, ministries ignored each other's activities, each office pursued its own policy, the Empire was pulled in every direction. For a mind set on clarity, the temptation to put some order into this medley was very great. Catherine brought a lamp and a broom to it. The senators and ministers, hearing her criticisms and proposals, recognized that she was right. But in their heart of hearts they wondered what right this young German princess had to stir up the dust of the Russian State.

In fact, Catherine loved Russia's faults, whilst swearing to reform them. She was fundamentally a Westerner, with her clear mind, her desire to classify everything, her practicality and her unconquerable vitality, and she was both irritated and charmed by the dreaming nonchalance, the fatalism and impulsive extravagance of this nation that had become her own. She found it large and beautiful, and she wanted to be worthy of it. She was to write, in a kind of delirium: 'Never has the world produced a more masculine, steady, honest, humane, charitable, generous, obliging person than the Scythian (in other words the Russian). No other man can equal the regularity of his features, the beauty of his face, his dazzling colour, his carriage, girth and height, his limbs being either very well-covered or very muscular and active, his beard thick, his hair long and bushy. He is naturally alien to all trickery and guile, and his rectitude and honesty make him abhor such devices. There is no horseman, foot-soldier, sailor, nor steward on earth to equal him. No other individual is more affectionate towards his children and next of kin. He has an innate respect for his parents and his superiors. He is prompt, quick to obey and loyal.'

This declaration of love, which could have been addressed to Gregory Orlov, applied in fact to the whole country. Catherine, in the same way, was to say to her doctors one day: 'Bleed me of my last drop of German blood, and leave only Russian blood in my veins.' With her passionate attachment to Russia, Catherine took the name 'little mother' which her subjects honoured her with, very seriously. She wanted to embody for all of them warmth, safety and providence. She wrote: 'Be gentle, humane, accessible, compassionate and liberal. Never allow your greatness to prevent you from descending with charity to the lowest, and putting yourself in their place, but never let that goodness diminish your authority, nor their respect.' She personally examined the petitions sent to her and promised to repair injustices. However she was soon submerged by the flood of letters and she left three quarters of them unanswered. When she walked to church or to the Senate there were so many petitioners in her path that one day she found herself encircled by a human wall. The police wanted to intervene with their clubs, but the Empress spread out her arms to protect her people. This symbolic gesture brought sobs of gratitude from the crowd. The incident was retold a thousand times, exaggerated and embellished, and became part of the legend of the 'little mother's' glory. To increase her popularity she stopped the balls and masquerades which Empress Elisabeth had so much enjoyed, and which had bored her so much when she was Grand Duchess. Her own parties were, it is true, to cost a hundred times more than those of her predecessor, and yet no one could reproach her for it, as she would not be spending the money for her own pleasure, but for the renown of the Empire. Every braid on her dress, every pearl in her necklace, every chandelier in her drawing-room, every cracker in her firework display, was there to enhance her prestige, and consequently Russia's prestige in the eyes of the world. Although thrifty by nature, she wished to be extravagant for the sake of others. That would certainly show at the coronation! The tailors, dressmakers, jewellers and boot-makers of St Petersburg were overwhelmed with orders. The outfits of the Empress and her court must, it was said, outshine anything seen at previous ceremonies in the greatest nations of Europe.

Between fittings and gatherings of the Senate, Catherine sorted out the Courland business by secretly supporting the Duc de Biron's cause, since he was loyal to her. Thus, she calculated, Courland would fall under the Russian influence before becoming re-attached to the Empire. Then she turned to Poland. Like Courland, Poland, in her view, must re-enter the Russian sphere. Later on, when years of chaos had prepared all minds for a radical solution, this unfortunate nation was more or less totally annexed. Since the king, Augustus III, was gravely ill, France or Austria must not be allowed to supply a successor of their choice. Russia must have 'its own king' ready when the moment came, to suggest or, if necessary, impose on the country. Catherine had long since decided who this king should be – none other than her inconsolable lover, the handsome Stanislaus Poniatowski. Exiled far from St Petersburg, he had not the slightest idea of this official future being prepared for him. His own dream had nothing to do with politics. He wanted to come back to this woman whom he had never ceased to love, to rediscover the taste of her mouth, the softness of her voice, and the movement of her hips. He said as much in his passionate letters, never realizing that he had long since been supplanted by Gregory Orlov. When he heard the news of Peter III's death, he was exultant: free, now she was free, she would summon him, he would rush to her, perhaps she would marry him! Once again he bombarded her with letters. She was worried by his insistence. Had he not understood anything? She wrote to this hare-brained child, to tell him the details of the palace revolution and to beg him to keep calm:

'I beg you urgently not to make haste to come here, because your visit under present circumstances would be dangerous for yourself and very harmful to me. The revolution that has just taken place in my favour is miraculous; it is incredible with what unanimity it came about. I am overwhelmed with work, and am not able to give you a full account. All my life I will seek to serve and honour you and your family, but everything here is critical and important. I have not slept for three nights and have only eaten twice in four days.'[1]

A month later, she wrote to him again:

'Minds here are still in a ferment. I beg you to restrain yourself from coming here, for fear of increasing it. I received your letter. A regular correspondence would be subject to a thousand drawbacks, I have to be endlessly cautious, and anyway have not time to write dangerous love letters. I am embarrassed... I cannot tell you everything, but this is true... I feel the weight of government. Farewell, there are strange situations in the world.'

The beginning of the letter surprised Stanislaus Poniatowski even more than the melancholy warning at the end. As if she were announcing the arrival of a barrel of oysters, Catherine offered him, out of the blue, this crown: 'I am immediately sending the Count Kayserling as Ambassador to Poland, with the aim of making you King of Poland on the death of Augustus III.'

[1] Letter, 2nd July, 1762.

He could not believe his eyes. And, instead of being pleased, he was miserable. What would he do with the Polish throne? This honour, which he had never wished for, would keep him apart from the woman he loved. What he wanted was Catherine's bed, not Augustus' throne. Although she had begged him not to write to her any more, he took to paper again and scrawled, one after the other, a series of despairing letters. She replied: 'I am running a great risk with this correspondence. I am watched. I must not be suspected. I must keep to the straight and narrow path. Keep calm. It would be indiscreet for me to impart to you my innermost secrets ... If they tell you that there has been more unrest amongst the troops, please believe that it all comes from an excess of love for myself, which is becoming a burden to me. They die of fear that anything should happen to me. I cannot go out from my room without receiving cheers. Their enthusiasm resembles that shown in Cromwell's time.'

Later, she was more precise: 'If you come here, we could both be murdered.' And again. 'It is a lot that I should even be answering you: I should not do so ... My role is to be perfect. People expect the impossible of me.'

However he wanted nothing 'impossible'. His goal was earthly, ordinary happiness, without any politics or crowns. He wrote saying this to Catherine, despite her warnings. In his passion he called her by her real name, Sophie, the one she had been baptized with at Stettin, and not the assumed name of the Empress of Russia, which had stood like a barrier between herself and him for years:

'You are making me King, but are you making me happy? You could not take away from me the memory of the happiness I enjoyed, nor the wish to recapture it. One does not love twice in a lifetime and I have loved you, and so what is there left for me? A void, a terrible emptiness in the bottom of my heart that nothing can fill. Ah! I do not know how other people are made, but I feel, for myself, that ambition is a foolish thing when it is not sustained by peace and a contented heart ... I beg the Lord to return you to me every day, every hour of my life ... Great God, is it my fault that it was not me who gave you the crown that you wear? Is it possible that someone other than myself can love you as perfectly, as truly as I do? Ah! Sophie, you have made me suffer cruelly.'

These epistolary outbursts came, nobody quite knew how, to the knowledge of the foreign diplomats. Frederick II secretly warned Catherine that, if she should ever plan to appropriate Poland by a marriage with the future King Stanislaus Poniatowski, she should realize that such a move would turn the whole of Europe against her.

However, Catherine had not the slightest intention of marrying this mad Pole, who once was lucky enough to attract her, and of whom she remained quite fond. She quickly told Kayserling in Warsaw: the order was to marry the impetuous Poniatowski to a Polish girl as soon as possible, and let it be known in the diplomatic corps that this union was the wish of the Russian Empress. But Stanislaus bridled at this. He did not care to be thus disposed of. He would remain a faithful bachelor . . .

Catherine, already exasperated by her ex-lover's claims, was also having to deal with the whims of the present lover. His demands were certainly flattering but they were also a nuisance. He complained that the Empress worked too much. She preferred her papers to him. In order to distract her from the cares of government, he brought young Potemkin to meet her – he had become famous amongst his comrades for his talent as a mimic. This was the same Potemkin who had given his pennant to Catherine on the day of the triumphal march on Peterhof. She had rewarded him for this by promoting him to second lieutenant after the *coup d'état*. She immediately recognized him – how could she forget such a face – and begged him to do one of his imitations. The first one he did was of herself. She could have been angry, but instead laughed until she cried. The young man was immediately allowed to join her intimate circle. In order to justify the presence of this charming boy at the Palace, with his vitality and wit, she made him a gentleman of the bedchamber. Gregory Orlov suddenly wondered whether he had not unluckily introduced her to a rival in this prepossessing clown. The official lover, devoured by jealousy, complained to his imperial mistress, and she, amused, allowed him to send Potemkin as a courier to Stockholm.

But Gregory Orlov, who had become the most powerful man in the Empire, was no longer satisfied with his role as lover. Although he was lodged in the Palace and received an annual salary of 120,000 roubles, he did not feel that he was being rewarded according to his worth. Not only did he presumptuously advertise his liaison with the Empress, but he even spoke of marrying her. His brothers encouraged this. So did Chancellor Bestuzhev, whom Catherine had recalled from exile. She herself was not fundamentally opposed to the idea of a secret marriage. And yet she feared public opinion. When rumours began to circulate on the subject of her matrimonial intentions, the officers and nobility became indignant. The subject came up before the Imperial Council. Most of the councillors were embarrassed and kept quiet, but Panin spoke: 'The Empress can do what she wishes, but Mrs Orlov will never be Empress of Russia.' With these words he stood up defiantly, and his powdered wig left a white trail on the hangings behind his chair. His colleagues silently rose, went over to the mark and, one after the other, rubbed their heads against it, as a sign of approval. However Bestuzhev did not admit that he was beaten. According to him, Alexis Razumovsky,[1] the old lover, had in the past contracted a similar marriage with the Empress Elisabeth. If this was so, it would create a precedent which Catherine could use to justify her behaviour. It was likely that Alexis Razumovsky possessed documents establishing the exact nature of his relationship with the dead Tsarina. To persuade him to hand them over, Catherine sent Chancellor Michael Vorontsov to see him. He found the old man reading his Bible, and begged him, in the name of the Empress, to hand over the proof of his clandestine marriage. If he did so, he would, as a widowed Prince Consort, have the rank of Imperial Highness, along with the substantial pension attached to this title. Alexis Razumovsky closed his Bible, took out of a cabinet an ebony box encrusted with silver and mother-of-pearl, and from it produced a roll of parchment tied with a pink ribbon; he placed his lips on it and threw it into the fire. When the document was reduced to ashes, he murmured: 'No! There is no proof. Tell that to our gracious sovereign.'

The 'precedent' no longer existed. Without totally abandoning her plan, Catherine postponed it. To compensate her lover, she made him a Count, assigned to him the first place next to the throne, and gave him a portrait of herself in a heart-shaped medallion decorated with diamonds, with permission to wear it in his button-hole.

Showered with privileges, Gregory Orlov every day displayed more of his upstart arrogance. Princess Dashkova found him lying on a sofa in the Empress's room, opening official letters addressed to Her Majesty. When Catherine arrived and ordered that lunch should be served, he did not move, and the footman had to push the table over to him. The Princess, when she learnt about her idol's relationship with such a lumpish and boastful soldier, felt hurt and disappointed as if by a spiritual betrayal. She was virginal, naive and prudish and she could not understand how a creature of Catherine's talent and intelligence could be capable of succumbing to such vulgar fleshly attractions. But she was even more upset by the way the Tsarina honoured him than by his coarse manners. She considered that she, not Gregory Orlov, had been the spiritual force behind the 'revolution'. Therefore all honour should go to herself. But the Empress had been slow to broadcast the merits of her main collaborator. It was said that Frederick the Great had nicknamed her 'the busybody'. It was too much! To show her

---

[1] Not to be confused with Cyril Razumovsky, his brother, the Hetman of Ukraine.

importance, Princess Dashkova, who was not yet twenty, made secret visits, passed on drawing-room rumours, whispered advice and information to ambassadors, and let it be known that Panin was devoted to her. Keith, Breteuil and Mercy d'Argenteau listened to her gossip, and came to speak of the 'Dashkova government'. Was it the beginning of an insurrection? 'She (Princess Dashkova) has already joined half a dozen conspiracies,' wrote Sir George Macartney. 'She is a woman of extraordinary strength of mind, with almost manly courage, whose bravery makes her capable of embarking on almost impossible projects to satisfy a momentary impulse: a much too dangerous character for a country such as this one.'

Irritated by her young friend's restlessness, Catherine refused most of the time to let her into her office, and instructed those close to her not to speak freely in front of this hare-brain. But she did not yet feel strong enough to break with her. She could not afford herself the luxury of capriciously increasing the number of her enemies. She reluctantly conferred on the Princess the rank of lady-in-wating, and made her husband Chamberlain. Would that be enough? Caught in a web of intrigue, spied on both by foreign diplomats and Russian ministers, never knowing whether yesterday's ally would be tomorrow's enemy, obsessed by the fear that Peter's assassination would be the pretext for a counter-revolution, sure of herself but unsure of her people, she advanced in the dark towards the coronation festivities, which, she thought, would make her forever invulnerable.

CHAPTER XIV

Blood and Incense

Catherine gave the goldsmiths a pound of gold and twenty pounds of silver with which to forge the new crown she intended to wear in Moscow on Sunday the 22nd September, 1762. Four thousand ermine pelts would be used to adorn the imperial cloak. A mass of precious stones would be scattered over the coronation robe. A hundred and twenty small casks would contain the six hundred thousand roubles that were to be thrown to the people. The parties alone would cost fifty thousand roubles. Who, after all that, would doubt the legitimacy of the Empress?

On the 27th August, Catherine sent her son, Paul, aged eight, to Moscow, in the hands of Panin and Kruse, the Court doctor. She was held up by work, and would only set off four days later, but she would travel fast. And indeed she caught up with the child half-way, to find him in bed, shaking with fever, in a squalid post-house. The fever abated a little the next day. Catherine wanted to stay until he was completely better, but she was forced to continue her journey immediately, so as not to upset the programme of festivities. The people would never forgive her if she missed her entrance into the holy city. So, on the 13th September, 1762, she came to the ancient town with its multicoloured cupolas. Her son, better at last, had been able to rejoin her. He sat next to her, pale, bewildered and frightened. The yellow dust was lit by the soft autumn sunshine. The carriage rolled slowly along. Bells rang. The façades of the wooden houses were decorated with carpets and garlands. The long fences were topped with flowers. The crowds, in their Sunday best, jostled each other in the streets. Groups of onlookers leaned out of windows and waved from the roofs. They were cheering the Empress and His Imperial Highness, Grand Duke Paul. The celebrations continued for eight days, and foreign diplomats informed their governments that they had never seen so much jewellery, lace, fur and brocade as there was now in the drawing-rooms crowded with Russian nobles.

At last, on Sunday the 22nd September, in the cathedral of the Assumption, at the heart of the Kremlin, before fifty-five High Church dignitaries standing in a semi-circle 'the most serene and all-powerful Princess and lady Catherine the Second, Empress and Autocrat of all the Russias', at the age of thirty-three, let the ermine cloak slide from her shoulders and replaced it with imperial purple. After which, lifting the heavy crown from a gold cushion, she placed it herself on her head, took the sceptre in her right hand, the orb in her left, and appeared before all eyes as the incarnation of Russia. The congregation fell to its knees, and the choir burst into a joyful hymn. Catherine, seated on her throne in frozen dignity, never once let her head or hands bend under the weight of the massive crown and the sacred insignia of the Empire. The Archbishop of Novgorod anointed her. Now she was head of the Orthodox Church, and she celebrated the mass herself at the altar. Did she, at that moment, remember how her father had made her swear never to renounce the Lutheran faith?

Once the ceremony was over, Catherine returned to the Palace in a gold carriage whilst, behind her, silver coins flew into outstretched hands. Long tables, placed outside for the people, groaned under the weight of roast meats, cakes and casks of drink. After the procession had gone by, the crowd fell on the food, blessing and praising their 'little mother'. She, meanwhile, presided from her throne over a solemn banquet in the Granovitaya Palata, the hall of mirrors. She looked around at the assembled dignitaries. All the great names of Russia. Never had she been surrounded by so many people, and never had she felt so alone.

On the days that followed, for hour upon hour, delegates from all the peoples of the Empire filed past her; as did those from all classes of society, and all the guilds. She was exhausted. And she still had to appear at the ball, the firework display, the gala dinner, change her dress and hair style ten times, and between receptions, work with her ministers.

In fact she felt less at home in Moscow, a city of the past, than she did in St Petersburg, which represented the future. 'I do not like Moscow at all,' she wrote in her *Notes*. 'Moscow is the home of idleness. I have made a rule for myself that when I am here I never send for anyone, because one only hears the next day whether or not the person is coming... Also the population is surrounded by objects for their fanaticism! Miraculous images at every step, gaggles of priests, convents, bigots, tramps, thieves, useless servants in the houses – and what houses, what filth in those houses, with their enormous areas and muddy yards!... Here then is a massed population of all kinds always ready to disrupt law and order, rioting on the slightest pretext, as it has done from time immemorial, and then cherishing the stories of these riots, nourishing their minds with them. Each house still has its ancient password . . . At St Petersburg people are more polite and obedient, less superstitious, more accustomed to strangers.'

Yes, she found her stay in Moscow wearisome. One week after the coronation, just as she was about to succumb to exhaustion, she was seized by a hideous panic. Her son's strange illness was worsening. He was weak and feverish. Kruse did not know what to prescribe. Little Paul was dying before her eyes. Catherine, terrified, never left his bedside. She trembled both for her son's life and for her own future. News of his illness quickly spread around the court. If the Grand Duke died, the Empress would be held responsible for his death. After her husband, her son! It was logical. Little Paul should really have been crowned instead of his mother. To avoid any future complications, she was killing him – slow poison which left no traces. That is what they would say. That is what they were already saying. Tomorrow the same people who had knelt down as she passed, and blessed her with cries of joy, would accuse her of being a double murderess. Priests prayed around the bed. She promised that she would build a hospital if God spared her son. Was it the mother or the Empress making this pathetic vow? On the eighth day of the illness, he began to pull through. The child was saved. Catherine immediately ordered that plans should be drawn up for a large, light hospital that would bear Paul's name.

Despite this recovery, the atmosphere around Catherine remained charged. Whilst some reproached her for not having had her son crowned, and contenting herself with the role of regent, other, bolder people spoke of bringing from his cell the poor Tsar Ivan VI who lived, it was said, as a saint and martyr. Thus, this prisoner, whose sad memory had haunted the nights of both Elisabeth and Peter, now came to haunt Catherine's sleep. After the *coup d'état,* when she had planned to incarcerate Peter in the fortress of Schlusselburg, Catherine had had Ivan transferred to the fort at Kexholm. This was no doubt because it seemed inconvenient, and indeed amoral, to put two fallen emperors in the same prison. After Peter's death, there was nothing to stop Ivan returning to his former cell. However he spent another two months at Kexholm, and it was there that Catherine, driven by worried curiosity, went to see him. She saw before her a degenerated young man of twenty-two with a white face and wild-looking eyes. He had been proclaimed Emperor when he was two months old, and dethroned two years later by Elisabeth. He was the direct descendant of Ivan V, the Fool, Peter the Great's elder brother. His right to the crown was incontrovertible. But, since the age of six, he had only known the bare walls of his cell. Who were his parents? And where were they? Ivan did not know. He did not know that his mother had died sixteen years before, and that his father was incarcerated in another fortress.[1] To his guards, Ivan was the nameless prisoner, 'Prisoner No 1.'

Barefoot, wearing a dirty and torn sailor's uniform, he paced round and round his cell with its whitewashed panes, and barred windows, from time to time proclaiming that his destiny was to be emperor. His mind, in this isolation, had slowly atrophied. It was an effort for him to speak. In front of Catherine, who examined him with a cold stare, he could only stammer out his wild claims over and over again. 'Apart from a painful and almost incomprehensible stammer, he possessed neither intelligence nor human understanding,' she said later. This categorical verdict released her from feelings of pity, but not from worry. Peter III before her had been to see Ivan VI and he too had found him mentally retarded, but this was no reason for neglecting the threat represented by this pretender relegated to the shadows. For the humble people he was a fairy-tale prince, virtuous and unfortunate. They had affectionately nicknamed him 'Ivanushka'. The Russian people had always loved the feeble-minded, whose innocence, poverty and simplicity placed them in direct contact with God. It only needed a spark and 'Ivanushka' in his cell would become more powerful than Catherine in her Palace. The foreign courts realized this. Two months after Catherine's accession to the throne, Louis XV wrote to the Baron de Breteuil:

'Your research must include the fate of Prince Ivan. It is a great deal already that he is still alive. I do not know if it is possible for you, with skill and circumspection to form a bond with him, or if, supposing this to be possible, this would be dangerous for yourself and for him; try, without exciting suspicion to discover what can be done.'

The Empress, foreseeing problems, ordered that the guards around Prisoner No 1 should be reinforced, and that a doctor should not be called if he fell ill (only a confessor). Also, if anybody should approach No 1 without express orders from the Tsarina, the guards should 'kill the prisoner, and let no man take him alive'. These instructions had already been given by Elisabeth and renewed by Peter III.

Catherine very soon realized that she was right to be wary of 'Ivanushka'. In October 1762, after the Moscow festivities, she was still congratulating herself on the unanimous devotion of the army, when she heard that seventy officers of the guards regiments were plotting to put Ivan VI back on the throne. The leaders of the plot were a certain Peter Kruschev, and three brothers, Simon, Ivan and Peter Guriev.

---

[1] His father died in 1776, still exiled on the shores of the White Sea.

The enquiry revealed that they had indeed proclaimed Ivan's legitimacy before their comrades, and maintained that failing him, it was Grand Duke Paul who should have been crowned and not his mother. Catherine ordered the case to be brought in the utmost secrecy, refused to have the plotters tortured to provide more details, and punished them only by having them sent to faraway garrisons. Panin pointed out to her that such leniency, far from earning the gratitude of the eventual plotters, would only encourage them to continue, and that, by her generosity, she was risking her life. She replied, laughing, that she would rely on her lucky star. Then, instructing her personal guards to stay away from her, she defiantly visited the poorest quarters of Moscow in an open carriage. She was comforted by the cheers she heard. But the mob was so fickle! The same ones who adored you today, tomorrow would curse you, without really understanding themselves why they had changed sides.

She had hardly finished with this ridiculous business when the police uncovered another plot. This time the concern was not Ivan VI but Gregory Orlov. Rumours of the Tsarina's eventual marriage to her lover had spread through the army, and a young and noble officer by the name of Khitrovo had assembled a group of friends in order to kill the Orlov brothers and thus put an end to their ambitions. Troubles broke out in Moscow. The Empress's portrait hanging from a triumphal arch was torn down in broad daylight. Amongst the conspirators were some of those who had helped Catherine during the *coup d'état*. Her former friends, her most reliable allies! When he was interrogated, Khitrovo replied that the marriage plan was offensive to the Empire and that it was to protect Her Majesty from herself that he had planned to kill Gregory and Alexis Orlov. Once again Catherine ordered that the matter should be hushed up. Khitrovo was simply exiled to his lands in Orel. And a proclamation was made in Moscow, to the sound of drums, forbidding the inhabitants 'to interfere with things that do not concern them'.

At almost the same time, Catherine came up against Church discontent. When she had come to the throne, she had stopped the secularization of Church riches ordered by Peter III in order to gain its good will. However, during the winter of 1762–1763, she realized that the serfs who had belonged to the Church were refusing to return to their cruel and merciless masters. In order to avoid serious trouble, and also, obviously, to enrich the Treasury, she withdrew her promise and definitively handed over the administration of the ecclesiastical estates to the State economic body.

The main body of the clergy, although outraged, bowed its head. But at Rostov, Archbishop Matsievitch rose furiously to defend the sacred rights of the Church. He anathematized 'those who lay hands on the churches and places of worship, and who wish to appropriate for themselves the wealth given to the Church long ago by children of God and pious monarchs'. This was aimed directly at Catherine. When she heard that the Archbishop was also calling on the people to rebel against 'the foreigner' and speaking of 'the magnificent martyr' Ivan VI, she had him arrested and brought to Moscow. This was a brave move as the Archbishop was an important personality in the Empire. When he first appeared before the Empress, Gregory Orlov, Glebov, the Attorney General, and the chief of police, Chechkovsky, he burst out with oaths and biblical curses. The violence of his speech was such that Catherine, it was said, had to block her ears so as not to hear. The terrified judges dared not condemn this prophet with his black beard and flashing eyes. They thought that God would never forgive them for passing a sentence on one of His most eloquent servants. They asked Bestuzhev to intervene with Her Majesty and beg for leniency. But she refused. To give in now would be to recognize that the Empress, the earthly head of the Orthodox Church, was bowing down before one of her prelates. And when Bestuzhev insisted she replied: 'Go to the devil! You are tired! Go to bed and sleep well!' Impressed by the sovereign's firmness, the Holy Synod handed the Archbishop over to civil justice. Matsievitch was condemned to be degraded and interned in a monastery, where he would, by express order, be given the hardest jobs, such as carrying water or chopping logs.[1]

As for the Empress, these first conflicts had seasoned her for battle. The more she was challenged, the more unbeatable she felt. It seemed as though her legitimacy was only increased by the obstacles it had to surmount. Every day she was becoming more deeply rooted in Russian soil. From that time onwards she established a style in her government: a mixture of charm and harshness, of generosity and caution. 'It is a curious thing to observe, on Court days, the great pains the Empress takes to please all her subjects, the freedom of behaviour of most of them, and the pushing manner with which they importune her and tell of their business and their thoughts,' wrote Baron de Breteuil on the 9th January 1763. 'For myself, who knows the Princess's character, and observes her lending herself to all this with unequalled grace and gentleness, I can imagine how hard it is for her, and how much she

---

[1] After four years in a monastery, Matsievitch was deposed and under the name of Vral ('liar and gossip') was incarcerated in the fortress of Reval where he died of cold and hunger in 1772.

must feel the obligation to submit to all this.' And a month later: 'She (Catherine) said to me that from the moment she had set foot in Russia she had wanted to reign alone over it... However she confessed to me that she was not happy and that she had to lead people who were impossible to satisfy, that she was carefully searching for ways of making her subjects happy, but that she felt that they needed several years in which to become accustomed to her... Never had any court been so divided amongst itself.' And again on the 19th March: 'The Empress's fear of losing what she so boldly seized is easily seen in her daily conduct, which is such that nobody of the slightest importance feels her strength turned against them. Her haughtiness and arrogance only show in outside matters.'

Catherine, with time, was becoming plump. Although she was beneath average height, she bore her head so high that some people found her tall.

An English observer, Richardson, drew the following portrait of her: 'The Russian Empress is above average height, gracious and well-proportioned, but well covered. She has pretty colouring but seeks to embellish it with rouge, like all the women in this country. Her mouth is well shaped, with fine teeth; her blue eyes have a scrutinizing expression... Her features are mostly regular and agreeable. The whole is such that it would be insulting to say she had a masculine look, but it would not be doing her justice to say she was entirely feminine.'[1]

As for Favier, her French secretary, he described her thus: 'One cannot say that she is a beauty; her waist is long and fine but not supple, her bearing noble, her way of walking affected and graceless, her chest narrow, her face long, especially the chin; a permanent smile on her lips, a tight mouth, a slightly aquiline nose, small eyes... Pretty rather than plain, but not inspiring passion.'[2]

Although she did not eclipse all the ladies of the court with her beauty, Catherine easily dominated them with the extent of her culture and her spicy conversation. Lord Buckingham, the new English Ambassador, stated that, in the realm of ideas, there was a large gap between her and her compatriots. 'From my observation,' he wrote in a report to the Court of St James, 'the Empress is by her talents, her education and her application, quite superior to everybody else in this country.'

Catherine's reward, when she escaped from her papers, was conversation with distinguished strangers. She had very soon

---

[1] Waliszewski *The Story of an Empress.*
[2] Zoe Oldenbourg *Catherine of Russia.*

understood that if she wished her glory to extend beyond the frontiers of Russia she would have to find propagandists for herself in European intellectual circles. Thus, *nine days after the coup d'état,* she invited Diderot to St Petersburg, to continue the printing of the *Encyclopaedia,* whose publication had just been forbidden in France, although the seven previous volumes had been successfully published. Despite the insistence of the Russian Ambassador, Golitsin, and Count Shuvalov, Diderot refused on the pretext that the succeeding volumes could appear at Neuchâtel. In fact he had no wish to deliver his work or his person into the capricious hands of a sovereign who had installed herself on the throne so recently and in such suspicious circumstances. There was also d'Alembert, to whom Catherine offered a salary of twenty thousand roubles, a palace and the rank of ambassador, to come to Russia; she wanted him to pursue his encyclopaedic works there and teach science, literature and philosophy to the Grand Duke Paul; he politely refused the offer. In a letter he confided to Voltaire the real reason for his reluctance. Alluding to the manifesto attributing Peter III's death to a haemorrhoidal colic, he wrote: 'I am too prone to haemorrhoids; they take too serious a form in that country (Russia) and I want to have a painful bottom in safety.'

Hurt by this double rebuff, Catherine was all the more pleased to receive a certain Monsieur Pictet from Geneva who came on Voltaire's behalf. The old philosopher of Ferney was Catherine's 'teacher of thought'. Just before the *coup d'état* he had published the first two volumes of his *History of Russia,* which was a wild panegyric to the genius of Peter the Great. It was also said that he was very interested by the debut on the political stage of this Empress who patronized the arts and wanted to have the *Encyclopaedia* printed in her country. When Monsieur Pictet, who was built like a giant, gave Catherine a poem dedicated to her by Voltaire, she could hardly control her emotion. Was it possible that the greatest writer of all time had touched this paper, had written these regular lines? She read, and her heart swelled with happiness:

> *God who has deprived me of eyes and ears,*
> *Return them to me, I will depart at once!*
> *Happy the man who can see your majestic beauty*
> *O Catherine! And happy the man who can hear you!*
> *To please and to reign, those are your gifts;*
> *But it is the first which touches me most.*
> *You astonish the wise man with your wit,*
> *And he would cease to be wise if he saw you.*

Monsieur Pictet had hardly left when Catherine took up her pen to reply:

'I was so eager to read your ode that I have abandoned a heap of petitions, and many people's fortunes have been set aside. I am not even sorry. There are no casuists in my Empire, and until now I did not mind. But, seeing that it is necessary that I should return to my duties, I can see no better way of doing so than to give way to the turmoil in which I find myself and take up my pen to beg Monsieur de Voltaire, most earnestly, not to praise me before I have deserved it. This is for the sake both of his reputation and mine. He will say that it is for me to render myself worthy of this praise; but, truly, in the immensity of Russia, a year is one day, like a thousand before the Lord. That is my excuse for not yet having done the good that I should have done . . . Today, for the first time in my life I regret that I do not write poetry; I can only reply to your lines in prose; but I can assure you that, since 1746, I have been feeling the greatest obligation towards you. Before that time I read only novels; then by chance your works came into my hands; since then I have never stopped reading them, and would not have wished for books better written, or where there was as much to learn. But where to find them?'[1]

This letter opened the way to a correspondence which lasted for fifteen years, until Voltaire's death. From the beginning, Catherine realized that she had found in him the perfect singer of her praises. In a few months she became for him 'the Incomparable', 'the brightest star of the north', 'the Sovereign of his heart'. He took it upon himself to comment in hyperbolic terms on even her most doubtful decisions. He told her that her verse and prose 'would never be surpassed', that he was a 'Catherinite', that he would die a 'Catherinite', that he placed at her feet 'his adoration and his idolatry', that she must think of him as 'the old Swiss', the old solitary, half-French, half-Swiss, 'the old man of the Alps, the old Russian of Ferney'. Thanks to him, Catherine now possessed a publicity machine in the centre of Europe, whose sayings flew from drawing-room to drawing-room.

She would quite sincerely have liked to be worthy of the praise he heaped upon her. To govern firmly according to liberal ideas. But was it possible? As she left Moscow in June 1763, she was bubbling over with plans. In the carriage she travelled in, she studied, with Ivan Betsky, who was President of the Buildings and Gardens Commission, plans for an orphanage, a school for midwives, an establishment for popular health and an institute for young girls of the nobility. When her

---

[1] Letter, 15th October, 1763.

companion worried about the expense, she silenced him by saying that they would economize on other fronts. A few months later, the first stone of the orphanage had been laid, the walls of the midwives' school rose from the ground, the foundations of the girls' school were laid – this was to become the famous Smolny Institute. At the same time, Catherine brought German settlers in to cultivate the rich land of the Ukraine and the Volga; she exempted them from military service, lent them capital to establish themselves with, interest-free for ten years, freed them from taxation for thirty years, and guaranteed the free exercise of their religion. The presence on Russian soil of these honest, sober and energetic foreign workers would, she thought, inspire the moujiks to follow their example and improve their own methods of work and way of life. She was forgetting on one hand the powerful inertia of the people, with their deeply rooted customs, and, on the other, the submissive relationship of a serf towards his landlord. Instead of admiring his new neighbour, the German peasant, the Russian peasant merely envied or hated him. Catherine also summoned to Russia doctors, dentists, architects, engineers and artisans from the four corners of Europe. She stopped the State from intervening in commercial affairs. Anybody who wished to export tar, linseed, wax, tallow, iron, hemp, caviar or potash, should be encouraged to do so by the administration. Merchants were ordered to form corporations to fight apathy and disorder in commerce, and to promote a spirit of enterprise. A Finance Commission was established to oversee the re-striking of all the coins circulating in the Empire. Another commission studied the ways of abolishing corruption in business; a third set about reforming the army, creating arsenals and barracks and building military roads. Catherine personally attended most of the sessions, impatiently speaking to them, urging her counsellors to speed up their work. There was so much to do, time was so short and Russia so vast!

All the time she was reorganizing the interior, she never lost sight of changes in the Western world. In Poland, Augustus III held onto life by a thread. Stanislaus Poniatowski obediently waited in the wings for 'his' Empress's decisions. As a precaution, she had placed thirty thousand soldiers close to the Polish frontier. Fifty thousand remained in reserve. But what view would Berlin and Vienna take? What about Paris? And London? She realized that she was playing a hard game and that her adversaries were keeping their cards well hidden. Poland was a chaotic primitive country ruled by an arrogant nobility. A few great families ruled over peasants who were in theory free but in practice as miserable as any slaves. The Catholic Church reigned supreme. This strange country was governed by a Diet, which elected the king. The veto system was used, so that a single negative vote could annul any decision. But if a party defeated at the vote still wished to impose its will, it could form, with its members' private militia, a 'Confederation'; this, when it became strong enough, would defeat the legal opposition. Thus the rivalry between the great Polish families kept the country in a state of anarchy, judged by Catherine to be 'propitious'. Frederick II had recently conveyed to her the message that he would leave her free to present her own candidate for the Polish throne, as long as this intrusion into a neighbouring country's affairs did not start another war. She replied, 'I will make a king with as little noise as possible.' And, in the shadows, she continued to buy allegiance and loyalty from the most powerful Polish personalities.

One evening, as she chatted light-heartedly with her friends, Gregory Orlov came up to her and whispered some startling news in her ear. A messenger had just arrived : the King of Poland had died, in Dresden. She sent away her guests and retired to her room to think. That night a second messenger came – from Berlin: Frederick II was worried and wanted to know what the Empress intended to do. Advance Stanislaus Poniatowski of course! Since he was in love with Catherine he would be a docile king. As long as France and Austria did not intervene with their armies! Catherine feverishly awaited the opposition's reaction. But Versailles hesitated, despite Breteuil's reports about the Empress's 'unbridled ambition'. And Vienna was intimidated by the concentration of Russian troops. Catherine soon saw that she had tricked her enemies by pretending to be extremely determined. Perfect. She quickly scooped her winnings off the green baize. Stanislaus Poniatowski was elected King of Poland by the Polish Diet on the 26th August 1764, under the name of Stanislaus-Augustus. He immediately had to accept a Polish-Russian alliance against Turkey, an adjustment of the frontier in Russia's favour and the admission of Orthodox Christians to all public posts. It was the end of a proud nation's independence. Chained to Russia, Poland was ready to be shared out. It was Catherine's first international success.

She was travelling through Courland, and her 'Polish victory' still appeared uncertain when, after a day of celebration in Riga, she heard another piece of news, so serious that it kept her awake for part of the night. The next day she did not appear in public, cancelled the final celebrations and set off in a hurry. When she arrived at Tsarskoe Selo, she summoned Panin and questioned him. Was it possible that Ivan VI had been assassinated? What exactly had happened at Schlusselburg? Who was this Basil Mirovitch of whom she had never heard? Panin placed before her the first findings of the inquest. According to these papers, Basil Mirovitch was a twenty-four-year-old lieutenant, an impoverished and ambitious gambler and swashbuckler, hot-headed and in debt. He was descended from a Ukrainian family whose wealth had been confiscated by Peter the Great for its part in the Mazeppa betrayal. When he came to St Petersburg he had hoped for the restitution of his estates, or at least some improvement in his lot. Why could he not, like the Orlovs, achieve money and fame in the Empress's scented wake? But all his petitions had remained unanswered. His very existence was ignored in high places. He became embittered and rebellious. The thought of a *coup d'état* entered his mind. And then he was posted to Schlusselburg. He immediately became intrigued by the layout of the fortress with its inner enclosure under permanent special guard. Two sworn officers, Vlassyev and Chekin, were permanently attached to Prisoner No 1. These unusual jailers were in fact as pitiable as the man they guarded. Like him they had no contact with the outside world. They too were buried alive. They had several times begged Panin to replace them. 'We are at the end of our strength!' Panin advised patience. Who was this faceless unknown prisoner? Mirovitch tried to find out. Gradually tongues began to loosen in the guard room. He learnt with amazement that No 1 was without doubt 'Ivanushka', the martyr-Emperor Ivan VI. Crowned in his cradle, then thrown into prison in early childhood, this miserable man crouched in a cold dark cell, half-naked and dying of hunger, when he should be reigning in purple and gold over the biggest empire in the world. They never saw him – they only knew that he was twenty-three years old and had a red beard, that he was very thin and very miserable, that his mind was exhausted, that he stammered and that he had learnt to read from prayer-books; sometimes he argued with his two personal guards who mocked and despised him, and sometimes, exasperated by their sarcasm, he would curse them and, throwing his pewter mug at them, shout that he was the real Emperor. Nevertheless he never even asked to see the light of the sun. When he had been transferred to Kexholm the previous summer, on Catherine's orders, his head had been covered by a sack. He could not imagine a world different from the stone pit, the tightly barred window whose glass had been chalked over, the dented bowl and the hateful guards. Space, fresh air, wind, games, love, a ride in the forest or a friend's laughter were things he could not even dream of. Everything as far back as he could remember, was solitude, ugliness and brutality. These thoughts obsessed Mirovitch during his long nights on guard at Schlusselburg. At first he was moved only by personal interest. If he succeeded he would become a new Gregory Orlov. Then he gradually persuaded himself that God had entrusted him with a holy mission. In his excitement he confided his plan to one of his comrades, Apollo Oushakov. Together they would raise the garrison, free 'Ivanushka' and proclaim him emperor. Certain of the outcome, they swore loyalty to each other in a church, and drew up a proclamation justifying their action. The moment was well chosen, since the Empress was preparing to travel through Courland. But Oushakov drowned accidentally, on the eve of the day chosen for the attack. It might have been suicide. Mirovitch decided to act alone. He thought he could be sure of sympathy from his fellow-soldiers at Schlusselburg, as most of them felt a sort of mystical fondness for Prisoner No 1. During the night of the 4th and 5th July 1764, when he was on guard at the fortress, he harangued his men, ordered them to free the true Emperor, and made them load their guns and bring forward a small cannon. Woken by the noise, the Commander of Schlusselburg appeared in his dressing-gown. Mirovitch knocked him down with his rifle butt shouting: 'Why do you keep your Emperor prisoner?' and rushed towards the casemates where the permanent guards were. Shots were fired on both sides. The guards laid down their arms at the sight of the small cannon. The way was open. In the gallery, Mirovitch met Chekin, seized his arm and shouted: 'Where's the Emperor?' Chekin replied imperturbably: 'We have an Empress, not an Emperor!' Mirovitch pushed him furiously forwards and ordered him to open the door of Prisoner No 1's cell. Chekin did so. It was dark. They brought a light. On the floor, in a pool of blood, lay a body covered in wounds. It was the Emperor Ivan VI, murdered. He moved feebly and his throat rattled. Mirovitch threw himself upon him in despair, hugged him and, sobbing, kissed his hands and feet. There was another, more violent spasm. It was over. Ivan VI was dead. Vlassyev and Chekin stood in the background numb and silent. They did not feel guilty in the least. When they had heard the shots, they had simply carried out the order issued by Elisabeth, confirmed by Peter III and renewed by Catherine II: not to surrender Prisoner No 1 alive. In any case Mirovitch did not appear to hold it against the murderers. He took no notice of them. The body was placed on a bed and carried into the courtyard. Mirovitch called the assembled soldiers to arms, and military honours were performed for His Majesty. Then he said: 'See brothers, your Emperor Ivan Antonovitch. Now we are plunged in disaster. I in particular will suffer for this. You are innocent. You did not know what I was going to do. I have assumed all responsibility for you, and take all punishment upon myself.'

When she heard details of the execution, Catherine underwent complex feelings of relief and embarrassment, as she had done at her husband's death. 'God's ways are mysterious and unpredictable,' she said to Panin. 'Providence has shown clear favour towards me by bringing this affair to a satisfactory conclusion.'[1] Of course for a 'philosophical mind', crowned or not, the massacre of an innocent man must always be a reprehensible action. However, Catherine thought, there are circumstances in which reason must take precedence over mortality. The order to kill the prisoner in the case of attempted abduction was a logical one, since his freedom would have represented danger to the throne. This wild Mirovitch, by hastening events, had cleared the land. Thanks to him and the two guards who had so faithfully carried out the imperial orders, Catherine could now breathe freely. Certainly she would once more be held responsible for a death that served her interests. But she had not been directly implicated in the assassination. She could even deplore it in public. Thus the advantages of this business heavily outweighed the disadvantages. Of course there could be no question of Catherine protecting Mirovitch from the workings of justice, as she had previously done for the Orlov brothers. Such mercy, if it were repeated, would be interpreted as an admission of guilt. Mirovitch was interrogated by the secret service and Catherine examined the file on her return to St Petersburg. She found in it the 'manifesto' drawn up by the accused man: this incredibly violent document accused her of being no more than a usurper, of having poisoned her husband, of having linked herself 'out of weakness of character' with an unscrupulous officer, Gregory Orlov, and even of considering marriage with him. These accusations did not come as a surprise to Catherine. She guessed that a large proportion of her subjects thought the same. She had to accept, against her will, the burden of unpopularity. She would soon be able to shake it off with some kind of festivity.

Mirovitch was condemned to death. The sentence did not surprise the people or the Court. But they were surprised that the part played by the main accomplice, Oushakov, was not clearly defined during the inquest. He was suspected of having been paid to incite Mirovitch to do this senseless thing, and of having faked suicide so as to disappear before the uprising. He could therefore have been an instrument of power, Catherine's agent. In any case, everybody thought that the condemned man would be reprieved at the last minute as had been all political criminals during Elisabeth's reign. Ostermann, indeed, had been informed of the imperial reprieve just as his head rested on the

[1] Bilbassov *The Story of Catherine II.*

block. Perhaps Mirovitch was encouraged by the memory of this. He climbed onto the scaffold with the calm confidence of a visionary. The crowd, massed in the square, waited in religious silence for the arrival of a messenger bringing a reprieve from Her Majesty. No messenger came. The executioner raised his axe. As the blade came down on the condemned man's neck a sigh of horror went through the crowd. An eye-witness, the poet Derzhavin, said that the whole square seemed to shake. The parapets of a bridge collapsed under the weight of the mob. The corpse of the executed man was burnt, so that he could not be resurrected. A few soldiers who had followed the lieutenant were condemned to run a gauntlet of birches from three to ten times, through the ranks of a thousand of their comrades, chosen from the toughest in the army. Catherine had not forgiven. From that day onwards, there were many who no longer thought of her as the merciful 'little mother'. Vlassyev and Chekin were rewarded for their loyalty and zeal. They confirmed in an official report clearly inspired by the Empress that Prisoner No 1 had been retarded, was incapable of stringing two thoughts together and was a piece of human refuse whose death could sadden nobody.

The foreign diplomats were astounded, but continued to smile officially at this sovereign who was responsible for two regicides in two years. Bérenger wrote in a report on the 20th July, 1764: 'The Empress is suspected of having premeditated and ordered the murder!... What a woman, my lord, is this Empress Catherine! What a stage is Russia!' And on the 7th August: 'The moment and the circumstances of this murder have made people suspect the Empress of having instigated it herself with the object of removing a source of continual worry to herself.' Count Sacken, the Ambassador from Saxony wrote on the same day to his own government: 'The people believe that this performance took place only to decently get rid of Prince Ivan.'

In reply to the wave of suspicion which was gathering inside the country and abroad, Catherine issued a self-justifying proclamation on the 17th/28th August. This document stated that Ivan, the unlawful pretender, had been from his earliest childhood 'deprived of reason and human intelligence', that Mirovitch had wished to push himself to the fore by taking advantage of 'a bloody popular riot' and that the guards Vlassyev and Chekin had acted to 'safeguard public peace'.

The proclamation impressed nobody. 'The Russians, in private, tear both the contents and the wording of this proclamation to pieces,' wrote Sacken. And also: 'I have been told that some people have prayed for Mirovitch's soul as for that of a martyr, on the very spot of the execution.'

Madame Geoffrin declared to King Stanislaus; 'I consider that her (Catherine's) manifestos on Ivan's death were ridiculous. She need not have done anything; Mirovitch's trial was quite sufficient.'

To Catherine herself, she dared to write: 'It seems to me that if I were on the throne, I would do what I thought suitable for my own interests and those of my people, without publishing manifestos about my behaviour. I would wish my actions to speak for themselves, and I would enforce silence upon my pen.'

Catherine returned: 'I am inclined to tell you that your arguments about this manifesto are those of a colour-blind person. It was not drawn up for the foreign powers, but merely to inform the people of Ivan's death; it was necessary to say how he died ... If I had not done so, people would believe the evil rumours spread by ministers from courts that envy and hate me ... they criticize this manifesto in France, people have also criticized the Good Lord, and here they sometimes even criticize the French. But it is nonetheless the case that here the manifesto and the criminal's head have effectively silenced all criticism. Therefore the aim has been fulfilled, and my manifesto has achieved its object: *ergo* it was right.'

Despite this splendid defence, Catherine's friends abroad keenly felt the shock of disappointment. Voltaire stated that, 'the Ivan affair was conducted in such an atrocious manner that one might swear that bigots were involved.' D'Alembert reinforced this: 'It is very tiresome to be obliged to get rid of so many people, and then to have to print that one is very annoyed, but that it is not one's fault.' Then the philosophers gradually calmed down and accepted the argument of reasons of state. Their admiration for the distant and generous Catherine brought out in them a sort of resigned indulgence. To overcome Voltaire's scruples, d'Alembert quoted this proverb: 'It is better to kill the devil, than be killed by him.' And he continued: 'I agree with you that our philosophy does not want to boast of too many pupils like her. But what can we do? One must love one's friends with all their faults.' Voltaire was happy to let himself be persuaded and to forget these 'trifles'. 'These are family matters which do not concern me,' he said. Hearing the opinions of the wise man of Ferney, Horace Walpole wrote to Madame du Deffand; 'Voltaire and his Catherine disgust me.' And the Duchesse de Choiseul wrote; 'Now she (Catherine) is as pure as snow, she is the idol of her subjects, the glory of her Empire, the object of admiration of the whole world, a marvel of marvels.' Voltaire and his 'Cateau' were lumped together in the drawing-rooms of Paris and London.

From the depths of her Palace Catherine watched and evaluated the importance of this turbulence. She was sure that the storm would soon die down. A true sovereign had to be able to look beyond the every-day foam, to the line of the horizon. When Panin complained of the world's ill-will towards Her Majesty, she retorted; 'As long as it is only about me I don't mind what anybody says. I only become upset when Russia's honour is at stake.'[1]

Her two main rivals had been eliminated, and so only one remained: Catherine's own son, Grand Duke Paul, heir to the throne. Now that Peter III and Ivan VI had both been assassinated, the hopes of the Tsarina's enemies would surely rest on this child of ten. Certainly there was no question of her killing him as well. In her way she loved him and was sincerely alarmed at his slightest illness. But she was an empress before being a mother. The exercise of power was her main object. As long as she lived no one else would rule Russia. Paul must grow up in her shadow, educated but submissive, as a possible successor, not as a hidden rival. Despite her innumerable tasks, she found time to spend a few moments with him each day; she would bend over his games in his room, watch over what he read, and try to tame him. This was a difficult job as the boy was nervous, wild and sickly, and subject to convulsions. He was jealous of Gregory Orlov and said so to his mother. She would reason with him. He suffered secretly from his ugliness. His face, fresh and charming in the past, with a little upturned nose and fair hair, had become a terrifying caricature with a squashed nose and thick lips. Would he look like Peter III even though he was not his son? Catherine worried about the future, especially as Paul was now asking people about his father's death and what his chances were of reigning. Hearing about these conversations from the child's valet, Bérenger wrote to the Duc de Praslin: 'This young Prince (Paul) is showing ominous and dangerous tendencies. It is well known that his mother does not love him and that, since she has been in power, she has, in an unseemly fashion, withdrawn any signs of affection previously shown ... A few days ago he was asking why his father had been killed, and why his mother was on the throne that was rightfully his. He added that when he grew up he would put the situation right. One might say, My Lord, that the child makes such remarks so often that the Empress must hear of them. Now nobody can doubt that the Princess will take every step needed to prevent any effect they might have.'

[1] M. Lavater-Sloman *Catherine II and Her Times.*

CHAPTER XV

Legislomania

In the spring, the country was ravaged by a smallpox epidemic; Catherine longed to introduce vaccination into Russia. What a prestigious thing it would be if she were to overtake France and impose this measure on a country which was thought by others to be so backward! She discussed it with Baron Cherkassov, President of the Institute of Hygiene, who was a sensible and cultivated man. However, he respectfully warned Her Majesty of how her subjects might react. Even the most advanced of them, he said, would be terrified at the thought of receiving into their bodies germs of such an illness – even if, in theory, it was to increase their resistance to it. Supporters of 'inoculation' were few and far between. Only a few philosophers and scholars were prepared to praise 'the diabolical lancet'. When Catherine told Frederick II of her plan, he begged her to abandon it, for fear of a disaster. Gregory Orlov depicted to her the hatred that would arise amongst the courtiers and the people, if the experiment were to fail. How would she defend herself, faced with hundreds of dead bodies? She would be blamed even for natural deaths! Catherine decided then to submit herself to an ordeal too dangerous for others. She ordered Cherkassov to bring a good specialist over from England. Cherkassov was horrified at the responsibility he would have to bear, and begged Her Majesty to think again. What would happen to him in the event of her death? Or if the Empress was even disfigured by the pustules? She burst out laughing. She was aware of the danger. Smallpox was a disease she had feared more than any other since her youth. Since she now had an opportunity of wiping it out, and of persuading others by her own example, she would take the risk. She always wanted to be at the head of any movement, in the front line, tempting fate and drawing attention to herself. She held to her decision, some said out of love for her people, others out of her longing for fame. Cherkassov brought from London the great Thomas Dimsdale, who was a proponent of inoculation against smallpox. As soon as he arrived in St Petersburg, in October 1764, the doctor prepared for the operation. When they heard of the Empress's intention, her friends sobbed and begged her to abandon it. One morning, Thomas Dimsdale with his lancet made a light incision in the majestic arm stretched towards him. The news spread throughout the Court from the Empress's room. It was as though Her Majesty had decided to kill herself. Gregory Orlov immediately had himself inoculated as well, without waiting, so as to share the fate of the woman to whom he owed so much. For the following nine days, everybody chafed, cursing the English quack and imagining Russia in mourning for her sovereign. Only Catherine remained composed. Even before the critical period was over, she confirmed her interest in progress by founding an enlarged Academy of Sciences, set up according to her own theories. In the order of the foundation, which she drew up herself whilst awaiting the results of the smallpox 'insertion', she declared: 'Anybody who has reached the required standard may, even if he is a serf, become a member of the Academy. All members, associates as well as academicians, as well as their children and all their descendants, will remain free men forever; nobody will have the right to make them or their descendants serfs again.'

There were indeed in Russia at that time serfs whose masters had encouraged them to educate themselves and become secretaries, painters, musicians, actors or poets. But they represented an infinitesimal proportion, and by proclaiming the members of the Academy automatically free, Catherine was hardly shaking the foundations of society.

The same combination of unconscious cynicism and social concern was apparent in the founding of the orphanage. On the curriculum, which consisted mainly of manual work: 'The boys will begin to work in agriculture and gardening, whilst the girls will learn to cook, make bread etc. following the example of the much praised women in the Bible, and the hard working ones sung by Homĕr. Thus we will see emerging a generation of men to whom sloth, carelessness and idleness and all the vices that ensue, are unknown things.' The foundation decree of the establishment adds that at the end of their studies the inmates would be free men and that nobody could 'appropriate or enslave them' and that this 'freedom' would apply to their descendants: 'Our pupils will therefore not be slaves or convicts who can be sent to the galleys or the mines.' This was really saying the best way a serf could better his child's lot would be to abandon him. Foundlings had the privilege of being free. Delighted with this discovery Catherine said, explaining the motives of the decree: 'There are only two classes in the Russian Empire, the nobility and the enslaved, but through the privileges allowed to this establishment, our pupils and their descendants will be forever free and will form a third class.'[1] This did not prevent her from extending serfdom in the Ukraine at the same time and with the same calmness. The peasants of this province now no longer had the right to leave the land. The post of Hetman of the Ukraine was abolished. The whole of central Russia was weighed down with iron laws.

The days went by and the Empress showed no sign of illness after her inoculation. She pretended not to be surprised at this. Everybody around her praised her courage: she seemed brilliantly to personify scientific progress. There were services of thanksgiving in the churches. Messages of congratulation and devotion poured in from the most distant provinces. Cherkassov and Dimsdale were in transports of delight, and now all the courtiers wanted to be vaccinated. Grand Duke Paul followed suit, on his mother's instructions. Dimsdale was made a baron in recognition of his services, named Counsellor of State and awarded a pension of five thousand pounds. Little Alexander Markov, aged seven, who had provided the lymph for Catherine's inoculation, was made a hereditary nobleman and allowed to count himself amongst Catherine's personal *protégés* under the name of 'Ospenny' or 'carrier of smallpox'.[2]

Enthusiasm spread from Russia to other countries. Catherine's detractors had to recognize that here she had scored a point. With public opinion as changeable as it is, it appeared that the scratch from the lancet had almost brought her forgiveness for the sword wounds which had killed Ivan VI. Voltaire wrote triumphantly to 'his' sovereign:

'Ah! Madam, what a lesson Your Majesty has given to our French fops, our wise Masters at the Sorbonne, our Aesculapiuses of the medical schools! You had yourself inoculated with less display than a nun having an enema. The Imperial Prince followed your example. Count Orlov went hunting in the snow after being given smallpox. This is how Scipio would have behaved if the illness (which came from Arabia) had existed in his time.'

When General Brown, the Governor of Livonia, also congratulated the Empress on her bravery, she replied with modest calm: 'Your compatriot, the honest and skilful doctor Dimsdale, makes everybody in Petersburg adventurous, and he had clients in every great house.'[3]

It remained only to spread the practice from the capital to the

[1] Olga Wormsev *Catherine II*.
[2] The family bearing this name has, as a result, been held in high esteem in Russia.
[3] M. Lavater-Sloman *Catherine II and Her Times*.

provinces, from the Court to the people. Judging from the reports she received, Catherine felt confident about the future. The population had suffered too much from the regular round of epidemics not to see the advantages of inoculation. No subject could possibly refuse what the 'little mother' Catherine had dared to submit to save herself from smallpox.

Now that the smallpox business had been settled Catherine embarked on more innovations. Reform had become her craze – she wanted to knead the thick dough of Russia. She drew up, with Ivan Betsky, a *General Rule for the education of children of both sexes,* inspired by the ideas of Locke and Rousseau. The parents, on sending their children to school, had to engage themselves not to remove them 'under any pretext'. But where would they find teachers? Catherine gave Schlözer the job of rounding up from abroad all the educated men who would agree to impart their knowledge to upper-class little Russians. It had to be done quickly. Too bad if the quality wasn't there. Betsky, when he was organizing the Cadet School, appointed as headmaster an ex-prompter from the French theatre, and as inspector of classes an old valet of Catherine's mother's. Later, these improvised teachers would be sent to England, France and Germany to learn their job. Catherine's proudest achievement was undeniably the Smolny Institute for young girls of the nobility. The régime was strict, following the Empress's directions. Twelve years of seclusion. Almost no holidays. No outings, except from time to time to the Court where the Empress received pupils who had attracted her attention. Lay teachers. Priests kept in their proper place. A sort of humanist convent, with no windows onto the outside world and only one door opening into the paradise of the Imperial Palace. A few young girls of the bourgeoisie were admitted amongst the aristocratic ones. However, although they all wore the same colour an apron singled out the lower-class girls.[1] Equality according to Catherine had its limits. There was more preaching than practice. The letters she wrote to Voltaire, to Frederick II, to Madame Geoffrin and to Diderot, are the letters of a liberal queen, but the decisions taken were those of an autocrat with no illusions. Thus, on the 11th/22nd February, 1763, she formed a commission charged with detailing and enlarging Peter III's proclamation on the privileges of the aristocracy. In a month she had drawn up a report which contained the main part of the Charter for the Nobility, issued twenty-two years later. All the time-honoured advantages enjoyed by the aristocracy were, here, formally confirmed and extended by the new sovereign. The list of

[1] Waliszewski *The Story of an Empress.*

orders demonstrated her solicitude towards the grandees of her régime. One of these decrees stipulated that any nobleman, when he left military service could assume the rank of officer, whether or not he had reached it on retirement from the army; this was so that he would be in a superior position to commoners. Another specified that noblemen were entitled, on their own authority, to sentence their serfs to forced labour. A third granted to the nobility a monopoly on the distillation of brandy. As well as all this, on the 3rd/14th July, 1763, after some unrest amongst the peasantry, Catherine indignantly made a special announcement that she was resolved to 'vigorously protect the lands and the wealth of gentlemen landowners'. From the beginning of her reign she instinctively knew that one must in theory pity the serfs, but, in practice, rely on the noblemen. Russia was too enormous and diverse to be ruled with eclecticism. And she alone had to hold together this polymorphous mass. She was a hive of energy; she saw, controlled and directed everything, whether it was the reorganization of the Senate or the Grand Duke's education, building works in the capital, or negotiations with the sculptor Falconet for a monument to the glory of Peter the Great.

This mass of activities did not prevent her from strictly observing the programme of life at Court. Each day of the week was marked: on Sunday 'court'; on Monday, a French comedy; Thursday, a French tragedy or opera, with the audience adjourning afterwards to Maître Locatelli's ballet; on Friday, a fancy-dress ball at the Palace; Saturday, nothing. Catherine made a point of appearing at all these occasions. She would always leave before the end, as she was in the habit of rising at dawn and did not wish to go to bed late. Sometimes, at six o'clock in the morning, she would light the great china stove herself. Once, as she was putting a match to the kindling she heard piercing shrieks in the smoke duct. She quickly put out the fire and apologized to the black-faced, crestfallen little sweep who appeared before her. To apologize to a chimney-sweep! The incident was retold at the Court, as an example of the Empress's exceptional goodness. In general those who served her praised her simplicity and good-nature. Maids and valets adored her. She never beat them and hardly ever scolded them. One evening after having rung her bell in vain, she went into her antechamber to find her servants playing cards. Calling one of them, she politely asked him if he would take the letter she had just written whilst she replaced him at the card-table. She did not dare to sack a hopeless cook, and when it was his week on duty she would merely say to her friends: 'We must be patient. We've got eight days of fasting ahead of us.' She confided to Grimm: 'My valets provide me with two fresh pens every day, which I have the right to use. But when they are worn out, I dare not ask for more, I just turn them round as well as I can.' She added: 'I never see a new pen without smiling at it and feeling a strong temptation to use it.' Thus, the first light of day found her happy and hard at work, two conditions necessary to one another. As soon as she opened her eyes, her greyhounds, who slept on a silk and lace cushion, leapt onto her bed and, yapping with delight, licked her hands and face. After playing with the little pack, she would go into her dressing-room where her chamber-maid awaited her. A few mouthfuls of warm water, a piece of ice rubbed on her face, and she would go into her study. There in the ample folds of a linen dressing-gown, with a white crêpe bonnet on her head, she gulped down coffee so strong that it would have given anybody else palpitations. A pound of coffee was used to make five cups. Biscuits, sugar and cream were shared with the dogs. When the sugar bowl was empty, Catherine would open the door and the dogs disappeared for a short walk. All her life she would only be happy if she had around her a few of these unruly and affectionate four-legged companions. She gave them funny names, laughed at their tricks and devoted whole pages to them in her letters. 'I have always loved animals,' she wrote, 'animals have a lot more spirit than one might suppose.' And also: 'Lady Anderson (a little five-month-old bitch) tears up everything she can find, jumps forwards and bites my visitors' legs, hunts birds, flies, deer and other animals four times her size; she makes more noise than all the rest of her family put together.' Whilst the dogs careered around her desk, she read reports, annotated memoirs, drew up orders and wrote the odd love-note to Gregory Orlov – who was still asleep. She took snuff as she worked. But only from the left hand, out of concern for her entourage. 'One of the demands of my job,' she said, 'is that I often have to have my hand kissed. It would hardly be right, I think, to make everybody around me smell of snuff.'

At nine o'clock, while still in her dressing-gown, she returned to her bedroom and received officials with their problems. When a footman whispered to her that her lover had arrived she waved everybody else away. Then the audiences would begin again and continue until mid-day, at which time Catherine would return to her private dressing-room; there she finished washing and dressing, and had her hair arranged. Her brown hair was so long that it touched the ground when she was seated. She wore neither powder, rouge, mascara nor beauty spots. Some friends watched the 'petit lever' in Her Majesty's official dressing-room. The ceremony lasted for a few minutes. Then they ate. It was a frugal meal, consisting of boiled beef and salted cucumbers, with redcurrant syrup and water to drink. The meal did not last for more than an hour. There were about ten guests with the Empress. All complained secretly about the poor food. Catherine, however, did not notice it. She had as little taste for food as she had for music. In the afternoon, the high officials reappeared, presenting reports and asking for instructions. Then there was a reception for courtiers in the drawing-rooms. Everybody gossiped and played whist or piquet. When there was no performance, Her Majesty retired at ten o'clock, hardly touching the supper prepared for her. Back in her apartments, she would drink a large glass of boiled water and then go to bed. Leading, as she did, this sober, regular and hardworking life, which was both homely and philosophical, the only excesses which she allowed herself were those of physical passion.

Tuesdays and Saturdays – the days when there was no reception – were the most eagerly awaited days of the week for Catherine. These were given over to long and lighthearted conversations with her close friends, Gregory Orlov, Panin, Naryshkin, Monsieur Pictet from Geneva, Princess Dashkova, Betsky... She would read them some of the most brilliant letters she had received from abroad, comment on the latest pile of French books and marvel at the liveliness of the *Literary and Artistic Correspondence* of Grimm and Diderot: this was a bi-monthly journal which she received from Paris, as did most of the crowned heads of Europe. In it Grimm gave detailed descriptions of the painting and sculptures that he had admired in the drawing-rooms. As Catherine read these accounts, she dreamed of founding her own art gallery, a place of beauty and meditation which she would retire to alone, or with a few chosen friends, a 'hermitage'. Whilst they awaited the creation of this intimate museum, a 'small session' continued in a friendly and simple atmosphere. In this circle of friends, it was forbidden to slander anyone, to lie, to swear, to lose one's temper, or even to rise as Her Majesty came and went through the room. There was a fine of ten kopecks. They played society games with joke punishments and wagers. The Empress talked a lot, fooled around, laughed at trifles: it was everybody's duty, she thought, to search after pleasure. She had, from her earliest youth, cultivated this optimistic outlook. It was a systematic policy, a sort of health cure for the mind. Every time she was about to give way to her worries, she would react by drawing on this *joie de vivre*. 'One must be cheerful,' she wrote. 'It is the only way to overcome and bear everything.' 'She would laugh at some common-place remark, some quotation, some foolishness...' said the Prince de Ligne, 'it was this contrast between the simplicity of her society conversation and the great things that she did which made her so fascinating.' All the same, this strong woman was easily reduced to tears.

But they were only passing showers. Crying was a relief to her and brought back her good humour, and laughter was soon heard again in the 'hermitage'. Clean laughter of course, as the Tsarina would never tolerate any coarse remarks in her presence. If a guest produced some smutty joke, she would freeze over and reprimand him. She considered that love, which played such an important part in her life, should not be made a subject for jokes. She was carried away in the darkness of the bedroom, but prudish in the bright light of the drawing-room. However much she enjoyed sensual pleasures, she always made them subject to some rules of conduct, stemming perhaps from her Protestant upbringing. Foreign diplomats very much appreciated the honest friendliness of these gatherings. After the splendour of Versailles, the Baron de Breteuil was charmed by the familiar welcome he received from Her Majesty in Russia. The English Ambassador, accustomed as he was to the dull formality of Saint James's Palace, wrote: 'There reigns there an atmosphere of harmony and good humour such that one might be in a paradise of peace.'

Catherine spent the winters in St Petersburg charming everybody with her performance as a home-loving woman. In summer, she was at Tsarskoe Selo. Casually dressed, without powder on her hair, she would walk, early in the morning, in the dewy park. She carried a pencil and pad with which to write down her thoughts. She held audiences out of doors, under a tree, in an arbour, or on a balcony. One of the most talented of her chosen collaborators was undoubtedly the young economist and agronomist Jean Jacques Sievers, who had been introduced to her on her visit to the Courland. She made him Governor of Novgorod. She also, against all advice, made a man of thirty-four, Prince Alexander Vyazensky, Attorney General – the most important political post in the Empire. The Attorney General presided over the Senate and administered finance, home affairs and justice. He was Her Majesty's spokesman and closest collaborator. When she drew up the document establishing his functions, Catherine added a letter enlightening him on his ruler's political views:

'The Russian Empire is so vast that any form of government other than that of an absolute Emperor would be harmful to it; all other forms of government are slower in their workings and leave the field open to upheavals, which waste the power and strength of the State...' She pointed out also that what suited other countries did not necessarily suit the Russians and that 'the internal establishments of a nation must be developed to suit the national character'. Anyway the inertia of the Russian authorities 'which dare not speak or act for themselves' alone would justify, if necessary, the need for an inflexible central power. On the other hand, the ethnic populations had the right to a special status. 'Little Russia, Livonia and Finland,' she wrote, 'administer themselves according to confirmed privileges and to disparage them would be more than a mistake, it would be foolishness. These provinces must be treated with great tact, so that they will become friendly towards us and no longer live like wolves in a forest.'

The Empress ended by giving the new Attorney General a splendid description of herself:

'You must realize whom you are dealing with. You will be in daily contact with me and you will realize that my only aim is the happiness and glory of this country, my only desire the well-being of my subjects, whatever class they may belong to. My only thought is that all should be peaceful and satisfactory both inside and outside the Empire. I love truth, and you can speak to me without fear. You can also argue with me without worrying, as long as you are only moved by a concern for our work . . . I will also add that I dislike flattery, and do not expect any from you. All I ask from you is frankness in our relationship and energy for the job.'

These principles for collaboration between a prime minister and his sovereign seemed to aim so high that eventually the whole of Europe heard about them. Catherine soon had another opportunity of impressing the intellectual circles. She heard through her Ambassador in France, Prince Golitsin, that Diderot was short of money and wished to sell his library for fifteen thousand pounds; she offered sixteen thousand, and added as a condition that the precious volumes should remain with the famous writer for as long as he lived: 'It would be a cruelty to separate a wise man from his books.' Diderot thus became the Tsarina's librarian without moving from his house, and received, as well, a salary of a thousand pounds a year, paid in advance for fifty years, so as to avoid any delays. Diderot, overcome, wrote thus to the Empress:

'Great Princess, I bow down at your feet; I stretch my arms towards you; I want to speak to you but my mind has contracted, my brain is confused, my ideas jumbled, I am as emotional as a child, and the true expression of the feeling with which I am filled dies on my lips . . . Oh Catherine! Remain sure that you rule as powerfully in Paris as you do in St Petersburg!'

'We three, Diderot, d'Alembert and myself build altars to you,' wrote Voltaire to the Empress. And also: 'Could one ever have suspected, fifty years ago, that one day the Scythians would so handsomely reward virtue, science and philosophy in Paris, where it is so badly treated?'

And Grimm wrote: 'Diderot received not the smallest reward for thirty years of work. It pleased the Empress of Russia on this occasion to pay off France's debt.'

Proof came, in letter upon letter, that Catherine had spent her money well. Those who had previously thought of Russia as a backward country, buried in snow and infested with wolves, now began to believe that perhaps over there generosity and intelligence also throve. Diderot beat the drum. His house became an employment agency. Men of letters, scholars, artists, artisans, architects and engineers came to get information from him and to obtain work in St Petersburg. He would send them on to Prince Golitsin or Betsky. Catherine savoured her success. Thanks to this one gesture, which had cost her little, she had become according to Voltaire 'the benefactress of Europe'. She had only been crowned for three years and she reigned now not only over the millions in Russia but also over those abroad who had devoted their lives to study. She was the protector of literature and art. A sort of secular madonna, dispensing roubles. The little mother and patroness of St Petersburg, who recognized only talent and ignored frontiers.

With this revival of her prestige, Catherine wanted more than ever to be known as a thinker. One day she tasted a potato, to the horror of her fellow-guests, and thought this 'Indian foot' so good that she ordered Sievers to develop the cultivation of the tuber. The plantations had to be watched by armed guards to prevent superstitious peasants from destroying this 'devil's grass'. Other peasants worried her more: these were the 'Raskolniks', the Old Believers, who when threatened with persecution by the Church as heretics, decided to burn themselves to death to escape a world ruled by the devil. The Tsarina was horrified, and instructed Sievers to proclaim that she personally would protect the dissidents. But they had acquired a taste for mass suicide. They continued to throw themselves to the flames, not to escape persecution any more, but to enter the Kingdom of Heaven as quickly as possible. Sievers had to send in troops to prevent these holocausts. A proclamation was issued, allowing the 'Raskolniks' to live according to their religion. They were not in the least grateful to the Empress. By allowing them to exercise their religion, they thought she belittled their mystical fervour. The path to Heaven had to be a path of suffering. Tolerance only softened the soul – it was a trap of the devil. Catherine was astonished by this deeply Russian conception of redemption through suffering. It seemed to her that the heretics' mistrust of earthly happiness was shared by the illiterate and fatalistic masses. Perhaps the serfs were secretly afraid of being emancipated and changing their state from that of irresponsible animals to that of men conscious of their rights and their duties? Perhaps these liberal ideas, so elegantly defended in Parisian drawing-rooms, were not suitable for this sombre empire? Thus, with extreme caution, the Empress began what she considered to be the great work of her life, her *Nakaz, Instructions with a View to the Elaboration of a Code of Law*.

Russia still lived under the complicated and barbaric code which Tsar Alexis Mikhailovitch had established in 1649, the *Ovlogenia*. A few adjustments by Peter the Great, Catherine I, Peter II and Anne Ivanovna had hardly clarified the situation. This decayed apparatus had to be dusted off and modernized. Catherine, in great secrecy, took on this gigantic task. Only Gregory Orlov and Panin were allowed, from time to time, to read a page of her manuscript. They were overcome with admiration. Panin exclaimed: 'These axioms will bring down walls!' Pen in hand, Catherine felt herself guided by two beacons: Voltaire and Montesquieu. She wrote to d'Alembert: 'For the benefit of my Empire, I have plundered the works of President Montesquieu, without naming him. I hope that if he can see me at work from the other world he will forgive me this plagiarism. For the good of twenty million men. He loved humanity too much to mind. His book is my Bible.'

And to Frederick II: 'I have behaved like the jay in the story who puts on the peacock's feathers.'

In fact she stole 'feathers' not only from Montesquieu, but also and mainly from the Italian jurist Beccaria, whose *The Punishment of Crime* had been published in 1764. However, all these borrowings were assembled into a whole different from their original intention. The *Instruction* was, paradoxically, an autocratic interpretation of the liberalism of the writers who had inspired it. Montesquieu and Beccaria appeared in it disguised as potentates with scales in one hand and clubs in the other. This was not a code of law, but an enumeration of principles to guide the future legislator. In these principles, which took up six hundred and fifty-five paragraphs, there was constant vacillation between progressive thought and the maintenance of traditions, desire for equality and respect for privilege, the need for absolutism and the benefits of tolerance. On every line, Catherine called for charity, fairness, patriotism and reason. But the flock's progress towards happiness had to be conducted in an orderly fashion and under the crook of a muscular shepherdess. She alone knew that what her sheep needed was gentle firmness. Although she was a champion of the monarchy, she did not wish to be accused of tyranny. To her, autocracy meant love rather than despotism. She generously enjoined the rich not to oppress the poor, castigated torture, disapproved of the death penalty except in the case of political crime, and declared that people had not been created for rulers but rulers for people. But this did not prevent her from pronouncing herself in favour of privileges for the nobility, and from saying that people must only be made slaves for a good reason. Thus no abolition of servage, but a recommendation to treat serfs humanely. International liberalism adjusted by national empiricism – European theories in a Russian sauce. Despite its diffuse nature, this work, which Catherine toiled at for more than a year, bore witness to her courage, tenacity and sincere desire for change. Her 'legislomania', as she described it, was on a grand scale.

In the autumn of 1766, she personally presented it to the Senate, with orders to form a legislative commission, or Great Commission, charged with codifying the principles expressed in the *Instruction*, after first finding out what the people wanted. To consult the people on their wishes! To expect each province, each class of society to express its wishes in respectful 'Notebooks'! To associate the masses, no matter how indirectly, with the making of laws! What a revolution! The senators did not know whether to be horrified or impressed by such boldness. They chose to break into sobs and cheers.

Those called to take part in the Great Commission were representatives of the Senate, the Synod and the Electoral bodies: but there were also delegates from the nobility, the townspeople and the peasantry – excluding of course the actual serfs. The nobility elected one deputy for each district, since all nobles had the vote. Each town elected a deputy but only householders could vote. In order to be elected as deputy for the nobility or the townspeople one had to be over twenty-five, and have a faultless reputation. To be elected deputy for the free peasants of the State, one had to be at least thirty-five and married with children. The deputies received from the electors a book of wishes drawn up by a committee of five. Their expenses were met by the Treasury and they were exempted for life from torture, capital punishment, physical punishment and confiscation of wealth. In fact these elections took place with little enthusiasm; there were many abstentions; everyone dreaded the burden of obligation and responsibility that came with the office. And then the distances were so great for most of those concerned, candidates and voters alike, between their homes and the district capital! So one stayed at home, one counted on one's neighbour, and one let the world go by. At last, despite this apathy, the Great Commission was set up on the basis of 1,441 Books of Wishes.

When they met in the spring of the year 1767, the deputies began by asking themselves what title they should give the Empress to thank her for her initiative: 'Catherine the Great', 'The Very Wise', 'The Mother of the Nation'. The discussions continued for several sessions.

Catherine became impatient. 'I assembled them to examine the laws,' she wrote to Count Bibikov, President of the Assembly, 'and instead they occupy themselves with an anatomy of my qualities.' The title 'Catherine the Great' drew the most votes. She pretended to be annoyed. But in fact this new name did not displease. Having thus baptized their sovereign, the Great Commission set to work. It was made up of twenty-eight representatives of State institutions, and five hundred and thirty-six deputies elected by all social classes except the serfs. The job of these men of such diverse origins was to find laws which would suit both Christians and Muslims, both the inhabitants of the steppes and those of the rich lands of the Ukraine, both Muscovites and Siberians. They very soon realized that this enterprise was beyond their capacities. Catherine was present at most of the meetings. Her first disappointment came when the 'Notebooks' were read out: she had hoped to find out from them what the state of mind of her subjects was. But she was forced to accept that in Russia there was no such thing as public opinion. Nobody dared to complain for fear of reprisals. On matters of government, they all entrusted themselves to 'the wisdom and maternal care of the Empress'. At most, the nobles humbly hoped for an extension of their privileges, and the merchants for the right to possess serfs themselves. The serfs of course were not consulted. To simplify things the Great Commission divided the work between nineteen special committees, which then wasted their time with cautious chit-chat. 'It is a comedy,' wrote the French chargé d'affairs, Rossignol, 'the Empress's favourites and confidants run everything; they read out the laws so fast or so quietly that one can hardly hear them . . . They then ask for the approval of the assembly and get it, although nothing has been either heard or understood.'

In December 1768, after two hundred sessions, Count Bibikov on the Empress's orders quite simply dissolved these fake States-General. His pretext was Turkey's declaration of war against Russia. In fact the Tsarina had had enough of the Commission's sloth. When a delegate asked if the work of the assembly would start again later, he was answered by the sound of a chair being violently knocked over. The Empress had stormed out of the room in a rage.

Catherine learnt from the failure of this enterprise how incompetent deputies were and how diverse were their opinions on such serious problems as servage, taxation, privileges and justice. This disappointing experience led her to rule the country with an even firmer grip. After a few feverish months, Russia returned to its age-old sleep.

In contrast, Western Europe was most enthusiastic. Catherine had had her *Instruction* translated into Latin, French and German, so as to make sure that it would be read in all enlightened countries. She could count on the usual flatterers. There they all were at their posts, trumpets raised. Voltaire pretended to think that this monument of wisdom was not just an 'introduction' but a complete and detailed code, already being put into practice. He wrote; 'The Empress, in her new code, the best of all possible codes, gives the custody (of the laws) to the Senate composed of the great men of the Empire.' He saluted 'the finest document of the century, worthy of Lycurgus and Solomon'. Justice and Humanity guided the pen of Catherine II, she has reformed everything: Diderot and d'Alembert outdid him. Even Frederick II was impressed. As if to complete Catherine's success abroad, the *Instruction* was suppressed in Paris by the police authorities. She was indignant in public, but privately she was thrilled. Never had anyone shown two such different faces at home and away. She was an autocrat in Russia but a republican in France. Her courtiers consisted on the one hand of nobles defending servage, and on the other of freedom-loving philosophers. And she maintained this double standard with no effort, sometimes following her heart, sometimes her mind; sometimes indulging her taste for orderly western behaviour, sometimes her penchant for Russian volatility.

CHAPTER XVI

The French and the Turks

There was worrying news from Poland. In February 1768, in the small Polish town of Bar, near the Turkish frontier, a confederation of patriots was formed, which swore to shake off the Russian yoke and limit the civil rights of non-Catholic Poles. Thus, paradoxically it was the Russian oppressor who was defending religious tolerance, and the oppressed Pole who wanted unequal treatment for members of different denominations. Catherine was delighted with this imbroglio since it spared her from any guilt for her repression. She would re-establish order in Poland in the name of freedom of thought. Her troops, who had been ready for a long time, brutally attacked and defeated the disorganized bands of confederates. Voltaire, as usual, applauded: 'The Empress of Russia's example is unique in the world. She has sent forty thousand Russians to preach tolerance with fixed bayonets...' And elsewhere: 'She has set armies marching...to force people to live together.' Stanislaus Poniatowski, who was a man of straw, gave in.

In Warsaw, Catherine's ambassador behaved like the governor of a conquered province. In France, Louis XV's court boiled with indignation. However, the French government had no intention of intervening directly in this Polish business. Its anger was tempered by caution. The French preferred to take their revenge through an intermediary, and they looked around for one. Two years beforehand, the Duc de Choiseul had written to Vergennes, who was then the French ambassador in Constantinople: 'The surest way of toppling the usurper Catherine from her usurped throne would be to cause her to go to war. The Turks alone can render us this service... Your sole object must be to cause the Turks to go to war.'[1] Catherine, far from dreading it, was longing for such a war. She was confident of the strength of her army and fleet. Perhaps she would be able to fulfil Peter the Great's old dream: to annex the Crimea and gain access to the Black Sea and the Dardanelles; thus she would wipe out Turkish power and conquer Constantine's holy city, the cradle of the Orthodox Church. Then

[1] Letter of 21st April 1766. Daria Olivier: *Catherine the Great*.

indeed could she call herself Catherine the Great! She prayed for a spark to ignite the powder-keg. There was a frontier incident in the nick of time. During a skirmish with some Poles, a detachment of Ukrainians entered Turkish territory and took Balta, an Ottoman town in Bessarabia. The sultan, urged on by France, protested and ordered Russia to evacuate Poland. Catherine, delighted, refused to do so. The Russian ambassador in Constantinople, Obreskov, was imprisoned in the Seven Towers citadel. The Turkish government declared war on the enemies of the prophet.

The Turks began to mobilize, and so did the Russians. Frederick II suspected how ill-prepared both sides were and spoke of a war between 'the blind and the crippled'. Certainly the Russian army was disorganized, ill-equipped and badly fed. But the Turks were even less well provided for. France had backed a loser. In September 1769 Count Peter Rumyantsov defeated the 'infidels' at Khotin, occupied the principalities of the Danube, took Azov, Taganrog and prepared to invade the Crimea. In 1770, seventeen thousand Russians carved up fifty thousand Turks on the Kagoul river. In the same year, the Russian fleet under the 'Scarface' Alexis Orlov left the Baltic, crossed the Channel, entered the Mediterranean and put into Venice; then it continued into the Aegean to meet the Turkish fleet. There followed a terrible battle in the Bay of Khios, before the port of Chesme, in which the Turkish ships were dispersed and blown to pieces. When news of these successive victories reached Catherine she said to Panin that she thought she would 'die of joy'.

Meanwhile in Europe the kings began to panic. Frederick II and Joseph II met in order to work out a way of stopping 'this torrent which would engulf the world', if possible without bloodshed. At Versailles the Duc de Choiseul cursed himself for having overestimated Turkish military strength. The English government felt bitter at the fact that the Russian fleet had dared to come through the Channel, and was worried that this new naval force would upset the old balance of power. The Swedes were distressed at the Russian threat to the Baltic and the Gulf of Finland. Catherine, who had hitherto been treated as a political dilettante, now appeared to the Western ministries as an evil genius, a sort of calculating and fast-moving ogress. What irritated the foreign courts most was the fact that, although she was simply and greedily enlarging her Empire, she managed to use liberal philosophy as the justification for her conquests. She even, with her pen, supported the cause of Paoli's Corsicans against the French oppressors. 'I pray every morning,' she wrote to Count Tchernychev, her representative in London, 'My God, save Corsica from the hands of those wicked

Frenchmen.' She saw the French as the Turks of the West – the fleur-de-lys and the crescent represented the same thing. 'The Turks and the French,' she wrote again, 'have woken the sleeping cat . . . And now the cat is going to chase some mice, and now you will see what you will see, now they are going to pay attention to us; they never expected such a commotion as we have caused, and now that the Turks have been defeated, the French will be treated everywhere as the Corsicans are treating them now.' Frederick II said that Catherine had 'a sort of revulsion for everything French'. And the French chargé d'affaires, Sabatier de Cabre, told his government that she 'loathes and hates the French' and that 'her main concern is to automatically and venomously do the opposite to whatever France wishes for'.

In fact, when Catherine spoke of the French with such bitterness, she did not include the whole nation, only Louis XV and his ministers. A few French scribblers were also rapped on the knuckles. A priest, Chappe d'Auteroche, who was also an astronomer and geographer, returned from a journey to Siberia and proceeded to write a slanderous book about Russia. He dared to criticize all the imperial institutions, claimed that the Lithuanian peasants were short of bread in winter and stated that Siberian vegetation was extremely sparse. To prove that this was not true, Catherine sent Voltaire nuts from a Siberian cedar. She was sure that this frightful book had been set up by the Duc de Choiseul. She wanted a famous French writer to produce a lightning reply to it. But, as the famous French writers were not all that eager, she had to set about the task herself. This avenging rebuttal was entitled *The Antidote*. The first two parts appeared in a splendid edition in 1771; a sequel was promised, but never saw the light of day. Catherine, by this time, had lost interest. She had other enemies to deal with now in the shape of the Turks. In 1773, she told her friend Madame de Bielke that *The Antidote* would remain unfinished, 'as the author has been killed by the Turks'. She went on refusing to admit officially to the authorship of this work. Another provocation appeared in the shape of an ex-secretary at the French embassy in St Petersburg, Claude Carloman de Ruhlière. He had just brought out in Paris a pamphlet relating Catherine's seizure of the throne. She was described in it as an adventuress who had murdered her husband. When she heard that she had been libelled, Catherine first thought of buying back all the copies in circulation; then she told her ambassador, Prince Golitsin, to get the French authorities to seize them. The government, to pacify the Empress, threatened Ruhlière with the Bastille if he did not hand over his papers. It was a mere formality. Almost immediately Monsieur, the king's brother, made Ruhlière his private secretary, thus protecting him. The affair remained there and the pamphlet continued to circulate. Diderot tried to mollify the Empress by writing: 'If, Madame, you regard respectability and virtue, the tattered rags of your sex, as all-important, then this work is indeed a satire against you; but if you are more concerned with a broader view, with masculine and patriotic ideas, then you appear there as a great princess, and taking all in all he does you more credit than not.'[1] Catherine accepted this flattering interpretation and swallowed her rage. She was relying on the finest minds of the century to defend her in the eyes of posterity: Voltaire, Grimm, d'Alembert, Diderot ... As usual it was Voltaire who set the tone for the panegyrics. But was he totally disinterested? Catherine did not only send him letters. Nice sums of money often travelled from St Petersburg to this corner of Switzerland. At the end of 1770 Voltaire spoke to the Empress of the good watchmakers of Ferney, who would be so honoured if she ordered some watches from them. She answered that she would like 'a few thousand roubles' worth'. He sent her a whole caseful, with a bill for 39,238 pounds. She was horrified by this figure, but resigned herself to paying. After all it was not too much to pay the high priest of her cult. The war against the Turks whipped up the imagination of 'the old dotard of the Alps'. He called Sultan Mustapha III 'the Crescent's fat pig', and, despite being an enemy of violence, called for a war without mercy. 'Why make peace, when you can push on so far with your conquests?' he wrote. 'War is very useful to a country, when it is successfully waged on one's frontiers. The nation then becomes more active and industrious, as well as more powerful.'

And again:

'Madame, Your Imperial Majesty has brought me back to life by killing the Turks. The letter I had the honour of receiving, of the 22nd September, made me leap from my bed crying: "Allah! Catherine!" I was right, I was a better prophet than Mohammed! God and your soldiers heard me when I sang: *"Te Catharinam laudamus te dominam confitemur!"* The Angel Gabriel had thus informed me of the complete destruction of the Ottoman army, of the capture of Khosin, and pointed out to me the road to Yassi. I am, Madame, really overjoyed; I am delighted and I thank you.'

He went even further: he wanted to actually take part in the glorious Turkish campaign, disembowel a few infidels, enter Constantinople, replace the cross on the dome of St Sophia, liberate Athens, and wander with Catherine, talking philosophy in the Agora. It was a pity he was too old at seventy. However, he said, he was able to render a great

[1] Waliszewski *Around the Throne*.

service to the Russian people who were fighting so bravely. A few years beforehand he had invented a war machine, modelled on Assuern's chariot with scythes. The plans for this murderous machine had not received the approval of the French government. Voltaire firmly believed that if Versailles had adopted it, France would have won the Seven Years War. So now he was offering his invention to enable Catherine to speed up the extermination of the Turks.

'I am not in the killing business,' he wrote to her. 'But yesterday two charming German murderers assured me that these chariots would have an overwhelming effect in their first battle, and that it would be impossible for a battalion to resist the novelty and speed of such an attack.'

Catherine was mistrustful, and replied evasively that these assault vehicles would no doubt be a fearful weapon but that for the moment her soldiers' courage was sufficient to impress the enemy. Voltaire's pride was wounded, and he pretended to believe that his project had not been turned down, but simply set aside for future consideration. Much harder to bear was the insult he received from the Council of the Genevan Republic when they refused to allow young Swiss girls to travel to Russia to become governesses to the children of Russian aristocrats. At Catherine's request, he had personally overseen the recruitment of the young ladies. And now it had all collapsed at the last minute. What a fool he would look in front of his 'Semiramis'! He protested. The scholar Tronchin replied in the name of all his compatriots: 'Monsieur de Voltaire, the Council regards itself as the father of all its citizens; consequently it cannot allow its children to establish themselves in a country whose sovereign is strongly suspected of having allowed her husband to be murdered, and where the wildest behaviour is allowed to flourish!'[1]

Really these Genevans wouldn't use their eyes or ears. They accused the Russians of barbaric behaviour when, in the midst of a war with Turkey, Catherine was planning to build a museum in her capital. Yes, she had made her dream a reality. The new Winter Palace, built by the Italian, Rastrelli, had an annex built on to it by the Frenchman Vallin de Lamothe. This elegantly proportioned building was baptized 'The Hermitage'. It was linked to the main building by a sort of covered bridge. The first masterpieces began to appear in the gallery. The Empress commissioned Diderot, who was a great connoisseur, to buy paintings, statues, furniture and medallions. The more absorbed she was in her political life the more she felt the need, from time to time, to

[1] Jean Orieux *Voltaire*.

escape with a few friends to rooms full of beautiful shapes and colours. It was true, and she admitted it herself, that her artistic taste was not perfect, but all the monarchs she admired, Louis XIV in particular, had been collectors of one sort or another. And she loved amassing possessions. 'It is not love of art,' she said, 'it is greed. I am a glutton rather than a taster.' She bought from everywhere, things that were sometimes very expensive, sometimes given away, both singly or in bulk. The first thing she bought was a lot that Frederick II had refused for reasons of economy. Then she obtained, for 180,000 roubles, the personal treasures of Count Brühl, the King of Poland's ex-minister. In 1772, thanks to the efforts of Tronchin, Diderot, Prince Golitsin and Count Betsky, she acquired for 438,000 pounds the five hundred and sixty-six masterpieces forming the Crozat Collection. There were Raphaels, Guidis, Poussins, Van Dycks, Rembrandts, Teniers', Veroneses, Titians, Clouets, Watteaus, Murillos ... An avalanche from the French, Italian, Dutch and Flemish schools. Diderot wrote to Falconet: 'Ah! my friend Falconet, now we have changed! We sell our paintings and sculptures in peace-time. Catherine buys them in the midst of war. The sciences, the arts, good taste and wisdom are moving north, and barbarism, with its attendants, is approaching the south.' But Diderot was worried at the thought of all these masterpieces travelling to their new country. In the previous year, the ship carrying the Braancamp collection, which Catherine had bought in Holland for 60,000 crowns, had gone down in the Baltic sea. This time, however, the journey went well and the seventeen crates arrived safely at the Hermitage after several weeks on board ship. A few months later, Catherine had the pleasure of buying up the collection of her declared enemy, the Duc de Choiseul, at a public auction. Quite insatiable, she bought, as one lot, all the Duc d'Orléans' engraved stones, ordered paintings from Chardin and Vernet, and had a Diana by Houdon sent over, which had been turned down by the Louvre for being too scantily clad.

She wandered amongst these riches which were scattered through the enormous rooms, ruminating on her own glory. 'My little museum is such,' she wrote to Grimm, 'that to go to it and come back to my room takes three thousand steps. There I wander amongst a quantity of objects that I love and enjoy, and it is these winter walks which keep me on foot and in good health.'[1]

To give herself even more pleasure during the winter she had an enormous greenhouse with a glass roof built on the second floor of the

[1] Waliszewski *The Story of an Empress.*

Winter Palace, with lawns, trees, flower-beds, fountains and birds flying freely around. Outside the snow slowly came down, the runners of sledges grated as they slid along, the Neva was ice-bound, and the white guards outside looked like great clumsy bears; and in here the gentle warmth of summer made the plants flourish. Catherine loved the thought of denying the existence of winter. In any case, she was attracted by any idea that seemed humanly impossible: she decided to have an enormous rock brought to St Petersburg, as a plinth for the equestrian statue of Peter the Great that she had commissioned from Falconet. She had seen it in Finland in 1768, with Falconet and Betsky, when builders were looking for granite suitable for building the quays of the Neva. It was a gigantic, sparkling primitive stone shaped like a wave about to break. According to the specialists' calculations, it must have weighed over three million pounds.[1] It was twenty-two feet high, forty-two feet long, thirty-four feet wide, and deeply sunk into soft earth. Catherine dreamt of this pedestal for two years – it seemed that it was rooted for ever in a deserted landscape. But she had to have her rock, even if it meant forcing half her subjects to drag it to St Petersburg. Peter the Great would not have hesitated. A reward of seven thousand roubles was offered to the person who could think up the best way of moving it. After several attempts, an ingenious system was installed: beams with carved gutters, with brass balls in them on which the monolith could be rolled. A hundred horses were used to pull it. Catherine herself watched over the mechanism being installed. The journey lasted for a year, on a road built for the purpose. When the monumental block of stone arrived at last in the Admiralty Square near the banks of the Neva, the populace was struck with religious awe: the 'little mother' Catherine could not only defeat the Turks, she could move mountains.

However, it was easier for Catherine to tear out of the ground a rock implanted there since the beginning of time than it was to shape the characters of her nearest and dearest. As he grew up, her son, Grand Duke Paul, became uglier and more tormented. In 1770, at the time of the victories over the Turks, he was sixteen. His bulging, washed-out blue eyes had a wild expression and his bull-dog features twitched uncontrollably. He suffered from epileptic fits, and saw his murdered father in nightmares. Very early on, he listened to the Court rumours and began to hold his mother responsible for this death. He was finally convinced when he read Ruhlière's pamphlet which was slipped to him by trouble-making advisors. He saw himself as Hamlet. Vague ideas of

---

[1] Two million pounds more than the largest of the obelisks brought to Rome.

vengeance went through his mind. He was disgusted by the Empress's relationship with Gregory Orlov, and reacted by idolizing the father he had hardly known. Like him, Paul had a passion for military exercises. The regiment, with its smell of leather, cartridge grease, powder and sweat appeared to him as the best escape from the boredom of everyday life. He lived from one parade or shooting-match to the next. At the same time, he suffered from persecution mania. Despite his mother's solicitude towards him, he was always afraid that she was about to have him poisoned or stabbed. He only had to see her to think of death; the atmosphere of the morgue hovered around her. One day, he found tiny pieces of glass in a dish that a servant presented to him; he turned pale with fury, leapt out of his chair, ran gesticulating through the Palace to the Empress and shouted to her face that she was trying to kill him. Catherine lectured him very calmly and he gave in, with his head bowed. As these scenes repeated themselves, however, she became less and less fond of this shifty and sour adolescent. She knew all too well that he was impotently cursing and insulting her behind her back. He reminded her of Peter III. She saw in him the disruption of her peace of mind. And indeed of her position. 'He is thought to be vindictive and single-minded in his views,' wrote the French chargé d'affaires, Sabatier de Cabre, on the 20th April 1770. 'He is only to be feared if, through the repression of a strong character, hatred, dishonesty and perhaps petty-mindedness should emerge instead; thus the nobility that might have developed in him will have been forever stifled by the terror that his mother has always inspired in him ... It is true that the Empress, who sacrifices everything else for the sake of appearances, observes none towards her son. Before him, she always behaves and speaks like a sovereign, and she disgusts the young Prince by the dryness and neglect she shows towards him. She has never treated him as a mother should. The Grand Duke behaves with her as if he were before a judge.'

Catherine's other son, little Count Bobrinsky, who had been brought up in a gentle atmosphere, exasperated her by his laziness and inconsequence. His father, Gregory Orlov, was also worried and dissatisfied. His liaison with the Empress had been going on for ten years when the Turkish war broke out. The original passion had gradually given way to a sort of voluptuous affection interspersed with quarrels. They were seen as a couple of old lovers, tired of each other but unable to separate. Gregory Orlov suffered from being a mere provider of nocturnal pleasures, and tried to prove that he was able to keep up with her thoughts as well as her frolics. He started to read, and began a correspondence with Jean-Jacques Rousseau; he became interested in painting, then agronomy, but each time his enthusiasm died down. This lazy and superficial sybarite, built like a giant, was now bitterly aware that without the Empress, he was nothing. The larger Catherine's figure became in the political landscape, the smaller he appeared in the shadow of the imperial skirts. Whenever he offered an opinion on public affairs she would silence him with kisses. It was as if he was the female part of this unusual couple. And it was true – the little German princess had not only changed countries on coming to Russia, she had also changed her sex. It was a double emigration. When she thought about women, Catherine did not feel she belonged to this weak, frivolous and whining species. Only her entrails had the same demands, the same pulsations as those of her sisters. But her mind was that of a conquering male. When he took this Amazon, Gregory Orlov was surprised that, once in bed, she was still capable of behaving like a mistress. He became depressed and complained; he wanted at least to cover himself in glory in the war, like his brother Alexis. But when he spoke of going to fight the Turks, Catherine refused to let him go. She claimed that she needed his presence and his advice. In fact he knew quite well that she was keeping him purely for his services in bed. The only battlefield he was allowed to enter was Catherine's bedroom. And he was summoned there less and less often. She was totally preoccupied with affairs of State. She was forty; he was thirty-four. In order to distract himself, he was secretly unfaithful to her with any chance meeting. Anyone would do, whether she was aristocrat or commoner. But these furtive conquests in alcoves did not satisfy his ambition. He never stopped thinking of Catherine even in the arms of others. He longed to amaze and subjugate her once and for all. He at last had an opportunity to do so, just as he was beginning to see no escape from his state of gilded slavery: a plague epidemic had broken out in Moscow. The local authorities were soon unable to handle it. Orders were given that, to avoid contagion, there were to be no gatherings at markets or in church; the people refused to obey. Since this was a scourge from God the only remedy, thought the faithful, was prayer. And now they were being forbidden to kiss their miracle-bearing icons. They rebelled, cried out treason, and broke down the doors of the churches. Faced with this assault the Archbishop of Moscow decided to remove the holy images. When he arrived in person from the Kremlin to see that his orders were carried out, he was recognized by the mob, attacked, thrown to the ground, trampled underfoot and killed. The whole city then collapsed into disorder, despair, fear, violence and madness. Gregory Orlov begged Catherine to allow him to travel to Moscow to bring the crowds to their senses. He enjoyed danger, had great physical courage and could take the initiative. He had shown this at the time of the *coup d'état* which had brought Catherine to the throne. She must now allow him to display these qualities once again. After years of softness and idleness, he needed to prove himself, in his own eyes as well as those of the Empress. Catherine's decision might seem surprising: while she remained opposed to Gregory Orlov returning to the army, she consented to his departure for Moscow. Did she not realize that he was running a far greater risk there than he would be in some luxurious army headquarters far from the battlefield? Some people around her whispered that she was sending him to his death because she was bored with his emptiness and his pretensions. Others said that the hope of seeing him gloriously succeed in this mission had overcome all considerations of safety. Others again mentioned the name of a possible replacement, Wysocky... And indeed it did appear that Catherine wanted to get rid of her tiresome lover for a few weeks whilst at the same time, out of charity, providing him with a chance to carry out a noble and vital mission.

On the 2nd October, 1771, Gregory Orlov set off, full of energy, for Moscow. There, with astonishing boldness and efficiency, he imposed sanitary measures on the hostile inhabitants, accompanied doctors to patients' bedsides, watching over the distribution of medicine, and helped with the removal of bodies which were rotting in the houses and even in the streets. Seven or eight hundred people were dying every day. Gregory Orlov had the victims' clothes burnt. He was everywhere at once, and hardly slept at all. His authority gave heart to those who had hesitated, and appeased the rebels. He seemed to be in control of the illness. In three months the epidemic had died down. He returned to St Petersburg a conquering hero. Catherine put up a triumphal arch for him at Tsarskoe Selo. A French artist, Mademoiselle Collot, a pupil of Falconet, sculpted a bust of Moscow's saviour. A medal was struck at the same time bearing a portrait of the hero with a symbolic one of the Roman hero Curtius,[1] and the inscription: 'Russia also has such sons'. However, these marks of admiration and gratitude did not quite suffice to convince Gregory Orlov of his complete return to favour. Catherine might well show great joy at his return; there was, nonetheless, a curious contradiction between the honours showered on him in public and the coldness of his reception in private. Now that he was the hero of the battle against the plague, he wanted to return to his position as lover. But the door of the imperial bedchamber was now only rarely opened to him. His vanity suffered, even if his flesh did not. Desire for

[1] Curtius, according to the legend, had thrown himself off a precipice to save his country.

Catherine had long since died down, but desire to appear, dominate and shine had not. Whatever happened, he would not surrender his place to anybody. He would kill, if need be, any rival who dared to present himself. Catherine knew this and discreetly kept an eye on her splendid and moody companion.

CHAPTER XVII

The Grand Duke's Marriage

Bender, Ackerman, Braila and Bucharest all fell before the victorious Russians. Frederick II sent his brother, Heinrich, to St Petersburg, to persuade Catherine to begin peace negotiations with the Turks. She was being difficult – she had to have Moldavia and Wallachia. Indeed her counsellors urged her to be even more demanding, since the enemy was collapsing. Thereupon, Austria decided to occupy the county of Zias, in Poland, on the false pretext of making itself more secure. Catherine was not angry and let them carry on. By accepting the Austrian occupation, she justified her own intervention in advance. Since Austria had helped herself, 'Why shouldn't we take something as well?' she declared cynically. In January 1772, she concluded a secret agreement between herself, Frederick II and Joseph II on the partition of Poland. The feeble Stanislaus Poniatowski learned afterwards of the amputations higher powers had decided to make on the body of his country. Russia had annexed White Russia with the towns of Polotzk, Vitebsk, Orcha, Mogilev, Mstislavl – a total of 1,600,000 inhabitants. Russia took Warnia and the Palatinates of Pomerania, except for Danzig, with 900,000 inhabitants. As for Austria, despite Maria-Theresa's pious protestations, she took the lion's share – Galicia with 2,500,000 inhabitants. Poland thus lost a third of its territory. The final treaty, signed in St Petersburg (on the 5th August 1772), stated in its preamble that these amputations had been made 'to re-establish order in the interior of this country, and to give it a political existence which conforms better with the interests of its geographical position'.

These presumptuous excuses fooled nobody. Stanislaus Poniatowski, as usual, accepted the Empress's decisions but the Polish nobility shook with rage and humiliation. Throughout Western Europe cries of indignation were heard about these three robbers who had pillaged an unprotected country. Lampoons, scurrilous pamphlets, caricatures, and avenging poems poured out of the garrets and into the drawing-rooms. Even Maria-Theresa, whose son Joseph II had happily taken part in the carve-up, declared: 'I blush with shame.' The Poles, in desperation, called on France and England to help them. But in France, the fiery

Duc de Choiseul had been replaced by the Duc d'Aiguillon, a cautious man who had no wish to start a war 'for the sake of Poland's lovely eyes'. And England was content to deplore the situation without moving a single pawn on the chessboard. There remained the philosophers. Would they castigate the woman they normally worshipped? Of course not. Once again, they defended this 'enlightened monarch' whose troops had crossed the Polish frontier purely in order to 'combat fanaticism'.

As Helvetius used to say, 'Anything becomes legitimate, even virtuous, if it is said to be for the public good.' And Voltaire, describing the three accomplices in the dismemberment of Poland, declared: 'Now we have three good and fine figures under the same umbrella.' After the first partition he expressed the wish 'that they do not stop in the midst of such a fine venture'. The Polish rebellion appeared to him as an 'Italian-style farce, representing everything that is disgraceful and craven about this century'.[1] He finally dared to write: 'It might appear amusing and, indeed, paradoxical to support freedom and tolerance by violent methods, but really the Poles' intolerance is so insupportable that they do deserve to have their ears boxed.' And again, to Catherine: 'I am not a murderer, but I think I could become one for your sake.'

So the pacifist philosopher became a propagandist for aggression, out of devotion to his 'Semiramis'. She, for her part, confessed to Grimm: 'I may be good, and I am as gentle as anybody, but I find that, by nature, I cannot help terribly wanting what I want.' And she 'terribly wanted' Poland; and she was to get it, piece by piece. She was quite carried away by this first success. She also 'terribly wanted' the Crimea, access to the Caucasus and the basin of the Danube, and the freedom of the Black Sea. To achieve this she would have to bring the Turks to their knees. By the spring of 1772, they showed signs of being willing listeners. Peace negotiations began in the small town of Foksàny in Moldavia. The Empress decided that her lover Gregory Orlov should represent her at this meeting, triumphant as he still was after his victory over the plague in Moscow. Should he consider this posting as an honour or was she once more trying to remove him from her presence for a few months?

He set off in great splendour, accompanied by a royal suite. Catherine had given him a costume embroidered on every seam: he looked so splendid in this outfit, that, at the moment of separation, she was once more overcome by the sight of him. One look brought back all the emotions she had felt when she was Grand Duchess. She wrote to her

[1] Waliszewiski *Around the Throne*.

friend, Madame de Bielke: 'My angels of peace (the envoys) are at this very moment, I believe, face to face with the horrible bearded Turks. Count Orlov, who, I am not exaggerating, is the handsomest man of his generation, must seem like a seraph compared with those bumpkins; his attendants were selected for their brilliance ... But he outshines everybody else. He is such an unusual ambassador; nature has been outstandingly generous to him in all aspects – appearance, wit, heart and soul! ... '

When he reached Foksàny, Gregory Orlov dazzled the Russians and Turks there with his arrogant splendour. The mission had gone to his head – he now saw himself as the Tsar in person, not just the lover. He strutted and preened himself, held forth with his hazy ideas, and foolishly pontificated about everything. Although his business was to make peace, he longed to start the war again, to take command and outshine all the other Russian generals on the battlefield. He argued with General Rumyantsov in front of the whole assembly, and threatened to have him hanged if he disagreed with him; he ignored the instructions sent to him by Panin, and considered seizing Constantinople. He would muddle the discussions with his untimely interruptions, and then he suspended the proceedings altogether in order to throw a series of splendid parties, where he would appear in the famous diamond-studded costume.

Catherine received worrying reports from Foksàny about her flamboyant 'ambassador'. Still more unsettling were the rumours which were flying around the capital. Orlov's enemies took pains to let Her Majesty know about his extra-imperial adventures. Once she was certain that she had been deceived, Catherine tried to control her wounded pride. There was no question of recalling the unfaithful Gregory in order to punish him, or even simply to ask for explanations. Their relationship had for a long time been no more than an old habit. While appreciating her lover's beauty and energy, she no longer felt the excitement of newly-discovered pleasure when she was with him. The best thing to do was to replace him – and quickly. There was no shortage of candidates. Catherine reviewed the choice. There was, obviously, Potemkin, that poor, noble and witty young officer who had given her his pennant on the day of the fateful march to Peterhof. Since then, he had participated in the works of the Great Commission with a great deal of spirit and competence. He had been picked out by Catherine, and had become both a member of the inner circle at the Hermitage and an object of the Orlovs' jealousy. The gigantic and violent Alexis had quarrelled with him over a billiard game, and put out his eye in the fight. The Empress remained interested in Potemkin even though he only had one eye, and a squint in the remaining one. His charm was both intellectual and sensual – a combination much appreciated by Catherine. She followed her protégé's career very closely, and kept him informed about matters of state; she provided him with a French tutor and urged him to rejoin the army. His bravery at the battle of Khotin earned him medals and the rank of major general. The more irritated she was by Orlov's whims, the more Catherine thought about 'the other one'. Unfortunately 'the other one' was detained by faraway military operations. She would have to look elsewhere – she could not wait. Nikita Panin recommended a certain Alexander Vasilchikov – a twenty-eight-year-old ensign in the Horse Guards. He belonged to a distinguished Russian family, was handsome and strong, but not very intelligent. However, he was not required for his conversation. Catherine looked him over at Tsarskoe Selo, where he was one of the capering escorts around her carriage. One glance was enough, and that same evening Vasilchikov came to dine at Her Majesty's table. When she left Tsarskoe Selo for Peterhof, she gave him a gold snuff-box inscribed: 'For the good bearing of the bodyguards.' Other gifts followed, and finally the supreme one – access to the Empress's bed.

The interim lover fulfilled his task so well that Catherine made him a Gentleman of the Bedchamber, bestowed on him the order of St Alexander Nevsky, and installed him temporarily in Gregory Orlov's apartments. At forty-three she could have been the mother of this young man who was so energetic in bed and so shy in the drawing-room. She was attracted to young flesh. All her life she chose men much younger than herself, so as never to be disappointed. This one renewed her vitality and good humour.

At Court, everybody was amazed. They had all become accustomed to Orlov's failings; after ten years he had become an institution. Would they now have to bow down before this pretty little officer? The Tsarina had capriciously picked him out of the crowd, and was now imposing him upon them with brazen calm. The foreign diplomats were very disturbed. 'In general, most people at Court disapprove of the affair,' wrote Baron de Solms to Frederick II. 'She has caused a great commotion amongst them, and amongst the friends and relatives of Count Orlov, as well as all the servants. They look sulky and discontent . . . ' As for Gunning, the English ambassador, he was even harsher: 'This successor of Orlov's finally proves how weak and blemished is Her Majesty's nature.' Catherine took no notice of public opinion and enjoyed herself by coddling her new lover. She gave him a house, an estate with seven thousand serfs, jewels, paintings and trinkets, all for the pleasure of hearing him stammer out his gratitude. 'I was no more than a kept woman,' Vasilchikov was to say later, 'and I was treated as such.' However, at the time he was naively thrilled by his new position.

Gregory Orlov, of course, soon heard about his demotion from his friends in St Petersburg. The shock affected his reason. He decided that peace negotiations could go to the devil, and he set off at speed to St Petersburg, leaving the Turkish and Russian delegates dumbfounded. The fastest courier took sixteen days to cross Russia from south to north. Gregory Orlov rode without stopping, exhausting one horse after another, and reached the outskirts of the capital in two weeks. But the Empress, meanwhile, had been warned of his intentions, and was both angry and apprehensive. Anything could happen with this hothead around. She had the locks of her new lover's apartment changed just in case, and placed guards at the approaches to St Petersburg. Then she sent a messenger to Gregory Orlov with orders that he should proceed to his castle at Gatchina, and there await her decision on his fate. He agreed to go into quarantine, and she was grateful to him for his apparent resignation. Although she was angry that he had abandoned his post as negotiator, she could not help being moved that he had done so out of love for her. The Empress condemned him, but the woman forgave him. She had no wish to see him again at Court but she sent Betsky, Tchernychev and Alsouviev, one after the other, to assure him of her good will. She demanded that he should voluntarily resign from all the positions he held, but at the same time wrote to him every day. Although she publicly flaunted her new lover, she still wanted to know what the old one was eating and drinking, and whether he had enough linen. She showered him with farewell gifts: a few thousand peasants, a set of silver, another 'for everyday use', furniture, and all the objects from Orlov's apartment in the Imperial Palace ... Her ministers were worried at seeing her neglect the affairs of the realm. One day, on an impulse, she sent Panin to Gatchina to demand from Gregory Orlov the diamond-framed miniature that she had given him, and that he always wore on his costume. The supplanted lover proudly handed the diamond mounting over, but refused to be separated from the portrait. When he heard that he had been declared out of office, but was allowed to travel 'for his health', he burst out laughing: he was in excellent health, and the only journey he wished to make was the one between Gatchina and St Petersburg. To soothe this madman's feelings, Catherine conferred on him the title of Prince on the 4th October, 1772.

He immediately assumed that he had been forgiven and he

reappeared at Court one evening at Her Majesty's card-table. She received him coldly but did not send him away. Everybody thought that he was in a strange state – he twitched, his eyes shone, his speech was jerky. 'He behaved,' wrote Sabatier de Cabre, 'like a man who wanted to be locked up if he could not return to his previous position.' In a lucid moment he told this same Sabatier de Cabre, 'that he would be quite happy to live in a tavern, and would not miss his past glory at all, but that he could not bear to see the Empress making a fool of herself before the whole of Europe.' He added that 'the Empress writes the most glowing notes to Vasilchikov, and loads him with endless gifts.'[1]

However, far from bearing a grudge towards Vasilchikov for having replaced him in the Empress's favours, he made friends with him, and took to joking in public about his own disgrace. These unsuitably high spirits in the face of misfortune began to embarrass and irritate even his friends. He frequented both drawing-rooms and slums, flirted with ladies-in-waiting and slept with prostitutes, guzzled, got drunk, rambled and generally gave the impression of a man bent on self-degradation. The new French minister, Monsieur Durand de Distroff, wrote; 'Nature has made Gregory Orlov a Russian peasant, and he will remain thus until the end ... He is with the young ladies of the Court from morning until night. He dines and sups with them; the table is dirty, the food disgusting, and the Prince delights in this way of life ... His moral conduct is no better. He loves childish things; his soul is like his taste – anything is good enough for him. He loves in the same way as he eats – he is as happy with a Kalmuk or a Finnish girl as with the prettiest woman at the Court; that's the sort of oaf he is.'

At last the 'oaf-prince' agreed to travel. As he journeyed through Europe, he dazzled the crowds with his splendid baggage; he played everywhere for high stakes, and met several great men, one of whom, Diderot, remarked: 'He is like an ever-boiling pan of water which never cooks anything.' On his return, the Empress gave him a marble palace. So as to keep up with her, he gave her, on St Catherine's day, an enormous blue Persian diamond the 'Nadir-Shah' (later known as the 'Orlov diamond'), worth 460,000 roubles. Although there was no longer any physical relationship between them, Catherine had so many memories in common with him that she put up with behaviour from him which would have been intolerable in another. 'He has a primitive mind which goes its own way,' she wrote to Grimm, 'and mine simply follows.'

This 'primitive mind' suddenly fixed itself onto a charming young

---

[1] Dispatch from M. Sabatier de Cabre, 30th October, 1772.

girl called Catherine Zinoviev. He was forty-three, she was fifteen and his first cousin. The old rake forgot all about the Empress at the sight of such innocence. He was in love again, but now his only aim was to attract her: Catherine Zinoviev was bowled over by this prince who had seduced so many women, and when he proposed, she eagerly accepted. But their union was forbidden by the Senate, as marriages within families were against both the civil and religious laws. But Catherine was watching. She felt no jealousy about her erstwhile lover, and she cancelled the Senate's decree. The young couple set off on their honeymoon, loaded down with gifts.

There is no doubt that it was Gregory Orlov's fault that the Foksàny talks broke down. Catherine did not hold this against her 'envoy extra-ordinary', and ordered others to continue the peace negotiations, this time in Bucharest. But the Turks were being obstinate. As the war dragged on, Catherine wrote to the Russian ambassador, Obreskov, now released from the Seven Towers and conducting the talks: 'If we cannot obtain independence for the Tartars, free navigation on the Black Sea and a few bases between the Sea of Azov and the Black Sea, we will have gained nothing, despite our victories.' Meanwhile, Rumyantsov had crossed the Danube and defeated the Turks at Choumla.

Catherine, now at Tsarskoe Selo, ordered a new recruitment drive, organized the financing of the military operations and studied plans for a hospital for pensioners, and a savings bank for war widows and orphans. At the same time she would peruse reports from provincial governors and, for her own pleasure, oversee the transformations of the Palace and the park. 'At the moment I am mad about English gardens with their curves, gentle slopes, ponds shaped like lakes and archipelagos in solid earth; I now despise straight lines and parallel alleys,' she wrote to Voltaire. 'I hate fountains which torture the water into unnatural courses; statues are relegated to galleries and halls – in short my plant mania is now subject to my Anglomania. It is in the midst of such occupations that I calmly await peace.'

She was concerned with another 'occupation' which is not mentioned in this letter, and that was the planning of some sort of future for her son, whose moody and changeable nature was fast deteriorating. How was she to settle the nineteen-year-old Grand Duke's mind, and ensure a balanced way of life for him? Nikita Panin suggested that he should be married to a healthy and attractive young girl. This retarded child would only be brought to his senses by a union with a person of quality. And Her Majesty might then have a grandson whom she could bring up according to her own views. Catherine was attracted by the idea. But how was one to find the ideal fiancée? They must ask Frederick II, obviously! Had he not already shown his good judgment by producing Catherine for Peter? He could find another Catherine for Paul, thirty years later. When Frederick heard what was expected of him, he immediately thought of the daughters of the Landgrave of Hesse-Darmstadt. In this way he would reinforce the links between Russia and the German confederation. The two eldest daughters were already married, but the three youngest, Wilhelmina, Amalia and Louise were still available. Frederick could not decide which was the most suitable as future Empress of Russia, so he offered them all. Catherine, therefore, invited the mother and the three candidates to Russia; the father, as had happened in her own case, was not asked. That sort of person might only obstruct the marriage negotiations, with his Protestant scruples and worries about his offspring's happiness! The three young ladies hastily perfected their knowledge of French, improved their dancing, practised their curtseys, and completed their wardrobes. Their first stop was Berlin, where the King of Prussia inspected the 'merchandise', as he had done with Figchen. He was pleased with what he saw and gave the Landgrave 10,000 thalers towards his expenses. Catherine had sent a flotilla of four ships to carry the ladies. Andrew Razumovsky,[1] who was Grand Duke Paul's best friend, was in command of the frigate bearing the young ladies and their mother. He was immediately attracted by these charming passengers as they sailed towards a princely future, especially Wilhelmina. She, although she had one chance in three of becoming Tsarina, responded to his attentions. The weather was beautiful, with a calm sea, and the cabins were luxuriously furnished. And there, at the end of this dream of waves, sun and salty breezes, stood the Empress of all the Russias. As the three girls kissed her hand, one by one, Catherine remembered that day in February 1744 when she too had bowed for the first time before the Empress Elisabeth. But she had now reached such a level of power and glory that she could not allow herself any nostalgia about those distant and childish emotions. Success had wiped out any regrets she might have had. She received the terrified young girls with great kindness, and tried to put them at their ease.

Two days after the princesses' arrival, the Grand Duke had already chosen: he picked the eldest, Wilhelmina. She was pretty and high spirited, and Andrew Razumovsky liked her. Paul relaxed when he was with her, and found himself laughing at the slightest thing. But what did Wilhelmina make of this skull-like oaf who would soon be her husband? Catherine guessed at the young girl's disappointment, and

[1] The son of Cyril Razumovsky.

remembered her own feelings at the sight of Peter. It was all happening again, in the same place, but with different characters. The Landgravine, describing her daughter's reactions, was significantly reserved: 'The distinction that the Grand Duke has honoured her with does not appear to be disagreeable to her.' No more than that. The engagement was lavishly celebrated, and Wilhelmina became a Grand Duchess. She had to change her religion and her name, as Figchen had done in the past. She became Natalia. Her mother begged her never to cross the Empress. She regarded Catherine as incomparably great, 'a historical event'. Paul sneered when he heard his mother's praises being sung.

The Empress, too, held the Landgravine of Hesse-Darmstadt in high esteem. This wise and energetic woman reminded her of her native country. They had long conversations in German: Catherine spoke with the rough accent of the Stettin tradesmen. She described Russia in German to her guest, who listened, amazed. The Russian soul, she said, was like the steppes, whose horizon blends with the sky – unlimited, calm and sleepy at times, and then whipped by raging winds. The people were imbued with religious feeling and yet sometimes gave way to bestial instincts. Those who bowed down before icons were also capable of hacking up a priest, or disembowelling a nobleman. Russia was given to excess, in good as well as in evil. That is what Catherine said, but her criticism was tempered by love. She was as proud of having become Russian as she was of governing this great country. She wanted foreigners to admire the marvels of her capital. President Moser, Grimm and Louis, the Landgrave's eldest son, arrived to attend the wedding, and she insisted on showing them around herself. They saw the new painting in the Hermitage, the 'hanging gardens' in the Winter Palace, the Smolny Institute, where a bevy of young girls in uniform surrounded the Empress in silent adoration, and the apartment where she was bringing up some orphans – a little Turk found in a destroyed village, an orphaned Tartar girl, a little Russian boy who had been found half-naked in the snow... She had developed a great passion for children, having neglected her own when she was young. Although still in love and presumably actively so, she longed to be a grandmother. She looked tenderly at her daughter-in-law's slender figure and looked forward to it changing shape. The German visitors were highly impressed by their imperial hostess's goodness, good taste and intelligence. Grimm, whose literary correspondence she had subscribed to for ten years, paid her extravagant compliments but declined her invitation to him to settle in Russia. He said he could serve her cause better in Paris than in St Petersburg. In fact he dreaded the intrigues of this Court whose splendour he pretended to admire.

There was a succession of parties at Tsarskoe Selo: banquets, balls and picnics celebrating both the engagement and renewed victories over the Turks. The Landgravine was in poor health, and exhausted by the round of festivities: she suffered from vapours, gastric troubles and fever. She was attended by a doctor lent by Frederick II for the journey, and he prescribed bleeding and medication. Catherine laughed at her friend's little weaknesses. She had always scorned illness, even in herself. If her stomach was upset, she would starve herself; if she caught a chill she would order a ball with several hundred guests, so as to sweat out the infection in the crush. So, on a hot afternoon, she invited the Landgravine to plunge with her and the other ladies of the Court into a cold water bath. All the bathers wore fustian shirts, with their shoulders covered with cloaks, and their necks and heads wrapped in white scarves. They submerged themselves up to the chin and began to paddle and splash about, giggling. The Landgravine thought that the Empress and her women must have iron constitutions; she, who was afraid even of warm water, would never stand up to this ordeal. However, she let herself be dragged into the water and, after the first shock, was thrilled by this new Russian invention.

As the wedding-day approached, a problem emerged which reminded Catherine uncannily of her own beginnings at the Court. Natalia's (alias Wilhelmina's) father, a Protestant as Catherine's father had been, was also opposed to his daughter changing her religion. Catherine, Orthodox as Elisabeth had been, refused to give in on this point. Negotiations took place. Against his will, the Landgrave was forced to give in to his wife's arguments, but he did not attend the ceremony.

The wedding took place on the 29th September/10th October 1773 with great display and splendour. Paul was in Heaven. Natalia consoled herself for her amorous disappointment by looking to a glorious future. Catherine observed the couple with a mixture of hope and fear: now again there was an old court of which she was the centre, and a young court revolving around the lively young Grand Duchess. The present was imitating the past, and sometimes even aping it. Catherine felt slightly sad. The Landgravine prepared to return home with the two daughters still on her hands. Her son, Louis, entered the Russian army as commander of a brigade; he was eager to join the spring campaign against the Turks. The first snow began to fall in St Petersburg.

CHAPTER XVIII

Diderot and Pugachev

The Landgravine of Hesse-Darmstadt, her daughters and suite, and Grimm, were all still in St Petersburg when another guest arrived to join Catherine's charmed intellectual circle: Denis Diderot. The old philosopher who was home-loving and felt the cold, and who had hitherto only travelled as far as Montmorency to visit Madame d'Épinay, had at last decided to set out for this distant country. He wanted to thank his benefactress and speak to her about the financing of his next project: a new *Encyclopaedia*, a sort of index of ideas, to add to the index of things, a giant philosophical dictionary covering all human thought from the beginning of time. He was less awed by this ambitious project than he was by the prospect of crossing half of Europe to reach his beloved Empress's frozen and violent land. He suffered from stomach cramps and dreaded Russian food; he was also terrified of draughts. However he set out in May 1773, and at last arrived, exhausted, coughing and spitting, at La Haye and stayed there for three months with Prince Golitsin, resting. Then, as autumn was approaching, he set out for St Petersburg with Count Naryshkin, despite a violent attack of 'colic'. Huddled in the depths of his post-chaise, he hoped to arrive before the onslaught of winter. But it was already snowing as they entered the capital. Diderot was horrified and went straight to Falconet's house hoping to find there at least a little bit of France. But Falconet was most unwelcoming: he had no room for his compatriot and he was beset with problems, and not interested in anybody else's. Rejected by the sculptor, Diderot accepted Naryshkin's hospitality. He was woken the day after his arrival by the sound of bells and gunfire – it was the wedding day of Grand Duke Paul and Princess Wilhelmina, now called Natalia. After the nuptial ceremony, the celebrations continued for a fortnight. Diderot took no notice of the merrymaking and called on the Empress. His black costume scandalized the gaily-dressed courtiers. Catherine welcomed him with great warmth and friendliness, and he was immediately won over by the simplicity of her manner. She received him every day in her study, to converse 'for an hour or two'. This 'hour or two' would often continue until dinner-time. Diderot was completely at ease and would hold forth, yelping and gesticulating, until the Empress collapsed with laughter at his lively familiarity. 'He would seize her hands,' wrote Grimm, 'shake her arms, bang the table, just as if he were in the synagogue of the rue Royale.'[1] Catherine told Madame Geoffrin that she always made sure there was a table between her and Diderot, as she otherwise ended these conversations with 'bruises on my knees and my thighs'. Sometimes, in the heat of the argument, he would tear off his wig and throw it into the corner. The Tsarina would pick it up and hand it back to him, smiling. He would cry 'Thank you' and continue to harangue her, stuffing it into his pocket. First of all, he insisted on giving his views on Grand Duke Paul's education. After he had served a sort of statesman's apprenticeship in different departments of the administration, the young man should travel throughout Russia in the company of geologists, jurists and economists so as to learn about all aspects of his country. Then, after he had made his wife pregnant to ensure the succession, he should visit Germany, England, Italy and France.

Catherine would have been delighted if Diderot had limited himself to these wise suggestions. But his advice did not remain confined to education: he also wished to enlighten the Empress on the best way of governing her people. Was he not the apostle of liberal philosophy? Full of his role he set the Empress a forty-eight-point questionnaire covering a wide range of topics: How much did each province produce? How were veterinary colleges organized? How many Jews were there in the Empire? What was the relationship between 'masters and slaves'? Stung, she replied that there were no 'slaves' in Russia, only peasants attached to the land: the serfs, she declared, had free minds, even if their bodies were subject to some constraint. This was a strange euphemism indeed. Did she really think that, by giving thousands of moujiks to her lover, she was making free men of them? Diderot contradicted her, calling her 'my good lady', and quoting the Greeks and Romans, urged her to reform these institutions while there was still time. Having said that, he did admit that there was such a thing as a 'benevolent dictator', but that 'if two or three benevolent dictators succeed each other, people forget the value of opposition and freedom of opinion'. She shrugged. Really, her beloved philosopher had no conception of the realities of Russian life. 'Monsieur Diderot,' she said, 'I have listened with great pleasure to the outpourings of your brilliant mind; but your great principles, which I understand perfectly well, make fine theory but hopeless practice. When you plan all these reforms, you forget the

[1] Baron d'Holbach's house in Paris.

difference in our positions: you work with paper, which is supple and even, and places no obstacle in the way of your imagination, whilst I, poor Empress that I am, work with human skin, which is irritable and ticklish.' However he continued to give advice at random, and on all subjects: the schools curriculum, the plays that the pupils should perform, even foreign policy. Durand de Distroff had asked him to use his influence on the Empress to make peace with Turkey, and to draw closer to France: she roundly told the diplomat that she considered Diderot both too old and too young for this role as intermediary: 'He appears in some ways to be a hundred years old, and, in others, ten.' And when Diderot railed against the sycophantic courtiers, saying they should be damned in Hell for their flattery, she asked abruptly: 'Tell me, what is it they say in Paris about my husband's death?' Diderot was disconcerted and tried to change the subject, but she stopped him again: 'It seems that you are on your way, if not to Hell, at least to Purgatory.'

Diderot had come to sow the seeds of liberal thought in this uncultivated ground, but he gradually came to realize that the Empress had no intention, in the near future, of putting into practice the fine theories that he endlessly expounded to her. She nodded and smiled, and Russia continued as it always had done. All the same, he assembled his advice to her in a volume entitled *A Philosophical and Historical Mixture*. She greeted this document with great interest, and then put it away in a casket, out of sight and out of mind. As winter came to an end, Diderot began to think of returning home. He was not urged to stay. The Empress gave him a ring, a fur, his own carriage and 'three bags of a thousand roubles'. 'But,' he wrote to his wife, 'if I deduct from that the price of an enamel plaque and two paintings which I am giving to the Empress, the expenses of the journey, and the presents I must give to the Naryshkins . . . , we will only be left with five or six thousand francs, perhaps even less.'

Catherine had made no definite commitment on the publication of the new *Encyclopaedia*. That did not matter: for Diderot she possessed 'the soul of Brutus and the charms of Cleopatra'. There was a sad parting, in March 1774. Diderot was dreading the return journey, and with good reason: as they crossed the Duna, the ice gave way and the carriage began to sink slowly into the water. Just as he was about to disappear the old man was dragged out by his servants, while the horses drowned. The old philosopher escaped with a good fright, a fever and a bout of colic, and had to take to his bed. Three quarters of his luggage was lost. When he reached La Haye, however, he gathered enough strength to write his *Observations on Her Imperial Majesty's Instructions to the Deputies on the Making of Laws*. When she read this heartfelt document, Catherine could hardly control her rage. After a few months of talking to Diderot, she saw him as a fraud and a hollow dreamer. And now he had the cheek to criticize her *Nakaz*. 'This piece (the *Observations*) is a real hotch-potch, without any common-sense, judgment or insight,' she wrote to Grimm after Diderot's death. 'If my *Instructions* had been to Diderot's taste, everything would have been turned upside down.'

However, as soon as Diderot reached Paris, he sent an ecstatically grateful letter to his benefactress: 'I have the honour of writing to your Majesty from the bosom of my family. Fathers, mothers, sisters, children, grandchildren, friends, acquaintances – all fall at your feet to thank you for the kindness with which you overwhelmed me at your Court. You are now placed alongside your friend Caesar, and a little above your dangerous neighbour Frederick. There is still a place waiting beside Lycurgus and Solomon, and your Majesty will one day sit there. That is what the Franco-Russian philosopher is hoping for.'

Another 'Franco-Russian philosopher' was sourly observing his rival in the Empress's esteem. Voltaire was so irritated by Diderot's accounts and anecdotes about his long stay on the banks of the Neva, that he actually fell ill with jealousy. The old hermit had not received a letter from St Petersburg for months! Had Catherine turned away from him and become infatuated with another? He could no longer bear it, and wrote to his 'Semiramis of the North,' on the 9th August 1774:

'Madame, I am clearly in disgrace at your Court. Your Imperial Majesty has abandoned me for Diderot, Grimm or some other favourite. You have no regard for my age. I would understand it if your Majesty were a French coquette; but how can a victorious and lawgiving Empress be so flighty?... What crimes have I committed to cause such coldness? I realize that all passions come to an end, and this thought would make me die of sorrow, if I were not on the point of dying of old age...' Signed: 'Your admirer, the abandoned old Russian of Ferney.'

Catherine replied, in the same light tone: 'Live, sir, and let us make it up; we have no cause to quarrel... You are such a good Russian that you could not be Catherine's enemy.'

Voltaire was satisfied and said that he would lay down arms and 'return to his chains'. Now he dreamt of ending his days on the banks of the Neva (without, of course, believing in it). 'Why should I not have the pleasure of being buried in some corner of Petersburg, whence I could see you passing to and fro under your triumphal arches, crowned with laurels and olive branches?' He and Diderot tried to outdo one another with their compliments, each one more extravagant than the last. When Voltaire expressed a wish to die in Russia, Diderot, or so he said, longed to live there, because nowhere was there an easier exchange of ideas. 'I remember saying to Your Majesty that I had the mind of a slave in the land of so-called free men, and that I had discovered in myself the mind of a free man in the land of so-called slaves,' he wrote. 'These were not the words of a courtier, they were the truth.'

In fact, the departure of the Landgravine and her suite, and then that of Diderot, were a great relief to Catherine. For weeks she had had to suppress the fear inside her, in the midst of Court festivities and idle conversations with her philosopher. To have to listen to a hazy-minded French philosopher's views on the happiness of the serfs, while a popular revolt was simmering in the Urals, about to shake the foundations of the Empire – really she needed nerves of steel to bear it! The chief rebel's name, Emilian Pugachev, was already on everybody's lips. Who was he? A simple Cossack from the Don, who had fought in both the Seven Years War and the war against Turkey. He had deserted, been condemned, escaped, been caught, escaped again and disguised himself as an Old Believer monk; then he claimed to be Peter III, miraculously escaped from his assassins. Four fake Peter III's had already appeared in the South Western provinces between 1762 and 1770: Bogomolov, Kremenyev, Aslanbekov and Yevdomikov... perhaps the fifth was the real thing! The popular belief was that the tombs of great men were never completely closed. Who but a tsar could claim the gift of resurrection? To be sure Pugachev did not look in the least like Peter III. The Emperor had been tall, narrow-shouldered and spoke mainly in German. Pugachev was of medium height, broad-backed, had a black beard and spoke perfect Russian. But one shouldn't quibble with a ghost over details. The people were so desperate for a saviour that they immediately believed in this one. The country was suffering: Catherine had distributed so much land that the number of serfs had rapidly increased. The Polish and Turkish wars had put a heavier burden of taxation on the shoulders of the poor. Despite the Empress's promises, the Old Believers were being hunted down and persecuted. Workmen suffered in hideous conditions in the armament factories and the mines of the Urals, and troops often had to be called in to put down riots. The Cossacks' autonomy had been limited by order of the Empress, and these proud, free and brave men found it hard to accept the new regime. They formed a small and adventurous nation within the amorphous grey Russian mass. They had their own customs, their own laws, and their own leaders, and they wanted to carry on this proud way of life. And now this character Pugachev appeared in Yaik, south of the Urals, claiming to be Peter III and making inflammatory declarations. They were aimed at the rabble of discontented serfs from the farms and the factories, the Bachkirs, the dispossessed Kirghiz Muslims, and the Cossacks from all parts of the country. He promised them all freedom and riches. The Cossacks from Yaik were told that they would own the whole length of the Yaik river[1], and that they would receive payment in corn, silver and lead. The news spread like a burning fuse: Peter III had returned, after eleven years, to free his people from the yoke of servitude. His wife had tried to kill him because he wished for the good of his people. But God had saved him at the last minute because God loves Russia. The time had come to make 'the German, the Devil's daughter' pay for the crimes she had committed against the Tsar and the nation. The Cossacks rallied round this new leader in their thousands, and the peasants from the Urals and the South West gathered, armed with forks, scythes and axes to seize by force the right to happiness. Did they all believe that the leader was really the Emperor? Of course not. Perhaps the illiterate and superstitious peasants saw in him the 'little father' resurrected from the dead, but most of the more sharp-witted Cossacks regarded him simply as one of themselves, and capable of helping them towards victory. 'Does it matter whether he is the Tsar or not?' they said. 'We could make a prince out of muck. If he cannot conquer the Muscovite Empire, we will make our kingdom in Yaik.'[2] Thus in October 1773 he had assembled around him a strange army consisting of battle-hardened Cossacks, escaped serfs, mystical peasants, rebel factory workers and highwaymen. Carried away by the mob's enthusiasm, he no longer knew himself whether he really did have a holy mission to perform or was merely a clever charlatan. In any case he possessed the gift of moving crowds with his speeches. He often appeared in public, wearing a gold-embroidered caftan and a fur hat, with his chest covered in medals. His 'officers' surrounded him, also dressed in barbaric finery. This general staff travelled through the countryside with sabres drawn and banners blowing in the wind – Pugachev mockingly named his companions after the grandees of the Empire: Count Tchernychev, Count Vorontsov, Prince Orlov, Count Panin. He had roubles struck with his image on them and the inscription: 'Peter III, Emperor of all the Russias'. The human torrent gathered new strength in every village. A huge mob, fuelled by hatred, poured along the roads or sailed up the Volga, as they had done in the time of Strenka Razin, a bandit who had terrorized the country a hundred years before. The rich were abandoned by their servants and, as the rebels approached, holed

[1] Quoted by Gaissinovitch *The Pugachev Revolt*.
[2] The present-day Ural.

themselves up, terrified, in their vast houses. Their capture brought out a sort of demented brutality: the children were massacred, the women raped before being strangled amid coarse laughter, the noblemen mutilated, flayed alive, burnt and cut to pieces. The world had turned head over heels – now the starving and down-trodden were the master, and the masters lay dead in the mud. Pugachev handed out rewards; a hundred roubles for a dead nobleman or a sacked mansion, a thousand roubles and the title of general for ten dead noblemen and ten sacked mansions. The small forts, with their weak and terrified garrisons, fell one after the other as the howling mob streamed towards the North. Catherine sent a few regiments to the Volga region, but the soldiers had no wish to fight these 'brothers', whose rebellion they understood all too well, and they often changed sides during the night. General Karr, whom the Empress had great faith in, could not halt the advance of the rebels. So, while Catherine was peacefully conversing with Diderot, Orenburg was under siege. Pugachev wrote to the governor: 'You are tempting your luck, vermin, and putting yourself in the service of your father, the Devil.' On the 10th December, Catherine wrote to Sievers: 'Two years ago, we suffered from the plague in the heart of the Empire. Now, on its frontiers, we have a political plague ... With God's help we shall defeat this band of disorganized and lunatic vagabonds; they are nothing more than a collection of brigands led by a rash and shameless impostor. It will all end with the rope. But what a prospect – I hate the gallows! European public opinion will think we have returned to the era of Tsar Ivan Vassilievitch.' What exasperated Catherine more than anything was the fact that her husband, so unpopular in the past because of his Germanophilia, had become a sort of hero of Russian legend, a liberator, a martyr to the people's cause, who had miraculously reappeared on earth to chase away the usurper, drag down the great, and bring justice to the lowly. Her logical mind could not understand this murky crowd's *volte-face*. She was trying to judge an Eastern phenomenon with a Westerner's mind. Despite all her armies, all her cannons, all her fortresses, she felt a growing sense of panic. How long would this absurd and pitiful ghost pursue her? It was vital to defeat Pugachev, for the sake of both her country's and her own health. She replaced Karr, who had suffered many setbacks, with Bibikov, who methodically organized the attack. Pugachev had to retreat, surrounded by regular troops. But then Bibikov died and was replaced by the idle Prince Michael Shcherbatov. Pugachev immediately returned to battle and took the town of Kazan. In Nizhny Novgorod the serfs rose and devastated the whole region. Everybody expected the rebels to begin a march on Moscow and St Petersburg. Moscow was already preparing its defences: the police hunted down Pugachev's envoys, who were already busy promising the inhabitants that they would become free, that the poor would own the land, that the wicked would die and that the Empress would end her days in a convent.

The situation was exacerbated by the fact that the war against Turkey was continuing, with its ups and downs, and that the Grand Vizier's messengers were inciting the Muslim tribes of the Urals and the banks of the Caspian to rise and join Pugachev. Catherine wanted to finish with the foreign enemy as quickly as possible in order to concentrate on re-establishing order at home. She secretly instructed her envoys to conclude the peace negotiations. But the enemy finally laid down arms only after Suvorov's victory at Kozlodui and Rumyantsov's at Choumla on the Danube. In July 1774, after six years of war, a treaty was at last signed at Kutchuk-Kainardji. Russia gained the fortresses on the coast of the sea of Azov, a protectorate in the Crimea, the Khabardas and the steppe between the Boug and the Dnieper, access to the Black Sea and the Aegean, war compensation of 4,500,000 roubles, and the right to protect the religious freedom of the Sultan's Christian subjects.

Having thus fulfilled Peter the Great's dream, Catherine ordered her army to return North and disband Pugachev's rabble. Peter Panin[1] was made General in command, and Suvorov himself was summoned to the Volga. Pugachev was terrified by this enormous concentration of troops: he gave up his plan to march on Moscow and turned South again. His men were disappointed by a retreat they did not understand, and began to fear the consequences of their revolt. The impostor's magical authority began to fade rapidly, and more and more of his followers deserted him. Now he was surrounded only by desperate vagabonds and marauders. With General Mikhelson's regiments at his heels, he suffered a serious defeat on the 24th August/4th September 1774 at Sarepta; he tried to flee but his own men seized him, tied him up and handed him over in exchange for their own safety. Pugachev, brought before Panin, fell to his knees and publicly admitted to being an impostor, and to having sinned against God and Her Imperial Majesty. Chained up and locked in an iron cage, he was paraded on a cart, like a wild animal, through the provinces that had previously greeted him as a saviour. He was accompanied by a large armed escort, for fear of any popular movement. However, after his capture, the insurrection died out as if by magic.

When Pugachev reached Moscow, the end of his journey, he was exhausted and despairing and longed for death. He was not put to the

---

[1] The brother of the minister Nikita Panin.

rack, despite the nature of his crimes, as Catherine had forbidden the use of torture. But he had fallen from so high that his mind and health were affected and he fainted several times during his trial. The judges feared that he might cheat the executioner by dying before the appointed day. 'The Marquis de Pugachev[1] of whom you speak,' wrote Catherine to Voltaire, 'has lived a scoundrel and will die a coward.' And also: 'He cannot read or write, but he is a tough and determined man. Up to now there is no evidence that he was anybody's instrument . . . One must accept that Monsieur Pugachev was a master brigand and was not the servant of any living soul. Nobody since Tamburlaine has caused such destruction. He is hoping that his courage will bring him mercy. If it were only me he had offended, his reasoning would be correct and I would pardon him; but the Empire has its laws.'

Pugachev was condemned to be racked and then decapitated. Catherine wanted to appear more humane than Louis XV had been towards Damiens. The execution took place in Moscow, on the 10th/21st January 1775 before a great crowd. The nobility rejoiced but the people murmured in consternation. Could the real Emperor have been murdered once again? The impostor's accomplices were quartered, hanged or beheaded. Others were beaten, had their nostrils torn out and were condemned to penal servitude. The Tsarina reprieved the nine bandits who had betrayed their chief. Order had been restored and Catherine could breathe freely. For the past year she had felt the ground moving beneath her feet, as if she were on the deck of a storm-tossed ship. But she had held the wheel: she had kept on course; she was satisfied.

In the countryside however there were merciless reprisals. Sometimes the landlords took the law into their own hands. Accounts were settled on a national scale. Each village had a scaffold in the main square. People were hanged, beaten and deported. The Yaik river, with its bloody connotations, was re-named the Oural. It was forbidden to mention the name of 'the wicked rebel' Pugachev. In 1773, Bibikov had written: 'What matters is not Pugachev, but the general discontent.' And indeed, although Pugachev was gone, the discontent remained. Mistrust and hatred rose like fog between the propertied classes and the under-privileged, between the Empress and those at the bottom of the pile. But Catherine did not care. She could have learned from experience and tried to diminish the people's hostility by applying the principles contained in her *Instruction*. But she preferred toughness to conciliation. If she had in the past, even very vaguely, considered

---

[1] Catherine's ironic name for the rebel chief.

freeing the serfs, she now recoiled with horror from the idea. What atrocities might these primitive people perpetrate if they were suddenly freed? She had idealized them in her philosophical meditations; now they had shown their true face. For the same reason she thought that it would be dangerous at the moment to restrict the nobles' powers over their slave livestock. The nobles and the landlords were the pillars of the Empire. The schismatics, towards whom she had previously displayed some sympathy, had shown by following Pugachev that they were not worth the rope needed to hang them. And this was not the moment to reduce taxes either, with famine raging in the provinces devastated by the rebels, and the state coffers empty! Let everything remain as it was. Immobility would be Russia's salvation, at least for the time being. When the people were ready for reform, she would consider it. Meanwhile it was still permissible to talk about it with the French philosophers.

Catherine had hardly finished with Pugachev when her peace of mind was once again threatened by another impostor. She had heard that for two years a very beautiful young woman with auburn hair and dark blue eyes had been claiming that she was the daughter of the Empress Elisabeth I and her lover, Alexis Razumovsky. This so-called granddaughter of Peter the Great had been travelling in France, Italy and Germany, changing her name according to her circumstances – calling herself Ali Emettée, Princess of Vlodomir, the Princess of Azov, Countess Pimberg and Princess Tarakanova. But whatever title she used, she always proclaimed that she was the legitimate heir to the Romanov throne usurped by Catherine II. She possessed, she said, her mother's secret will, in a box, leaving her the Russian throne. Her beauty, easy ways and political ambitions attracted several gentlemen in search of romance and adventure and she was lavishly entertained by all and sundry. She gave a variety of replies when questioned about her past, but always the same one on the subject of her future: she would regain the sceptre that belonged to her by right. The Duc de Limbourg and Prince Radziwill took up her cause with child-like credulity. They planned to set sail for Turkey, so that the real Tsarina Elisabeth II could lend her support to the Turko-Polish cause against the false Tsarina, Catherine II. The signing of the Treaty of Kutchuk-Kainardji dashed their hopes to pieces, and the journey to Constantinople was abandoned. All the same, Alexis Orlov, who was at Leghorn with his flotilla, asked Catherine for her instructions regarding the 'adventuress'. Catherine, of course, did not believe a word of the Tarakanova's story. She knew for a fact that Elisabeth I had never had a child. Anyway if the dead queen had had one, she would have had it brought up at the Court, as Catherine had done with Alexis Bobrinsky, her natural son by Gregory Orlov. No, clearly this woman who was challenging the Empress of all the Russias was a pathological liar, a 'crookess' according to Catherine herself. Her fantasies deserved nothing but contempt. But the Pugachev uprising had made Catherine extremely sensitive. She could no longer bear that anyone, even a whimsical mad-woman, should cast doubt on her legitimacy. In a letter dated the 12th November 1774 she ordered Alexis Orlov to seize 'this creature who has so insolently assumed a name and a lineage to which she has no right'. He was to use 'threats in case of insubordination and punishments if necessary'. He was to bombard the town of Ragusa if necessary, to force the authorities to hand over the wretch. But it would obviously be better to operate quietly, so that everything should happen 'without noise, if possible'. Alexis Orlov obediently chose duplicity and hatched a diabolical plan. He let it be known to the 'pretender' that he was convinced of the authenticity of her claim and that since his brother Gregory's disgrace he felt nothing but hatred and malice towards the Empress. He begged the young woman to join him in Pisa so that he could discuss with her the best way for him to help her in her struggle for power. She did not smell the trap: she came to Pisa and was delighted to be received like a queen by such a grandee of the Empire. The 'Scarface' installed her in sumptuous surroundings, gave parties in her honour and finally declared his passion for her. Yes, said he, he had fallen in love with her at first sight. If she consented to marry him he would share the government of Russia with her. She was dazzled and accepted at once; she then followed her suitor to Leghorn and with him embarked on the flagship, where a fake nuptial benediction took place. A naval officer disguised as a priest united the couple; guns were fired and there were cries of 'Long live the Empress!' The bride burst into sobs of happiness. Then suddenly Alexis Orlov disappeared. Soldiers surrounded 'Her Majesty', pushed her roughly into a cabin and locked her in with no explanation. The ship set sail with Admiral Grieg in command. He was in charge of bringing her to St Petersburg. Alexis Orlov, having played his dirty trick, remained in Leghorn.

As soon as the boat reached Kronstadt on the 12/23rd May 1775, the Tarakanova was thrown into a cell in the fortress of Saint Peter and Saint Paul. Field Marshal Prince Golitsin was charged with interrogating her.

From his first report, the prisoner appeared to have a fine bearing; she looked Italian; she spoke French and German but not a word of Russian; the doctors found her to be suffering from severe consumption; she said that her name was Elisabeth and that she was twenty-three years old. Later, after relentless questioning, she admitted that she did not know who her father and mother were, what nationality she was or where she had been born; she said that she had lived in Baghdad, then Isafahan, contradicted herself, and ended by writing to Catherine promising her 'great favours' if 'all the stories invented against her' were forgotten. The letter was signed 'Elisabeth'. 'What an arrant villain!' cried Catherine when she read the note. Meanwhile the consumption diagnosed by the doctors was progressing rapidly. She was kept in harsh conditions, shivering with cold, short of food, watched by day and night; she wrote once again to the Empress begging her to forgive her her crimes, and to remove her from her cell as 'her condition made nature tremble'. Catherine remained unshakeable. In normal times she was capable of pity, and even mercy, but when reasons of state demanded it she was as hard as nails. She became armourplated, and no longer felt human warmth; it was as if she had turned into a statue of herself. She considered that, in political affairs, merciful decisions always rebounded against their originator. The Tarakanova had gambled and lost – now she must pay. Catherine, as well as refusing to free the prisoner, also refused to better her conditions. The weeks went by, and everybody lost interest in the woman buried alive in the fortress of Saint Peter and Saint Paul. She died at last, on the 4th December 1775, not, as was later rumoured, by drowning when the rising waters of the Neva flooded her cell, but of tuberculosis: she died exhausted, breathless, and spitting blood, in the icy darkness of her cell.[1]

A year later, despite the death of 'the horrible rebel' pretending to be Peter III, and the incarceration of 'the madwoman' pretending to be Elisabeth II, a third impostor was arrested, claiming this time to be Pugachev returned to earth.[2] Catherine could not understand. What a strange country Russia was! Legend often meant more than reality. Ruling this irrational country, one had to struggle as much with spirits as with human beings.

---

[1] The flood only took place two years after Tarakanova's death, in 1777.
[2] Marquis de Juigné's (French ambassador's) report, 24th February 1777 – (French foreign office archives).

CHAPTER XIX

Potemkin

Catherine was beset by problems and wanted to be able to lean on a man whose love and strength would help her to persevere in her task. Pretty little Vassilchikov with his 'head full of straw' was useless to her for this. This gimcrack lover's smiling acquiescence seemed to her unworthy of her great destiny. She could talk to him about nothing and never felt so lonely as with him; the mind played no part in their gloomy contortions. In other words he bored her, and she regretted the privileges she had weakly allowed him. Her thoughts turned more and more towards the funny, rough and brave Potemkin, fighting then beneath the walls of Silistra; she had had him at the back of her mind for a long time. Several times she had sent him short but sympathetic notes via her secretary. On the 14th December 1773 she wrote in her own hand: 'Lieutenant-General, I dare say you are so busy gazing at Silistra that you have no time to read my letters; and although I do not yet know whether your siege has been successful, I am nonetheless certain that everything you undertake is inspired only by your ardent feelings for my own person, and generally for your beloved country. But, since I want to preserve such zealous, intelligent, good and wise men, do not waste time wondering with what purpose this is written. To that I can reply that it is to confirm to you my feelings towards you, as I am, always, your well-wisher, Catherine.'

This ill-disguised declaration of love threw Potemkin into a frenzy of impatient happiness. He had in the past considered becoming a monk out of chagrin at not gaining the Empress's favours, at that time reserved for Gregory Orlov. 'Oh God, what torture it is to love somebody to whom I cannot declare it, and who cannot be mine,' he wrote then. 'Cruel Heavens, why did you make her so beautiful, and so great? Why must it be her, and her alone, that I can love?' And now the 'unattainable one' was calling to him in a soft voice above the clash of battle. In January 1774, he asked for leave, left the army and hurried to the Court.

He was badly disappointed on his arrival, to find Vassilchikov still at his post. He was so handsome that Potemkin, seeing himself in a mirror, lost all hope of being chosen as a replacement. If in the past he had resembled 'Alcibiades', at thirty-five he now looked heavy and contorted. He had black hair and a brown complexion, and did not wear a patch over his missing eye. His features were bloated, and his large strong body had become heavy and shapeless. All the same he gave an impression of wild freedom and primitive strength. Women were impressed by him. Some found him hideous, others were pleasantly troubled by the light in his one eye and the flash of his teeth. They sensed an air of passion about him. He resembled a cyclops dressed up as a courtier. 'The cyclops has a charming habit,' wrote Ribeaupierre. 'He bites his nails with frenzy, right down to the skin.' The English ambassador, Sir Robert Gunning, wrote that the newcomer was 'gigantically tall and out of proportion', and that 'his physiognomy is far from pleasant'. He added however: 'He seems to have a wide knowledge of humanity, and is more discerning than most of his compatriots.'

Potemkin was jealous of Vassilchikov and feared that he could not compete with him in terms of love-making, so he announced once again that his love-sickness was driving him to take holy orders. He hoped in this way to move the Empress who, like all women, would judge the sincerity of the passion by the extremity of the measures it inspired. Catherine did not ask so much. Her suitor had hardly reached the monastery when Countess Bruce arrived to summon him back to the world, where all his hopes would be fulfilled. He replied with a long letter humbly begging for the honour of being named 'general and personal *aide-de-camp*' to Her Majesty; in other words, asking to become her lover. 'It could not offend anybody,' he wrote, 'and I would be the happiest man alive if, finding himself under the special protection of Your Majesty, I could have the honour of receiving your wise orders, and, studying them, become better able to serve Your Majesty and the country.' Catherine heartily granted his request and ordered Vassilchikov to leave the capital for 'health reasons'. To reward him for twenty-two months of loyal service the discharged lover received one hundred thousand roubles, seven thousand serfs, diamonds in bulk, an annuity of twenty thousand roubles and a palace in Moscow, where he was told to stay. As soon as he had vacated his apartment, previously Gregory Orlov's, Potemkin moved in. It was still warm. It was only two paces and a spiral staircase away from the Empress's bed. The hairy one-eyed giant would appear there punctually at night naked under his dressing-gown. She found him handsome despite his tormented appearance. And vigorous – both in body and mind. He amused, astonished, charmed, dominated and bullied her – he made her feel young again. She wrote to Grimm: 'I have drawn away from a certain excellent-natured but extremely dull character, who has immediately been replaced, I don't quite know how, by one of the greatest, most amusing and original people of this hard century.'

The day after the new lover's installation in the palace, Field-Marshal Rumyantsov's wife wrote to her husband: 'Some advice my treasure: if you want to ask for anything, speak to Potemkin.' Cyril Razumovsky's daughter was indignant: 'How and why could anyone court that blind monster?' Sir Robert Gunning wrote to his minister, Lord Suffolk: 'He (Potemkin) can justifiably hope to reach the heights towards which his blind ambition drives him.' 'She is mad about him,' wrote Senator Yelagin to Durand de Distroff. And also: 'They must love each other as they are completely alike!' One day, as he passed Gregory Orlov on the steps of the Palace, Potemkin amiably asked him, 'What's being said at the Court?' 'Nothing,' replied Orlov, 'except that you're going up and I'm going down.'

Potemkin was 'going up' so high that it appeared that nobody before him had ever achieved such physical and intellectual intimacy with the Empress. For the first time in her life she abandoned herself completely to a wild and enriching love-affair. She forgot about her powerful position and worried about her lover's happiness. She was forty-five – ten years older than he. Not a minute passed when she did not think of him. When he was not beside her she would write him a note, even if she was in a council meeting, or in the middle of the night, or at dawn, when the Palace was still asleep. A trustworthy valet would carry the messages; Potemkin would reply; she would burn his letters. He kept her letters in his coat pocket next to his heart. They consisted of a few hastily scribbled lines of feverish and senseless outpouring. The Empress of all the Russias called her lover the most ridiculous names: 'My sweet darling..., my soul's sister..., my beloved doll..., my little plaything..., my tiger..., my little parrot..., my Arab..., my little Gricha..., my gilded pheasant..., my golden cockerel..., my lion of the jungle..., my wolf-bird...'

She admired him physically and told him so: 'My marble beauty..., my beloved, better than any king..., no man on earth can equal you...'

Suddenly the strength of her passion would frighten her, and she would pretend to try and suppress it.

'I have given strict orders to my body – down to the last hair – to stop showing you the smallest sign of love. I have shut my love up in my heart, under lock and key; it is miserable and suffocates in there – I fear it will burst out.'

Then she would admit defeat: 'A torrent of stupid words is flowing through my brain. How can you bear a woman with such incoherent ideas?' And she added proudly: 'Oh! Monsieur Potemkin! What trick have you played to unbalance a mind previously thought to be one of the best in Europe!... What a disgrace! What a sin! Catherine II a prey to such mad passion! You will disgust him with this lunacy, I say to myself.'

Carried away by her enthusiasm, she would sometimes address him quite roughly: 'There is a woman living who loves you and deserves a kind word from you. Fool, Tartar, Cossack, barbarian, Muscovite, damn you!' Or, unable to find words in her uusal vocabulary, she would launch into bold improvisation: 'My flower-bud..., my sweet-meat...' She was grateful to her 'barbarian' for the stories he told her: 'Darling what tales you told me yesterday! I cannot stop laughing as I think of them... We are together for four hours at a time without a shadow of boredom, and I always leave you reluctantly. My dear pigeon, I love you very much. You are handsome, intelligent and amusing.' At other times she would refer, not to the pleasures of their conversation, but to the perfection of their physical relationship. She was a great connoisseur of sensual pleasures and she appreciated the way her new lover treated her. She thought that their sexual compatability enhanced their romantic understanding. She humbly confessed her greed for this heavy, smelly and vigorous body: 'Every cell in my body reached towards you, oh!, barbarian!... Thank you for yesterday's feast. My little Gricha has fed me and quenched my thirst, but not with wine... My mind is like that of a cat on heat... For you I will be a "woman of fire" as you often say. But I will try to hide my flames...' 'The doors will be open, and all depends on the will and capacity of the one concerned; for my part I am going to bed... Darling, I will do what you order, shall I come to you, or will you come to me?'

Potemkin had a changeable temperament, sometimes lunatic and vainglorious, sometimes surly and jealous, passing from wild happiness to morbid depression; one day he reproached her for having had fifteen lovers before him. She was wounded and only admitted to five: 'I took the first because I had to, and the fourth out of despair!' she cried. 'As for the other three, God knows it was not for debauchery's sake – I have never had any inclination for that!'[1] He asked her about Vassilchikov. Wasn't she still in love with him? She replied: 'You have absolutely no reason for fear. I really made a fool of myself with that idiot Vassilchikov... You can read my mind and my heart... I love you

[1] Solveitchik *Potemkin.*

infinitely.' Sometimes he would appear aloof and distant or irritated for no reason – the sky was grey, or he had got out of bed on the wrong side. She would then scold him warmly in her notes: 'Kindly inform me when your stupid bad temper has passed... You are a wicked Tartar! I come to tell you how much I love you, and find the door closed! You are torturing me for nothing! Just as I am feeling quite safe, an avalanche comes down on me... Really we must try to live in perfect harmony. Don't torment me by your ill-treatment, and then you won't suffer from my coldness... My little soul, I have a string with a stone at one end and all our quarrels at the other, and I have thrown the whole thing into a bottomless pit. Good-morning my darling! Good-morning, without quarrels or arguments...'

She felt so close to him in the flesh that she did not conceal her most intimate problems:

'I won't come to you, as I sweated all night and all my bones are hurting, as they did yesterday... I have got slight diarrhoea today but, apart from that, I am well, my beloved... Don't worry about my diarrhoea, it cleans out the intestines.'[1]

She was carried away by passion to the extent, it was thought, of actually marrying Potemkin. The nuptial ceremony, according to some evidence, took place towards the end of 1774 in the St Samson church in St Petersburg in the presence of her faithful maid Perekusikhina, Count Samoylov, Potemkin's nephew, and the chamberlain Chertkov. The documents relating to this secret wedding have disappeared. On the other hand the language used in twenty-three of Catherine's letters to her lover, lead one to believe in the conjugal nature of their relationship. 'My beloved husband... My darling, most gentle and kind husband... My dear, sweet husband... I beg you not to humiliate me any more... It would not be kind to anybody, but particularly not to your wife... I kiss you with my heart and my body, oh my dear husband. Why believe your sickly imagination rather than the facts which confirm what your wife has said...? Have I not been attached to you for the past two years by the most sacred of bonds...? I remain your faithful wife, who loves you eternally.'

Whether or not they were married, Catherine and Potemkin were an exceptional couple, a conjunction of two forceful, violent characters, both healthy and intelligent and gluttons for work and pleasure. Potemkin, although bound to the Empress's bed, was never, from the beginning, merely a temporary lover. She was dominated by her companion and consulted him about all important political decisions,

[1] Love-letters from Catherine II to Potemkin – published by G. Oudard.

and sometimes even took his advice. Before or after making love, by day or by night, between kisses, they would discuss matters of state; they examined ministers' reports and ambassadors' despatches, they planned reforms, dreamt up new alliances, took Russia and Europe to pieces and put them together again. 'Our disagreements are always about power, never love,' she wrote to him. 'Talk to me about yourself and I will never be angry.' In fact she enjoyed their differences of opinion. She was delighted to have before her, for the first time, a strong character who sent the ball back into her court. Now she no longer ruled Russia alone.

Potemkin rapidly took up important positions. He became a member of the Privy Council, Vice-President of the Council of War, with the rank of general, and was generally showered with duties and honours: he became a Knight of St Andrew; Frederick gave him the Prussian Black Eagle; the King of Poland, Catherine's ex-lover, gave him the White Eagle; Denmark, the White Elephant; Sweden, the Order of St Serafina; Joseph II, despite Maria-Theresa's opposition, made him a Prince of the Holy Empire. There were, however, two exceptions: France refused to award Catherine's lover the Order of the Holy Spirit, which was only for Catholics, and England withheld the Garter. Meanwhile, during the festivities celebrating the peace with Turkey, Catherine made him a Count of the Russian Empire, and gave him a miniature of herself framed with diamonds. He wore it on his coat, as Gregory Orlov had done. Contemporary Russian poets wrote pompous verses in his praise. The Court was at his feet. Foreign ambassadors sought his friendship. He was surrounded by a murmur of base adulation. He installed his whole family in the Palace: his mother, sister and five nieces, who were so pretty and bold that he eventually seduced them all one after the other. He soon became Governor of the southern provinces, 'New Russia'. When he had to take an important decision he would shut himself up in his study and play with precious stones on his desk, arranging and re-arranging them until the solution to the problem occurred to him; or he would clean the stones in his rings for hours, lost in thought. Gifts of silver, jewels, land and peasants rained down on him. He received twelve thousand roubles a month and his household was entirely paid for out of the imperial purse. His food and wines came out of the Court budget. The Court carriages and livery were at his disposal. The impoverished little officer risen from the ranks was now basking in luxury. And he spent money without counting it, losing it at the gambling table, accumulating debts – each time he would turn to the Empress, who would smilingly settle his bills. She was far too extravagant herself to reproach her lover for this failing.

All the same, this man, whose successes so astonished the world, had bouts of despair and self-disgust that made him wish he had gone into a monastery. He had exceptional talents as a musician, poet, connoisseur of art, soldier, administrator, diplomat, economist and builder, and he broached every problem with enthusiasm; then suddenly he would collapse, lose interest in everything, and spend whole days half-naked on a sofa, unwashed and unbrushed, eating crusts of bread and chewing his nails. One day his nephew, Engelhardt, who was dining with him, complimented him on his good humour. Potemkin's face immediately darkened and he said; 'Could there be a happier man than myself? All my hopes and dreams have been magically fulfilled. I wanted important duties – I have them; medals – I have them all; I enjoyed gambling – I have lost incalculable sums of money; I liked giving parties – I have given splendid ones; I liked buying land – I possess as much as I want; I liked building houses – I have built palaces; I loved jewels – no individual owns rarer or more beautiful gems. In a word I am entirely happy.' With these words, he smashed a valuable plate on the floor, disappeared into his bedroom and shut himself in.[1] He was a man of extremes, a Slav to the roots. From one moment to the next he could be gentle and violent, happy and sad, lazy and active, coarse and refined. He was a great eater and drinker, and indiscriminately gulped down the finest food and drink as well as the roughest. At his table in St Petersburg, oysters, sterlets, figs from Provence and water-melons from Astrakhan would appear, but first he would greedily chew up cloves of garlic and *piroshki* watered down with *kwass*. He appeared in Court in costumes sparkling with gold, diamonds and medals but at home he would wear nothing more than a large dressing-gown. He wore no trousers or underwear beneath this comfortable garment and dressed like this would receive not just the Empress, but ladies-in-waiting, ministers, ambassadors even. When the Comte de Ségur called on him, on his arrival in St Petersburg, he found a hairy one-eyed giant stretched out on his bed, who did not even rise to meet the King of France's envoy. Ségur left an excellent description of him: 'Nothing could compare with the liveliness of his mind and the flabbiness of his body. He never flinched before danger or turned back in the face of difficulties, but was bitterly disappointed by all his successes... Everything had to be complicated with him: business, pleasure, moods, surroundings... He was rude to people who were deferential towards him, and friendly to those who behaved in a familiar manner. He always promised things and rarely fulfilled his promises; he never forgot

---

[1] Waliszewski *Around the Throne.*

anything he had seen or heard. Nobody had read less than him, but few were as well informed... Because of his unstable temperament his general behaviour and way of life were indescribably eccentric... His eccentricities, although they often irritated the Empress, made him on the whole more interesting to her.'

The Prince de Ligne wrote: 'He is the most extraordinary man I have ever met. He appears lazy and yet works ceaselessly... always lying down and yet never sleeping by day or night – he is kept permanently awake by the frenzy of his adoration of the Empress... He is melancholy in the midst of pleasure, made miserable by his own happiness, *blasé* about everything, easily disgusted, morose, changeable; he is a profound philosopher, an able minister, a brilliant politician and a child of ten;... enormously rich but never has a penny; discusses theology with his generals and war with his archbishops; never reads anything but amasses information by talking to people;... like a child he wants everything, but like a great man he can do without everything... What is his magic then? Genius, genius and more genius!'

By this mixture of enthusiasm and disaffection, and of polite and coarse behaviour, Potemkin permanently held the Empress's attention. Even when, with time, the sexual passion died down between them, she always turned to him in the end. Was he the first to become slightly weary of this ageing woman? Or did she tire of his moodiness and long for a new and more ordinary liaison? In any case after years of mutual enjoyment he began to ogle young girls and she turned towards young men. Neither was upset by the other's disenchantment, and the weakening of their sexual appetites in no way diminished their affection and admiration for each other. Potemkin's first concern, when he saw the change in their relationship, was to choose his own replacement, thus retaining his influence over Catherine. So, although possessed by another, she never completely stopped belonging to him. This 'other' was to be a young and charming Ukrainian, Peter Zavadovsky. He was approved and put to the test as soon as he was introduced to the Empress as a successor. The test was conclusive. Everybody at the Court thought that Potemkin was out of favour when they heard about this boudoir revolution. Some rejoiced. 'His arrogant behaviour whilst he was in power made him a great many enemies, and he can expect the same treatment now that he is in disgrace,' wrote Sir Richard Oates in a coded report. 'It would not be surprising or unexpected for him to end his career in a monastery, something he has always professed to want.'

He underestimated Potemkin. He returned to St Petersburg after a short journey to Novgorod, and gave up his apartment to Zavadovsky for the sum of a hundred thousand roubles. The new lover was thus paying key money for access to the imperial bedchamber, a commission, as their paths crossed, to the previous beneficiary. But the latter had no intention of being separated from his beloved; certainly he did not hope to return to her bed, but neither would he allow the intruder to remain for any length of time. He was now the Empress's purveyor rather than her lover. His power over her was proportional to the brevity of her affairs and so he encouraged her taste for change and variety. Paradoxically the more single-minded and jealous he was, the more he wished for a rapid turnover of young men in his beloved's bed. As long as she only sought physical satisfaction from these men, he would remain the master. His calculations were correct. He installed himself in a private house linked to the Imperial Palace by a covered passage. The Empress could therefore visit him at any time without attracting attention. And she did so. Never had she needed her Gricha's advice so much. Her life fell into two sections. Wild night-time activities with a minor character, and rewarding and friendly exchanges with the man she considered to be her husband. From now on, all the Empress's 'chosen ones' would be chosen by Potemkin. They never lasted more than a few months. Zavadovsky was relieved from his post in June 1776. 'He received fifty thousand roubles from Her Majesty, a pension of five thousand and four thousand peasants in the Ukraine, where they are worth a lot,' wrote Chevalier de Corberon, the new French chargé d'affaires, to his brother. And he added: 'You must admit, my friend, that it's a good job to have over here,'[1]

Simon Zorich succeeded Zavadovsky – he was nicknamed 'the Adonis' by the Court ladies. The Empress affectionately called him 'Sima' and thought he had 'a beautiful head'. The same Corberon wrote: '(Potemkin), who is more in favour than ever and now plays the same role that La Pompadour did at the end of her life with Louis XV, has presented her (the Empress) with a certain Zorich, a major in the Hussars, who has been promoted to lieutenant-colonel and inspector of all the light infantry troops. This new favourite dined with her. Apparently he received 1,800 peasants for his trial run! After dinner Potemkin drank to the Empress's health and sat at her knee.'

The handsome Zorich, who was Serbian by birth, was so happy with his promotion that he offered Potemkin a hundred thousand roubles to thank him. To hell with scruples! Potemkin accepted, and a custom was thus established amongst the 'chosen' to give the go-between a hundred thousand roubles on the day of their accession. It was not too great a

---

[1] The Chevalier de Corberon *A French diplomat at the court of Catherine II*.

price to pay for the certainty of ending one's career in riches and grandeur having known for a time the glories of the imperial bed. Then Zorich began to falter. The new ambassador from England, James Howard Harris, wrote in a despatch to his government: 'The present favourite, Zorich, seems to be in decline. It is likely that Potemkin will be charged with finding a successor, and I have heard that he is already casting his eyes on a certain Akavov.' And again, in a private letter: 'Zorich is expecting to be dismissed but they say that he is determined to obtain satisfaction from his successor. "I know," he said the other day, "that I am about to go but by God I'll cut the ears off anyone who tries to take my place."[1]' Suspecting his 'boss' of already having a candidate up his sleeve, Zorich provoked a violent scene, hurling insults and even challenging him to a duel. Potemkin treated the outburst with scorn and asked the Empress to get rid of the trouble-maker without further delay. That same evening the young man was told that his presence was no longer required at the Palace, and that he would do well to travel. He was furious and rushed to his mistress's apartments – to find the doors closed. Potemkin's words and the promise of an annuity and some good land with seven thousand peasants soothed the feelings of the demoted lover. He packed his bags and one Rimsky-Korsakov, urged forward by Potemkin, timidly approached, under the encouraging eye of the Empress. Others were to follow.

Thanks to Potemkin, who had taught her the delights of perversity, Catherine – the good, faithful, steady Catherine – began to discover the pleasures of variety and choice. Each new lover was seen as a rare gem. She was rejuvenated, revitalized, in love yet again, and she would present him at the Court as some sort of superman; he would be beautifully dressed and then dragged around official receptions; she would fawn over his mildest witticisms but forbade any sign of intimacy in public. He was on duty twenty-four hours out of twenty-four, expected to be a gallant escort by day and a tireless lover by night. The fear of not coming up to the mark, when the time came, often became an obsession. Thus when the young Lanskoy became ill, in order to avoid disgrace he resorted to aphrodisiacs which finished off his health. Certainly Catherine, experienced as she was, would from time to time allow a failure in the execution of duty, but if it happened too often they were out. Once a lover had ceased to be attractive, he would be loaded with gifts, assured of a large pension, and would then discreetly move out of his apartment, whilst Potemkin looked around for a new *aide-de-camp*. The 'one-eyed genius' knew the Empress's tastes better than

---

[1] The letter and despatch are dated 13th February 1778.

anybody. She very rarely returned the goods he sent her. These licentious dealings took place with an openness verging on cynicism; the enthronement procedure involved elementary precautions. Once he had been chosen by Potemkin and accepted by the Empress, the young man was summoned to the Court where Her Majesty's English doctor, Rogerson, examined him with the greatest care. Then he was introduced to Countess Bruce who would engage him in a friendly interrogation to ascertain his intellectual capacity and depth of character. Finally the same Countess Bruce (later it would be Miss Protassof) would submit the candidate to a more intimate test, to find out about his physical capabilities.[1] A detailed report by the 'tester' or 'éprouveuse' was then submitted to the Empress, who made the final decision. If it was a favourable one, the young man would be taken to the tied apartment, now vacated by its previous occupant. There he would find in a desk a box containing a hundred thousand roubles, the customary first present – the first of many. That evening he would appear before the assembled Court at the Empress's side, with a conspiratorial Potemkin looking on. At ten o'clock when the gambling was finished, she would retire to her apartments, followed by the new favourite. A murmur of envy would go with him, but he would be aware of the tight corner he was in – his future to be decided upon in the following hour.

Catherine agreed to be supplied by Potemkin because she was too busy to worry about these minor romantic matters. Above a certain intellectual level one must be able, she thought, to place the responsibility for supplying objects of pleasure onto other, safe, shoulders. There was no secrecy about her sexual preferences. For her, sexual satisfaction was a basic necessity about which one need neither blush nor boast. Few women have disregarded as she did the obscure passages of the unconscious, the secret whirlpools and tremors in the depths of the human mind. She was totally transparent, a diurnal genius.

The foreign diplomats were scandalized by the Tsarina's licentious behaviour. 'Her Court', wrote Harris, 'has little by little turned into a scene of depravity and immorality ... One can at present no longer hope that she will leave this mire, and, short of a miracle, one cannot

---

[1] Byron alludes to this in a famouse verse in *Don Juan*
　　　' ... As also did Miss Protassof then there
　　　Named from her mystic office 'Eprouveuse'
　　　A term inexplicable to the muse.'
Ref: Waliszewski *Around the Throne*.

expect her, now that she is too old to reform herself, to improve either her public or private behaviour. Prince Potemkin rules her absolutely. He knows intimately all her weaknesses, desires and passions and he satisfies them at will. Apart from having this ascendancy over her, he keeps her in constant fear of the Grand Duke and he has persuaded her that he is the only man on earth who could discover in time any enterprise launched against her from that quarter, and protect her from it.' The same Harris analysed Catherine's character thus: 'It appears to me that the Empress has a manly strength of mind, is obstinate in the pursuit of a plan, and fearless in its execution. But she lacks other masculine virtues such as deliberation, moderation in expenditure, and balanced judgment. Indeed she possesses in the extreme the weaknesses attributed to her sex, love of flattery and the vanity which is tied to that, disinclination to listen to and follow beneficial but unwelcome advice, and a taste for sensual pleasure dragging her towards excesses which would dishonour any woman whatever her station in life.' And the Chevalier de Corberon, the Versailles cabinet's envoy, continues on the same theme: 'How, they will say, can this State be governed, how can it support itself? I reply that it is governed at random and supported by its own natural equilibrium, like a great piece of matter whose immense weight makes it solid, resisting all attacks, giving way only to uninterrupted assaults from corruption and old age.'

This harsh judgment was certainly very different from Catherine's own view of herself and her work. When she looked back she saw only a line of successes. At forty-six, faced with a hostile and mocking Europe, she had annexed a part of Poland and installed her very own king in what remained of that miserable country; she had defeated Turkey, pushed back the Russian frontiers in the south, opening up new channels for her naval fleet; she had held French diplomacy in check; she had put down the Pugachev rebellion; she had dazzled the philosophers by the vision of her great ideas; she had pushed aside the threat to her throne represented by Ivan VI...

At present her main worry was still her son. Paul's marriage was a failure. 'The Grand Duchess likes extremes in everything,' wrote Catherine to Grimm. 'She does not listen to advice and I can see in her no attraction, wit or sense.' And again: 'Everything is excess with this lady! She is always spinning around!' This stupid creature, as well as refusing to learn Russian, was also an intriguer. She longed to place her husband on the throne. A list of conspirators was circulating in the Palace. Catherine heard about it, summoned the Grand Duke and Grand Duchess, and before their eyes threw the tell-tale paper into the fire. The two conspirators learnt their lesson and withdrew with their heads bowed.

If Natalia longed for power so much, it was because, as a woman, she was deeply disappointed. She had overestimated her own adaptability when she had married this ugly sneering, limited and cruel prince. Luckily, right beside them there was Andrew Razumovsky, Paul's best friend. Natalia soon fell in love with him, and into his arms. The two lovers used to slip opium to the husband after supper so that, in the words of Comte d'Allonville 'their trio became a *tête-à-tête*'. The whole Court was aware of the Grand Duchess's infidelity. The Empress wanted to remove Andrew Razumovsky from the Palace. But Paul, who was aware of nothing, refused to let go the person who was dearest to him after his wife. Catherine could have told him of Natalia's behaviour. But one scruple prevented her from doing so. Natalia was pregnant. By Paul or by Andrew? It did not matter. She was carrying the heir inside her, and was therefore consecrated, as Catherine had been at the time of Elisabeth, now that she was 'officially' pregnant. Paul was wildly proud at the thought of having a son. Catherine encouraged him in his delusion.

When Natalia felt the first pains, the Tsarina tied a big apron over her dress and helped the midwife with her business. The birth was protracted; the mother shrieked with pain for three days; doctors were called in to help. 'My back is hurting as much as hers,' Catherine wrote in a note to Potemkin. 'It must be because of the worry I feel.' The child was at last torn from his mother's stomach – a silent little lump of flesh. It was a boy, enormous and still-born. They had not wanted to perform a Caesarean operation. Natalia could not be properly delivered of the baby. Gangrene set in and the stench filled the room. Soon afterwards, towards six o'clock on the evening of the 15th April 1776 the young woman died, exhausted. Catherine was shattered, but remained calm: she had to as Paul, driven mad with grief, was smashing all the furniture in his apartment and trying to throw himself out of the window. She tried to reason with him but he would not listen. He would not let his wife be buried, and demanded to keep her with him. She was alive – the doctors had lied to him! Catherine wrote to Madame de Bielke: 'No human help could save the Princess – she was blocked up . . . After her death, when they opened up the body they found that there were only four fingers of space and the child's shoulders were eight fingers wide.' The Chevalier de Corberon was of a quite different opinion. After speaking to the doctor, Moreau, during a dinner party, he wrote: 'To me, he (Moreau) said that the Court doctors and physicians were asses. The Grand Duchess's death should not have happened. It really seems surprising that more care should not have been taken of a Grand Duchess. The people are angry and embittered and in tears. Yesterday and today people were saying: 'The young women die; the old *babas*[1] are still alive.'

The Empress was certainly grieved at the loss, but she ended her letter to Madame de Bielke with cold lucidity and cruel practicality, in these words: 'Anyway as it has been shown that she (Natalia) could not have a living child, or at least could not give birth to one, we must not dwell on it any more.' This strange funeral oration was not enough for Catherine. As usual when faced with catastrophe, she had to fight back. She hated sadness and resignation, undermining as they did the individual will. Living meant looking forwards not backwards. The most important thing now was to replace the dead woman, and quickly. On the very day of the Grand Duchess's death, Catherine sent Potemkin a hastily scribbled note in pencil, telling him of her intentions. She had drawn up a six point plan leading up to a re-marriage for the Grand Duke. He would be sent to Berlin where another German princess would be chosen for him; the young woman would be forced to convert and the engagement ceremony would take place in St Petersburg: 'All top secret until it has been set in motion.' They were still laying out the body, and the Empress was already enumerating in her mind the possible successors: Sophia Dorothea of Württemburg seemed straight away to be the best placed. But she would have to please that idiot Paul! And he continued to sob, howl and curse his entourage. As often happens with weak people, unhappiness increased the hatred he felt for his mother. He held her responsible for everything. Faced with these outbursts, Catherine decided to use extreme methods. She forced open Natalia's little desk and found there, as she had expected, the dead woman's correspondence with Andrew Razumovsky. Charity should have made her burn the letters and leave her son in ignorance. But reasons of State were always the strongest for Catherine, and she also wanted to bring this lunatic to his senses with a salutary shock. So she cruelly and boldly pushed under the miserable man's nose proof of his wife's deception. He read the letters, was confused, cried out with misery, shame and anger, and then, broken, agreed to do anything that his mother wished. Catherine was triumphant. She wrote stiffly back to Grimm, who had sent her a moving letter of condolence: 'I never reply to lamentations... I have not been wasting my time. I have my irons in the fire already; I am planning to repair the loss, and we have thus distracted ourselves from the profound unhappiness we have

[1] The 'old ladies'. Allusion to Catherine.

suffered... And then I said: The dead are dead, let us think of the living...! If one believed oneself to be happy and then lost that belief, must one despair of regaining it? Come, in short, find another. But who? – Ah! I have one in my pocket. Who is it...? Is she dark, fair, small, large? – Gentle, beautiful, charming, a gem, a gem... And so low spirits begin to rise.'

Andrew Razumovsky was sent to Reval. The Grand Duchess was buried in the midst of wails and sobs. The Grand Duke, in mourning, was so stunned that he appeared almost indifferent. The Court moved to Tsarskoe Selo; and there in the midst of delightful picnics and rural excursions, Catherine and Prince Heinrich of Prussia, on a diplomatic mission to the Russian court, considered the possibilities of a meeting in Berlin between the young widower and little Sophia Dorothea of Württemburg. They wrote to Frederick II, who reigned over a fish-pond wriggling with marriageable princesses. He happily accepted to take up the search once again, to reinforce the links between the two countries. Mysterious messages flew between Berlin, Stuttgart and St Petersburg. Everyone feverishly prepared for the Grand Duke's journey. He set out from Tsarskoe Selo in great style, with an entourage worthy of his rank. Prince Heinrich accompanied him. At Riga, the first stop, Prince Heinrich received this letter from Catherine: 'I do not think there is any precedent for an affair arranged like this one,' she wrote. 'It is the result of the most intimate friendship and confidence. This princess (Sophia Dorothea) will be the proof of it. I will not be able to see her without remembering how this affair was begun and carried to its conclusion by the royal houses of Prussia and Russia.'[1] She anxiously awaited news of the first interview between the young people. As long as her fool of a son did not weaken at the last minute! He was quite capable of doing so if only to annoy her. What would she do if he refused Sophia Dorothea? Just in case, she ran through other names in her mind – all German.

[1] J. Castéra *Life of Catherine II*.

CHAPTER XX

Catherine the Great

It was a success! As soon as he met Sophia Dorothea of Württemburg, who had been summoned to Berlin by Frederick, Paul became wild with enthusiasm. For the third time in thirty-two years, the King of Prussia had shown his talents as marriage-broker to the Russian royal family. Sophia Dorothea had originally been promised to the heir of Darmstadt. But on Frederick's instructions, her engagement to this secondary figure was broken off, and the young girl, now free, and excited and consenting – she was sixteen – offered herself to the very different attentions of Grand Duke Paul, the heir to Russia. Paul, who had forgotten his mourning, and even his conjugal misfortune, could hardly wait: he dreamt only of getting Sophia Dorothea into his bed. The fact that Frederick II recommended her made her doubly desirable, as, following the example of his supposed father, Peter III, he had unlimited admiration for this king, and for all things Prussian. Frederick found Paul 'haughty, arrogant and violent, it makes anyone who knows Russia apprehensive about his ability to remain on the throne.'[1] The Grand Duke's head was completely turned by the parties, ceremonies and artillery salvos. To reward the Berlin matrimonial agency, Catherine renewed her treaty of alliance with Prussia. She eagerly welcomed the young German princess, who disembarked in Russia soon after her fiancé, with that bitter-sweet mixture of hope and fear that she, Catherine, had known long ago. She was delighted with her future daughter-in-law and wrote to Madame de Bielke:

'I confess that I am completely and utterly charmed by this princess. She is exactly as one would wish her to be: she has a slender figure, a complexion like lilies and roses, the most beautiful skin on earth, and is tall and with good bearing; she is light; gentleness, kindness of heart and candour are written all over her face.'

The young girl immediately converted to Orthodoxy, assumed the title of Grand Duchess and changed her name from Sophia Dorothea to Maria Feodorovna. The day after the engagement ceremony she wrote to her intended: 'I swear in this paper to love and adore you all my life and to

[1] Frederick II *Memoirs.*

always remain attached to you, and nothing on earth will make me change towards you. These are the feelings of your tender and faithful fiancée.'

Paul, on his side, wrote to Heinrich of Prussia: 'She (the Grand Duchess) has the gift not only of chasing away my dark thoughts, but she also restores in me the good humour I had completely lost in the last three miserable years.' And to Sacken: 'You see, I am not made of marble, and my heart is not as hard as many people think; my life will show this.'[1]

Preparations for the nuptial ceremony were hastened. Less than a year after Natalia's burial, the bells rang out for Maria and Grand Duke Paul's wedding.

From the begining Maria was completely satisfied with her lot. 'This dear husband is an angel, I love him madly,' she wrote to the Baroness Oberkirch. Catherine was relying on her daughter-in-law to bring Paul to his senses. In a supreme attempt at reconciliation, she gave up her precious time to devote two mornings a week to his political apprenticeship. But he refused to show any interest in State affairs. What interested him were the petty details of military life. And he thought he knew where that leaning came from. It was a curious mimesis; obviously, in this court, where the smallest unpleasant rumour was repeated a hundred times, he must have heard it whispered that his father was perhaps not Peter III, but Saltykov. He refused to believe this gossip, and firmly thought himself to be the son of the assassinated Tsar. And to prove it to himself and others, he adopted the dead man's obsessions. He made himself Prussian, violent-natured, and military-minded, to be like Peter. Indeed he rapidly overtook the latter, when dealing with the army, by his contradictory orders and cruel punishments. His obsession was to reduce the troops to a collection of automatons. A badly sewn button, or a mistake in the manoeuvres, would result in beatings and deportations. He would tirelessly review the troops, make them manoeuvre in the mud, organize mock battles, shout, rage, threaten, playing sometimes at being a genial strategist, and sometimes an NCO drunk with power over his men.

The Empress was horrified to see signs of this military madness, but she consoled herself with the thought that he at least, unlike Peter III, was capable of fathering a child. Maria was very soon pregnant. Catherine was triumphant, she could hardly have been happier if it had been herself. This grandson – it could only be a grandson – already belonged to her in flesh, blood and mind. He would inherit her life's

---

[1] Constantin de Grunwald *The Assassination of Paul I, Tsar of Russia.*

work, and continue it. He would be what Paul had failed to be. Yes, before the child had even been born, the idea grew in his grandmother's mind of leaving everything, not to her unworthy son, but to her unknown grandson. After all, she was only forty-eight years old, she would have plenty of time to shape her young successor. She wanted this imperial scion to be perfect both in body and mind. To be sure of bringing him up properly she plunged herself into educational treatises, despite all the work calling for her attention. She read through Rousseau's *Emile*, found out about Pestalozzi's latest discoveries and absorbed the theories of Basedow and Pfeffel. Grand Duchess Maria admired the works of Lavater and advised her mother-in-law to read *Fragments of Physiognomy*. Catherine noted down on a piece of paper the principles of child-rearing that she wanted to put into use, almost all of which went against the customs of the time: 'It is better that children should not be dressed or covered too warmly in winter or in summer. It is better that children should sleep without a cap at night. Children to be washed as often as possible in cold water ... It is a good idea to teach a child to swim when he is of the right age ... Let him play in wind, sun and rain without a hat ... ' She counted the days until this quasi-holy birth would occur. The whole Court watched the Grand Duchess's stomach. At last on the 12th/23rd December 1777, after a few hours of labour, and without the slighest complication, Maria gave birth to a boy. He was heavy, lively, well-built, noisy – a future Emperor. Catherine was overcome and fell to her knees before her icons, praying. Her eyes were filled with tears. Then she had the baby bathed, wrapped up and pressed him convulsively to her breast. This future potentate could only have one great name: Alexander. Forgetting her own unhappiness when Elisabeth had taken away her son, Catherine removed the new-born baby to her apartments. The parents would be allowed to see the child from time to time but she would bring him up. A young and inexperienced couple could not be entrusted with the upbringing of the Tsarevich. Cannons were fired, bells in the churches rang out joyfully, a *Te Deum* was sung in the Kazan cathedral and on the day of the birth the famous court poet, Derzhavin, composed an interminable *Lullaby for the Young Eagle's Nurse*:

> *Ah! in these cold times*
> *When the furious North Wind*
> *Whips the plains*
> *of the north, a child*
> *Is born, and the North Wind*
> *Immediately ceased to howl ...*

Alexander was placed in a little iron bed rather than a cradle, so that nobody would be tempted to rock him. His wet nurse was the wife of a gardener from Tsarskoe Selo, judged by the doctors to be a good milk-producer. Voices were not lowered in this room, even when he was asleep. The temperature in his room was never more than 14 or 15°C. In winter and summer he was washed in cold water. 'At four months so that he would not always be carried, I gave him a carpet for his room,' wrote Catherine to King Gustave III of Sweden.[1] 'There one or two women sit on the floor and Master Alexander is placed on his stomach. He lies kicking and is a pleasure to watch... He never gets cold, he is big, fat, healthy and happy; he has no teeth yet and almost never cries.'

She soon installed the 'divine infant' right next to her desk. Grimm, whom she nick-named jokingly her 'whipping boy', heard all the smallest details about the character, games, education and first words of the little prodigy. 'I dote on this child,' she wrote to him. 'In the afternoon my boy comes in as often as he likes and spends three or four hours a day in my room...' And again: 'I am turning him into a delightful child. It is surprising that, without being able to speak, he knows, at twenty months, far more than most children of three. Grand-mother is making him into what she wanted. He will be delightful!' Or: 'For the last two months, as well as doing a little legislating, I undertook for my amusement a small dictionary of sayings, for Master Alexander's benefit, which is most astute. All who see it have the highest praise for it... The sayings, like a string of pearls, lead on one from the other; I only have two aims: one is to make the mind receptive to things, and the other is to elevate the soul by developing the heart.'

She sent Grimm a sketch of a garment she had designed for her grandson: 'It is all stitched together, you put on all at once, and it closes at the back with four or five little hooks. There are no bindings and the child hardly notices that he is being dressed; one pushes his arms and legs into the costume all at once, and that's it. This garment is a stroke of genius on my part. The King of Sweden and the Prince of Prussia have asked for and obtained copies of Master Alexander's costume.'

Catherine was convinced that 'Master Alexander's' father and mother would never have been able to develop the child's mind and heart to such an extent. He was her creation, her property. He loved and obeyed only her. One day the little prodigy asked one of the Empress's maids, whom he resembled.

'Your mother to look at.'

'What about my temperament and my manners?'

'Your grandmother.'

---

[1] King Gustav III was, through his father Adolf-Frederick of Holstein Gottorp, Catherine's first cousin.

'I hoped so!' cried Alexander, hugging the maid.

Catherine was delighted with this remark and repeated it to everybody. She wrote again to Grimm, speaking of her grandson: 'He will become a most excellent person, as long as *secondaterie* does not hold me up in his progress.' *'Secondat, secondaterie,'* were scornful terms devised by the Empress to describe 'the seconds', her son and daughter-in-law.

However, the *secondaterie* was not being idle. Maria was a fine brood-mare. Hardly time to breathe and she was pregnant once again. Seventeen months after Alexander's birth she gave brith to another son. Catherine was in Heaven. She called this second grandson Constantine, in the hope that one day he might reign over the Empire of Constantinople.[1] A medal was struck for the occasion: on the front, Sophia of Constantinople, and on the back, a map of the Black Sea surmounted by a star. Lines from Homer were read at the festivities organized by Potemkin to celebrate the event. But the baby had a sickly constitution. His disappointed grandmother wrote coldly: 'As for the other (Constantine), I wouldn't give tuppence for it: I would be most surprised if it remained alive.'

However 'it' did remain alive; 'it' grew in strength and intelligence, so much so that Catherine, by the child's bed, slowly regained her confidence and her hopes of a Byzantine hegemony. They had to have milk from Olympia to feed this future Emperor of the East, so a Greek wet-nurse was obtained. She brought with her all the ancient virtues in her swollen breasts. There were now two 'divine infants' on the carpet of the imperial study, and Catherine, as she checked files, dictated reports, and signed proclamations, would melt with happiness when her grandsons' laughter broke through her political preoccupations.

She had more of these worries than ever now. The whole of Europe was changing around her. A few days after Alexander's birth she learnt of the death of the Elector of Bavaria, Maximilian Joseph, on the 30th December, 1777. In the international balance of that time, one king's personality, his friendship, his dislikes, his family bonds, his secret hopes, all played such an important part that his disappearance could totally transform a nation's destiny. Every time a sovereign died, Catherine would compute the consequences of the resulting upheaval, so as to extract the maximum benefit for Russia. She had already seen several major historical figures die: Charles VI and Charles VII of

[1] Paul and Maria had ten children: the future Tsar Alexander I (1777–1825); the future Viceroy of Poland, Constantine (1779–1831); Alexandra (1783–1801); Helena (1784–1803); Maria (1786–1859); Catherine, future Queen of Württemburg (1788–1819); Olga (1792–1795); Anne, future Queen of the Netherlands (1795–1869); the future Tsar Nicolas I (1796–1855); Michael (1798–1849).

Germany, Tsarina Elisabeth, Augustus III of Poland and in 1774, Louis XV.

This last change of ruler provoked a complete about-turn in the Empress's attitude to France. She felt scorn amounting to hatred for Louis XV, and had the highest regard for Louis XVI. The Marquis de Juigné, the new French ambassador, remarked on this subject in 1776: 'I do not think that Catherine's prejudices against France are unchangeable. Indeed I think they have diminished towards the government, and on essential matters.' Catherine, for her part, wrote to Grimm: 'Your Monsieur de Juigné has arrived. I saw him yesterday. He doesn't seem to be a fool. I pray that God will elevate his mind above the hollow dreams, high fevers, heavy and cruel slander, stupidities and brainstorms of his predecessors, and above all preserve him from the rambling of the last one,[1] and the gall, bile and black and atrabilious hypochondria of that little scoundrel of a minister who preceded both of them.' And again: 'I have such a high opinion of everything that is being done under Louis XVI, that I would scold anyone who slandered him.'

The tide of French public opinion, as unpredictable as it was powerful, and previously hostile to Russia, suddenly began to flow in her favour. Everything Russian became popular. The theatre borrowed subjects from Russian history: *The Scythians* by Voltaire, *Peter the Great* by Dorat, *Menshikov* by La Harpe... Hotels 'de Russie' and cafes 'du Nord' appeared everywhere in Paris. A dress shop called itself 'Au Russe galant'. Another boutique-owner dedicated his business 'to the Empress of Russia'. A tailor called Fagot made a fortune manufacturing children's garments on the pattern sent by Catherine to Grimm. The smartest Parisian mothers wanted their darlings to be dressed like little Alexander. Catherine was most amused. 'As for Monsieur Fagot,' she wrote, 'I am sure he is doing his job, but it does seem strange that fashion should come from the north, and stranger still that the north, and especially Russia, should be in fashion in Paris. After they thought, said and wrote such bad things about us!'

Nonetheless, if Louis XV's death had somewhat ameliorated the Franco-Russian relationship, the death of the Elector of Bavaria had a quite different effect on the international scene. The disappearance of Maximilian Joseph and the extinction of the Bavarian line left the field open for Austria to enlarge her territory – something she had long hoped to do. But the other German princes, in particular the Hohenzollerns, would not accept any extension of the Hapsburg influence, under Joseph II. 'Rather an eternal war than live under the thumb of those arrogant Hapsburgs!' cried Frederick II. Once again

---

[1] This was Durand de Distroff.

Austria and Prussia embarked on a war of words, which threatened to come to blows. But neither felt confident of his own strength. Since they were equally balanced militarily and diplomatically, the issue could only be decided by a war of attrition – unless Russia immediately began to support one of the adversaries.

Catherine realized this and calmly took stock of her prestige in a world which had hitherto treated her as an adventuress. Frederick II, after supplying her with a second daughter-in-law, begged his 'Russian sister' to be the 'arbiter of Europe'. Peace or war, he said, depended on her alone. She must declare herself ready to support Prussia, that is to say the German princes, and thus make Joseph II and Maria Theresa give in.[1] But Maria Theresa, who hated Catherine, now wrote extremely friendly letters asking her of course to settle the issue in favour of the Austrian monarchy. Catherine, canvassed by both sides, hesitated before pronouncing. She was friendly towards both Frederick and Joseph. She also needed them both if she wanted to finish dismembering Poland with impunity, and to chase the Turks off their European territory. She could only pursue her Eastern policy if both these kings closed their eyes and crossed their arms. How could she favour Prussia without upsetting Austria, and vice-versa? Catherine was proud of having been chosen, but tormented by the decision awaited from her by both Hapsburgs and Hohenzollerns. 'Who the devil can be right?' she wrote to Grimm. 'Who is wrong? Where is the liar? Oh, my God! If only the question of the Bavarian succession could be resolved simply and justly!' In April 1778, the King of Prussia, receiving no assurances from Catherine, lost patience and launched a campaign. Catherine still waited, evading questions, suggestions and pressure from the queue of diplomats at her door.

The truth was that, without for a minute losing sight of the quarrel over the Bavarian succession, she was deeply enjoying the pleasures of private life. She was fulfilled as a grandmother and once again as a lover. Zorich, the Hussar officer had, thanks to Potemkin, just been replaced by the Russian sergeant, Ivan Nikolayevich Rimsky Korsakov, also from the regiment of Hussars. The new lover was twenty-four and came from a noble family in Smolensk. When Grimm cautiously teased Her Majesty for being 'infatuated' with her new lover, she burst out with adolescent enthusiasm:

'Infatuated, infatuated! This term is quite inappropriate when one is speaking of Pyrrhus the King of Epirus, the wreck of portrait painters,

[1] Joseph II was Emperor of Austria, and co-regent with his mother, Maria Theresa, after the death of his father, Franz I, in 1765.

the sculptor's despair: It is admiration, sir, enthusiasm, that this master-piece of nature inspires . . . When Pyrrhus takes up his violin, the dogs stop and listen; when he sings, the birds come to hear as they did with Orpheus. Never did Pyrrhus make a movement or gesture that was not noble or gracious; he shines like the sun, spreading light around him; he is not effeminate, but very manly – everything one could wish for . . . All is harmony. There is no jarring note; that is the result of the great gifts accumulated in his beautiful . . . '[1]

And later: 'Only say that Pyrrhus is handsome, and has a proud and noble bearing, and know that if you heard him sing, you would cry as you did hearing La Gabriella singing at Elagin's.'[2]

Rimsky-Korsakov did indeed sing and, to accompany him, the greatest Italian artistes were brought to St Petersburg. He also wished to learn about art and literature. A librarian was instructed to form a library for him. 'What books would Your Lordship like to possess?' asked the librarian. 'You know,' he answered, 'big volumes at the bottom and little ones on top, like the Empress has.'

The Chevalier de Corberon, who knew Rimsky-Korsakov well, wrote about him: 'He was a model of small-minded self-satisfaction, and would not even have been tolerated in Paris.' It was no doubt the young man's beaming foolishness that had inspired Potemkin to push him into Catherine's arms. He realized that such a fop could never be a dangerous rival. As usual he distracted the Empress with others in order to keep the better part, her heart and mind, for himself. Pyrrhus, who had been made *aide-de-camp* and Knight of the Polish White Eagle, and was covered, as was the custom, with titles, decorations and gifts, became dizzy with his own good fortune and decided to introduce a bit of variety into his life. So he took Countess Stroganov as his mistress. But this was not enough for him: he had happy memories of Countess Bruce, who had been his *'éprouveuse'*, and returned to her for another test. Catherine surprised them voluptuously enlaced with one another. This time, Countess Bruce could not claim that her frolics were in the course of duty to the Empress. Catherine lost her temper; but it was only a passing storm – her heart wasn't in it. Her Majesty was already, no doubt, slightly bored with Pyrrhus. Countess Bruce was sent to Moscow for a time and Rimsky-Korsakov was discharged after fifteen months' service, with generous remuneration. The Tsarina never bore grudges against her old lovers.

Whose turn was it now? In the past when Voltaire had reproached her for being changeable, she had replied that, on the contrary, she was

---

[1] Letter, 1st October, 1778.
[2] Letter, 7th May, 1779.

'absolutely faithful'. 'Who to? Beauty of course! That alone attracts me!' Now she would like to have gossiped about this with the old hermit of Ferney. But he died, on the 30th May, 1778. Catherine felt deeply the loss of this man whom she had never met.

'I have a feeling of general discouragement, and a very profound contempt for all worldly things,' she wrote to Grimm. 'Why did you not seize his body, in my name? You should have sent it to me, and, by God . . . ! I promise you that he would have had the most splendid tomb possible . . . Buy his library and all that remain of his papers, including my letters. I am quite prepared to handsomely pay his heirs who, I think, do not fully realize the value of all these papers.'[1]

And again: 'Since he died it seems to me that there is no more honour attached to high spirits; he represented divinity and mirth. Also he was my master, it was he, or rather his work, which formed my spirit and my mind.'

With Grimm as her intermediary, Catherine acquired Voltaire's library from his heirs. This library, in which most of the volumes were annotated by the patriarch of Ferney, went to join that of Diderot and was for a long time buried in total oblivion. A statue of Voltaire by Houdon came with it. Catherine even, for a moment, considered building a copy of the Château de Ferney at Tsarskoe Selo, then she gave up the idea. Meanwhile she was fiercely opposed to the publication of her correspondence with the dead man. She feared that her letters would appear too badly written, and Voltaire's too flattering to her and disrespectful to other monarchs.

Finally, in the midst of these sorrows, joys and intimate worries, she reached a decision on the Austro-Prussian conflict. After sleepless nights she took the bull by the horns. Prussia, she decided, was in the right. She let Maria Theresa and Joseph know that if they did not abandon their claim over Bavaria, she 'would not allow an iniquitous war, and would feel constrained to take steps to safeguard the interests of Russia and of her friends the German princes, who had turned to her for help.' Frederick II was jubilant, Maria Theresa indignant. Joseph II was disappointed, but tried to put a good face on it, and even thought of concluding a treaty of friendship with Russia. Catherine very cleverly forewarned Versailles. The French and Russian ambassadors stirred themselves: a feverish diplomatic ballet resulted, on the 13th May, 1779, in the signing of the Teschen agreements between Prussia and Austria.[2] Ironically, Russian political interests benefited most from the whole affair, although Russia had played only an indirect part in it.

---

[1] Letter, 21st June, 1778.

[2] The Teschen Treaty gave Austria the Inn area, and Prussia the promise of the Duchies of Anspach and Bayreuth, and guaranteed the succession of the Palatine Elector, Charles Theodor (who died in 1799) to his cousin Maximilian.

From beginning to end of this imbroglio Catherine had shown a clear-sightedness, practicality and firmness that won her the respect even of her enemies. She had suddenly become, in her own words, a sort of 'magistrate of Europe' issuing judgments to the other bewildered sovereigns.

That same year, she refused to take sides between Great Britain on the one hand, and France and Spain on the other, on the issue of American Independence; she declared that she would not allow the fleets of these three countries to interfere with merchant vessels from neutral countries such as Russia. Urged on by her 'legislomania' she drew up a 'Declaration of Maritime Neutrality' to guarantee freedom of trade and movement to non-combatants. This project of the Empress's was hailed throughout the European courts as a masterpiece of equity. 'Not least among all the wonders which have enlightened your reign is your recent proclamation of a maritime code,' wrote Frederick II. 'And she who has given such wise laws to the greatest monarchy of Europe has the same right to extend them to the empire of the seas.' Most of the states adhered to the convention. Only England fulminated, but the deterioration of Anglo-Russian relations paved the way for an improvement in Russo-French ones.

As for relations between Russia, Austria and Prussia after the Treaty of Teschen, they evolved, to say the least, curiously. Frederick II, who had obtained Catherine's support, was less popular in St Petersburg than Joseph II, who should have been the one with a grudge. The Prussian diplomats tactlessly maintained friendly relations with the Grand Duke and the young court, which irritated the Empress, whereas the Austrian Emperor sang her praises wherever he went, which flattered her. Since the Bavarian business he had been thinking more and more seriously of drawing nearer to St Petersburg. He announced, to his mother's amazement, that he would like to pay Catherine a visit. Maria Theresa choked: her son, Emperor of the Germanic Holy Roman Empire, descendant of Charles Quint, to venture into that barbarous country and beg for the friendship of a 'Catherinised Princess from Zerbst', a murderess and fornicatress, whose amorous exploits were the talk of all the European courts? He held his ground. Maria Theresa gave in, but wrote to her daughter, Queen Marie-Antoinette, that she was very worried about her son's plan. She even confided to her chancellor, Kannitz: 'This is more evidence that I am powerless to impede my son's plans. And yet I will be the one who is blamed!' Catherine declared herself deeply 'honoured' by the prospect of such a meeting. She was indeed curious to meet face to face this young emperor who, she had been told, possessed the culture of a Voltaire and the simplicity of a Rousseau. Mohilev was chosen as the meeting-place. Joseph II planned to go there, with two gentlemen, under the name of 'Count Falkenstein'. He would travel as a private individual, without any pomp, staying in inns and begging peasants, as he passed, for the simplest food – a glass of milk or a hunk of bread. Catherine could not help smiling when she heard about this plan for rustic sobriety. She thought of Joseph II's sister who played at being a shepherdess in the Trianon gardens, tying pink ribbons around sheep's necks. If the 'young man from Vienna' refused to stay in the castles of Russian nobles at different stages of his journey, his democratic whim would be respected. But how could it be? There were no 'inns' in Russia. At best there were some nasty post-houses full of bed-bugs and quite unsuitable for a Hapsburg, no matter how partial he was to rural simplicity. Catherine decided to practise a little deception and had private houses prepared, with hotel signs above the door. The owners were ordered to remain out of sight during the so-called Count Falkenstein's stay, and the servants to behave like waiters and maids in a common lodging-house.

By contrast, Catherine travelled in all possible splendour, making a triumphal entry into each town she passed. At Mohilev the two sovereigns immediately started trying to charm one another. Catherine was impressed by Joseph's youth, air of distinction and enormous culture. But this did not prevent her from immediately discerning that he was 'two-faced', a sort of 'Janus', whose honeyed words concealed a total lack of scruple. He, on the other hand, admired the Empress's political genius, but deplored her behaviour at a personal level. He filled his letters to Vienna, which he knew would be intercepted and read by the Russian secret police, with flattering remarks about Catherine, but his private messengers carried a different story back. 'One must realize,' he wrote, 'that one is dealing with a woman concerned only with herself, and no more with Russia than I am; so she has to be stroked. Her vanity is everything; wild happiness and exaggerated adulation, which is the envy of all Europe, have spoiled her. However one must cry with the pack: as long as the end is obtained, the means matter little.'

If he 'stroked' Catherine during this meeting, she 'stroked' him at least as much. They vied with each other in exaggerated friendliness. Of course they discussed politics, but soon moved on to other subjects and they roared with laughter 'whilst the whole of Europe wondered what was being said in there'. 'Some people said, seeing us always together and hanging on each other's words, that we were going to be married,' wrote Catherine to Grimm. A match was indeed being made, first at

Mohilev then at Tsarskoe Selo, where Joseph joined Catherine, but it was a match on the level of political ambition. Joseph was happy to listen to Catherine's plans for carving up the Turkish territories: she would take the Greek archipelago, Constantinople and of course the Crimea which was under Russian influence; Joseph would have Serbia, Bosnia and Herzegovina. He readily agreed. In any case, he swore that Austria would henceforth undertake nothing without first consulting Russia.

Catherine wrote to Potemkin: 'Little father prince! In my opinion there is no other living sovereign to equal him (Joseph II) in terms of breadth of knowledge, manners and general merit. I am delighted to have made his acquaintance.' This declaration, written in French, was followed by a few lines of Russian: 'Believe that my friendship for you is quite equal to your attachment to me, which is priceless in my eyes. Alexander Dimitrievich (Lanskoy) sends his regards; it is ridiculous how much we miss you!'

Potemkin, to whom this note was addressed, had of course taken part in the Mohilev meeting, as the Empress's personal adviser. He had hardly left her than she felt the need to communicate her 'friendship' to him from afar. As for love, that was kept for others. On the 9th February, 1779 Harris wrote to the British cabinet; 'The Empress has expressed her intention of changing lovers and a great many candidates have put themselves forward.' He named a few names, made some predictions: Strakhov, Levaskov, Svykosky, all *protégés* of Potemkin and Countess Bruce. 'Prince Potemkin is the supreme arbiter of everything concerning business and pleasure,' he wrote, 'the Countess is only involved with the pleasure – her role is similar to that of the nobleman in the past who would taste the wine and food before the sovereign partook of them.' In the end Alexander Lanskoy, the one mentioned in the Empress's letter to Potemkin, defeated the other candidates.

'A handsome and well-built young man,' Harris noted. Lanskoy was made *aide-de-camp* after Rimsky-Korsakov's fall from grace, and was installed in the official lover's quarters. So when Joseph II met the Empress he found her flanked by her past and present lovers. The past one was a massive old lion with a powerful snout and menacing eye; the present favourite was a slender and handsome young man of twenty-five, with extremely elegant manners. Was he a sort of spiritual son of Catherine, as some maintained,[1] or as others would have it, a jealously guarded lover? Khrapovitsky, Her Majesty's private secretary, wrote in

[1] This was Madame Lavater-Sloman's theory.

his journal: 'Monsieur Lanskoy appears to be in the highest favour. Even in public, the Tsarina shows preference and attention to him with demonstrations of affection, which without being quite incompatible with strict decorum appear (to a newcomer like myself) a little extra-ordinary.' The Chevalier de Corberon had no illusions about the young man's position vis-à-vis the Empress. 'Nothing is more natural than this feeling on the part of a woman dominated, at her age, by this sort of passion; at the same time there is nothing more tiresome, as it leads to minor weaknesses on the sovereign's part. One would wish that her lovers were purely physical; but that is a rare thing in older people, and, when their imagination has not been deadened, they are a hundred times as hare-brained as any young man.'

What one can certainly say is that, for Catherine, Lanskoy was a quite different matter to Rimsky-Korsakov or Zorich. She did not merely seek nocturnal satisfaction with him. She was moved, interested and distracted by him, and she envisaged a fine political career for him. She had known him for a long time. He was brought up at the Palace at the same time as Catherine's illegitimate son Bobrinsky (who was eighteen in 1780) and a protégé of Potemkin's, Plato Zubov (thirteen in 1780) The three young men had been carefully taught by the best possible tutors. By bringing them up according to her own theories the Empress hoped to make them into the ministers of the future. The most gifted and refined of them was undoubtedly the elegant Lanskoy. How different he was from the half-mad, moody and violent Grand Duke Paul or the futile-minded, dissipated Bobrinsky, both of whom were incapable of taking part in public affairs! Catherine, disappointed in her two sons, turned onto Lanskoy her frustrated maternal feelings, and her need to educate a young person according to her theories. She saw him as a disciple – one who would, one day, replace Potemkin. But was it conceivable that this passionate woman who normally could not be without a man for a month should resign herself, out of love for Lanskoy, to years of chastity? Surely, while loving him like a mother, she opened her bedroom to him at night: he was both her lover and her son. A delightful blend where body and soul received equal satisfaction, where the gap between generations closed, where the pleasure of teaching a child gave way to the thrill of giving way to a man.

Everybody at the Court knew about the new imperial craze. As usual, Her Majesty made Lanskoy general, chamberlain, head of the cuirassier regiment and awarded him the Order of the Polar Star. Gifts flowed from her hands: money, palaces, land, peasants, diamonds, to a total value of seven million roubles. She hired a French teacher for Lanskoy, encouraged him to read, became ecstatic about every progress he made: 'He began by "devouring" poems and poets one winter, historians the next,' she wrote to Grimm in June 1782. 'Novels bore us . . . Without having been educated we know a great deal, and we only enjoy the best and most intelligent company. Apart from that we are building and planting; we are charitable, cheerful, honest and full of kindness.' In fact, in these descriptions addressed to Grimm, all the lovers appear alike. She tirelessly sought the ideal companion, from one relationship to the next. Reading her letters, it might always be the same man, under different names, in her bed and her mind. However by general consent, the newcomer was truly goodnatured and intelligent. Masson, who was so hostile to the Empress, wrote in his *Secret Memoirs* about Lanskoy: 'He is a model of goodness, humaneness, amiability, modesty and good looks . . . He loves art, and encourages talent, and is kind and charitable . . .' Little by little Catherine got into the habit of summoning Lanskoy to work with her for two hours at a time on her ministerial reports. He collaborated so closely with her that Potemkin began to take umbrage. Catherine was amused rather than alarmed by the great favourite's little bouts of jealousy towards the little favourite.

Meanwhile in Europe, the Prussians were worried about the meeting between Joseph II and the Empress. Frederick II refused to believe that 'after the duet has been sung, nothing will remain' as his ambassador put it, and decided to send his nephew and heir, Frederick William, to St Petersburg. Hearing of this Joseph II wrote to his mother: 'The Prussian Prince is coming . . . to try to spoil everything I have achieved.' His fears were groundless. Catherine did not change her plans so easily. She received Frederick William with cold formality, found him clumsy, limited and boring, and showed it. She hardly addressed a word to him, leaving Potemkin and Lanskoy to try and amuse the unwelcome visitor. The latter was annoyed by this treatment and made friends with Grand Duke Paul, which irritated the Empress even more.

As if to finally disrupt the Prussian Prince's mission, the Prince de Ligne suddenly appeared at the court, straight from Vienna. He was forty-five years old and Joseph II's chamberlain, married to Princess Françoise of Liechtenstein. He was the arbiter of culture and cosmopolitan refinement: his looks, gallantry and sharp wit had earned him the nickname of 'Prince Charming' in Paris. Here is how he described himself: 'I enjoy good life and bad life, I am religious but not pious, a Christian and not a Catholic, but ready to become one and mutter an ode by Homer instead of a Kyrie. I have six or seven countries: The Empire, Flanders, France, Spain, Austria, Poland and, almost, Hungary.'[1] He was officially Austrian, since Belgium was then part of the Austrian Netherlands, and he was in the service of Joseph II, but in fact he was from nowhere. All drawing-rooms wanted him, women were mad about him. His international adventures were whispered about everywhere. As soon as he appeared at St Petersburg other reputations faded. Catherine immediately fell under his charm. He wrote laconically: 'She was still quite handsome.' At fifty-one she obviously could not hope to compete with the young girls he usually fell for. But her mind was as sharp as ever. Conversation with the Prince de Ligne was like a fencing match. During the little evening gatherings at the Hermitage she delighted in her guest's anecdotes and *bons mots*. To make the repartee more direct, she suggested that they call each other *'tu'*. Quite unmoved the Prince de Ligne began, 'Que pense ta Majesté de . . .' He was stopped by a roar of laughter from the Empress. Another time she was showing him her new Palace in Moscow, and said, 'You must admit this is a beautiful suite!' He replied coldly, 'It has all the beauty of a hospital!' And she was delighted with his effrontery. She wrote to Grimm: 'We have the Prince de Ligne here, one of the most delightful people I have ever met. He is the most original man – thinks deeply but behaves like a child.' Compared with this mischievous visitor, Frederick William appeared even more of a nonentity. He only had to cross Catherine's field of vision for her to be irritated. Her expression would immediately turn hard and authoritarian. Frederick William realized this and his bad temper, uneasiness and awkwardness increased accordingly. When at last he left, realizing that his mission had been a failure, Catherine heaved a sigh of relief. 'I swear to you,' she wrote to Grimm, 'that he (Frederick William) made the rheumatism in my arm considerably worse by the boredom he inflicted on me, and the pain has been diminishing ever since he left.'

Frederick II soon realized the harm his nephew had done to the Austrian cause by his clumsiness. He lost his temper and suffered an attack of gout. In the meantime Catherine and Joseph II had exchanged handwritten letters which in fact constituted a secret agreement for the sharing out of the Ottoman Empire.[2] Frederick II, when he heard about this unnatural collusion, pulled in his claws and choked with rage. His correspondence with the Tsarina slowed down, then stopped altogether. The treaties between Russia and Prussia, which had expired in 1780, were not renewed. Maria Theresa's death on the 19th November of that year, liberated Joseph from maternal tyranny and brought him even closer to the Empress. Catherine, although a disciple

[1] Ref: Henry Valloton *Catherine II*.
[2] Two letters from Catherine, dated the 12th April, 1781, and two similar letters from Joseph II, dated the 18th May, 1781.

of Voltaire, sometimes felt that Heaven was helping with her boldest enterprises. There was certainly no mysticism in her attitude. But she carried within her a deep and irrational conviction that she was an exceptional person, born for success. If there was a God, he was certainly on her side. Did he inspire her in her efforts to carry on Peter the Great's work? She must think seriously about that monument that she intended to put up to the glory of her predecessor.

Falconet had been working for many long years, and in the face of general incomprehension, on his colossal statue of the Tsar. So that he could catch the movement of the rearing horse, a groom came for months to manoeuvre the Empress's two favourite horses, Brillant and Caprice, in front of him. The head of the great builder was carved by a French pupil of the artist, Mademoiselle Collot.[1] In the spring of 1770 the maquette was finished. Diderot, when he visited St Petersburg, exclaimed: 'I knew you were a very skilful man, but strike me dead if I thought you had anything like.this in mind!' However Falconet's worries were only just beginning. Old Betsky, President of the Academy of Art, treated him like a humble artisan, 'a foundry slave', and tried to give him advice. According to him, Peter the Great should be looking both towards the Admiralty and towards the Twelve Colleges. They had great trouble explaining to him that this would make the Tsar squint. Falconet had dressed his subject as a Roman emperor, and this made the Church dignitaries protest to Catherine: by what right could this little Frenchman represent the Tsar of all the Russias, head of the Greek Orthodox Church, as a pagan monarch? To tell the truth she was a little baffled by this ancient horseman, in whom she could not recognize the rough Russian Peter, Tsar of the people. However she had great confidence in Falconet and calmed the prelates by saying that this Peter I was not dressed as a pagan, but was wearing 'an idealized Russian costume'. This announcement satisfied the churchmen but upset the nobles: why put the Emperor in 'idealized Russian costume' when all his life he had fought to introduce European costume to his country? Once again Catherine sent would-be advisers away with a few cutting words. Four years were spent, from 1770 to 1774, in a vain search for somebody capable of striking such an enormous mass. In the end Falconet became exasperated and decided to try it himself. Twice running his workmen took fright and ran away in the midst of the casting. It was another setback — possibly the final one. There was no money, Falconet was growing impatient. The months went by in

---

[1] Later Mademoiselle Collot married Falconet's son.

inactivity and despair. Finally a third casting succeeded. The statue was upright. But Catherine was busy elsewhere and did not think of inaugurating the monument. Some people could not understand why the Tsar was three times life size: he looked less 'real' because the artist had made him into a giant. As for the horse, where had anyone seen a horse like that before? Fed up with the critics, the delays, exhaustion and illness, Falconet cursed the ungrateful Russians with whom he had spent twelve years, and begged his leave of Her Majesty. She refused to see him but paid him his due and let him go. He returned sadly to Paris, to old age, grey hairs and honours.

The inauguration of the statue took place later, without the artist.[1] Guards regiments stood to attention on the Senate square, facing the veiled monument. Catherine was surrounded by ministers, ambassadors, courtiers and distinguished guests; she gave the signal. An artillery salvo burst out, the cloth fell, and the crowd gave a cry of admiration at the sight of the bronze Tsar, mastering his rearing horse beside a chasm. The monarch's left hand firmly held the reins of power, his outstretched right hand ruled over the Neva, that inhospitable river on which he had built his capital; he gazed towards the horizon, and his horse's hooves crushed the twisted serpent of envy. In this grand finale, the artist was quite forgotten. Nobody mentioned his name. It was as if nature had produced the statue, as it had done the rock which supported it. Peter the Great and Catherine the Great faced each other alone. She knew already that this monument celebrated the glory both of her forerunner and of her own self. When they asked her what inscription she wanted to have engraved on the plinth, she replied proudly: 'To Peter the First, Catherine the Second.'

[1] 7th August 1782.

CHAPTER XXI

Lanskoy

Catherine patiently nursed her 'Greek project': Potemkin built small forts all along the Turkish frontier; Suvorov encamped his troops firmly in the Kuban region. Bezborodko, the Empress's new private adviser, talked of attacking Perekop and taking the Turkish citadel of Otchakov, everywhere armies trained, arsenals were prepared, generals consulted each other – the excitement mounted. Catherine and Joseph II, in an exchange of letters, considered more and more seriously the question of expelling the Turks from Europe. Catherine suggested founding an Empire of Dacia, governed by an Orthodox monarch, comprising Moldavia, Wallachia, Bessarabia, the fortress of Okakov, the land between the Bug and the Dniester and a few islands in the Archipelago. As for the Crimea, where 'happy anarchy' reigned, she considered that it virtually belonged to Russia already. Joseph II agreed in principle to all this, but demanded for himself Bosnia, Serbia, part of Wallachia, Orsova, Vidin and the mainland Venetian possessions. Catherine thought these demands altogether 'immoderate', and coolly said so to her colleague. He bridled at this. They were already quarrelling over the Turkish cake, without even having raised the knife to slice it. Frederick II, 'the old fox of Sans-Souci', was amused by this dispute, and predicted that Vienna and St Petersburg would never agree over the Turkish question. But Catherine remained optimistic – a good war would clarify the situation. And, one day, if God really was on Russia's side, Grand Duke Constantine would be on the Dacian throne. So the Tsarina's two grandsons would, after her death, rule over the two greatest empires in the world. Of course the order of succession would have to be changed so that the charming Alexander would succeed her, and not that demented maniac Paul. She had secretly decided on this long ago. And that was why she insisted on keeping the two young Grand Dukes with her as if they were her own children. She knew only too well that if she gave them back to their own parents, who demanded them, they would be brought up to hate their grandmother and despise her political achievements. To console herself, Grand Duchess Maria had the two girls who were born, one straight after the other, after

Constantine. They were willingly left to her. She was even urged to have more to distract her. But she complained: 'We dare not place anyone with the children (the boys), the Empress even chooses the wardrobe maids.' As for the Grand Duke Paul, deprived of his male offspring, he felt he had lost all paternal power, and his grudge towards the Empress became an obsession. Why did his mother, who had never looked after him, prevent him from looking after his own sons? By what refinement of cruelty did she stop him from leading an ordinary family life? Wherever he turned he found her blocking his path. In his deluded mind he saw her as a giant octopus with ever-moving tentacles. She tied him up, hypnotized him – she would stifle him, kill him perhaps, to give the throne to Alexander. He was encouraged in these feelings by Nikita Panin who, at sixty-three, had just been removed from office by Catherine and could not forgive her. Since his retirement, the old minister had drawn close to the young court, flattering the Grand Duke, who considered himself the legitimate heir to the throne.

Joseph II, who had witnessed the friction between mother and son on his visit to St Petersburg, suggested to Catherine that the Grand Ducal couple should travel to Europe. Away from the Empress, Paul, he said, could find the peace he needed so much and the foreign courts might smooth the rough edges of his character. Catherine thought this an excellent plan – but how could she get the Grand Duke to accept it? Any idea coming from her was automatically suspect. He was only interested in plans to annoy her. So she resorted to trickery. Young Prince Repnin was to say to Paul that the time had come to defy his mother's will, and demand that he be allowed to set off, with his wife, to visit the European capitals. Paul and Maria, spurred on like this, became enthusiastic. Certainly it was necessary, considering their future political responsibilities, that they should meet all the best minds of the contemporary world. Also, by making a detour by Württemburg, the Grand Duchess would be able to visit her family. They would go as far as Switzerland and call on Lavater, whose vague mysticism fascinated the young couple and exasperated Catherine. And Paris and Versailles of course...! Joseph II, Marie-Antoinette, Louis XVI, Grimm, Diderot... A complete itinerary. Quite carried away by the idea, Paul begged his mother to allow him to carry out this political and social tour, which he thought he had dreamt up himself. She pretended to be astonished, then suspicious, then indignant. How could he, the heir to the throne, think of abandoning St Petersburg? He begged her on his knees; Maria sobbed; Catherine pretended to be upset and finally gave in. Joyful preparations for the journey began. The planned itinerary took in Poland, Austria, Switzerland, Italy, France, Holland

and Belgium. But Catherine forbade her son to go to Berlin, knowing his unhealthy passion for Frederick II. All the foreign courts were officially informed. The young couple would travel *incognito*, under the transparent name of Comte and Comtesse du Nord.

However, amid the general elation, old Nikita Panin decided to throw a spanner into the works. His grudge against Catherine had made him Machiavellian. In order to ruin the Empress's plans, he convinced Paul that it was all a trick of his mother's. If he went she would not allow him back into Russia, and would take advantage of his absence to proclaim Alexander as her direct heir. Paul and Maria, horrified, saw themselves already exiled, deprived of the crown, separated for ever from their children. Having begged the Empress to allow them to go, they now begged her to allow them to stay. She refused, saying the foreign courts would already have made their arrangements. She was answered with cries, sobs, and curses. Paul shouted that he would not move. Maria was fainting with misery. Catherine tried in vain, in scene after scene, to reason with the young couple. On the day of departure they refused to leave their apartments. Catherine had to drag her son by the arm to the carriage; behind her, Prince Repnin carried the Grand Duchess who had fainted. He placed her inert body next to the pale Grand Duke, who looked as if he had been condemned to death. The coachman whipped the horses. Catherine sighed with relief. Would she really one day have to place Russia in the hands of this idiotic son of hers?

Her fears were confirmed by the reports she received at each stage of their journey. At Florence, before Leopold of Tuscany, Paul criticized his mother's expansionist policies, expressed his admiration for the King of Prussia, and made threats against the Empress's friends, saying they were all in the pay of the Austrians: 'As soon as I have any power, I will have them whipped, I will break them, I will expel them.' In Brussels, in the presence of the Prince de Ligne, he told ghost stories and spoke of the hallucinations which no doctor could cure him of. At Versailles, where he was received with splendour and friendliness, he confided to Louis XVI and Marie-Antoinette that at St Petersburg he was kept 'in darkness and discomfort', and that his mother's favourites persecuted him, that his life was hell. And when the Queen asked him if it was true that he could trust nobody, he cried: 'I would be very sorry to have with me a dog who loved me, because as soon as we left Paris my mother would have had it thrown into the Seine with a stone round its neck.' There were intimate suppers, the opera at Versailles, a party at the Petit Trianon, a grand ball in the Hall of Mirrors, a review of the French Guards on the Champ de Mars, a concert at Bagatelle, a visit to the Institute, a reception given by the Prince de Condé, at Chantilly –

the 'Comte du Nord' felt more important in France than he did in Russia. He puffed himself up, almost bursting with pride, and was quite unable to hold his tongue. Although Grimm, fawning as ever, assured Catherine that her son and daughter-in-law had been a great success in Paris 'without an if or a but',[1] it seems that the passage of this moody, talkative and resentful couple caused some embarrassment to sovereigns, ministers and courtiers. After Paul's stay in the Grand Duchy of Baden, the Minister of State, Edelsheim, summed up the general feeling thus: 'His mind is crooked, his heart straight, his judgment a matter of luck. He is suspicious, touchy... Plots, but feels persecuted... a disaster for his friends, enemies, allies and subjects...! He detests his own country, and said things about it to me, at Gatchina, which I cannot repeat.' When Paul visited Vienna and was due to see a performance of *Hamlet*, the actor Brockman refused to perform it before him for fear that he might see an allusion to his own unhappiness in the tragedy of the Prince of Denmark.

Possibly what irritated Catherine most was to learn that her son and daughter-in-law had been to see Lavater in Zurich. She was very suspicious of the influence the Protestant theologian's hazy theories might have on a hysterical nature, and she deplored the fact that the Grand Duchess encouraged her husband in his leaning towards the supernatural. She loathed Rosicrucians, Freemasons, Martinists and other parasites on the next world. She had forbidden Cagliostro to appear at Court. It was this wandering spirit that had given birth to the myth of Ivan VI and the Pugachev rebellion. To govern them they needed a clear well-organized and rational mind. A Peter the Great, a Catherine II. Not a Paul I.

If she had previously been impatient for her son to leave, she now wanted him to return, for fear of what more foolish things he might do on his journey. When the couple returned she was infuriated by the amount they had bought abroad and ordered them to send back all the foolish samples of French fashion, with which their luggage overflowed. There were, wrote Harris, 'two hundred cases filled with chiffon, pompoms and other toiletries from Paris'. Faced with this disastrous refusal, the famous seamstress, Mademoiselle Bertin, gave cries of rage. 'She defended her flounces,' wrote Grimm. After questioning the Grand Duke, Catherine realized that the flattering receptions Paul had received had only increased his folly and arrogance. More than ever she found it necessary to keep her grandsons away from their father. But she felt that she should not, for all that, neglect her granddaughters, who

[1] Letter of the 7th June, 1782.

had unfortunately been left in their parents' charge. The young princesses must have an exceptional governess, who would, by her gentle authority, counteract the pernicious influence of the family circle.

Sievers, on instructions from Her Majesty, chose Charlotte de Lieven, the widow of a general, who lived modestly with her four children on the outskirts of Riga. When Madame de Lieven was informed of the honour that awaited her, she tried to refuse: she had no wish to leave her retreat and face all the intrigues of the Court. However an Empress's orders could not be disobeyed. If she would not go willingly to St Petersburg, Madame de Lieven would be taken there by force. She was bundled into a carriage and taken under escort to the Winter Palace, where she was questioned by one of Her Majesty's secretaries. She was exhausted and furious, and spoke of the children she had had to abandon, of her distaste for the ostentation of public life, and of her desire for peace and solitude! A female voice interrupted: 'You're the person I need! Follow me!' The Empress, who had been listening behind a curtain, came up to her, embraced her and swore that she alone could supervise her granddaughters' education. Madame de Lieven was touched and gave in. Her four children later joined her.[1]

While the new governess was trying to gain her charges' affection, Paul's only supporter and last adviser, Nikita Panin, died. After the old minister's death, he felt a deathly void around him. He did not know where to turn for support in his follies. He bitterly began to think that even his wife and daughters belonged to a hostile clan.

Catherine was worried by another case of insanity. Her old lover, Gregory Orlov, had lost his young wife at Lausanne on the 16th June, 1782, and was trying to forget his unhappiness by travelling through Europe. From Karlsbad to Ems, and Ems to Vichy, he pursued water and rest cures, which had little effect on his miserable condition. He was destroyed by remorse and regrets. When he reappeared at St Petersburg, Catherine was horrified by this living corpse, the fleshless features, white hair and wild eyes – where was the fiery companion of her youth? He felt responsible for the death of his wife whom, he said, he had been unable to understand or love. Another ghost also haunted his dreams. In his wanderings, he would see the spirit of Peter III

---

[1] Madame de Lieven remained at the Court for nearly half a century. She organized Catherine's granddaughters' education, and, partly, that of the grandsons, with dignity and good sense. Alexander and Nicholas regarded her as a grandmother. She died in 1828, loved and respected by all, after having been made a Countess, then a Princess. She was the mother-in-law of the famous Princesse de Lieven, who seduced Metternich, held a salon in Paris, became Guizot's muse, and was nicknamed 'the Sibyl of Europe'.

before him. Orlov confessed that he was the assassin and cried: 'This is my punishment!' Catherine brought him to stay at the Palace, under medical supervision. Sometimes he screamed with terror. She would then be summoned by a servant and rush to his bedside where she would talk to him gently and fondly until he calmed down. Little by little Orlov's insanity became worse, until he finally had to be moved to an isolated house in Moscow. He died there in April 1783. 'Although I was prepared for this sad event, I confess to you that I have felt the greatest sorrow,' wrote Catherine to Grimm. 'They say to me, and I say to myself, all the things one does say on these occasions: I reply with waves of sobbing – I am suffering terribly... Prince Orlov's genius was very great... For all his great qualities his mind was incoherent... Nature had spoiled him, and as regards anything that didn't immediately spring to his mind he was lazy... There is a strange coincidence about Prince Orlov's death; Count Panin died about fourteen or fifteen days before him, and neither knew about the death of the other. These two men will be most surprised to meet each other in the next world, disagreeing and disliking one another as they did.'

To replace these two men, Catherine had by her young Alexander Lanskoy, her dear 'Sacha', so young, intelligent and agreeable, and out 'on the field' the impetuous and idle Potemkin. He decided to win the Crimea for the Empress. 'The Crimea by its position cuts our frontiers,' he wrote to Catherine. 'Whether we have to confront the Turks on the Bug or the Kuban, the Crimea will be in our way... Now imagine that the Crimea is yours, that this wart is removed – in one blow the frontier position becomes perfect.' In April 1783, Potemkin, backed by General Samoylov's troops, began talks with the pro-Russian Khan Chagin Ghirey, who had been elected in the Crimea in the same way as Poniatowski, in the past, had been elected in Poland. And, just as Poniatowski had consented to the dismembering of his country, so Khan Chagin Ghirey, after taking the opinion of the Tartar tribes of the Kuban, agreed to surrender the Crimea, which then became a Russian province. Catherine followed the whole business very closely, as she hoped, while taking the prize, to avoid a European war. Joseph II recognized it as a *fait accompli*. France only made a diplomatic protest: she offered to appease the Turks on condition Russia promised not to push any further. Catherine refused to tie herself to such a promise. 'I have taken a firm decision to count on no one but ourselves,' she wrote to Potemkin. 'When the cake is cooked, everybody will be hungry. I count very little on my allies, and am not at all impressed by French thunder, or rather, hot air.' Sultan Abdul Hamid, abandoned by all, realized that his army was not strong enough to re-open hostilities, and things remained at that. On the 21st July, 1783, the Tsarina proclaimed the annexation of the Crimea, and congratulated Potemkin on his success. Now Russia controlled the Black Sea as well as the Caspian.

Now that he had joined the Crimea to the crown, Potemkin began to lead the luxurious life of an Eastern potentate. Named 'Prince of Taurida' by the Empress's wish, he was seized with administrative frenzy and began to build on the virgin territories under his power. He founded cities in the desert, built roads, created universities, designed parks, planted vineyards, dredged out ports, opened shipyards, and attracted settlers by subsidizing their establishment. He had his own harem on the spot, his 'hen-run' as he called it, consisting of his five pretty Engelhardt nieces. One by one they became his mistresses. The age difference and blood connection did not worry him. As the Empress's unofficial husband, he swore everlasting love to her whilst at the same time enjoying all this young flesh. The letters he wrote to one of his favourites, the little Barbe, show how passionately he felt; 'I love you, oh my soul, but how? As I have never loved before ... I kiss you everywhere ... My friend, my beloved little lips, my little mother, my treasure ... My tender mistress, your victory over me is strong and eternal ... Come, oh my mistress, hurry, oh my friend, God's own priceless gift ... I am happy when you are happy, satisfied when you are satisfied. I follow you everywhere, right up to that swing you like to balance on; although I worry when you go too high.' Had Catherine ever received such spicy letters from her lover? In any case she was not jealous. How could she be when she was living through the perfect love affair, at fifty-four with her twenty-five-year-old Sacha Lanskoy?

In that year, 1783, she was as happy as possible with Lanskoy. Attempts to seduce him away by foreign monarchs, whether it was Joseph II or Gustavus III of Sweden, left him cold. He was devoted to Catherine and wished only for his mistress to be happy, and his country great. The gentleness of his nature had gained him the confidence of the Grand Ducal pair. The Court was astonished to see that he kept out of all intrigues. He was eager to cultivate his mind, and spent all he had enlarging his library. He was like the Tsarina, passionately interested in Russian history. They would sit side by side studying old archives from convents. Catherine had worn reading glasses since 1772, and did not hesitate to wear them in front of her lover. They were so close that vanity did not enter their relationship. Indeed the exchange of ideas may have been their chief pleasure. This collaboration was shown to particular advantage when it came to reviving the Russian Academy which had slid into lethargy under the direction of Domachnev. Lanskoy suggested that this muddled and extravagant man be replaced by the exuberant Princess Dashkova. She had just returned to Russia, and regarded herself as a victim of ingratitude as, she said, Her Majesty had not sufficiently recognized the services she had performed during the 1762 *coup d'état*. It was an excellent opportunity to stuff some sweetmeat into her greedy mouth. And what an example it would be to the enlightened minds of Europe to have a woman at the head of the Russian Academy!

Catherine approved of the idea. But Princess Dashkova bridled: 'Make me head laundress instead!' she replied in the midst of a Court ball. Perhaps she had been hoping for a more important position. When she got home, still in her ball-gown, she wrote a long epistle to the Empress, saying that she had refused for fear of not being up to the task. At seven in the morning she sent the letter to the Palace, and an hour later received a friendly reply in which there was no question of accepting the refusal. 'You rise earlier than I do, my lady,' wrote Catherine, 'and you have sent me a note for breakfast... First, since you do not entirely reject my proposal(?) I will forgive you... Please remain assured that it will be a pleasure to me on all occasions to serve you both with words and actions.' Upon which, that same evening an edict was sent to the Senate naming Princess Dashkova, Directress of the Academy. She foamed with rage but it was too late to escape. A few days later, angry but honoured she entered on the arm of the octogenarian, Euler, to preside over the inaugural session of the Academy. In any case she very soon acquired a taste for the work. Inspired by the example of the French Academy, she charged the Russian one with the task of producing the first dictionary of the language, and fixing the spelling, grammar and prosody. The lexicographers classed the words in etymological rather than alphabetical order. The result disappointed Catherine. 'The work is... thin and dry,' she wrote to Princess Dashkova. 'In its present form, all I can see is a simple list of words which are not naturalized or in general usage. For my part, I cannot understand it... the French Academy has purified the national tongue by removing all foreign elements.' Princess Dashkova was discouraged by the Empress's lack of comprehension but nonetheless pursued her task. She set about tidying up the language and the premises with a housewife's energy. When she was reorganizing the Museum of Fine Art, she was horrified to discover two jars containing the pickled heads of victims of Peter the Great: that of the Tsar's mistress, Marie Hamilton, who had been found guilty of infidelity, and that of William Mons, the Tsarina's lover.[1] These

---

[1] Marie Hamilton was decapitated in 1719 and William Mons in 1724.

macabre remains had been in the gallery since 1724, attracting public curiosity. Princess Dashkova took it upon herself to get rid of them. She also began to print Catherine's historical writings at the Academy press, and asked for her help in a magazine she had just created: *The Companion to Friends of the Russian Language*. The Empress was delighted and anonymously wrote a series of light-hearted little articles, portraits of her friends, funny memories, harmless banter, all interspersed with brackets and NB's. Lanskoy corrected Her Majesty's spelling mistakes. But the sharp and ironical style was very much her own. 'You must know,' she wrote to Grimm, 'that for the last four months a magazine has been appearing in St Petersburg, where the NB's and other remarks are sometimes quite hilarious. This magazine is in general a hotchpotch of amusing things.' Still anonymously she wrote plays for the theatre which were performed on the Hermitage stage. 'You ask,' she wrote to Grimm, 'why I write so many comedies... First because it amuses me; secondly because I would like to encourage the national theatre which was becoming neglected for lack of new plays; and thirdly because it is a good thing to mock the visionaries who turn up their noses. *The Impostor* and *The Victim of Delusion* have had enormous success... What was most delightful was that they called for the author at the first performance... Of course he kept the most perfect incognito.' In *The Impostor* and *The Victim of Delusion* Catherine presented a sort of Cagliostro surrounded by his foolish admirers. Most of her plays were badly put together political satires with somewhat feeble characterization. It is likely that she was secretly helped in this work by some publicist who was well in with the Court. The general inspiration of these little works is a mixture of Voltairian philosophy and Russian tradition. She replied gaily to Grimm, when he made a few mild criticisms of them! 'Well these dramatic works have been pulverized, have they? Not at all. I maintain they are perfectly good for the lack of anything better, and since people went to see them and laughed, and they stemmed sectarian enthusiasms, they got the success they deserved despite their faults. When somebody has been found to write better ones, we will stop writing them and enjoy theirs.' She even tried her hand at poetry, in Russian, French and German, but realized her weakness in this field. 'I have been versifying for the past four days, but it takes too long and I started too late.'

Comedy was the literary form she liked best. She loved laughing – but simply, with no undercurrent of meaning. Thus she was shocked by *The Marriage of Figaro*. 'As for comedy, if I write one,' she wrote to Grimm, 'I will not take *The Marriage of Figaro* as my model... as I have never found myself in worse company than at this famous wedding.

Apparently these trends, which I thought had been purged, have been brought back to imitate the Ancients. Molière's expression was free but sprang from a sort of natural gaiety and effervescence; but the thought was never unpleasant, unlike this play where the implications are always disagreeable – and it goes on for three and a half hours. In addition it is a permanent struggle to follow the tissue of intrigue, which is quite untrue to life. I did not laugh once at the reading.'[1]

In fact what she really held against *The Marriage of Figaro,* although she did not say so, was the author's subversive ideas, which emerged from the rattle of the dialogue. She guessed that Beaumarchais was one of the firebrands she so hated. In any case the French theatre, which had amused her so much in the past, now bored her. 'Most French plays put me to sleep,' she confided to Grimm. 'There is no energy, no spice in them; I don't know, but it seems to me that vitality, accompanied by an eye for what is beautiful and great, matters more and more in this world... Oh Voltaire! You knew how to relight the sparks that lay amongst the ashes.' She would like to have rewritten all these disappointing French plays, but didn't have time. She didn't like being put to sleep by a comedy, but neither did she enjoy crying at a tragedy. A work could often be saved by the modification of a few sentences. Catherine was not deterred by any respect for an author's wishes, even when the author was the great Voltaire himself. She was so upset by the tragic ending of *Tancred* that she ordered it to be changed on the Hermitage stage. No more killing – at the end of the play, Tancred, after having saved Aménaïde, marries her instead of dying in front of her. Surely it was better that way? In any case, at about this time Catherine was beginning to detach herself from French literature. Apart from Voltaire who had 'given birth' to her, Corneille who had always 'elevated her soul' and the inimitable Molière, it was not worth even leafing through the works of the others. Salvation now lay in German literature. With her usual impetuosity, Catherine spoke of dumping all French writers and forming an exclusively German library for herself. Strangely she ignored her great contemporaries, Lessing, Schiller and Goethe and became infatuated with minor German writers instead. 'This Teutonic literature is making giant strides – it leaves the rest of the world standing,'[2] she wrote.

As for German music, she splendidly ignored it – as she did all other music. However, to please her charming Sacha Lanskoy she engaged the famous conductor, Sarti, and organized concerts at the Hermitage.

[1] Letter of the 22nd April, 1785.
[2] Waliszewski *The Story of an Empress.*

Unfortunately she hated remaining seated for one hour, submitting to this disagreeable barrage of notes. Her reward was to hear Lanskoy afterwards explaining solemnly to her the spirit and the structure of the piece they had just heard. Anything coming from him revived and comforted her. She allowed him to find a tutor for the Grand Dukes, Alexander and Constantine. Sacha Lanskoy insisted on having César-Frédéric de La Harpe, a shy Swiss republican.

La Harpe, a native of Rolle on the Lake of Geneva, exasperated by the pestering of the Berne governemnt, had originally decided to go to America to help found a perfect society, free from constraint. His fellow pupil, Ribeaupierre, who was a foreign member of the Russian Academy, suggested that he should go instead to Russia. And indeed at that moment the Empress's favourite was searching for a tutor, not for the Grand Dukes, but for his two younger brothers, the badly-behaved Counts Lanskoy, who had been travelling in Europe and were to be brought back to St Petersburg. After long hesitation, La Harpe accepted the post. But once he found himself in Italy with the two rogues, he became discouraged by their aimless stupidity and insolence. He was both irritated and amused by his own position and wrote to Ribeaupierre about it with such irony and good sense that the latter showed the letter to Lanskoy who in turn passed it on to Catherine. The young lover was immediately struck with an idea: a man of such character was wasted on the job of bringing home those two scoundrels – he must be entrusted with the Grand Dukes. Catherine agreed. As a friend of the philosophers, how could she resist the temptation of placing her grandsons in the hands of a lover of justice and freedom? La Harpe, she thought, as the republican tutor of two future autocrats would instil in them respect for the individual without calling into question the legitimacy of their power. La Harpe, in Rome, received an official letter then, inviting him, the enemy of tyranny, to come and educate two princes who were destined to be tyrants over millions of men. He was told in the letter that he must work at making 'men' out of these rulers of the future. He was fired by the idea and already saw himself shaping liberal monarchs as if out of clay, thus saving Russia from the yoke of absolutism.

When he arrived in St Petersburg, La Harpe received an extremely warm welcome from Catherine, who gave him an 'Instruction', a sort of educational programme she had drawn up with the help of Sacha Lanskoy. The new tutor was thrilled as he read the document, finding it worthy of a permanent place in the history of pedagogy: 'Children must love plants and animals and learn how to care for them . . . Nothing must be more forbidden or more severely punished than lies . . . The aim of education must be to inspire children with love for their fellow-men. Children's minds must be prepared to listen with composure to the most opposed and contradictory views... The knowledge they acquire must serve purely to understand better their princely role... The main aim must be to inculcate virtue and good habits; once they have taken root, the rest will follow with time.'

These admirable principles were of course difficult to put into practice immediately as the Grand Dukes were only aged six and four at the time. Until their Highnesses could properly appreciate the teaching of the republican ideas, La Harpe was asked to teach them a few words of French, and take them for walks. He jibbed at this and, braving protocol, wrote to the Council for the Education of the Young Princes, asking whether he had been brought to St Petersburg as an educator or as a French teacher and child's nurse. Catherine, far from being offended, was delighted at this direct language. At last a man who knew what he wanted, despised Court favours, and stated his conditions without being in the least impressed by the splendour of the Imperial machine! He had to be accepted for what he was, or else he would pack his bags and return to Switzerland. Catherine would not dream of parting from this inspired and outspoken scatterbrain. She wrote the following appreciation in the margin of La Harpe's curriculum: 'The man who wrote this is capable of teaching more than just French.'

At the beginning of the summer of 1784, Catherine was at Tsarskoe Selo: Sacha Lanskoy, Alexander and Constantine formed a magic triangle on which her happiness rested. Leaning on her lover's arm, the passionate grandmother gazed fondly at her grandchildren playing on the lawn. The weather was beautiful, the park sparkled with new greenery, the first roses were opening in the shrubberies, fountains played, the Grand Dukes' English ponies galloped in the field, Potemkin was expected back after his prodigious achievements in the south, Russia was all-powerful, the air was pure and Catherine, despite her fifty-five years, felt as if she had wings on her feet and sunshine in her heart. Then suddenly, the crash, the shock, darkness. On the evening of the 19th June, Sacha Lanskoy took to his bed, shaking with fever, with his throat inflamed and almost closed up. His breathing became more and more laboured. Soon he could no longer speak. The doctors pronounced that it was diphtheria and begged the Empress to stay away for fear of infection. She refused and moved into what she called 'her child's' room. She never changed her clothes, slept or ate and, like a mother, helped the feverish youth struggle against death. On the 24th June the famous doctor Wickard was urgently summoned to Tsarskoe Selo: on his arrival he examined the patient and pronounced him lost. The Empress refused to believe it: 'You have no idea how strong he is!' She was thinking of their nights together. Doctor Wickard in his *Memoirs* implies that this 'strength' was the result of the cantharides powder he took in large quantities before going into action.[1] It might even have been this that had destroyed his health. Others, such as Masson, said that he had been poisoned by a jealous Potemkin. But whatever the cause, the beautiful, irreplaceable Sacha died in Catherine's arms on the 25th June, at the age of twenty-six.

He was buried in the park at Tsarskoe Selo. After the funeral, Catherine took to her bed, broken with grief. The doctors feared that she had had a stroke. For a week she collapsed unable to do anything. She got up at last on the 2nd July and found on her desk an unfinished letter to Grimm. She picked up her pen, and continued sadly:

'When I began this letter I was in the midst of happiness and joy and my thoughts came and went so rapidly that I never knew what happened to them. It is no longer like that; I am plunged in the utmost misery and my happiness is gone. I have thought of dying myself from the irreparable loss of my best friend, eight days ago. I hoped that he would be the support of my old age. He worked, he learnt, he had acquired all my tastes. I was bringing up this young man and he was grateful, gentle and honest; he shared my sorrows, when I had any, and was happy when I was happy. In a word, I weep and must tell you that General Lanskoy is dead ... My room which until now was so pleasant has become an empty cavern into which I drag myself like a ghost ... I cannot see anybody without being choked by sobs. I cannot sleep, nor eat. Reading bores me and writing exhausts me. I do not know what will become of me, but I do know that I have never been so unhappy in my life since my most beloved friend left me. I opened my drawer and found this letter begun, I have written these lines, and now I am exhausted ...'

For several days she declared herself unable to deal with political matters. 'Since Monsieur Lanskoy's death, she has not seen any of her ministers, nor indeed any of her private circle,' wrote the English Ambassador, Fitzherbert. At last she pulled herself together and doggedly returned to her task. Potemkin was with her. He 'howled' with grief with Her Majesty. But really he could not have been very ill-pleased at the disappearance of such a gifted rival. Catherine was happy to have at her side the powerful figure of her erstwhile lover and clandestine husband. He helped her back onto the tracks. 'Do not believe that I have neglected the smallest matter demanding my

[1] Waliszewski *Around the Throne*.

attention,' she wrote to Grimm two months later. 'During the worst time they asked for instructions about everything and I gave them, sensibly and intelligently . . . I have become a very sad soul; I only speak in monosyllables . . . Everything upsets me, and I have never enjoyed inspiring pity.'

She had a funeral urn erected in the private garden at Tsarskoe Selo engraved with the following inscription, in French: 'A mon plus cher ami.' Later she had a church built as a mausoleum for the whole Lanskoy family. But only Sacha was buried there. None of his relations accepted the offer to join him there one day. As far as they were concerned, he had dishonoured himself by becoming the Tsarina's lover. It was the only time a Russian family took Catherine's 'favours' towards one of their members as a disgrace. Jacques Lanskoy, the dead man's brother, built a church on his own land, and had it decorated with icons of saints with the faces of various members of his family; the handsome Sacha only appeared, amidst eternal flames, in a painting depicting Hell. Catherine ignored the Lanskoy clan's animosity and, the day after his death, wrote a very moving letter to the dead man's mother. The months went by and her heart 'still bled as it had done at the first moment'.

To fight her melancholia she plunged herself into the comparative study of languages, and surrounded herself with dictionaries. Finnish, Turkish, Abyssinian, all were included. She corresponded with the naturalist Pallas; she begged the Berlin publisher Nicolai to obtain documents for her; she tried by every possible means to find a Slav presence in all the great historical movements of the world; finally she struck up an epistolary friendship with Doctor Zimmerman, the Swiss doctor and philosopher of the Hanoverian court, whose book *On Solitude* had helped her to bear the first few days after Lanskoy's death. Zimmerman who was a witty, cutting, sometimes even cynical writer, became another Diderot for her. She sent him her works, she commissioned him to find literary and artistic treasure for her, she asked him to recruit, in her name, scholars and scientists to come and work in Russia. Her greatest wish was for Zimmerman himself to come and live in St Petersburg. But Zimmerman's price for expatriation was the sum of at least eight thousand thalers. 'He's an expensive man,' Catherine declared. And she dropped negotiations. But she continued her correspondence with the doctor-philosopher, broaching every possible subject, history and mysticism, art and morality, politics and the way to make cheese.

All the same these futile exercises of the mind could not replace the warm nourishment of love. Potemkin understood this, and as soon as he felt she was available, he cautiously advanced a new candidate: Alexander Ermolov. He was thirty-one, tall, blond, with almond-shaped eyes and a slightly squashed nose, which earned him the nickname from Potemkin of 'the white negro'. He seemed to possess neither wit nor good-humour. Minister Bezborodko saw him, however, as modest, serious and well-educated. As for the Empress, she wrote to Grimm: 'In a word I have a capable and worthy friend.' But after her great sorrow she did not feel ready for a really important love affair. No doubt she took this lover for her health, out of habit and need for a bedfellow. But her heart was not deeply involved. At Court, the new lover's chances were calculated, the Tsarina's smiles, words and silences in his presence carefully observed; courtiers approached him, hoping for favours, and drew away at Her Majesty's frown; ambassadors wondered which political faction the new favourite belonged to, and described in their despatches the smallest fluctuation in the imperial affair, as if it were a State matter. Most estimated that Alexander Ermolov would not last for long – he was not of high enough calibre. He soon betrayed the interests of the man to whom he owed his position and foolishly passed into the camp of Potemkin's enemies – who were many and powerful. Urged on by them, the young man told Catherine that Potemkin was subverting funds destined for the colonization of White Russia to his own use. Potemkin immediately defended himself by saying that it was only a loan and that it would be repaid as soon as he had sold one of his estates. Then on his friends' advice, Alexander Ermolov showed Catherine a letter from the ex-Khan of the Crimea, now interned at Kaluga, complaining that he no longer received his pension because the Prince of Taurida was appropriating it for himself. Catherine's confidence was shaken and she began to show marked coldness towards Potemkin which was of course noticed by all the courtiers. The English envoy, Fitzherbert, wrote to London: 'Confidence in Potemkin has largely diminished owing to his presumption and arrogant manner and also his numerous abuses of power, and his various whims. Hatred for him is such that one might be seriously worried.'

However, when Potemkin was warned against probable disgrace, he replied proudly: 'Do not fear, I will not be overthrown by an urchin. Anyway, who would dare?' And then he disappeared from the Court, so that it would be understood that he was offended, and suffered. Then on the anniversary of the coronation he reappeared in a splendid costume sparkling with diamonds, looked furiously at Ermolov who thought he had already won the battle, and rushed unannounced into the Empress's boudoir. She was in the hands of her hairdresser. Without any preamble, he shouted: 'Madam, you must choose between

Ermolov and myself; because as long as you keep that white negro, I will not set foot in your house!' Catherine was moved by this passion, and in any case had grown tired of her insipid lover. She was flattered by Potemkin's jealousy. A wave of memories came into her mind. How could she hesitate between 'the white negro' and 'the one-eyed lion'? She sacrificed her young lover without the slightest regret. Sacked out of the blue, the latter begged permission to see the Empress for the last time before leaving the Palace. Catherine refused to receive him. But, as always, she was generous with the parting gifts: a hundred and thirty thousand roubles and four thousand peasants.

The lover's quarters were empty. There was no creak of footsteps on the spiral staircase leading to Her Majesty's bedroom. All was scarcity, abstinence and gloom. Potemkin's enemies were dismayed by Ermolov's dismissal, and began the search for another champion capable of satisfying the Empress's passions. For a moment they thought they had succeeded with a certain Mengden from Courland, but that proved to be a false hope – Catherine didn't want him. In most people's opinion she had become more difficult than usual. She was enormous, short of breath, and ageing, and would only be satisfied with the best. She was not taken with any of the candidates. At last Potemkin picked out a young guards officer, Alexander Mamonov, who was twenty-six years old and handsome and elegant. Potemkin felt sure that he would fill the bill. And, as he had arranged with the Empress, he sent his protégé along bearing a watercolour. Catherine pretended to examine the painting, while running a practised eye over the bearer. Then she wrote on the back of the paper. 'The contours are fine but the choice of colours is less fortunate,' which meant that the boy was well-built but his yellowish complexion left something to be desired. Mamonov brought the annotated painting back to Potemkin. Was he a failure? No, in the end, not – Her Majesty overlooked the 'colours' out of esteem for the 'contours'. Mamonov was accepted. There was great excitement at Court over the new favourite, who moved into his tied quarters. He was said to be a keen Francophile. He came from a good family, spoke Voltaire's language fluently and was a witty conversationalist. Catherine immediately felt revived, forgot her mourning and became like a young bride beside the man she called 'Mister Redcoat' because of his uniform. She wrote to Grimm:

'The red coat covers a man with an excellent heart and a great fund of honesty, he has the wit of four people, he is an inexhaustible well of merriment, shows great originality in his view of life, and his manner of describing it; he is excellently educated, and most well-informed on all subjects needed for a sharp mind. We conceal our love of poetry as if it were a murder; we love music passionately; we have an unusual facility for quick understanding; God only knows what we don't know by heart. We recite, we tell tales, we can hold our own in the best company; we are most polite; we write in Russian and French, with a style and character unusual for this country; the exterior corresponds perfectly with the interior; our features are regular; we have two beautiful dark eyes with finely drawn eyebrows; above average height, a noble manner, and an easy bearing; in a word we are as solid inside as we are able, fine and strong outside. I am convinced that if you met this Redcoat you would ask who he was, if you had not already guessed it.'[1]

Two weeks later: 'Mister Redcoat is no less than an ordinary person, he sparkles with wit without forcing it; he can tell stories perfectly well, and is unusually good-humoured. Finally he is stuffed with honesty, good manners and wit; in a word, he is no fool!'[2]

And again: 'This Redcoat is anyway so amiable, witty, merry, handsome, obliging, and such good company that you must love him without even knowing him.'[3]

How could this fifty-seven-year-old woman, this practitioner of every sort of political trick, speak so naively about the 'honesty' of this very young man whom she had commandeered into her bed? Did she really believe that he was physically attracted by her fading charms? Should she not admire him more for his blind energy than for his over-accommodating morals? When it was a matter of love, at least at the beginning of a relationship, Catherine's self-delusion was staggering. She wanted to believe, and thus surrender more completely. Her 'uterine passions' to use Masson's expression[4] were always surrounded by veils of poetic feeling. She was both sensual and sentimental. She had to have with her a new man, handsome, tall, strong and able to satisfy the needs of her passionate temperament; but he had to also be a friend and adviser, a charming companion and sometimes even a child whom she could comfort and rock. The pleasures of the flesh never excluded those of tenderness, friendship and devotion. She was in no way a hysteric or a nymphomaniac. She was completely healthy and simple in her tastes, and needed men not simply for her physical well-being, but also so that she could blossom spiritually. She liked a masculine atmosphere; few women attracted her, but if a man showed

[1] Letter, 17th December, 1786.
[2] Letter, 2nd January, 1787.
[3] Letter, 2nd April, 1787.
[4] Masson *Secret Russian Memoirs*. Masson was Grand Duke Alexander's mathematics teacher.

courage and spirit she was won over to him – even if she had no intention of making him her lover. She had been conquered in this way, in the past, by the Prince de Ligne, and was again now by the new French Ambassador, Count Louis-Philippe de Ségur, who had just arrived at the court.

Ségur was thirty-two years old, and was worldly, seductive, subtle and cultivated; Vergennes had picked him to improve relations between Russia and France, and prepare negotiations for a commercial treaty. Catherine was, from the beginning, intrigued by this unusual character who, despite his great name, espoused democratic ideas and applauded the revolutionary enemies of his class. He had set off with twenty young noblemen to fight with Lafayette in America. Back in France where he was acclaimed as the 'hero of liberty', he dreamt of both serving the king and bringing happiness to the people. The Tsarina was not ill-pleased by this unlikely combination of ideas. Had she not, herself, engaged a Swiss republican as tutor to her grandsons? She still saw herself, sometimes, as a sovereign with philosophical ideals. With her pen she followed in Voltaire's footsteps – but came to her senses as soon as one of her subjects wavered. She wrote to Doctor Zimmerman:

'Philosophy has been extremely important to me, because I have always had republican leanings. Such leanings may seem strange combined with the complete power of my position, but nobody in Russia can say that I have abused it... As for my political conduct, I have tried to follow plans which were to the best advantage of my country, and the most bearable for others... Humanity in general has in me a never-failing friend.' And she composed a humorous epitaph for herself, in French:

'Here lies Catherine II, born in Stettin on the 21st April/2nd May, 1729. She went to Russia in 1744 to marry Peter III. At the age of fourteen, she made a threefold vow – to please her husband, Elisabeth, and the nation. To fulfil this vow, she neglected nothing. Eighteen years of boredom and solitude made her read a great many books. When she reached the Russian throne, she wanted the best and tried to procure happiness, freedom and ownership for her subjects. She forgave easily and hated nobody. She was indulgent, easy-going, good-humoured, had a republican soul and a kind heart – and she had friends. Work came easily to her, and she loved company and the arts.'

Thus she saw herself, and thus she wished her friends to see her. Especially Ségur, whose opinion mattered most to her at the time. She was enchanted by his conversation. She would ask him about America, about the puritan immigrants, about his ride through the virgin territories of Venezuela, and about Versailles as well; also about Voltaire who had praised his youthful verses, about her beloved Diderot who had died in 1784, about Frederick II, who had died in 1786, leaving in his place his lumpish nephew, Frederick William, about Madame du Deffand, about Marie-Antoinette. Ségur soon became one of the mainstays of the intimate suppers in the Hermitage. Nobody could beat him at literary parlour games. Rhymes were his speciality. Challenged to compose a quatrain rhyming *amour, tambour, frotte* and *note*, he wrote without hesitation:

> 'D'un people très heureux Catherine est l'*amour;*
> Malheur à l'ennemi qui contre elle se *frotte;*
> La renommée aura pour elle son *tambour;*
> L'histoire avec plaisir sera son garde-*notes.*'[1]

Everybody exclaimed in admiration. Catherine wrote to Grimm: 'There is no doubt about it, the best poet in France is the Comte de Ségur. I know of nobody who approaches his talent.' Potemkin liked the Frenchman, and Mamonov, the Redcoat, sought his company and his advice. Catherine saw Ségur more as a friend than a diplomat. To show her goodwill towards him she had a play of his, *Coriolanus*, performed. He was not ungrateful for these marks of esteem. Ségur found Mamonov 'very distinguished both in face and mind', appreciated Potemkin's jerky and muddled genius, and judged Catherine's love-life with the greatest tact: 'One can close one's eyes indulgently at the error of a woman in a great man's position, when she shows such self-control, charity and generosity even in her very weaknesses. It is unusual to find combined absolute power, jealousy and moderation, and only a man without a heart or a prince without weaknesses could condemn such a nature.' The French ambassador was less kindly disposed towards Grand Duke Paul, whose 'unstable character' made him worry about Russia's future. He wrote: 'Never has there been a more lightweight, cowardly, capricious character – he is quite incapable of making anybody happy, particularly himself. He is obsessed with the history of dethroned or assassinated Tsars... These thoughts come back to him like relentless ghosts which cloud his mind and derange his senses.'

Since his return to Russia, Paul had retired to Gatchina with his wife and daughters. He treated them brutally and cursed the Empress who

---

[1] 'Catherine is loved by her happy people;
Woe to the enemy who brushes against her;
Fame will beat a drum for her;
History will happily record her life.'

prevented him from seeing his sons, except from time to time and by special permission. He himself only saw his mother at official ceremonies. They maintained contact by exchanging cold and formal letters. 'My Dear and Good Mother, Your Imperial Majesty's letter gave me great pleasure. I beg you to receive the expression of my gratitude,' he wrote. And she would reply: 'I received, my dear son, your letter of the fifth of this month with the expression of your sentiments, which mine reflect. Goodbye, I hope you are in good health.'

Paul gave full rein to his military passion at Gatchina. Surrounded by his good German troops, he chose the officers, dressed the men according to his own ideas, submitted them to iron discipline, and brutalized them with daily manoeuvres. Enclosed in his fantasy world, he had lost all contact with his country's political life. Catherine was less and less inclined to involve him in government plans. And yet she was preparing to set out on a peaceful journey which logically should have included the Grand Ducal couple. Potemkin had invited her to make an official and splendid journey to the Crimea. By visiting the newly acquired southern provinces the Tsarina could see for herself the administrative, architectural and military accomplishments of the Prince of Taurida. The foreign ministers accompanying the Empress would report back to their respective cabinets on the Russian miracle. The Turks would finally be convinced of the Empress's interest in these territories, and of the power she had to defend them, and they would hesitate before once again trying to re-draw the frontiers by force. The whole Court was swept up in preparations for this exceptional expedition. Catherine invited Joseph II and the Prince de Ligne to join her on the route. She chose which foreign diplomats would accompany her: Count Cobenzl, the Austrian Ambassador, Fitzherbert the English Ambassador and the French Comte de Ségur. The imperial escort also included Russian ministers, important functionaries, ladies-in-waiting and of course Mamonov, the lover of the moment.

Potemkin set off in advance to prepare for the sovereign's reception. Catherine looked forward eagerly to this change of scenery. She wanted to take her two grandsons with her. But the parents protested: why the children and not them? Catherine did not dare say that their very presence would ruin the journey for her, whereas she would have been happy and proud to parade Alexander and Constantine through her empire. She wrote to Paul and his wife: 'Your children belong to you, me and the State. From their earliest infancy I have made it a duty and a pleasure to take the tenderest care of them . . . This is how I reasoned: it would be a consolation to me, separated from you, to have them with me. Of the five, three would remain with you.[1] Must I be the only one, in my old age, to be deprived of the pleasure of having one of my family with me for six months?' In the end Alexander and Constantine were left behind with their parents, as it was feared that they might become exhausted by the journey.

Sledges were quickly prepared, horses gathered at all the staging-posts; wardrobes were replenished, and messengers were sent forward to all the large towns on the way. At the end of December, 1786, all was ready for the departure. On the 1st January, 1787, the Empress received the Court and diplomatic corps' New Year's greetings, as she always did. But as she listened to the commonplace and stale compliments, and bowed her head to the curtseying courtiers, her mind was already far away on the snowy roads that led to the fabulous riches of the south.

[1] In 1786 the Grand Ducal pair had had a third daughter, Marie.

CHAPTER XXII

The Journey to the Crimea

It was extremely cold (−17°C) at the beginning of this month of January, 1787 as the imperial procession set off to the sound of gunfire and cheers from the crowd massed in front of the Palace. There were fourteen sledges carrying Her Majesty, her ministers, functionaries and diplomats. They were like little houses mounted on runners with three windows on each side, equipped inside with cushioned benches, carpets, sofas and tables. A man could stand up inside them. These princely quarters were drawn across the snow by eight or ten horses. The 'suite' and the servants piled into a hundred and sixty-four more modest sledges. Six hundred horses waited at each staging-post. To guide the drivers across the deceptive snow Potemkin had had bonfires lit all along the road, which were kept burning night and day by stokers until the convoy had gone by.

Lodgings were provided in houses belonging to the crown which had been carefully furnished for the occasion, or in private houses, whose owners were provided with funds with which to prepare their homes. A horde of servants arrived ahead of the sovereign and her guests. As soon as they stepped out of their sledges they would find hot food awaiting them on richly decorated tables. New crockery and linen were used at each meal, and then would be left behind as a gift to the owner in the case of a private house, or to some member of the escort if it was a state dwelling.

Despite the uncertainties involved in travel, Catherine kept to a very strict timetable. She rose at six o'clock, worked alone, or with her ministers until eight and then summoned the little group forming her court to join her for breakfast. They would set off at nine o'clock and skim across the snowy wastes until two in the afternoon when they would stop at some hastily built wooden palace to eat, and then set off once again. At four o'clock the procession would halt in open country, and the servants would busy themselves placing boiling samovars on the snow, pouring tea and running from one sledge to another with glasses of tea and cakes. During this halt, the travellers would change places to find new conversation and company. Catherine would choose whom she wanted wih her. Ségur was most frequently chosen. He always found 'the spoilt child', the 'Redcoat' Mamonov, at Her Majesty's side. The group would amuse itself with gossip, charades and little rhyming games, as they did in the Hermitage. The Empress would set the tone by telling comic stories from her long past. She had known so many different people, and lived through such strange events! She would laugh heartily as she recalled them. But if any of her guests began telling any *risqué* anecdote, she would stop him immediately. Despite the relaxation of etiquette necessary for the journey, licentious talk was as little tolerated in her sledge as it was in her Palace.

At the frontier of each province the Empress was greeted by the governor-general, who would then accompany her through his territory. She would spend one or two days in the largest towns where crowds massed and fell down on their knees before her. Her appearance seemed almost miraculous to people accustomed to thinking of her as an unreal, all-powerful and quite inaccessible figure. It was as though the Queen of Heaven had come down to earth.

On the 9th February, 1787, the procession reached Kiev, after covering four hundred leagues. Catherine stopped there to rest and await the coming of spring. Delegates from all countries arrived to pay homage to her. She even received Chinese, Persian, Indian and Tartar dignitaries, who came loaded with gifts. Ségur wrote: 'The astonished eye sees a sumptuous court, a conquering Empress, a rich and aggressive nobility, proud and extravagant princes and grandees, merchants with long robes and beards, officers of all kinds, those famous Cossacks from the Don wearing rich Eastern garments, Tartars, Russia's conquerors in the past, now humbly subjected to a woman and a Christian, a prince from Georgia bearing to the foot of Catherine's throne presents from Phasis and Colchis, several envoys from the numerous tribes of Kirghiz, and finally the savage Kalmuks, replicas of the Huns whose hideous looks inspired as much terror in Europe in the past as the fearful sword of the ferocious King Attila. All these envoys were lodged and fed at Her Majesty's expense. She forbade us to pay for anything,' Ségur remarked gratefully.

The *deus ex machina* of all this splendour, Potemkin, after installing his guests in these palaces, eccentrically chose for himself a cell of the convent of Petchersk. Those who wished to pay their respect had to abandon the worldly bustle that surrounded the Empress for the peace and contemplation of the holy place.

'It was like attending a vizir's audience in Constantinople, Baghdad or Cairo,' wrote Ségur. 'There was silence and a feeling of fear. This powerful and capricious favourite of Catherine's, who sometimes appeared in grand-marshal's uniform, covered with diamond insignia, edged with embroideries and lace, powdered and be-wigged like the most ancient courtiers, now, either out of natural indolence or affected arrogance, wore nothing but a fur-lined cloak, with bare neck and legs, feet in large slippers and with his hair flat and uncombed; he would remain limply stretched out on a large sofa, surrounded by a crowd of officers and the greatest people in the Empire – he hardly ever invited them to be seated... Quite unconventional and insatiable for sensual pleasure, power and luxury, he wanted to enjoy every form of glory but was tired and depressed by fortune... Such a man could become rich and powerful but never happy.'

Ségur joyfully greeted the arrival of the Prince de Ligne amongst the important figures surrounding Catherine at Kiev, who came as a fore-runner to his sovereign Joseph II. 'His presence,' he wrote, 'revived the languishing spirit, dissipated any shadow of boredom, and brought warmth into every form of diversion. From that moment we began to feel as though the rigours of the hard winter were about to abate and that a happy spring would soon reappear.'

Catherine too was delighted with this new companion, whose presence and vitality she had not forgotten. Their meeting was warm and friendly. Prince de Ligne baptized her 'Catherine the Great' and declared that 'bewitching genius had lured him to an enchanted visit'. Later, remembering their meeting at Kiev, he drew the following portrait of her: 'One could see that she had been beautiful rather than pretty; her stately forehead was tempered by an agreeable smile and friendly eyes, but the forehead told all. Without being Lavater, one could read in it, as in a book, brilliance, wisdom, fairness, courage, depth, an even temper, gentleness, calm and firmness; the height of this forehead showed the divisions of memory and imagination: One could see that there was room for everything. Her slightly pointed chin did not stick out very much... The shape of her face was not well drawn, but was very agreeable, thanks to the frankness and gaiety playing around her lips. She must have had some bloom and a fine breast, but this was at the expense of her waist which had been very slender; but people become very fat in Russia. She was clean, and she would have looked much better if she had not dragged back her hair, but had let it hang down a little, surrounding her face. One did not notice that she was small. She slowly told me that she had been extremely lively, something that was hard to believe... Everything with her was measured and methodical. She was a good listener and had so much presence of mind that she seemed to hear even when she was thinking of other things. She never talked for the sake of talking, and made those who spoke to her weight their words ... The Empress had all the good, that is to say great, side of Louis XIV. Her magnificence, parties, allowances, purchases and general ostentation resembled his. She controlled her Court better because there was nothing theatrical or exaggerated about her ... she did not demand explicit adoration. One trembled at the sight of Louis XIV, and one was reassured by that of Catherine II. Louis was drunk with his own glory. Catherine sought it and extended it without losing her head.'

Between the Prince de Ligne and the Comte de Ségur, Catherine felt constantly spiritually stimulated. She described them as her 'pocket ministers'. Anxious to impress them as much with her simplicity as with her munificence, she did not hesitate to receive humble peasants in their presence. These miserable people would tell her about a communal oven in ruins, lost crops, or a crumbling church and she would listen to them as attentively as if they were envoys from a king. What surprised the foreign diplomats most was the mixture of veneration and familiarity in the relationship between the sovereign and her subjects. The same moujiks who had bowed down before her as if before an icon, would then speak to her with a sort of unconscious freedom calling her 'thou' and 'little mother'. Catherine, although she had been Russianized for a long time, was still sometimes baffled and charmed by the many contradictions of her people. They were both mystical and pagan, dazzled by God and devoured by every kind of superstition; they easily accepted bodily slavery but extolled the freedom of the spirit; they were gentle but sometimes became drunk with cruelty; they hated war but fought with mad bravery; they beat their wives but venerated their mothers; they hated the nobles but could not exist without a master. At moments the Empress would wonder whether she could not learn more about Russia from these ignorant petitioners than from her well-informed ministers. But one could not go against the grain. Politics were for cabinets, not for the crowd outside. In order to act one had to remove oneself from the individual reality of faces and souls; to see things in terms of masses; to count people in millions; to move frontiers without worrying about individuals. Softheartedness was not a desirable virtue for a government.

The eagerly awaited spring at last began to warm the air, the snow melted, and artillery salvos announced that the ice on the Dnieper was breaking up. Potemkin had decided that the journey would be most comfortably pursued by water. To ease navigation in the southern part he had had rocks blown up and sand-banks dredged to unblock the river. Seven enormous barges painted in red and gold were provided for the Empress and her most important guests. Seventy other humbler ones were to carry the lesser fry. The total suite consisted of three thousand men. How many of those were galley-slaves chained to their oars? The diarists do not tell us – it was too banal a fact to record. They all joyfully embarked. The amazed passengers discovered in their cabins a toilet recess with its own water supply, a comfortable bed, a chintz-covered sofa, armchairs and a mahogany desk. Each luxury ship had a music-room, a communal drawing-room with a library, and a canopy on deck where one could be in the fresh air but sheltered from the sun. Twelve musicians played jaunty little tunes to announce the guests' entrances and exits. The orchestra on the imperial barge was conducted by the maestro Sarti himself. The intimate suppers took place on board Catherine's ship but there was a special one with a dining-room for seventy people where the guests would gather for important receptions. A swarm of launches and dinghies came and went all the time alongside this fleet which, as Ségur said, was like 'a fairy creation'. The twin beds that could be seen in the Empress's cabin left no doubt about her relations with Mamonov. One evening, Mamonov kept some friends with him for a card game. The Prince de Nassau was one of them and described the scene: 'We had hardly begun to play in the Empress's little sitting-room when she came in, in her dressing-gown, with her hair down, about to put on her night-cap. She asked if she was disturbing us. She then sat near us and was full of gaiety and friendly charm. She apologized for her dressing-gown, which was, however, delightful – it was made of apricot-coloured taffeta with blue ribbons ... She remained with us until half-past ten.'

The Prince de Ligne's cabin was next door to that of the Comte Ségur. In the morning Joseph II's envoy would tap on the partition to wake his neighbour, and recite impromptu verses to him. Then he would send his page round with a letter in which were mingled 'wisdom, folly, politics, pretty speeches, military anecdotes and philosophical epigrams'. Ségur would reply along similar lines. 'Nothing could have been more carefully pursued and precise,' he wrote, 'than this strange correspondence between an Austrian general and a French ambassador lying side by side on the same barge, not far from the Empress of the North, sailing down the Dnieper, through Cossack country to visit the Tartars.'

When the Empress was bored, she would have a flag raised and the regular court jesters would rush to her side; the witty Comte de Ségur, the elegant Prince de Ligne, the frivolous Cobenzl, Fitzherbert with his cold humour, the Prince de Nassau, Mamonov, Leo Naryshkin ... During their rambling conversations, politics were never completely forgotten. One or other of the ambassadors would slip an insidious

question in between two pleasantries, to try to discover what
Catherine's intentions were. Or it could be she who would suddenly embarrass her neighbour with a sharp inquiry. Thus she bearded Ségur: 'So you don't want me to chase away your protégés, the
Turks? That does do you credit! If you had neighbours in Piedmont
or Savoy who murdered and imprisoned thousands of your compatriots, what would you say if I suddenly decided to defend
them?'

From the beginning of this 'inimitable' journey, Ségur tried to find
the best way of fulfilling his mission which was to conclude a
commercial treaty; Fitzherbert was busy convincing the Empress of the
advantages to her of friendly ties with England; Cobenzl pointed out the
need for perfect understanding between Russia and Austria. Ségur was
lucky enough to have Potemkin's support in this matter. But the Prince
of Taurida was hardly ever on board. His job as producer meant that
most of the time he travelled ahead of the flotilla to prepare the scenery.
One day, finding himself next to Ségur on the boat, he pressed him to
immediately draw up a memorandum on the clauses of the envisaged
treaty, so that he could show it to the Empress that evening. Ségur was
thrilled at this opportunity, but realized that his servant had
disappeared with the key to his writing desk. Never mind: he asked
Fitzherbert if he would lend him his writing case for a moment. The
Englishman innocently did so, and thus it was with the English
ambassador's pen and on his paper that Ségur drew up plans for a treaty
quite abhorrent to England. It was signed soon afterwards and
Fitzherbert, hearing of the strange circumstances of its preparation,
managed, with his English sense of fair play, to be amused by this
diplomatic mishap.

The journey down the Dnieper continued in slow magnificence. The
orchestras played stirring melodies on the bedecked vessels. The flotilla
often dropped anchor so that the Empress and her guests could see more
closely the motley crowd of Her Majesty's adorers. The fronts of the
houses were decorated with garlands and carpets. Everything seemed
joyful, welcoming and prosperous. There were only happy people in
Russia. Not a single shabby hovel or ragged beggar. Unhealthy looking
individuals were sent inland and crumbling shanties were concealed
behind light façades of painted wood. These were the 'Potemkin
villages' – the Prince de Ligne wondered whether they possessed roofs,
doors, windows or inhabitants. What was real anyway was the vast
landscape, the blue sky, the flower-strewn steppes. Sometimes troops of
Cossack horsemen would appear from nowhere and perform wild
gallops and equestrian games, whose violence and skill left the travellers

flabbergasted. But were they not the same warriors who appeared in a different costume at the next halt? The troop moved with the ship. In the night gangs of workmen built roads which would only be used once, gardens which would receive only a single glance. 'Once the Empress had gone by, all these miserable people were sent home,' wrote Langeron. 'Many died as a result of this upheaval.'

Potemkin revealed himself as the magician of the moment, the king of *trompe-l'oeil*. However, not everything he accomplished was illusion. He really had raised an army of Cossacks, organized agriculture, founded cities, attracted nomad tribes and foreign settlers, built ships and opened up ports. All this was not enough for him. To be worthy of the Empress he added fiction for the fact. He dressed up the present in the colours of a possible future. Catherine realized quite well that there was a lot of fakery in this optimistic presentation of her country. But she could tell the difference between flattery and truth. She was so used to triumphal arches and artillery salvos that she found it almost normal that the truth should be embellished. The Comte de Ségur and the Prince de Ligne, on the other hand, felt as if they were living through a dream. Everything around them, objects and feelings, were fake. And yet they were charmed by everything. They felt as though they were outside time, part of Cleopatra's fleet. A modern queen of Egypt, 'Catherine,' wrote the Prince de Ligne, 'does not swallow any pearls but she gives many away.' De Ligne, Ségur, Cobenzl, Fitzherbert, Nassau – the whole of the Europe of embassies and drawing-rooms was travelling with her, enchained by garlands of flowers. As the days went by, Potemkin, who had organized the show, gradually became convinced that it was a success. By serving Catherine, he was building up his own glory. She was grateful to him. She was proud of her husband and of her country. And the accompanying ambassadors, without being completely duped, had to recognize the crushing greatness of Russia, and communicated it back to their worried governments.

'The plains were alive with great herds,' wrote Ségur. 'Groups of peasants enlivened the beaches; innumerable boats, with young boys and girls on board, singing rustic local tunes, surrounded us all the time; nothing had been forgotten... However by cutting out all that was artificial in these scenes, one had to recognize that some of it was real. When he (Potemkin) took possession of this great territory, it had only two hundred and four thousand inhabitants, and now, after very few years under his administration, the population has risen to eight hundred thousand.'

At Kaniev, the journey was interrupted for a strange meeting;

Stanislaus-Augustus Poniatowski, King of Poland, and Catherine's inconsolable lover, had obtained permission to see her again after twenty-eight years' separation. As he set foot on the imperial barge, he wished to show that he came not as a king but as a friend, and announced to the nobles assembled to greet him, 'Gentlemen, the King of Poland has asked me to recommend Prince Poniatowski to you.' He hoped that tender memories of their youth would brighten his meeting with the Tsarina. But there was no *tête-à-tête*. Catherine received him in the presence of Mamonov. Poniatowski saw before him, instead of the slender Grand Duchess he had known, a heavy matron with a prominent chin, a large bust and a proud eye. Nevertheless he was very much moved. Even though thickened by age, she remained for him the only woman he had ever loved. He tried to explain to her that the Russian ambassador in Poland, Repnin, had become the real ruler of the kingdom, that the country was suffering from this foreign tyranny, and that she alone could improve the lot of the miserable Poles. She listened to him with friendly indifference under the jealous gaze of 'Mister Redcoat'. Poniatowski left, pale and in despair. The past was now dead forever between them. He had just seen a woman without a memory, if not without a heart. Catherine, for her part, had been delighted to have the occasion to prick the vanity of her present lover by receiving the past one. And Mamonov simulated vexation and jealousy. He dared to timidly reproach Her Majesty, who was delighted to still be able to incite jealousy in such a young man. She told her intimate friends how sorry she felt for the moody 'Sacha'. Ségur and de Ligne were amazed by the Tsarina's ingenuousness. But nobody dared to tell her the truth. As for her the scene ended with the delicate pleasure of a sentimental victory. At the dinner Poniatowski gave in her honour she treated the Polish king with cold formality, whilst watching her present lover's behaviour with amusement. As he rose from the table, Poniatowski searched for his hat, which Catherine then handed to him. He murmured sadly: 'Ah! Madam you once gave me a much finer one!' He begged her to allow him one more day on board the ship. She refused. What good would it do to stir up the ashes? He seemed so shattered by this brisk dismissal that the Prince de Ligne whispered to him: 'Don't look so distressed; you are only giving pleasure to the court which surrounds you and which detests you!' He went away, broken, regretting, no doubt, that he had spoiled so many happy memories by this inopportune meeting.

He had hardly gone when the most eagerly awaited guest of all was announced – Joseph II. As usual, he was travelling under the pseudonym of Count Falkenstein, expecting to be treated like a simple tourist. He embarked at Kaydak, and was, in turn, enchanted by the magical voyage. Whilst ironical about the theatrical nature of the enterprise, he privately admitted that he was baffled by the size and richness of Russia. His supposed love for Catherine was mingled with a sharp stab of envy. On the site of the future city of Ekaterinoslav (or 'Catherine's Glory'[1]) the governor, dignitaries and clergy were gathered for the inaugural ceremony. Catherine laid the first stone and invited Joseph II to lay the second. He handed back the trowel and, turning to Ségur, whispered: 'The Empress laid the first stone, and I the last.' This prophecy was wrong, as the city was built and developed rapidly. 'We in Germany or France would never have dared to undertake what is being done here,' observed Joseph II sourly. 'Here human life and effort count for nothing; here roads, ports, fortresses and palaces are built on marshes; forests are planted in deserts; all this without paying the workmen, who never complain, are deprived of everything, sleep on the ground and often suffer from hunger... The master orders, the slave obeys... Also, Catherine can spend as much as she likes without running into debt. Her currency is worth whatever she wants it to be worth: she could strike coins out of leather.'[2]

At Kaydak, the Dnieper runs into cataracts. The party abandoned the barges and pursued its journey by road across the steppes. The foreign traveller could not avoid the sense of his own smallness when faced with this vast green expanse running under a fiery sky to the shimmering horizon. Absence of all human habitation makes him feel that he has finally left the world of men. He is defenceless, at the mercy of the sun, the grass, the dust and wind. What relief when he sees in the distance the smallest hill, the humblest village! The arrival at Kherson was greeted by all as a victory over the obsessive monotony of the southern plain. Catherine was exultant. It was only six years since this place had fallen into Russian hands, and already Potemkin had made it into a city of prime importance. White houses, straight streets, exuberant vegetation. The masts of hundreds of trading boats swayed above the estuary, the warehouses on the quays overflowed with merchandise, church bells rang, a mixed population crowded the streets, the fortress pointed its cannon towards the open sea, two bulging great warships lay in the dockyard, and Ségur, combing the shops, found to his amazement the latest fashions from Paris. The Empress wanted to push on to Kinburn, opposite Otchakov; but a small Turkish squadron had just dropped anchor in the Liman, near the Ottoman fortress, and her

[1] Now Dniepropetrovsk.
[2] Henry Vallotton – *Catherine II*. Compare with Possochkov's view, previously quoted.

Majesty wisely avoided the provocation. There was so much to see in the rest of the country. After a few days' rest, the convoy started again towards Perekop.

Nights were now spent in the middle of the steppes, in richly decorated and furnished tents. When Ségur complained of the flatness of the country, Catherine answered crossly: 'Do not be inhibited, Monsieur le Comte! If you fear boredom in the desert, nobody is preventing you from returning to Paris, where so many pleasures await you.' Ségur cried out: 'Madam, you must think me blind, ungrateful and lacking discernment and taste! I even dare add that I observe, with some pain, a remainder of prejudice against the French, who little deserve such unfounded opinion! Nowhere are you more admired and appreciated than in France!' Catherine relented.

One evening, on leaving the Tsarina's tent, Joseph II took Ségur by the arm and dragged him towards the steppe. The starry night with its unreal clarity seemed to weigh down on the unlimited dark spaces, which shimmered with silver. A caravan of camels was silhouetted on the horizon. In the lunar silence the cries of the drivers echoed as if from another world.

'What a strange journey!' sighed the Emperor. 'And who could have expected to see me with Catherine II and the French and English ambassadors, wandering in the Tartar desert? What a page of history!'

'It seems to me more like a page from *The Arabian Nights,* and that my name is Giafar and that I am wandering with the Calif Haroun-al-Rashid, disguised, as was his habit.'

A few steps later, the two men came across a nomad encampment. 'I do not know whether I am awake or whether your remark about *The Arabian Nights* has made me dream!' cried the Emperor. 'Look that way!' To their great surprise, one of the camel-skin tents was coming towards them. The Kalmuks, inside it, moved their shelter without dismantling it. Ségur and Joseph II visited them in their portable house. Then, overcome by their picturesque outing, they returned to their own encampment.

The important guests' tents were braided with silver. Those that held the Empress, the Emperor, Potemkin and the ambassadors were also scattered with precious stones which sparkled in the twilight. The highest and most spacious of these canvas structures was surmounted by a crown and a two-headed eagle![1] Beneath this proud emblem rested a small and satisfied woman who, with her unshakeable health and lively mind, had worked late into the night with her ministers. Lost in the

[1] M. Lavater Sloman *Catherine II and Her Time.*

midst of the southern steppes, she had, nonetheless, to rule her Empire with as much firmness as if she was in the Palace in St Petersburg. The capital of Russia was where the Tsarina was. At each stop, courtiers arrived from the four corners of the world. She followed, with particular attention, the dissension between England and France over an eventual conflict between Russia and Turkey. One day, irritated by the rumours coming from the courts of St James and Versailles, she assigned Ségur and Fitzherbert to the same tent, with one table to share between them. The two ambassadors had to sit face to face drawing up top secret and probably contradictory reports, exchanging suspicious looks from time to time. That evening, at supper, everybody laughed at this imperial joke.

The travellers' merriment turned to apprehension when the convoy entered the Crimea. To show her sympathy for the population of this recently annexed territory, Catherine decided not to be guarded any longer by Russian troops along the route. It was not yet four years since the Khan of the Crimea had surrendered his palace to her governor. In this fiercely Muslim country, Christian officials had taken the place of Muslims, gold-domed churches had sprung up among the minarets, the streets were invaded by unveiled women, all of which enraged supporters of the old order. Despite the danger, the Empress was confident of the loyalty of those tribes who had 'voluntarily' come under her flag. She knew that a man kept his word in the East. She insisted on making her entrance to Bakhchisaray surrounded by an indigenous escort. Suddenly the horrified ambassadors saw, coming towards them, twelve hundred Tartar horsemen, superbly dressed and armed to the teeth. How could these men, who scorned women and hated Christians, accept to be ruled by a Christian woman? The Prince de Ligne, riding in the same carriage as the Comte de Ségur, stared with some amusement at the fierce warriors with high cheekbones and olive skins who were riding along at their height. 'Do admit, my dear Ségur,' he said, laughing, 'that it would be a strange thing, and would cause an uproar in Europe, if the twelve hundred tartars surrounding us decided to gallop us to a small port nearby, there embark the noble Catherine and the great Roman Emperor Joseph II, and take them to Constantinople for the amusement and satisfaction of Abdul-Hamid, sovereign commander of the believers; and there would be nothing immoral about such a trick; because they could easily, without any scruples, steal away two sovereigns who had just ignored all human rights and treaties and stolen away their country, dethroned their prince, and removed their independence.'

But Catherine's new subjects, as she predicted, showed complete loyalty towards her. They even saved her life when, on the steep road down to Bakhchisaray, her carriage horses bolted. The vehicle raced at full speed down the hill, bumping and swaying from side to side. It was impossible to stop it. Another second and it would smash into the rocks. At last, at the entrance to the town, the horses reared and fell, the wheels went over their bodies, the carriage was about to topple over in the violence of the shock, when the Tartar horsemen charged forward and held it in balance. The occupants were unhurt. Joseph II, who was inside, admitted that he had been very frightened. However, he said: 'Catherine showed not the smallest sign of fear.'

At Bakhchisaray, the Empress installed herself in the Khan's old palace. 'As a sovereign, a woman and a Christian, she enjoyed seeing herself seated on the throne of the Tartars, who had been, in the past, the conquerors of Russia and who, very few years before their defeat, were still ravaging her countryside,' wrote Ségur. She willingly explained to her foreign guests that for more than ten centuries the wild inhabitants of this land had pillaged neighbouring territories and had sent thousands of white slaves each year into Asia Minor. Despite the grudge she might bear towards these arrogant people who still treated the Russians as 'infidels' and 'dogs', she had decided to protect the Tartars' religion, customs and language. This tolerance paid off. There was no revolt in the country, only apathetic indifference and an affected phlegmatism. In the street, passers-by, merchants and artisans pretended to ignore the splendour of the imperial procession. They looked elsewhere or turned their backs. 'They never stoop,' wrote Ségur, 'and never attribute their shame to stupidity: they only blame fate.'

The travellers were intoxicated by the pleasures of the Crimea. Beneath the warm southern sun they admired the silent white houses, the soft silvery foliage of the olive trees, and baroque fronds of the palm-trees with their varnished sheen, the gardens overflowing with roses, laurels and jasmine, the purple mountains and, far away, the hard, opaque emerald green of the sea. Could this luxurious paradise really be part of the same empire as that which contained the frozen plains of the north? Really, Catherine possessed all the fruits of the earth!

From Bakhchisaray the party continued down to the new port of Sebastopol. The guests gathered for a musical banquet in the hall of the palace. Suddenly the windows onto a large balcony swung open and the amazed guests saw, in the middle of the bay, a magnificent fleet: the ships, arranged in battle order, fired their cannons to salute the Empress. The din of the artillery seemed to be intended as much to intimidate Constantinople as to honour the Empress. The Russian ministers were hopping with aggressive enthusiasm. It had only taken Potemkin two years to build and equip this great Southern Armada. Her Majesty had only to say the word and all this fighting power would be turned towards the Turks. But Catherine kept a cool head – it was not yet the right moment. She reviewed the fleet, was present at the launching of three ships, and then gave Bulgakov, the Russian ambassador to the Turks, a friendly note for the Sultan. After visiting the new city of Sebastopol where crowds of workmen toiled on building sites, she asked Ségur what he thought of the city, the port and fleet. 'Madame,' he replied, 'by creating Sebastopol you have finished in the south what Peter the Great began in the north.'

Returning to Bakhchisaray, Ségur and de Ligne found themselves again in their apartments in the Khan's palace. They were, in fact, being lodged in the Prince's old harem. Each had an enormous room with marble walls and a tiled floor. A divan surrounded the whole room. In the centre a fountain played over a basin. The windows were half covered by intertwining roses, jasmine, pomegranate and orange trees. Staying in this 'volumptuous chamber', as Ségur described it, inclined the soul towards romantic matters. Prince de Ligne, although he was fifty, could hardly keep still. 'Before I leave Taurida I must at least see a woman without a veil!' he said to Ségur. 'Will you accompany me in this enterprise?' Ségur accepted and the two hunters set out. After they had wandered for a long time through the countryside, they saw three women, at the edge of a wood washing their feet in a stream. Hidden behind a clump of trees, they watched at leisure. The women took off their veils. But what disappointment – they were neither young nor pretty. 'My word,' whispered de Ligne, 'Mohammed was quite right to make them cover themselves!' He had hardly said these words when the three women turned, saw the watchers, screamed and covered their faces. Hearing them, Tartars appeared brandishing cutlasses. Ségur and de Ligne took to their heels, into the depths of the wood. The next day, at a great dinner, de Ligne, always anxious to amuse Her Majesty, told her about their adventure the previous day. A few of the guests burst out laughing but Catherine frowned. 'Gentlemen,' she said, 'this joke was in poor taste and set a very bad example. You are in the midst of a people conquered by me; I want you to respect their laws, religion, customs and prejudices. If I had heard this story without being told the names of those involved, I would, far from suspecting you, have thought some of my pages guilty, and I would have punished them severely.' The two criminals bowed their heads. The Empress, magnanimously, left it at that.

The journey continued in euphoria. Some of the triumphal arches raised for the Empress's passage bore the provocative inscription: 'The Road to Byzantium'. There were so many illuminations and fireworks that the Prince de Ligne 'feared he might turn into a fairy light himself from seeing so many'. To reward him for his good company and high spirits, Catherine gave him an estate as big as a French province. She took him out in her carriage to throw coins to the kneeling crowds. He dug handfuls of money from a bag beside him and scattered it. 'The people came fifteen or twenty leagues to line our route and see the Empress.' he wrote. 'They lie with their stomachs on the ground as soon as she arrives. Six times a day, I gallop past scattering gold on these backs and heads kissing the earth. I seem to have become, by chance, the grand almoner of Russia.'

Ségur, too, was showered with gifts. By Catherine, of course, but also by Potemkin. The Prince of Taurida was becoming more and more eccentric. Sometimes he would retire to fast and pray in a hermit's cave nearby, at other times, overflowing with energy, gaiety and inventiveness, he would invite the Tsarina and her guests to a party, whose splendour would exhaust and upset them. One day, he would receive the foreign diplomats slumped on a sofa, his hair unkempt and with a glazed stare, and complain about the empire's financial problems; then, during a lavish reception, he would present the Empress with a necklace of priceless pearls. His eccentricity, thought Ségur, bordered on madness. One morning, as the French ambassador was preparing to go out, he bumped into a young beauty in Circassian dress. He was astounded: this stranger looked, feature for feature, exactly like his wife. 'I thought for a moment that Madame de Ségur had come from France to meet me, and that somebody had taken it upon themselves to hide her and arrange this sudden meeting,' he wrote. As the apparition went away, Potemkin took him by the arm and said: 'Is the resemblance perfect then?' 'Complete and unbelievable,' replied Ségur. Potemkin burst out laughing. No doubt he had seen a portrait of the Comtesse in the ambassador's tent. 'Well! My little father,' he said, 'this young Circassian girl belongs to a man who will let me dispose of her; and as soon as you reach St Petersburg, I will give her to you.' Ségur was speechless, then stammered: 'I thank you, but I cannot accept – Madame de Ségur might find such an expression of affection somewhat strange.' Potemkin was wounded by this refusal, which he could not understand. To soothe the Prince of Taurida's feelings, the French ambassador had to accept another present: a young Kalmuk child called Nagun. 'I looked after him for a time,' wrote Ségur; 'he was taught to read; but . . . Countess Cobenzl, who found him most amusing, begged me so hard to relinquish him, that I gave in.'

At last the convoy set out on the return journey. For a week, Joseph II had been worried by news of trouble in the Netherlands. He wondered what he was doing on this fantasy expedition. 'We have been shown one illusion after another,' he said to Ségur. 'What is on the inside here (Russia) has great faults; but the exterior has as much reality as brilliance.' And he added, speaking of Catherine: 'What I cannot conceive of, is that a woman so proud and so mindful of her glory should show such a strange weakness for the whims of her young *aide-de-camp*, Mamonov, who is really no more than a spoilt child.' At Borislav, the Emperor took his leave of the Empress, recommending caution *vis-à-vis* Turkey and firmness towards Prussia.

A few days later, at Poltava a flamboyant display, mounted by Potemkin, awaited the travellers, who by now thought that they had exhausted all possibility of surprise. Fifty thousand troopers, some dressed as Russians, some as Swedes, re-enacted, by manoeuvres, the different stages of the famous battle of 1709 in which Peter the Great inflicted a crushing defeat on Charles XII. The Tsar, the King of Sweden, Menchikov and Sheremetiev were performed by Russian officers. There were cavalry charges, firing from the infantry, cannonshot – the amazed spectators felt as though they were in a real war. 'Happiness and pride shone in Catherine's eyes,' wrote Ségur. 'One would have thought she had Peter the Great's blood in her own veins.'

After this military display, the procession of carriages continued slowly northwards. In this part of the Empire there was no need for a brilliant stage-manager to build scenery and organize a cast. The prosperity of the country they were crossing was obvious. The cheers at the Empress's passage were sincere. Even the sceptical Ségur wrote: 'Here, the Empress was greeted like a mother, and the people now protected by her from the nobles' abuses of power, showed an enthusiasm inspired solely by gratitude.'

At Kharkov, Potemkin, seized with sudden lethargy, decided to leave Her Majesty and return to the south. Catherine was worried at seeing him so downcast after his triumph of organization. Was he ill? She wrote to him: 'By the great heat of the south, I beg you most humbly to give me the pleasure of looking after you, for the sake of our love and the love of God.' And again: 'You serve me and I am grateful, that is all! As for your enemies, you have rapped them on the knuckles by showing your devotion to me, and by your care for the State.' He replied to her: 'Mother Empress... you are far more than a mother to me, as your care for my well-being springs from an intentional impulse... Malice and envy have not succeeded in lowering me in your esteem and all the treachery has been in vain. This region will not forget this happiness. Goodbye my benefactress and mother. May God give me the opportunity to demonstrate to the whole world how much I am obliged to you, and how I will be your devoted slave until death.'[1]

The Empress approached the capital through Kursk, Orel, Tula, Moscow, amid receptions, balls, displays and fireworks. The days were hot and the stages exhausting. Sitting with Fitzherbert in Her Majesty's carriage, Ségur noticed that she was asleep. He continued his conversation with the English ambassador in low tones. The latter was maintaining that the American Revolution, which had removed thirteen colonies from the Crown, had been, all things considered, more advantageous than harmful to his country. Indeed, in a short time, having shed the expense of administering the distant provinces, London would make a great deal of money by trading with them. The discussion continued and the Empress, with her head slumped, continued to breathe evenly, never opening her eyes. The next day, she took Ségur aside and said to him: 'You had the most extraordinary conversation yesterday with Fitzherbert, and I find it hard to believe that, with his wits, he can really hold such strange opinions.' And as Ségur expressed astonishment that she could have heard everything while appearing to be asleep, she replied: 'I was careful not to open my eyes. I was too curious to hear the rest of the conversation. I do not know if George III holds the same opinion as his minister; but, for my part, I know that, if I had irretrievably lost a single one of the thirteen provinces taken from him, I should blow out my brains with a pistol.' Another remark of Catherine's astonished Ségur. He was with her when the arrival was announced of a provincial governor guilty of having taken no measures to fight famine. 'I hope,' said Minister Bezborodko, 'that Your Majesty will publicly issue the severe reprimand that he deserves.' 'No,' replied Catherine, 'it would humiliate him too much: I will wait until he is alone with me; because I like to praise and reward people out loud, and scold them quietly.'

The journey was almost over. Catherine distributed among her travelling companions medals struck for the occasion, with the Tsarina's profile on one side and, on the other, the itinerary of the journey to the Crimea. An inscription reminded one that the expedition had taken place to celebrate the twenty-fifth anniversary of her reign and another that it had been undertaken 'for the public good'.

When Catherine was questioned on what impression the tour of inspection had made on her she replied ironically: 'I, who speak to you,

---

[1] Daria Olivier *Catherine the Great*.

have seen the mountains of Taurida advance slowly towards us and bow down. Whoever does not believe me can go there and see for himself the new roads that have been built there! He will see everywhere sheer cliffs transformed into gentle slopes.'

On the 22nd July, 1787, after more than six months' absence, Catherine returned to St Petersburg. The procession dispersed, and each member of 'the enchanted circle' found it hard to re-adjust to the greyness of daily life. 'One had to return to dry political calculations,' wrote Ségur sadly. Catherine set off for Tsarskoe Selo, where she intended to spend the hot month of August. One joy awaited her on the way: her grandsons Alexander and Constantine, accompanied by La Harpe, came to meet her, and escorted her to her summer residence. No triumphal arch gave her more pleasure than the sight of these two young faces glowing with eager curiosity. The children asked her a thousand questions about the countries she had seen, and she asked them, just as eagerly, about their studies. The meeting with Grand Duke Paul was less uplifting. He was as sour and moody as ever. His wife, Grand Duchess Maria, was expecting a sixth child.

The political cauldron was bubbling hard, and had to be dealt with immediately. Joseph II bombarded Catherine with letters begging her to moderate her views on Turkey. She replied evasively. The area was beginning to appear explosive. At the same time she was feeling the ground as regards Gustavus III of Sweden, whose plans appeared ominous to her. And she also had to calm the English who were annoyed by the Franco-Russian commercial treaty. Not forgetting Prussia, whose susceptibilities had to be flattered, and whose new intentions towards Poland deserved closer examination. 'I am working like a horse,' she wrote to Grimm, 'and my four secretaries are not enough.' All decisions had to be taken by her. The whole of Europe was on her shoulders. One evening when she spoke of her 'St Petersburg office', where so many international affairs were dealt with, the Prince de Ligne said to her: 'I don't know of a smaller one, as it is only a few inches large: it extends from one temple to the other, and from the root of the nose to the root of the hair!'

CHAPTER XXIII

Wars

As one might have expected, Catherine's journey to the Crimea enraged the Turks, and the British, Prussian and even French ambassadors made every effort to calm them. Despite Catherine's appeasing assurances, Abdul Hamid felt personally offended by the Russian fleet and army manoeuvres in this area so recently snatched from his jurisdiction. The Taurida peninsula, he thought, was now no longer a province for pleasure, but a base for military expeditions, a war machine aimed at the heart of Turkey. He hastily assembled his troops. When Catherine pretended to be indignant at this, Ségur replied ironically: 'Suppose the Sultan, surrounded by his nobles and accompanied by a powerful ally, had appeared at Otchakov with an enormous fleet and a hundred and fifty thousand men, would it be suprising if you took a few precautions?' Ségur had been instructed by his government to issue a solemn warning to the Empress. She listened scornfully, teased him about his friendships with men in beards and turbans, calling him 'Ségur Effendi'.[1] She found it incomprehensible that most of the Western countries, instead of supporting the European Christians, took the side of the Asian Moslems. Were these so-called civilized countries so afraid of Russian power that they would give themselves to the Devil to thwart it? In any case, Louis XVI's France was politically so debilitated that one need not take much notice of its views. If there was any conflict, England and Prussia would show their teeth, but would not move. If only Austria could solve its difficulties in the Netherlands and give full support to Russia! The wisest course would be to wait before lighting the fuse. Especially as famine was raging in the eastern provinces, and the Russian army and fleet, despite their brilliance on parade, were not yet ready for battle. They needed to be reorganized, equipped, disciplined, trained and supplied... Meanwhile French officers helped to modernize the Turkish army and Russian emissaries infiltrated the Balkans, Egypt and Syria to buy local support. Catherine hoped that the Sultan, intimidated by the recent

[1] Effendi, Turkish title meaning Lord.

show of strength in the Crimea, would swallow his fury and hesitate to attack, thus leaving Potemkin time to organize the whole business properly. But Abdul Hamid, who was no doubt well-informed, handed Bulgakov, the Russian ambassador, an ultimatum, demanding that Russia should hand back the Crimea. Bulgakov, of course, refused and was imprisoned in the Seven Towers Citadel. It was war! England and Prussia declared themselves for the Sublime Porte, France declared itself neutral, and Sweden, which was hostile to Russia, decided to wait and see, in the hope of 'a propitious moment', and Joseph II, the delightful travelling companion, wrote to Catherine: 'I regret very much that we are not at this moment at Sebastopol, whence we could have proceeded to Constantinople to salute the Sultan and his unreasonable advisers with cannon-balls.'

Despite this avowal of friendship, Catherine was uneasy. Her secretary, Khrapovitsky, often saw her with her head in her hands, with a tired, lost, faraway look. She saw that this war would not be an easy one. For the Turks, it was a holy battle against the infidels. The Grand Vizir had travelled the streets of Constantinople, beneath the banner of Mohammed, calling on the people to sacrifice themselves for the great cause. On the Russian side, dissension amongst the high command added to the problem of disorganization and lack of equipment in the army and the fleet. Experienced generals like Suvorov, Repnin and Rumyantsov did not care to take orders from Potemkin, who had not yet proved himself on the battlefield. However the outcome of the war depended on him; by the Empress's command he had been made Field Marshal and Grand Admiral. But he was going through a period of depression and self-doubt. It seemed as though the preparations for the journey to the Crimea had used up all his energy and that he had not the resilience to face the hard realities of battle after so many agreeable fantasies. 'The show is over, the curtain has fallen, the director is asleep,' wrote the Prince de Ligne.

While the fanatical Turks were attacking the fort at Kinburn, Potemkin was advising Catherine, by letter, to conclude a peace before it was too late. Horrified by this disgraceful evasion, she tried to raise his morale from a distance. 'Fortify your mind and your soul against all these difficulties,' she wrote to him, 'and be certain that, with patience, you will conquer them; but it would be true weakness if, as you write, you were to cast aside all your talents and disappear.' In October, 1787, Suvorov defeated the Turks at the gates of Kinburn. The enemy suffered considerable losses. Catherine heaved a sigh of relief: if Kinburn had fallen it would have been impossible to defend Kherson. The whole south would have been open, soft and defenceless against the invader's onslaught. But the Russian fleet in the Black Sea had been damaged by a storm that had lasted for five days. And once again Potemkin despaired. Once again, Catherine shook him: 'I do not understand you at all. Why must we give up the advantages we have gained? When a man is on horseback, should he dismount and walk?' And, as he still considered withdrawing with the fleet and abandoning the Crimea, she exploded: 'What can one say? Perhaps that occurred to you in the heat of the moment, when you thought the fleet had perished! But what would become of the fleet after the evacuation? And how can you begin a campaign by evacuating a province that is not even threatened? You would do better to attack Otchakov or Bender, thus moving from the defensive to the offensive, which you have always said suits us better. Anyway the wind can't be blowing only against us. Courage! Courage! I am writing this to my best friend, my child, my pupil, who sometimes shows more resolution than myself; but at the moment, I am braver than you because I am in good health and you are ill . . . I feel that you are as impatient as a five-year-old child, when the work entrusted to you demands, at present, unshakeable patience.'

Potemkin continued to prevaricate, despite this gentle yet firm encouragement. Numbed by a kind of winter sleepiness, his main concern was not to capture Otchakov but to prevent the loss of human lives. He was extremely concerned with his soldiers' well-being: he eased the discipline, ordering officers to limit the floggings, and radically changed the soldiers' uniforms. The old inconvenient costumes, the high boots and heavy helmets, were replaced by comfortable great-coats, low boots and light helmets. He also ordered the men to cut off their 'rat's tail' tresses, and to stop powdering their hair, which would now be short. 'Is it a soldier's business to curl, powder and plait his hair?' he said. 'They do not have personal valets. What use are curling papers to them? Everybody agrees that it is much healthier to wash and comb hair, than fill it with powder, grease, flour, hairpins and plaits. A soldier's hairstyle should be such that it is ready as soon as he stands up.' This new regulation was enthusiastically greeted by the army, and the Empress expressed her satisfaction in a proclamation. But she continued to deplore the Field Marshal's lack of military aggression. With ridiculous obstinacy, Potemkin prevented Suvorov from exploiting his earlier successes. His personal strategy was not to assault but to mark time. He thought that time would wear down the enemy; the indignant Suvorov replied to this: 'You cannot seize a fortress just by looking at it.' Catherine was becoming exasperated, and pestered the Prince of Taurida: 'What has become of Otchakov? Are you going to take Otchakov? When will Otchakov fall?' Had he forgotten the reason for this war? Did he want to see the Crimea invaded? She was devoured by worry and claimed that all her dresses were having to be taken in. But she still worried too about the health of her lethargic hero. 'At this moment, my dear friend,' she wrote to him, 'you are not a private individual who lives and behaves how he pleases. You belong to the State, and to me. You must – I order you – look after your health.' Or: 'I am sending you a whole chemist-shop full of medicines, and I hope with all my heart that you will not need them . . . The second parcel will contain a fox-fur cape and a sable hat to keep the cold from you . . . As for the crown of laurels, that won't be ready for a fortnight or so.'

In June, 1789, the Turkish fleet suffered heavy setbacks in two successive engagements, and the Russian ships were at last able to besiege Otchakov from the sea, while Potemkin bombarded the target with a large land-based artillery. But although he could now have taken the fortress with one assault, he remained deaf to Suvorov's pleas and let the siege drag on.

Now Catherine's eyes were forced to turn to the west rather than the south. Thinking that his neighbour, the Empress, was now sufficiently entangled in the south, Gustavus III of Sweden conveniently remembered that he was an ally of the Sublime Port and declared war on Russia. He hoped that, by some military successes, he would impress the Swedish nobility who were still contesting his authority. Germany and England supported his aggressive plans. France disapproved. The King of Sweden, whom Catherine nicknamed 'Brother Gu', sent an ultimatum of such insolence that Ségur considered it totally 'devoid of reason'. 'It seems to me,' he said to Catherine, 'that the King of Sweden, carried away by a false dream, dreamt that he had already defeated Your Majesty in three great battles.' 'Even, if he had won three great battles, Monsieur le Comte,' replied Catherine fierily, 'and even if he were now master of St Petersburg and Moscow, I would show him what a woman of strong character, at the head of a brave and devoted people, could achieve, standing on the ruins of a great empire.'

To discredit her enemy, she had her own comic opera, *The Unhappy Warrior*, performed in St Petersburg; in it Gustavus III appears as a dwarf prince wearing a too large helmet that comes down to his stomach, and giant boots which come up to his waist. Thus equipped, he is put to flight by blows from the crutches of the crippled commander of a Russian fort. The diplomats watched this play with embarrassment and Catherine could see, through their weak compliments, the disappointment she had caused by this childish mockery. But she needed to let her bile flow freely, now that the country was fighting on two fronts under the unfriendly gaze of the great European nations. To satisfy the demands of the Southern campaign, she had had to strip the North of its best troops, and the capital therefore presented an easy target for the Swedes. Luckily, the new fleet, which she had intended to send round Europe to the Black Sea, had not yet left the Baltic. Catherine charged the Prince de Nassau, who had entered Russian service, with organizing naval operations in this sector. Under his direct authority, the brave and efficient Admiral Grieg tried to disperse the Swedish fleet. There was hope therefore in that area. On the ground, however, things were going badly. The Russian troops were demolished. The fortified town of Nyslott fell into enemy hands; Gustavus III marched on Friederickshamm. The road to St Petersburg was open. Certain of success, Gustavus III declared that he would give a great ball at Peterhof for the ladies of the court, that he would have a *Te Deum* sung in the cathedral of St Peter and St Paul, and that he would tear down the statue of Peter the Great. The capital was seized with panic. While recruiting sergeants rounded up and hastily drilled servants and workmen, trying to make soldiers out of them, pessimistic rumours flew through the drawing rooms. The town, they said, would be abandoned, and the Swedes were preparing for carnage. Haggard officials removed archives from government offices. Precious objects were crated up and heaved onto carts. The Court awaited the Empress's order to move to Moscow. Those whose duties did not oblige them to remain had already taken to the road in the general upheaval. Rich and poor, on foot, on horses, or in carriages, all fled the same danger. Catherine did not hold anyone back. She even joked. 'One must admit,' she said, 'that Peter I did build his capital very close to Sweden!' Did she intend to go herself? She could not risk being taken prisoner. And yet how could she, the heir and emulator of Peter the Great, bow down before these Swedes that he had defeated at Poltava? Not knowing what the Empress's plans were, the foreign ambassadors wondered whether they ought to flee the city with their files or remain until its surrender. Ségur was sent by them to the Winter Palace to try to discover what Her Majesty had in mind. When she asked what rumours were going round, he dared to answer: 'Everybody, everywhere is practically certain that your Majesty will be leaving for Moscow this night or the next.' Imperturbably, she asked: 'And do you believe that, Monsieur le Comte?' 'Madame,' replied Ségur, 'the sources of this rumour make it seem very likely; only your character makes me doubt it.' Catherine, with her straight neck and proud look, showed a self-assurance which left her companion speechless. Her certainty of a final victory had not been in any way shaken by the bad news of the last few days. If she had had five hundred horses gathered at each relay on the way to Moscow it was purely, she said, to hasten the arrival of reinforcements to defend St Petersburg. 'Tell your Court,' she said, 'that I am remaining in my capital and that if I left it, it would only be to confront the King of Sweden.'

Ségur thought that she was refusing to face reality. But the Empress was proved right. Admiral Grieg caught up with the enemy fleet and pushed it back into the port of Sveaborg. The Swedish nobility was in an uproar. Disappointed officers accused Gustavus III of having declared war without consulting the Diet. This dissidence, which went under the name of the Confederation of Anjala, stopped short the invaders' advance. Gustavus III's ambitious dream seemed to be in jeopardy.

Catherine was openly delighted with the breaking of the enemy's ranks. 'If the King had been another sort of man, one would have felt sorry for him,' she said. 'But what can one do? Since one is in a position to do so, one must seize the opportunity to bring down the enemy flag.' She had allowed her son, who was still haunted by the example of Frederick II, to take part in the military operations against Sweden. But she had placed him under the vigilant eye of General Mushin Pushkin, and, very soon, Grand Duke Paul, sickened by this state of subordination, returned to St Petersburg. Once again he had proved to be inadequate in the eyes of the world. As usual, he held his mother responsible for his humiliation. He suspected Potemkin of having arranged for him to be sent to the Northern front, so as not to have him by his side in the South.

As it happened, the Southern front was coming to life again. After the whole summer of 1788 had gone by with only a few pointless skirmishes, Potemkin at last decided to launch a major assault on Otchakov. Suvorov was seriously wounded. An epidemic broke out. Carried away by the fighting, Potemkin showed as much courage as any young officer eager for glory. To encourage his soldiers, he promised them pillage. On the 6th/17th December, 1788, they rushed forward, scaled the walls under gunfire, fought hand to hand in the streets, and conquered the town, house by house, massacring the inhabitants, raping, stealing, and burning as they went. Sixty thousand Turks and twenty thousand Russians were butchered. The booty was enormous. The finest piece was an emerald the size of an egg, and Potemkin sent it to Catherine. Colonel Bauer was charged with bearing the good news to the Empress. When he arrived in the middle of the night, Her Majesty was ill in bed. He handed the despatches to the lover, Mamonov, who, overcome, woke his mistress. She sobbed with joy. The next morning, at her levee, she declared: 'I was ill but joy has cured me.' Rewards poured down on the messenger, the Prince of Taurida, the officers and the soldiers. The poet Derzhavin composed an ode:

> *'Roar, Oh thunder of victory!*
> *Rejoice, Oh valiant Russia!'*

The Italian painter Casanova was commissioned to reproduce this great event in a painting. And Catherine wrote to Potemkin: 'I take you by the ears with both my hands, in my mind, I kiss you a thousand times.'

However, although the Turks had been defeated at Otchakov, they did not intend to lay down their arms, and the King of Sweden, who had now defeated the opposition from within the army, dissolved the Confederation of Anjala and resumed hostilities. At the same time, the Netherlands rose against Austrian domination, preventing Joseph II from turning his full strength towards Turkey. The year 1789 began, however, with some fine successes. The Prince de Nassau, commanding a new fleet, inflicted a severe defeat on the Swedes at Swenskund; Rumyantsov triumphed under Galatz. Suvorov and the Prince de Cobourg put the Turks to flight in the bloody battle of Foksàny... All this was not enough. The enemy fought on in the North as in the South, urged on by England and Prussia.

As for France, she was too much preoccupied by internal events to play much part in international affairs. Catherine was irritated by this democratic upheaval in France. 'Your Third Estate has very high pretensions,' she said to Ségur. 'It will arouse resentment in the other two and such discord could have dangerous and long-lasting results. I fear the King will find himself forced to make too many sacrifices, without satisfying any passions.' However, she said to Grimm: 'I am not one of those who believe it is leading to a great revolution.' And suddenly, the thunderbolt: the capture of the Bastille. Catherine heard of it through her ambassador in Paris, Simolin. This time, she could not contain her rage. 'What business is it of the cobblers?' she cried. 'A cobbler can only make shoes!' She loathed from her guts the stupid mob which dared to attack the monarchic principle. 'The atmosphere in your country is that of debauchery,' she wrote to Grimm. She declared that France 'in labour, had given birth to a rotten and stinking runt... The National Assembly is no more than a heap of hagglers... If you hanged a few of them and took away their eighteen thousand pound salaries the others might perhaps come to their senses.' She denounced the system of 'the thousand-headed hydra', whose heads would all have to be cut off to bring tranquillity back to the country. Grimm innocently asked her to send a portrait of herself to Bailly, the new Mayor of Paris, in exchange for one the latter would send to Her Majesty – she replied scathingly: 'It is as improper for the mayor of an assembly which has demonarchized France to possess a portrait of the most aristocratic Empress in Europe, as it would be for her to send one to the mayor of the demonarchizing assembly. It would be placing the demonarchizing mayor and the aristrocratic Empress in contradiction with themselves and with their past, present, and future duties.' She longed for a Caesar to come and enslave Gaul once again. 'When will this Caesar come? Oh! He will come, never doubt it!' Then, she prophesied: 'If the Revolution spreads in Europe, another Genghis or Tamburlaine will bring it to heel. That would be its fate; be assured of that. But it will not happen in my time, nor, I hope, in that of Mister Alexander.' She forgot that she had provided this same Mister Alexander with a tutor with republican convictions, La Harpe, and that she had always claimed to hold liberal opinions. Some fine ideas are very agreeable to play around with, but cannot stand being put into practice. One might be interested in one's subjects, try to better the lot of the most miserable, even allow a few liberties here and there, without having to tolerate a mob revolution. The role of the monarch was to rule, and that of the people to obey. Inverting this relationship could only lead a country to ruin. The subversive philosophers' hazy views could not alter the evidence. In fact, Catherine had never really liked France, the country of levity, agitation and disorder. She had loved French culture. And suddenly she was seized with fear: were those great French writers that she admired so much, Voltaire, Diderot, Rousseau, D'Alembert – were they responsible for plunging their country into such a hideous condition? Had they not, by their criticisms, disorientated a nation which had now completely lost its bearings? She asked Grimm: 'You say that one day you will exonerate Voltaire of the charge that he helped originate the Revolution, and that you will name the true culprits? I beg you, please name them and tell me what you know of them . . . I shall await . . . the moment when it shall please you to absolve, in my mind, the philosophers from having been a cause of the Revolution.'[1] She said quite simply to Ségur, whose democratic feeling made him look favourably at the abolition of the feudal system: 'I warn you that the English want revenge for their defeat in America. If they attack you, the new war will be a good thing for you as it will draw outwards the fire that is destroying you.'

[1] Letters of the 5th December, 1793, 11th February and 31st March, 1794, 6th April, 1796. Henry Vallotin *Catherine II*.

Ségur was eager to return to France to witness, on the spot, the benefits of liberty. Also, paradoxically, he was uncertain as to the fate of his family in the midst of the revolutionary turmoil. Catherine gave him his passports and allowed him a farewell audience. 'Tell the King how much I wish for his happiness,' she declared to him. 'It is with sadness that I see you go: you would do better to stay with me and not seek out storms of which you cannot know the extent. Your taste for the new philosophy and for liberty will probably lead you to support the popular cause; I would be angry at this, as I remain an aristocrat: that is my job. Think about it, you are going to find France most fevered and sickly.' 'I fear it is so, Madame,' he replied, 'but that is what makes it my duty to return.'

They separated with sadness and mutual esteem. But very soon the evolution of French political affairs made Catherine harden her heart towards Ségur. One day she was to write about him: 'There is a man whose foibles I cannot forgive: Ségur. Fie! He is as false as Judas.'[1] And again: 'With some people he passes himself off as a democrat, with others as an aristocrat ... We received the *Comte de Ségur* here ... Now it is *Louis Ségur* who is suffering from the national sickness.'

Russia had to be protected at all cost from this French revolutionary leprosy. On the 3rd November, 1789, Monsieur Genet,[2] the new French chargé d'affaires in St Petersburg, wrote in his despatch to the Comte de Montmorin: 'The wisest precautions are being taken here to prevent the dissemination of the news of the ferment in which France is plunged, and the cruel convulsions she is suffering. Only very short accounts of our home affairs are published in the papers; it is strictly forbidden to talk about politics in public places ... These prudent measures are intended as much for the maintenance of sovereign authority as for the safety of the State. If the Russian peasants, who possess no property, and who are slaves, were ever to break their chains, their first action would be to massacre the nobility, which owns all the land, and this flourishing country would once again be plunged into the most hideous barbarity.'

For the moment, Catherine had nothing to fear from her people. The pernicious theories of the French philosophers had not penetrated into their illiterate skulls. They had centuries of servitude instead of ideals. The Russians worked and fought. Successfully. Potemkin took Bender and Akkermann, Suvorov was victorious at Martinechti and Rimnik, the Austrians occupied Belgrade, and Repnin took the little fort of

---

[1] Letters to Grimm – 2nd May 1791.
[2] M. Genet was a brother of Mme Campan.

Hadjibei, which was to become Odessa. But the Turks were tough and still would not sue for peace. For Catherine the year 1790 began in sorrow, both personal and political: Joseph II, tired and ill, died in February. His brother, Leopold of Tuscany, who became Emperor, had no intention of continuing his predecessor's friendly relationship with Russia. He drew closer to Prussia, and even considered concluding a separate peace with the Sublime Porte.[1] Would Russia have to continue the fight against Turkey and Sweden alone? The Prince de Nassau then suffered a terrible naval defeat at Svenskund, the same place in which he had been victorious the preceding year. If Prussia now attacked, St Petersburg was lost. The Prince de Nassau, in despair, begged to be stripped of his command, and sent back to the Empress the medals he had received in the past, and which he no longer felt worthy of. She would accept neither his retirement nor his medals. 'My God,' she wrote to him magnanimously, 'who has not had set-backs in their life? The greatest captains have had their disappointments. The late King of Prussia was great even after a great defeat... The rest of the world thought that all was lost, while he was already defeating the enemy again.' By saying this, she was as much trying to convince herself as she was her correspondent. One morning Bezborodko found her reading Plutarch, 'to strengthen my soul,' she said. She often had sleepless nights. The naval defeat at Svenskund seemed to be an omen that worse was to come. But, curiously, the disaster had a good effect. Gustavus III, now that he had humiliated the proud Russian fleet, was satisfied, and declared himself ready for conciliation. In fact all the Swedish political parties were pressing him to end this absurd war. Catherine agreed to discuss conditions for an honourable peace. She did not surrender an inch of territory, but recognized the new form of government in Sweden. A treaty stating this agreement was signed at Varela on the 3rd/14th August, 1790. Gustavus III, now that he had been recognized as an absolute monarch, had obtained an indisputable moral advantage, and emerged victorious from a very risky quarrel. In a letter to his old enemy, he begged her to renew their friendship and to forget this war which had been 'like a passing storm'. A passing storm lasting two years! Catherine drew up the balance-sheet, with happy lucidity. 'We have one foot out of the mud,' she wrote to Potemkin; 'when we get the other one out we'll sing Hallelujah.'

The other 'foot' was deeply bogged down. There was no victory to celebrate. For months Russian troops had been besieging in vain the Turkish citadel of Ismail. King Frederick William of Prussia was

[1] The Turkish Government.

encouraging nationalist feeling in Poland. Taking advantage of Catherine's difficulties, he promised the Polish patriots that he would help them shake Russian hegemony, give them back the part of Galicia appropriated by Austria in the Partition, and defend them militarily if they were attacked. A mutual defence treaty was concluded between Prussia and Poland in March 1790. It was clearly aimed at Russia. Catherine had to swallow her pride at these affronts, as she was in no state to hit back. She had to finish with the Turks first. At last there was a break in the clouds: after three bloody assaults, Suvorov finally took Ismail. Fifteen thousand Russians perished in the fortress moats. 'Proud Ismail is at Your Majesty's feet,' wrote Suvorov to the Empress. Catherine's heart leapt – was this the end? No, the battles continued. She was tired. She was now sixty. She no longer believed in the realization of her Greek dream. Constantine would now, probably, never be Emperor of Dacia. However her grandson Alexander would rule over an enlarged, unified and strengthened Russia. Thanks to her. Peace talks cautiously began at Jassy. There was endless prevarication on both sides. Each tried to exhaust the other with their obstinacy and arrogance. The days went by. Men were still dying. The envoys separated, met again. Catherine was determined not to lose any part of the conquered territories. She was not like Louis XV who had given up Louisiana and Canada, or George III who had let go of his American colonies. Russia was under her skin – to remove a piece of it you would have to flay her alive. She had long since forgotten that she was born German. Her legitimacy was not a matter of blood, but one of choice, love, work and longevity. She had created her own country, and even her own ancestors. In her dreams, her father was not called Christian-Augustus of Anhalt-Zerbst, but Peter the Great.

CHAPTER XXIV

Zubov versus Potemkin

Catherine was over sixty and worn out by worry and work; she was now a small plump woman, with upright bearing, greying hair and a haughty look. 'I was, at first, extremely surprised to find her so small,' remarked Madame Vigée-Lebrun, after a visit to the Court. 'I had always imagined her prodigiously tall, as large in life as in reputation. She was very fat but still had a fine face ... Genius seemed to lie in her wide and very high forehead. Her eyes were soft and delicate, her nose was quite Grecian; she had a bright complexion and mobile features ... I have said that she was small and yet, on ceremonial days, with her head held high, her eagle eye – the expression which comes from the habit of command – she had such majesty that she seemed to me like the queen of the world.'

Even the spiteful Masson, the Grand Dukes' mathematics teacher, admitted in his *Secret Russian Memoirs* that the Empress combined corpulence with elegance, and an air of grandeur with a great deal of amiability. She walked slowly with small steps, 'her forehead high and serene', her eyes clear, bowing with a slight inclination of the head, stretching out her plump white hand for a courtier to kiss, and murmuring a few charming words. 'But it was then,' wrote the memorialist, 'that the harmony of her face would break up, and one would forget for a moment the great Catherine and see only the old woman; because when she opened her mouth, there were no teeth and her voice was broken and slurred. There was something rough and coarse about the bottom half of her face; her light grey eyes had something false about them and a crease at the base of her nose made her look somewhat sinister.'

Her costume, except on ceremonial days, was very simple. A floating dress of purple or grey silk, 'Moldavian-style', with double sleeves, no jewels and comfortable low-heeled shoes. All Catherine's vanity went into the arrangement of her hair: swept up at the back, and lightly powdered, it revealed a high and wide forehead. For large receptions she wore a diamond crown and replaced the 'Moldavian' dress with a 'Russian' outfit in rose velvet. In order to set a limit on the extravagances of costumes and to combat the influence of Parisian fashion, all the ladies of the Court were ordered to wear this unbecoming dress. They even had to renounce the 'à la Reine' or 'Bell-Poule' hairstyles, when a proclamation, on the 22nd October, 1782, forbade any capillary structures more than two and a half inches high. Severity was the rule. It was Versailles with Russian modifications. 'Here,' wrote the Comte de Damas, 'everything is like a fine sketch rather than a complete work of art ... The houses are still at the façade stage, the inhabitants don't quite know their parts ... The costumes, Asiatic for the populace, French for society people, do not look properly finished ... The people are muzzled rather than tamed ... There are many wenches at Court who would be quite happy to return to their villages, many clean-shaven men who still think a beard keeps you warm.'

In fact, despite the proclamations recommending greater sobriety in court dress, the aristocracy in the capital and the provinces showed a careless extravagance that amazed foreign observers. Following the Empress's example, the nobles built freely in all corners of Russia – palaces, rustic villas, greenhouses, riding schools, private theatres; they planted 'English' or 'French' gardens, dug lakes, built grottoes, gave parties and balls and set off fireworks. The imperial residences, Tsarskoe Selo, Peterhof and Gatchina were favourite places for such extravagances. The rule was always to live beyond your means. Wardrobes were superabundant: Marshal Apraxin possessed more than three hundred costumes. Recently ennobled small fry boasted of having hundreds of stockings and shoes. People rivalled one another with the splendour of their carriages, horses and harnesses. Many squires got into debt and ruined themselves in their desire to keep up their style of life. To remain afloat, they would sell or mortgage parts of their estates. The main thing was to maintain one's rank and to continue to appear in public. It was fashionable to have a mass of servants. A man's importance was measured by the size of his staff. The rich had between three and eight hundred servants each. For a man of moderate means, a hundred and fifty was a good number. An impoverished gentleman would have only twenty. Most of these servants were serfs whose masters had brought them up from the country. He did not know their names or their faces, and would complain continually of their idleness. They were fed and housed, received no wages, and performed every sort of function: certainly there were butlers, footmen, errand boys, chambermaids, cooks, cook's boys, pastry-cooks, bakers, stokers, washers-up, laundresses, linen maids, seamstresses, embroiderers, coachmen, equerries, stable-boys, huntsmen, grooms, porters, guards and night-watchmen; but there were also, in the great houses, tailors, bootmakers, saddlers, apothecaries, jesters, musicians, actors, singers and painters, yes, even artists were included amongst the great lord's livestock. The most talented of these moujiks were moulded and taught by teachers from abroad. Once they had been licked into shape, they served for the amusement of the master and his guests. Count Kamensky spent thirty thousand roubles mounting a gala performance in his theatre. Count Sheremetiev had, in his village of Kouskovo, a troupe of actors and singers envied by Catherine herself. To celebrate the signature of peace with Turkey, Leo Naryshkin had the major battles of the war re-enacted on his estates by extras in uniform. Skavronsky, who adored music, made his servants address him in operatic recitative.

On the whole, these specialist-serfs did well out of their masters' indulgence; as well as being status-symbols they became part of his capital. The others, like defenceless animals, were completely dependent on their master's will– he could overwork them, marry them to anyone he wished, punish them with the knout or deport them for the slightest misdemeanour. Only capital punishment was forbidden to him. Even the most good-natured landowners, who treated their peasants in a 'patriarchal manner', could not bring themselves to regard them as quite human. For the owning classes, the serf population of the countryside represented a separate zoological species, possibly with souls but certainly without rights. The most enlightened people bought or mortgaged serfs. The St Petersburg and Moscow papers carried strangely-worded advertisements: 'For sale, one hairdresser, four bedsteads, one eiderdown and other pieces of furniture.' Or: 'For sale, one sixteen-year-old girl, well-behaved, and one second-hand carriage, hardly used.' Prices were low for the ungraded product. A pedigree dog was worth two thousand roubles, while a peasant cost three hundred, and a young peasant girl less than a hundred. One could even buy a child for a few kopecks. On the other hand a good cook or musician could easily fetch eight hundred roubles. This trade in human flesh had flourished particularly since the beginning of Catherine's reign. She did not mind at all, despite her enlightened collection of liberal ideals. More than that, she took pleasure in giving whole villages as presents to those whose political, military or amorous zeal she wished to reward. Thus she had already distributed more than eight hundred thousand 'souls'. Favouritism was expensive. According to information gathered at the time from 'Well-informed persons', the French diplomat J. Castéra drew up an approximate account of these intimate imperial expenses. This is what they received in money, peasants, land, palaces, jewellery, china and pensions:

The five Orlov brothers	17,000,000 roubles
Vysotsky (an unaccounted extra)	300,000 roubles
Vasilchikov	1,110,000 roubles
Potemkin	50,000,000 roubles
Zavadovsky	1,380,000 roubles
Zorich	1,420,000 roubles
Rimsky-Korsakov	920,000 roubles
Lanskoy	7,260,000 roubles
Ermolov	550,000 roubles
Mamonov	880,000 roubles
The Zubov brothers	3,500,000 roubles
Lovers' running expenses since the beginning of the reign	8,500,000 roubles
Total	92,820,000 roubles

Or, according to the rate of exchange with French money at that time, 464 million francs. This colossal sum more or less corresponds to a similar account drawn up by Harris, the English ambassador, in a note to his government in 1782. As if to reply to these lists denouncing her amorous excesses, Catherine drew up in a letter to Grimm a list of her political achievements:

Governments organized according to the new plan	29
Towns built	144
Conventions and treaties signed	30
Victories won	78
Memorable edicts, making new laws or foundations	88
Edicts for the benefit of the people	123
Total	492

She proudly placed this total in opposition to the other. What weight did a few expenses for her own pleasure carry against the enormous benefits that Russia gained from each day of her government? It was not in her nature to recognize any fault in herself. The fact that she reigned meant that all her actions were excusable. 'It is not surprising that Russia should have had so many tyrants as sovereigns,' she wrote in the *Notes*. 'It is a naturally worried and ungrateful nation, full of informers and people, who under the pretext of zeal, only want to profit from what is convenient to them.'

'Tyrant' she was not, but she did expect blind obedience. And good-humour, if possible. And good French manners. Her house was open to all. According to a Swedish visitor, Count Sternberg, the audience chamber of the Palace, before the Empress appeared, was a noisy and heaving throng. All the languages of Europe and Asia mingled in one great roar. French, Russian and German were heard most. Anybody could mix with the crowd. All you needed was a sword at your side to be allowed through the doors of the throne-room, past the two guards in their splendid uniforms – with silver breast-plates struck with the imperial eagle and a silver helmet with black plumes, they stood at attention, staring straight ahead. Only those named on a special list could cross the threshold, but it was a long list. When the Empress appeared, silence fell and everybody bowed. Across the chest of her 'Russian' costume she wore the crosses of St Alexander Nevsky, St Vladimir and St Catherine; on one side she had the ribbon and emblem of St Andrew, and on the other those of St George, the two most important Orders of the Empire. She knew most of her visitors and her bright glance moved from one face to the next. She had not yet given up the company of young men. According to Engelhardt, Potemkin's nephew, there had never been so many young whipper-snappers greedy for sinecures, posing in front of her. They crowded into the chapel, the drawing-rooms and the gardens proffering smiles like nosegays as she passed. They were almost all from the minor nobility and all had major ambitions. Each one hoped that his pretty face would attract the attention of the aging but unrepentant collector. But she did not yet consider replacing the current favourite, the 'spoilt child', the 'Redcoat', Mamonov. Mamonov, on the other hand, after four years of hard work, was now feeling a certain lassitude and boredom towards his imperial mistress, which he scarcely tried to conceal any more. She lavished gifts and kindness on him, encouraged the young lover's taste for *objets d'art*, made him director of the Hermitage theatre, included him in political discussions; but nothing could distract him, he suffered from incurable melancholia, was indisposed, choked, fainted at the smallest harsh word, and generally considered himself more miserable than a prisoner in his cell.

One day, Mamonov reproached Catherine for her 'coldness' and spoke more insistently than ever about the sick depression that was gnawing him. What could he do? He was exhausted. He wanted advice from the woman who had made his fortune. She understood that he wanted his freedom. 'Since a separation has become necessary,' she said, 'I shall think about your retirement.' As always, she chose honesty in her relationships. There was nothing uglier than an old affair with tearful scenes dragging on through force of habit. After a night of thought, she sent Mamonov a note assuring him that he would be able to retire 'with a brilliant position' and that she had even decided to set him up by marrying him to the thirteen-year-old daughter of the very famous Count Bruce: 'She is only thirteen, but I know that she is already mature.' Instead of being pleased, Mamonov replied by letter to Her Majesty: 'My hands are trembling, and as I have already written, I am alone, and have no one but you ... I will not allow myself to be tempted by riches, and I will be obliged to nobody but you, and not to Bruce. If you wish to give a foundation to my life, allow me to marry Princess Shcherbatov, the lady-in-waiting ... May God judge those who have brought us to where we are at present ... I kiss your little hands and your little feet, and I cannot even see what I am writing.' Having thus explained himself on paper, he rushed round to the Empress, fell down before her, shaking and sobbing, and explained that he had been in love for the past year with the lady-in-waiting, Daria Shcherbatov, and that she had agreed to marry him. The blow hit Catherine in the heart. What wounded her most was not the confession of the fault, but the realization that she had been duped by a man she trusted. All that play-acting, the vapours, the absences – all so that he could meet Shcherbatov in bed! Mr Redcoat certainly did not pretend to be ill when he was with that twenty-six-year-old brat! She had been getting everything that he had been refusing the Russian Empress for the past few months! Never mind. She did not bear grudges. Let them marry since they had a taste for each other. Two days later, in the evening, she summoned her lover with his chosen wife, and publicly announced their engagement. Kneeling before their sovereign, the young people received her blessing and, sobbing, heard her wish them happiness and prosperity. Mamonov and the lady-in-waiting were, apparently, almost sick with emotion at the end of her little speech. Catherine gazed upon them with a motherly eye and, as always, promised them all sorts of gifts. But a few days later, she exploded with all the bitterness of an old and abandoned mistress, in front of her secretary Khrapovitsky. He carefully recorded the conversation in his *Journal*. In the midst of reading a report, Catherine cried: 'I have suspected him for the past eighteen months! ... He was avoiding me ... It was always chest trouble that kept him in his room! Then recently he began to talk about his conscience, which was making him suffer, and preventing him continuing with this communal life: Traitor! What was weighing on his chest all the time was his own duplicity – this other affair! But if he could not control himself, why didn't he honestly confess to it? ... He cannot imagine what I have suffered!' 'Everybody was surprised that Your Majesty consented to this marriage,' observed Khrapovitsky.

'God be with them!' she replied. 'I wish them all happiness... But you can see: I have forgiven them, authorized the union, they should be in Heaven, but all they do is sob! Ah! His old feelings are not quite dead. For the last week or two he has been staring at me everywhere!'

The wedding ceremony was hastily performed in the chapel of the Palace. According to the custom for ladies-in-waiting, the fiancée's toilette was supervised by the Empress herself. Mamonov received a hundred thousand roubles and a new estate with three thousand peasants, to which the couple departed in a flurry, straight after the blessing. There the ex-lady-in-waiting, who was already pregnant by the ex-favourite, gave birth to a child.

Still upset by this lamentable amorous upheaval, Catherine poured it out in a letter to Potemkin: 'I have never been a personal tyrant and I hate all forms of constraint.' Potemkin, from far away, sympathized. Certainly he had been responsible for introducing the 'spoilt child' to the Empress. But he had very soon advised her to 'spit on him'. Mamonov deserved nothing but contempt for having failed to stick to 'his job'. 'I was never mistaken about him,' wrote the Serene Prince of Taurida. 'He is a mixture of indolence and egoism – a complete Narcissus. He thought only of himself and asked for everything, giving nothing in return.'

Some time later, Catherine summed up her state of mind in a letter to Grimm. 'Mademoiselle Cardel's pupil[1] finds Mister Redcoat more deserving of pity than anger: he has been excessively punished, and for life, for his stupid passion, which failed to satisfy him, and branded him as an ungrateful fellow; all she did was end the affair as quickly as possible to the satisfaction of all concerned... There is a lot of evidence that the marriage is not a success.' And indeed Mamonov very soon realized that he had thrown out the baby with the bathwater.

Conjugal pleasures could never replace his extraordinarily privileged position as official favourite at the Court. He wrote to Her Majesty that he had died a thousand deaths since their separation, and that his only wish was to return to St Petersburg to find again the warmth he so sorely lacked. As always, Catherine, who was so perceptive in political matters, suffered from romantic delusions. At sixty, she had the imagination and simplicity of a teenager. One look in the mirror should have brought her to her senses, but she persisted in believing that a man could still prefer her to a young wife, despite her wrinkles, toothless smile and sagging bosom. She was touched and said to Khrapovitsky: 'I know it, he cannot be happy.' However, she refused to revive the

---

[1] This is how she sometimes described herself in her letters.

relationship: 'It is one thing to go out into the garden with him, and see him for four hours; living with him is a different matter.'[1] She replied to Mamonov's strange entreaties by advising him to wait for a year before seeing her again.

Catherine, when she wrote those lines, was feeling far from neglected. Even before Potemkin's *protégé*, Mamonov, had officially relinquished his position, the clique hostile to Potemkin – the Tchernychevs, the Rumyantsovs, the Saltykovs – had hurriedly begun the search for a replacement. They wanted to beat His Highness to it, and find a favourite who would not be under his orders. They had only too many to choose from, as it was a much sought-after position. The lucky man was immediately conveyed to the apartment by the Empress's confidante Anna Naryshkin. His name was Plato Alexandrovich Zubov. He was twenty-two, and a lieutenant in the guard. Catherine had known him for a long time, and had taken him under her wing when he was only an eleven-year-old schoolboy; later, she had sent him abroad to pursue his studies. That evening, however, she saw him in a new light. He pleased her, she accepted him, they dined by candlelight, and the following day he received ten thousand roubles and some rings, one of which went to buy the good will of Her Majesty's valet. In the week following his enthronement, Plato Zubov was made personal *aide-de-camp* to the Empress. He gave Anna Naryshkin, who had placed his foot in the stirrup, a valuable watch. One could see him now, wrote Masson, 'holding the Empress's arm in a familiar fashion, with his plumed hat, bedecked with his new uniform, followed by the great men of the Empire – who were bare-headed. Previously, he had had to dance attendance on *them*. In the evening, after the card game, Catherine would dismiss her guests and proceed to her bedroom, followed only by her lover.' She was so pleased with him that she wrote to Potemkin. 'I have come back to life like a fly in spring.' A fat sixty-year-old fly, moving and buzzing and greedy for new meat. This time, it was a particularly appetizing morsel. Plato Zubov was certainly the handsomest of all the Empress's lovers. He had fine features, a shapely mouth, soft brown hair, and, with his deep stare, gave an impression of aristocratic harmony and careless self-confidence. He was of medium height, but, Masson wrote, 'was supple, virile, and well proportioned'.

By a strange paradox of nature, this young man, who appeared so slender and amiable, immediately began to show signs of ambition, insolence, cynicism and a taste for intrigue. He very soon monopolized all the paths of influence, imposing his wishes in every sphere, and

[1] Waliszewski *Around the Throne.*

shamelessly demanding favours for himself and his family. He was surrounded by a court of flatterers. 'Every day,' wrote Langeron, 'his antechamber was crowded with ministers, courtiers, generals, foreigners, petitioners, people looking for positions and privileges. You mostly had to wait for four or five hours before being admitted... Then the doors would swing open and the crowd rushed forwards: they would find the favourite in front of a mirror having his hair curled, usually with one foot up on a chair or dressing-table. The courtiers would bow down and then stand before him, in a cloud of powder, in two or three silent and motionless rows.' And Masson corroborated: 'The old generals and other grandees were not ashamed of approaching his humblest valets. Stretched out on a sofa in a most indecent wrap, with his little finger in his nose and his eyes turned wearily to the ceiling, this cold and vain-looking young man hardly deigned to notice those around him.' Plato Zubov had a little monkey who leapt from one piece of furniture to the next, swung from chandeliers, emptied jars of pomade, and sometimes landed on a visitor's neck and pulled off his wig. It was a great honour to be thus distinguished by the animal, and nobody ever protested. As for Catherine, she regarded her lover's behaviour as innocent pranks. With age, she had lost all perception when in love. She wore rose-coloured spectacles; blinded and intoxicated, she made constant allusions to her happiness in her letters to Potemkin. She said that 'the child', 'the little dark one' had 'the most innocent soul, that he was without wickedness or treachery, modest, affectionate, and supremely grateful for everything, that he wanted to please everybody, that he was assiduous and even flatteringly demanding towards her. He cries like a child if he is not allowed to come into my room.' His tactfulness even made him want to be loved by his mistress's faraway husband. 'Goodbye my friend,' she wrote to His Highness. 'Cherish us so that we may be perfectly happy. ' And also: 'When he has a chance to write to you, he does so with great eagerness, and his agreeable character makes me more agreeable.'

In fact, when 'the little dark one' wrote so unctuously to Potemkin, it was to ask him for a commission for himself, and for his brother to be taken onto the general staff. Catherine, of course, backed this double demand with a flood of praise designed to make the Prince love the child, 'our child'. Potemkin could not refuse. Catherine thanked him effusively. 'The child thinks you are cleverer, wittier and nicer than any of those surrounding you, but keep it a secret as he does not know that I know it.'

Valerian Zubov joined the army in the Crimea. From there he sent malicious reports back to his brother, about the commander-in-chief's errors and general negligence. These confidential notes crossed no less confidential ones sent to Potemkin by his friends, describing the young lover's behaviour. According to these reports, Catherine was so infatuated by her 'little dark one' that she was thinking of making him a minister. Potemkin choked with rage. It was the first time the Tsarina had taken on a lover who was not his creation. And now this newcomer threatened to acquire great importance in the Court and the Government. Seen from a distance, this rise seemed to presage the fall of the Prince of Taurida, and that Potemkin could not allow. After the fall of Ismail, the army had taken up its winter quarters, but he had to remain on the spot to conduct peace negotiations which he did not believe in. So until he was able to escape these tiresome duties, he sent Valerian Zubov to St Petersburg with orders to say, literally, to the Empress that all was well on the front, but that the commander-in-chief was suffering from a bad tooth and hoped to come to the capital soon to have it removed. Now the Russian word for tooth is *zub* and with this simple pun on Zubov, Potemkin was warning the Tsarina that he counted on her to get rid of a tiresome rival. Catherine pretended not to understand, and continued, in her letters to Potemkin, to praise Plato's extraordinary gifts.

Then Potemkin lost patience and set off, abandoning his officers. An enormous suite, including several women, travelled with him. The Empress rejoiced in public when she heard of his departure, but was privately apprehensive. She had the road lit far into the countryside by equally spaced braziers. Since nobody knew exactly when he would arrive, these lights were kept going every night for a week. Every day, a messenger was sent to meet the travellers, and he would return at full gallop, to bring news of His Highness to the Empress. At last he appeared in person – big, heavy, sunburnt, half-blind, older, but beaming. At first sight he appeared in excellent spirits, and Catherine was able to write to Grimm: 'Prince Potemkin arrived four days ago, as handsome, agreeable and witty as ever, and in the best possible humour; a fine and glorious campaign like that does put one in a good humour.' And to the Prince de Ligne: 'Looking at the Prince-General Potemkin, one would think that success and victory make people beautiful. He has arrived from the army looking as handsome as the day, as merry as a lark, as bright as any star, as witty as ever, and not biting his nails any more.' This 'merriness' did not last long. From his first moments at Court, Potemkin realized that he had been right to fear Zubov's growing influence. Superbly dressed and covered with jewels, the new lover arrogantly put down even the highest dignitaries. They were all afraid of enraging the Empress if they displeased him. Even

Grand Duke Paul silently swallowed his insults. One evening at Her Majesty's supper, the heir to the throne loudly approved of a political comment made by his mother's lover. The latter cried out: 'What? Have I said something stupid?' An embarrassed silence fell around the table. Nobody dared flatten this young cock's comb. Catherine gazed at him with an enraptured stare. Potemkin could not bear the sight of this senile passion. Certainly, he had as his mistress his very young and pretty niece, Alexandra Engelhardt, Countess Branicka; but he never lost his head over her. He tried, with friendly firmness, to bring Catherine back to her senses, and make her see that she had become infatuated with a foppish idiot, who was both pretentious and an intriguer: the more importance she gave him, the more she compromised her own prestige; in any case she should never let him play any part in the conduct of public affairs. This wise advice came up against the radiant naivety of an old woman in love. Catherine was captivated by Plato Zubov – she refused to recognize her lover's faults, and took pleasure in her fantasies. But she did not hold Potemkin's remonstrations against him, taking them to be the result of quite understandable jealousy. How could he not suffer at no longer being first in Her Majesty's affections? To soothe his bitterness she showed him a great deal of tenderness and consideration. But, despite all the attentions he received, he soon understood that he was the loser. Plato Zubov was stronger than he. In a movement of angry pride, His Highness then decided to dazzle this sovereign who was drawing away from him with a party such as she had never seen before.

Potemkin was inspired in the preparations for this great day by wild extravagance, a kind of despairing folly and a deeply Slavic desire to go too far, to extremes of absurdity and uselessness. For months, hundreds of artistes – actors, dancers, musicians – rehearsed their parts in the Taurida Palace, under the eye of their fierce organizer. As he had done for the journey to the Crimea, he saw to every detail of the scenery and the cast. To warm the air in the main hall he had hot water pipes installed in the columns supporting the arch. The ground was carpeted with grass. A mass of tropical plants flowered between the marble walls. As well as the Empress and the Grand Dukes, the whole Court, the whole diplomatic corps, and all the representatives of the provincial nobility were invited, on the 28th April, 1791, on the pretext of celebrating the Russian victory over the Turks.

When Catherine arrived, at seven o'clock in the evening, in front of the Taurida Palace, she found herself in the midst of a noisy and violent crush of people, and began to fear a riot. But all it was was the natural movement of the ordinary people rushing to the tables, loaded with victuals and barrels of wine, which had been thoughtfully placed outside the princely dwelling. Descending from her carriage, the Empress passed between two long lines of footmen, in white and silver livery, holding candelabras. She was dazzled by thousands of candles. She knew that Potemkin despised tallow candles, and that all the wax from neighbouring provinces had been commandeered to provide illumination worthy of his sovereign. A triumphal tune, played by three hundred musicians, burst on her ears. Three thousand guests bowed down as she approached. The master of ceremonies advanced towards her, wearing a scarlet costume with gold embroidery. A long black velvet coat was held to his shoulders by diamond clips. His hat was so heavy with precious stones that he could not keep it on his head, and a page carried it behind him. The Empress was dressed in old Russian boyar costume. Her diadem shone out above her tired face. She held her head high. Potemkin knelt before her, bade her welcome, and led her by the hand to the ballroom. Seated on a throne, she watched the show. Grand Dukes Alexander and Constantine – now fourteen and twelve – danced graciously before her with forty-eight young boys and girls of the Court, all dressed in 'pink and sky blue' and studded with jewels. The famous Le Picq ended the ballet with some brilliantly skilful steps. After the applause, they moved to another room: there a scene took place in front of an artificial elephant covered with emeralds and rubies. Another ballet, followed by a short comedy and a procession of 'Asiatic splendour', in which representatives of all the races under Catherine's rule appeared in national costume. Next, the crowd of guests moved on to the winter garden, where they found, in the centre of a circular temple, a statue of the Empress in Paros marble. An ode by Derzhavin was then read, praising the heroine of the evening in pompous verse. Behind her, fountains played and gems glittered in the depths of the exotic foliage. Another room had walls hung with Beauvais tapestries, telling the story of Esther. Elswhere, on a lawn, there was an agate obelisk carved with the Tsarina's monogram. The courtiers assembled around the sovereign for a supper of five sittings for six hundred people each. Potemkin, standing behind her, wanted to serve her himself. She would not allow this, and made him sit down beside her. Thus they presided over the meal together, like an imperial couple. Not far away, Plato Zubov, resplendent in his sky blue costume, did not miss a single gesture; he was not in the least worried. He knew Catherine's real feelings: her show of affection for the Prince of Taurida meant nothing as far as the future was concerned. There was no promise in the looks she gave him, only a sort of sad compassion. Toast followed toast; they drank to the glory of Her Majesty and her host, to the Grand Dukes and

Grand Duchesses, to the army and the navy. The plates were of gold and silver. The gargantuan meal consisted of all the choicest dishes of Europe and Asia. The heat soon became suffocating, thanks to the hundred and forty thousand fairy lights and the twenty thousand candles which lit the room. Each guest received a royal gift. Potemkin bitterly savoured his triumph. The amazed foreign ambassadors, deafened by the music and the speeches, saw this giant, dressed in red and encased in medals, as a specifically Russian phenomenon, inexhaustibly rich, and of a futility that bordered on madness.

At two o'clock in the morning, Catherine took her leave. Plato Zubov followed her like a shadow. The orchestra played a hymn composed in her honour. She spoke a few words to Potemkin, thanking him for this incredible evening. He knelt down before her, kissed her hand and broke into sobs. Although she did not reveal her thoughts, he realized that this party had been his farewell to her.

The lights were out, the guests had all gone and Potemkin was suddenly aware of the uselessness of his existence. He was sickened by everything in St Petersburg, and yet he could not make up his mind to leave again for the South, where Prince Repnin now commanded all military operations. The latter, a brave and experienced soldier, crossed the Danube with forty thousand men and wiped out three times as many of the Grand Vizir's troops at Machin. Catherine was delighted and Potemkin, devoured by jealousy, bitterly regretted having allowed another to reap such military glory. These recent Russian victories made the Turks less demanding, and it therefore seemed an excellent moment to conclude an honourable peace. Plato Zubov and his friends were firmly in favour of this, which was all that was needed for Potemkin to be opposed to it. Anything coming from this Lumpkin made him bristle with rage. The Prince of Taurida, therefore, decided that the war must be pursued until the Turks had been totally annihilated. Catherine tried in vain to explain to him the country's precarious financial position, the exhaustion of the army, the internal problems – he remained obstinate. She hesitated to formally order him to return to Jassy and put an end to hostilities; in his present state of revolt, she feared that he might refuse to obey her. The most she could do was show him that by signing this peace, after four years of bloody fighting, he would be bringing her the greatest gift of her reign.

Suddenly, he changed his mind. Had he heard of talks with the Turkish envoys begun by Repnin? Did he think that he could impose his aggressive views better at Jassy than in St Petersburg? All of a sudden, he was ready to go. Catherine was touched by this new submissiveness, and personally supervised the preparation of the carriage, which was to take His Highness on his long journey. He left her, sad and disillusioned, with dark forebodings and crippled by debts. The florist's bill alone came to 38,000 roubles.

Bad news awaited the traveller at Kharkov. Prince Alexander of Württemberg, who had served under him, had just died. Potemkin attended the funeral in a dazed condition, and, when the moment came to return to his carriage, he realized, with horror, that, by mistake, he had gone towards the hearse to get into it. He was extremely superstitious and saw this as a fatal omen. His companions were struck by a sort of frenzy in his expression. Would he be strong enough to conduct the negotiations to a satisfactory conclusion?

He arrived at Jassy in July 1791, and learned that in his absence Repnin had signed the preliminaries to a peace treaty. In a fit of rage, he heaped coarse abuse on the General and tore up the document. Repnin replied that he had acted on secret orders from Her Majesty. Potemkin was bitterly wounded, realizing that, on a matter where their opinions differed, she had simply gone over his head. He could not accept such lack of confidence from his sovereign. As the talks began again on a different basis, his weakness and self-doubt increased. His enormous body, battered as it was by every kind of excess, was now devoured by a feverish infection. After his one burst of energy, he ceased to participate in meetings with the Turks. He lost interest in politics; worldly matters no longer concerned him. He was a difficult patient and refused to follow the prescriptions of his doctors, Linman and Massot; he would not even hear of a diet. 'The Prince was destroying himself,' wrote Langeron. 'I saw him, during a bout of fever, devour a ham, a smoked goose, three or four chickens, and drink *kwass*, *kliouvka*, mead and several different sorts of wine.' Between meals he would eat raw turnips, of which he was particularly fond. When he felt his temperature rise, he would have streams of eau de Cologne poured over his head, and would sprinkle himself with iced water. His niece, Alexandra Engelhardt, Countess Branicka, who was also his mistress, watched over the moods of this crushed giant. He did not understand what was happening to him. The Tsarina's letters were his only consolation: he read them over and over again, sobbing. With a superhuman effort, he would dictate his answer, scrawling his signature, in a trembling hand, at the bottom of the page. 'I am very weak,' he said. 'I beg you, choose and send me a Chinese dressing-gown, I badly need one.' When a messenger brought the Chinese dressing-gown, he claimed that he felt better. Anything from Catherine was beneficial to him.

At the beginning of October, 1791, he suddenly abandoned the Peace

Conference, and decided to go to Nicolaiev, a town that he had founded at the mouth of the Bug. Why this move? He did not know himself. A sick man's fancy. Health and happiness lay wherever he was not. He set off to search for them, and, before climbing into his carriage, he scribbled a despairing note to the Empress: 'Little mother, gracious sovereign, I can no longer bear these torments. My only hope is to leave this town; I have given orders that I should be taken to Nicolaiev. I do not know what will become of me. Your most faithful and grateful subject – Potemkin. The only way I can save myself is by going.'

His niece, Alexandra, got into the carriage with him. His Highness was accompanied by a doctor and three secretaries. The road was terrible, with deep ruts, and the patient groaned at every jolt. After a few versts, he asked them to stop the carriage and lay him on the grass. 'That is enough. No further. I am dying. I want to die on the ground.' They stretched him out on a carpet, at the foot of a tree. The doctor busied himself; Alexandra sobbed. At about midday, Potemkin, lord of so many estates, owner of so many palaces, died beside the road like a homeless vagabond. They looked around for a gold piece to shut his single eye with, as was the Russian custom. One of the Cossacks in the escort rummaged in his pocket and offered a brass five-kopeck piece, which was carefully placed on the dead man's eyelid.

On the 12th October, 1791, five and a half months after the evening at the Taurida Palace, a messenger dressed in black brought the news of his death to St Petersburg. Catherine fainted, and was bled, sobbed, locked herself up, refused to see anybody. Even her grandsons were not admitted. Strict mourning was enforced at the Court. The Empress withdrew into her grief, realizing more every day what an enormous loss she had suffered – he had been together her lover, husband, friend, adviser, confidant, minister and military leader. Even when far away from each other, they had never ceased to consult one another. He had increased his nation's territory by a third, he had brought wilderness under cultivation, he had created new towns, dredged out ports and built ships. He had known the greatest sovereigns of his time, loved many women, spent several fortunes and, in all things, had displayed a spirit full of vitality, both gentle and wild, both insane and far-sighted; and now this force of nature, this volcano of passion was nothing more than a lifeless corpse, buried at the end of the world at Kherson. 'How can one replace such a man?' Catherine said to her secretary, Khrapovitsky. 'He never betrayed me – he could not be bought. Nothing will be the same again. Who would have thought that he would die before Tchernychev and the other old men? Now they will stick their heads out, like snails out of their shells! But I am old, too.'

Thereupon, she seized her pen. At the height of her grief she had to write: she took a sheet of the gilt-edged paper she used for her correspondence. As usual she wrote to her 'whipping boy', her dear Grimm who understood everything:

'A terrible bludgeon-stroke has just fallen on my head. At about six o'clock in the afternoon, a messenger brought the very sad news that my pupil, my friend, my idol almost, Prince Potemkin of Taurida, has died in Moldavia, after about a month's illness. You cannot imagine how greatly I am afflicted: he combined an excellent heart with rare understanding and unusual breadth of mind; his views were always broad-minded and generous; he was extremely humane, full of knowledge, exceptionally agreeable, and always had new ideas; nobody had such a gift for finding the right word, and making amusing remarks. His military qualities, during this war, must have struck everybody, as he never failed either on land or sea. Nobody on earth was less led by others than he was ... In a word, he was a statesman, both in counsel and execution. He was passionately and zealously attached to me, scolding me when he thought I could have done better; with age and experience he corrected his own faults ... His most precious quality was courage of heart, mind and soul, which distinguished him from the rest of humanity, and which meant that we understood each other perfectly, and could leave the less enlightened to babble on at their leisure. I consider that Prince Potemkin was a very great man, who did not fulfil half of his capabilities.'

When Catherine reappeared at Court, everybody around her affected deep sorrow. But beneath their solemn expressions, Zubov and his friends were delighted. Some whispered that Potemkin had been poisoned on Plato's orders. In any case, the latter insisted to the Empress that she should not attach undue importance to the Prince's death. She resigned herself to muting her grief at the death of her old lover for the sake of her love for the new one. Since Plato requested it, she would not issue any proclamation on the death of the great man, nor would she erect any monument in his memory. Already Potemkin's innumerable enemies greedily began to calculate how they could carve up his political bequest. On the 25th December, 1791, a few weeks after the Prince's death, Count Rostopchin was able to write:

'The Prince's estates have not yet been shared out. He certainly left a few debts, but also seventy thousand peasant souls in Poland, six thousand in Russia, and a million and a half roubles' worth of diamonds. What is most extraordinary is that he has already been almost completely forgotten. Generations to come will not bless his memory. He possessed to the highest degree, the gift of doing harm as well as good, and of inspiring hatred against himself, while at the same time carelessly scattering favours and kindness. One might think that the main purpose of his life was to drag others down in order to raise himself above them. His greatest weakness was to become infatuated with all women, and want to pass as a rascal. This wish, ridiculous as it might seem, brought great success. Women sought his favours as eagerly as men sought position from him. He left St Petersburg after spending eight hundred and fifty thousand roubles, which were paid by the Empress, not counting all his other debts.'

His beloved Alexandra had a mausoleum built for him at Kherson, where he was buried in the church of St Catherine. But none of those who had paid their respects to the living Potemkin thought of doing so to the dead one.

CHAPTER XXV

Poland and France

Potemkin's disappearance led to a redistribution of roles around the Empress. She chose Bezborodko to replace His Highness at the Jassy Conference. He set off for Moldavia immediately, armed with conciliatory proposals. She wanted it over and done with as soon as possible! Peace was signed on the 29th December, 1791/9th January, 1792. The treaty left Russia all the land between the Bug and the Dniester, formally recognized that Otchakov and the Crimea were now Russian, and for the rest re-affirmed the agreements of Kutchuk-Kainardji. Although the whole north coast of the Black Sea now belonged to Russia, the sea itself was closed to the outside world by the Bosphorus. Four years of bloody fighting, with enormous casualties, and very few territorial gains to show for them. Catherine had not taken Constantinople; her grandson, Constantine, would not be crowned there. But Russia's prestige was untouched. Plato Zubov, who had advocated this hasty and unprofitable peace, was triumphant. Catherine made him President of the College of Foreign Affairs. She had total faith in him. By his prettiness and his application, he satisfied in her her pedagogic vocation, her maternal instinct, and the sensuality of a woman past her prime. He was 'a good pupil' and she went into ecstasies in front of her secretary, Khrapovitsky: 'What he does he does well and do you know why? Because he is impartial and has no special interest.'

He satisfied her in other ways too. If one is to believe Masson, 'Catherine's libidinous needs were still there and, once again, the orgies of the past were revived.' Without going so far as to say, as this diarist does, that the Zubov brothers and their friend Saltykov went in 'relays' with the Tsarina 'in a quarry so vast and so difficult to fill', one can believe that she still had a taste for physical love. Even if her burning sensuality had cooled somewhat over the years, she could not do without a warm young body in her bed. She would use any subterfuge to revive the sparks amongst the ashes. Toothless, breathless, and obese, she still sought the illusion of a willing embrace. And they would talk about politics, as she had done with Lanskoy. But Plato Zubov was tougher and greedier than his charming predecessor. He was not satisfied with being President of the College of Foreign Affairs, and he obtained from the Tsarina the Presidency of the College of War as well. Thus all foreign policy was now in his hands. Catherine, wild with gratitude, placed Potemkin's old apartments in a wing of the Hermitage at his disposal, showered him with gifts, bestowed on him the grand ribbon of Alexander Nevsky, the Order of St Andrew, and officially gave him her portrait on a medallion, as she had done in the past to the Prince of Taurida. Plato Zubov was so highly decorated that, according to Masson, 'he resembled a ribbon and hardware merchant'. His closest collaborators were appalled by his intellectual and moral insignificance, but the Empress thought him a miracle. 'Potemkin owed almost all his greatness to himself,' wrote Masson, who was a witness to this extraordinary promotion; 'Zubov owed his purely to Catherine's decrepitude. One could watch him gain power, wealth and influence in the same measure as Catherine lost her energy and genius... He was desperate to do, or appear to do, everything. The only thing that equalled his arrogance was the baseness of those who rushed to bow down to him... Everybody crawled at Zubov's feet; and because he remained standing he thought himself great.'

To help this curious minister, Catherine called Bezborodko, who had returned from Jassy. Could he not help this young man, who was full of ideas but short of experience, with some enlightened advice? Bezborodko was able to prevent a few blunders, and then handed the job of mentor to a certain Markov. He dealt only with the day-to-day problems; the wider strategy remained in the hands of Catherine and Zubov. They agreed on everything, and first of all, on the need to push back the Russian frontiers. A country's greatness depended, not on the happiness of its inhabitants, but on the extent of its territory. Now that the war with Turkey was over, they could turn their attention seriously towards Poland. Catherine coldly assessed the position of this unfortunate nation, ruled as it was by her sensitive and faithful old lover, Stanislaus Poniatowski. 'In political life,' she was fond of saying, 'one must be guided by humanitarian principles, or by self-interest... Each sovereign must make a clear decision in one direction or the other; if a government wavers between the two it becomes weak and sterile.' In the event she plumped for self-interest – she had never been inhibited by any scruples in her dealings with foreign powers. And Plato Zubov approved of her preference for immoral success over an ineffectual good conscience. It was he who organized the new move against Poland.

After the conclusion, in March 1790, of the mutual defence treaty between Poland and Prussia – which had so irritated Catherine – the

King and the Polish patriots decided to initiate a major political change. On the 3rd May, the Diet, many of whose deputies from the lesser nobility were on holiday, approved a new constitution: under its terms, the Polish throne, after Stanislaus Poniatowski's death, would become hereditary within the family of the Elector of Saxony, and the *liberum veto* and the dissident confederations would be suppressed. This amounted to the restoration of a democratic constitutional monarchy, which would do much to stabilize the country. But Poland's anarchic troubles were most useful to Catherine, and, without batting an eyelid, she declared that the 3rd May Constitution sprang from 'the spirit of revolution', that the King's plans for reform were inspired by 'the Parisian Jacobin clubs', that France was exporting its decadence to Poland and that, anyway, it broke clauses in the first treaty of partition. Thus, while refusing to participate in the Austro-Prussian alliance against France, she claimed to be fighting the 'revolutionary hydra' on territory closer to her own interests. While Prussia and Austria restored the *ancien régime* in France, she would do so, she said, in Poland. Now this was a very poor excuse, because, whereas the French Revolution lessened and even wiped out the power of the monarchy, the Polish Constitution of the 3rd May tended, on the contrary, to strengthen it and eliminate any cause for discord. Catherine, although she was reasonable both by temperament and education, refused to recognize the evidence when there was a practical advantage to be gained by ignoring it. It was worth twisting truth and justice a little, if one could carve up Poland as a result.

While the Austrians invaded Belguim and clashed with French troops, sixty-four thousand Russian soldiers entered Poland, and thirty-two thousand invaded Lithuania. A few Poles hostile to the Constitution formed a new Confederation at Targovicia, with the intention of collaborating with the Russians. The rest, the 'resistance', begged Prussia to come to their aid, in accordance with the 1790 pact. But Frederick William, who had suffered some reversals in Belgium and at the battle of Valmy, decided that he had the right to claim some 'reparation' from the Poles. Reneging on his promises, he declared that 'he was not obliged to defend a Constitution that had been drawn up behind his back'. Instead of helping his friends, he was prepared to profit from their downfall. Also, Austria, now that she was faced with Dumouriez' conquest of Belgium, had to abandon her original plan of exchanging Belgium for Bavaria, and was looking for compensation at Poland's expense. In January, 1793, Russia and Prussia signed a convention, with a view to a second partition. Stanislaus Poniatowski begged them not to amputate parts of his country yet again. Catherine categorically refused to listen. The Diet was assembled at Grodno, and, threatened by war, it ratified a new treaty. Russia took the regions of Vilna, Minsk, Kiev, Vilnius and Podolia, a total of 4,550 square kilometres, and three million new subjects. Prussia received Posen and its province, Torun, Danzig and a strip of territory along the Silesian border, a thousand square kilometres and a million and a half inhabitants. Austria did less well, but still managed to swallow up a few patches of ground. Once the second partition was complete, and Poland had been bled and dismembered, Russia concluded a treaty with her which effectively removed all political independence: the country's internal and foreign policies were now to be exclusively dictated by St Petersburg. Catherine, replete with her new conquests, preened herself, saying that she had 'quelled the Revolution in the East'.

But the Polish business was far from over. Secret patriotic groups were burgeoning under the direction of General Thadeus Kosciuszko, who had previously commanded the troops rebelling against the Russians. He had the support of Robespierre and of all other revolutionary spirits. No more was needed to make Catherine think of definitively wiping out this branch of revolutionary France. Sharp-shooters gathered around Kosciuszko, who had become a popular hero. He found himself carried away by his supporters' enthusiasm and obliged to lead a revolt he judged to be premature. Riots broke out. The Russian garrison, surprisingly, abandoned Warsaw. There was delirium in the insurgents' ranks. But the reaction was swift. Prussia sent in troops, and Austria promised to do the same, but only on condition she received Cracow and Sandomir. Catherine ordered Suvorov to reduce Warsaw to rubble. Kosciuszko was defeated at Maciejovice, wounded and captured. On the 22nd October/2nd November, Suvorov took Praga, a suburb of Warsaw and the furious Russian soldiers began a massacre. Stanislaus Poniatowski abdicated in tears, after thirty-one years of pitiful rule. He was brought to Grodno, on the Empress's orders. He must have felt some relief at relinquishing this crown he had never wished for, to finally be nothing more than a prisoner of the Russian government.

The three winners in this inglorious manoeuvre now occupied themselves with sharing out the spoils. Catherine was determined to encourage Austria and Prussia to energetically pursue the war with France, without herself becoming involved, so she declared herself ready to compensate her allies for their anti-revolutionary effort, by allowing them the best slices of cake. But they had to be equal slices. The bargaining and squabbling between the sovereigns went on for months. Catherine played a cunning game between Frederick William and Leopold, whose greed made her smile. The truth was that she was the greediest of the three. Poring over a map of Poland she carved and carved again into living flesh. She never for a moment felt guilty of any crime. She did what she called her 'household accounts': at her coronation she had had twenty million subjects, today she had thirty-six million. Which of the European monarchs could do better than that? Since she had strengthened her nation's power, she would be able to hold her head high before the judgment of history. As for the protests that could be heard here and there abroad, about the partition, these were surely only the result of jealousy or misunderstanding. Since she had nothing to reproach herself for, she scorned such back-biting. Anyway, the dismembering of Poland was the final result of a centuries-old struggle, dating from the time when the Slav empire in the west attacked the Asiatic Muscovite empire, when the Roman Catholic church armed its faithful against the Greek Orthodox church. All Catherine had done, she thought, was to place a full stop at the end of a process that had begun long before her advent on the scene. The third treaty of partition was signed on the 13th/24th October, 1795. Russia appropriated Courland and the rest of Lithuania as far as Niemen, Austria, as she had wished, got Cracow, Sandomir and Lublin, and Prussia the north-west of the country including Warsaw. It was all over. Poland no longer existed. The conquered bowed their heads. There was nothing left for them except 'useless regrets, painful memories, and despair.'[1]

Catherine worked day and night throughout the Polish affair. She confided to Grimm: 'Four posts arrive at once, delayed by adverse winds, three or four messengers from every corner of the earth, so that nine quite big tables are hardly sufficient to hold all the paper, and four people, in turn, read to me from six o'clock in the morning to six o'clock at night, for three whole days.'

She wanted to personally examine every detail of the operation. And yet, when Kosciuszko was brought captive to St Petersburg, she refused to see this unhappy champion of the Polish cause, declaring with cruel arrogance: 'He has been recognized as a fool in the full sense of the word, not up to the job at all.' She got his name wrong, calling him mockingly: 'My poor idiot Kostioushka.' Stanislaus Poniatowski was hardly treated any better. She had made him king in the past, against his will, now she made him her prisoner with the same tranquillity and ease. Already, on the boat travelling to the Crimea, she had seen him as

---

[1] Letter from Princess Lubomirska to Maurice Glayre, Poniatowski's private adviser. Daria Olivier *Catherine the Great*.

a defeated man. She could not understand how she, who so appreciated strength of character in a man, could ever have been in love with this gentle mollusc. She did not even pity him. She despised him. Let him end his days in soft captivity. He had withdrawn to Grodno, with a derisory little court, and could not take a step without bumping into a Russian sentinel. He was over fifty, a broken and bitter man, expecting nothing from the future; to console himself, he turned endlessly back to the memory of the happy moments he had had with Catherine. The *Memoirs* he wrote to occupy his leisure were little more than a nostalgic homage to the sovereign who had once given him everything, and who now scorned him. His real moment of power was when he had occupied Catherine's bed not the Polish throne.

While enlarging the greater Russian family by these annexations, Catherine remained actively preoccupied with her small personal family. She wanted to be sure that her successor would not destroy all that she had built. So she was more and more determined to remove her son, Paul, from the succession, replacing him with her grandson, Alexander. Paul, entrenched at Gatchina, abandoned himself to 'military mania' with ever greater fury. All those around him were silent, tense and afraid. He only ever relaxed at the sight of his Prussian-dressed regiments, whom he manoeuvred in all weathers, until they were utterly exhausted. 'The worst thing,' wrote Princess Augusta of Saxe-Coburg, 'is seeing these handsome Russian soldiers disfigured by the antediluvian Prussian uniforms, dating from the time of Frederick William I. The Russian must be Russian – he feels it; each one of them considers himself infinitely more handsome in a short tunic and pudding-bowl haircut, than with the plait and tight uniform that makes him miserable at Gatchina... I was pained to see this change as I love these people very much.'[1]

Paul's extravagances alienated even those whom he wished to have as his advisers, such as Count Rostopchin.[2] The latter wrote to Count Vorontsov, who was ambassador in London: 'The most odious thing in the world for me, after dishonour, is Paul's goodwill. The Grand Duke's mind is haunted by ghosts, and he is surrounded by people of whom even the most honest deserves to be hanged without a trial.' He described him quarrelling with everybody, arousing hatred and fear all around him, and trying to imitate Peter III's insanities. 'One cannot observe the Grand Duke's behaviour without a feeling of pity and

[1] Constantine de Grunwald *The Assassination of Paul I.*
[2] Count Theodore Rostopchin was the same who, as governor of Moscow in 1812, urged the inhabitants to burn the city as the French entered it. His daughter became the Comtesse de Ségur.

horror,' continued Rostopchin. 'One might think that he was searching for ways of making himself loathed and detested. He thinks that people despise him and seek to avoid him; as a result, he picks on anything, and punishes indiscriminately... The smallest delay, the slightest disagreement, make him lose his temper and he explodes...' Count Adam Czartoryski corroborated: 'Everybody is afraid of Paul. They admire his mother's strength and great capabilities all the more for it – but she keeps him dependent and far from the throne which belongs to him by right.' And the Swedish ambassador, Count Stedingk, wrote to Stockholm, in a coded despatch: 'Grand Duke Paul continues to behave extremely badly, and to lose the esteem of both great and ordinary people.'

More than ever, Paul felt isolated and pushed aside, as if under a curse. He could not forgive his sons, Alexander and Constantine, their adoration of their grandmother, and all three were enveloped by the same hatred. The tutor La Harpe's job was made difficult by this atmosphere of family discord. He remained faithful to his republican ideals and continued to expound to his pupils the benefits of liberty and sovereigns' duties towards their subjects. The agreeable Alexander was delighted with this teaching. Constantine, however, bridled. He was violent and choleric like his father, and, one day, cruelly bit his teacher's hand. Another time, he shouted at him that when he was in power he would invade Switzerland with all his armies and destroy the country. La Harpe replied, imperturbably: 'In my country, near the small town of Murten, there is a building where we keep the bones of all those who pay us such visits.'

Despite her indignation at the news of the French Revolution, Catherine continued to highly esteem this broad-minded and strong-willed educator. She made a distinction between the principles of social justice which had so inspired her youth, and with which she also wanted to inspire Alexander, and the chaos which befalls a country when the imbecile proletariat take power. The Grand Duchess in her favoured liberty, and the Tsarina, autocracy. She was as eager to condemn the brutal contortions of the Parisian populace, as she was to listen to suggestions for wise reforms. Pugachev must be executed, La Harpe must be listened to. It was a sort of intellectual – almost aesthetic – self-indulgence. She had no doubt that, thanks to all the wise words he had listened to, Alexander was well-prepared to become a great liberal sovereign. In order to better ensure the future of this exceptional grandson, she decided to marry him, and invited the two young and pretty princesses of Baden to the court. The eldest, Louise, was fifteen. Alexandra was sixteen. His future wife must be German. What other nation offered the same matrimonial guarantees? The Russian dynasty needed to be strengthened by German blood. Of course, Catherine did not tell Alexander of the exact reason for the arrival of the two sisters. She was laying a romantic trap for him. 'I am playing a diabolical trick,' she confessed to Grimm, 'as I am leading him into temptation.'

The princesses arrived by night, terrified by a storm. When the Empress received them, they fell at her feet, kissing her dress and her hands, until she made them stand up. The following day, according to well-established tradition, she brought them the ribbon of the Order of St Catherine, and jewels and materials, and asked to see their wardrobes. 'My friends,' she said, 'I was not as rich as you when I arrived in Russia!' She found the young girls worthy of their portraits. The elder was particularly attractive. 'Charming figure,' Countess Golovin wrote, 'Ash-blonde hair falling in curls on the nape of the neck, milky complexion, rosy cheeks, pretty mouth.' She and Alexander would make a fine couple. When he appeared, with his brother Constantine, Louise was dazzled. This marvellous young man 'was endowed with every natural grace'. Tall and slender, he had the shoulders of an athlete and the bearing of an angel; his face was noble and gentle with regular features, he had silky light brown hair, deep blue eyes and an enchanting smile. His whole physiognomy had an air of both strength and grace, of affability and mysteriousness. After this first meeting with the young girls, Alexander remarked that Louise was charming. 'Ah! Not at all!' cried Constantine. 'Neither of them is charming; they must be sent to Riga for the princes of Courland; they are only good enough for them!'[1] Alexander's eulogistic remarks were repeated to his grandmother, and she rejoiced. She had judged well. He had taken the bait. When the two young foreigners were presented at Court, Louise tripped and fell on a corner of the steps to the throne, collapsing on the ground. She was picked up, consoled, Alexander smiled at her and the incident was forgotten. The youngest sister, whom Constantine did not want, was sent back to the banks of the Rhine with a cart-load of presents.[2] The elder learnt Russian, gave up her religion, was baptized into the Orthodox church, proclaimed Grand Duchess and changed her name from Louise to Elisabeth Alexeievna. 'The Grand Duke is very much in love with his future bride,' wrote Stedingk, 'and one cannot hope to see a handsomer and more interesting couple.' As for Elisabeth, who was startled and amazed by Alexander's boldness, she wrote to her mother: When we were alone in

[1] Masson *Secret Russian Memoirs*.
[2] She later married the King of Sweden.

my room, he kissed me and now I think he will always do that. You can't imagine how strange I found it.'

Russia had just come to the end of three successful wars, and a crowd of bedecked generals attended the engagement ceremony. There were also many Swedish admirers of Catherine's 'humble and devoted' Polish grandees, Tartar khans, Turkish pashas, and Moldavian deputies. Catherine dined on a throne, raised above the other tables. 'Crowned and covered with gold and diamonds,' wrote Masson, 'she cast a serene gaze over this enormous gathering from every nation, which seemed to be entirely at her feet . . . A poet might have taken her for Juno seated amongst the gods.'

But even Juno had her worries. The brilliant festivities for her grandson were clouded, for her, by events in France. She had long considered that the country was going through a period of madness, and she was afraid it might be contagious. When she heard of Louis XVI's flight and arrest at Varennes, she was in despair. It was whispered that the Russian ambassador in Paris, Simolin, had secretly helped with the preparations for this unfortunate departure. It was only by a miracle that the diplomat escaped the vengeance of the revolutionary mob, which gathered, first at the Palais-Royal, then on the Champs-Elysées. 'They wanted to seize and murder me, as an accomplice in the organization of the King's flight,' he wrote to Catherine.

The first French refugees to arrive in St Petersburg were eagerly welcomed. They filed past the republican, La Harpe – the Sénac de Meilhans, the Saint-Priests, the Bombelles, the Esterhazys, the Choiseul-Gouffiers. All these uprooted people gossiped, complained and conspired, and settled in. 'Madame Vigée-Lebrun is soon going to think she is in Paris, there is such a crowd at these gatherings,' wrote the Prince de Ligne. And Count Rostopchin remarked bitterly: 'When one observes the French, one sees such levity in their natures, that one wonders how they remain on the ground. The scoundrels and imbeciles have remained in their country and the lunatics have left to swell the number of charlatans roaming the world.' The French chargé d'affaires, Genet, who supported a reasonable revolution, found himself in a difficult position. He tried in vain to maintain, against all the evidence, that Louis XVI enjoyed a certain amount of liberty. Catherine regarded him as 'a mad demagogue' and refused to receive him at the Court. She held it against Louis XVI that he had accepted the Constitution. 'Well! So my lord Louis XVI has signed that absurd Constitution, and then insists on taking oaths, that he has no intention of keeping to, and that no one has even asked him for, what is more!' she wrote to Grimm. 'But who are these people so lacking in judgment who have made him do these stupid things?... When you return to Paris, and if they have not yet been hanged, take a stick and give those schoolboy advisers to the King of France a good hiding.' Russians living in France were ordered to return immediately to their country. Simolin, the Russian ambassador in Paris, packed his bags. *Le Moniteur* described the Empress as 'the Messalina of the North'. She retorted by forbidding Russians to wear Parisian cravats, and by having Voltaire's bust removed to an attic. He was guilty. She knew it for certain now. What was the proof? On the 11th July, 1791, the French revolutionaries had solemnly removed his ashes to the Panthéon. An armed mob, it was said, escorted the funeral carriage. A delegation of literary people, headed by Beaumarchais, represented 'Voltaire's family'. Well! If he was resting in the Panthéon in Paris, he could rest under the eaves in St Petersburg. Yes, this time the beloved encyclopaedists had lost all credit in Catherine's eyes. After having admired them so much she now saw them only as monsters of intellectual duplicity. By preaching liberty, equality and fraternity they had made themselves the quartermasters of intolerance, hatred and murder. Utopians whose hands were red with blood. Their complete works were a scaffold for the guillotine. 'I suggest that all the Protestant powers embrace the Greek religion to save themselves from this irreligious, immoral, anarchic, wicked and diabolical plague, which is against God and the throne,' she wrote. And she declared to Grimm: 'I maintain that you would only need to seize two or three hovels in France, and all the rest would collapse by themselves... Twenty thousand Cossacks would be too many to make a green carpet from Strasbourg to Paris...' However she was careful not to order these twenty thousand Cossacks to set off.

When at the beginning of 1793, she heard of the death of Louis XVI, she suffered such a violent shock that her doctors feared for her health. She had far too high an opinion of the institution of the monarchy to be able to bear, without shuddering, the news of this ignominious death of a king on the guillotine. She felt the mob had hurled at *her*, that the blade had fallen upon *her* neck. 'At the news of the criminal execution of the King of France,' wrote Khrapovitsky, 'Her Majesty took to her bed, sick with grief. Thanks be to God, she is better today. She spoke to me about the barbarity of the French, of the obvious irregularity in the counting of the votes (which had pronounced in favour of the King's condemnation): It is a crying injustice, even for a commoner... *Equality* is a monster, and wants to be king.'

From then on, Catherine became more and more barbed. Her abuse made Genet shudder. In the Empress's words, Lafayette became 'The Great Booby', Paris 'a brigands' hideout', and the revolutionaries, 'scum'. 'We must wipe out even the name of France.' For her the French capital was no longer Paris, but Cobenzl, the *émigrés'* headquarters. She rescinded the commercial treaty concluded with Ségur on the journey to the Crimea; she forbade French ships access to Russian ports; she broke off diplomatic relations with France and sent the undesirable Genet back to his own country. 'They say,' she wrote to Grimm, 'that he left St Petersburg pulling a red woollen cap down over his head. This sounded so ridiculous that I burst out laughing when I heard about it.' Finally she issued an edict ordering all French people living in Russia to sign, under pain of immediate expulsion, a violently-worded oath: 'I, the undersigned, swear before the almighty God and his Holy Gospel that, never having adhered in fact or by intention to the seditious and impious doctrines now preached in France, I regard the government now installed there as a usurper in violation of all laws, and the death of the very Christian King Louis XVI as an act of abominable wickedness... Consequently, enjoying the secure asylum granted by Her Imperial Majesty of all the Russias in the State, I promise to live in it observing the holy faith in which I was born, and sincerely submitting to the laws instituted by Her Imperial Majesty, breaking off all correspondence to my country with Frenchmen who recognize the monstrous present government of France, and not resuming it until, after the re-establishment of legitimate authority, I have received the express permission of Her Imperial Majesty.'

Catherine had no doubt about the eventual return of personal power to France, after such bloody disorder and such stupid laws. With extraordinary prescience she wrote in 1794: 'If France pulls through, she will be stronger than she has ever been before... She just needs a great man, greater than any of his contemporaries, the greatest perhaps in a whole century. Is he born?... Will he come? All depends upon it!' The 'great man' had indeed already been born. In Ajaccio in 1769. He was twenty-four and had just distinguished himself at the siege of Toulon.

However, the French in Russia eagerly took the oath. Catherine already no longer considered them as guests but as new subjects, from whom she expected obedience. The arrival of the Comte d'Artois, in 1793, delighted her. She had hoped, before Varennes, to give asylum to Louis XVI himself. 'It would have been,' she said, 'the most remarkable gesture of my whole reign.' For a princess from Zerbst to offer protection to the grandson of her sworn enemy, Louis XV, and to the daughter of Maria Teresa of Austria, who had shown her such scorn – what a revenge! Failing that, however, she welcomed the Comte d'Artois with warmth and splendour. Her motto was plenty of friendly words and as little help as possible. The most important thing, she thought, with very feminine pride, was that the displays at the Winter Palace should rival those of Versailles. Her guest was treated by her and by Plato Zubov as a son of France and Lieutenant-General of the Kingdom. He turned out to be politically useless, but simple and amiable and 'without boastfulness'. His efforts to obtain from the Tsarina the military aid he hoped for were all in vain. All she did was to give him a million roubles with which to start the campaign, and open an account for him, with a credit of up to four million roubles, with the Russian ambassador in London. Then, to stimulate him in his holy war against the Revolution, which she called 'the debauchery', she gave him, after having had it blessed, a rich sword bearing the words 'Given by God for the King'. The Comte d'Artois was disappointed and accepted this symbolic arm, which he had no use for, thanking the Empress, as one witness put it, 'with too little expression on his face'. Catherine wrote, quite simply, to Vice-Chancellor Ostermann: 'I am racking my brains to find ways of involving the courts of Berlin and Vienna in French affairs . . . so that I can be left with a free hand. I have a lot of unfinished business. It would suit me if Prussia and Austria did not obstruct me.' Later, still preoccupied with the way 'French affairs' were going, she sought an understanding with England. A defence treaty was signed between the two countries. But Catherine never attached much importance to it. On the 26th April, 1793, the Comte d'Artois set off for England.

Grand Duke Alexander's wedding was celebrated on the 28th September of the same year. They were such an attractive couple that they were nicknamed 'Cupid and Psyche'. Catherine hoped to become a great-grandmother soon. That, she thought, would be another safeguard for the country's future. She would have built, not only in space, but also in time. But first she must find out Alexander's intentions. Nourished as he was on La Harpe's fine ideas, he scandalized his audience during one reception with his enthusiastic praise of *The Rights of Man*. Catherine thought it was just youthful exuberance. The horrible execution of Marie-Antoinette, after that of Louis XVI, soon shut up the Swiss liberal and his pupil. The hideous result must cast doubt on the fine principles. Salvation lay in the monarchy. Catherine wanted to convince Alexander of this, and, at the same time, inform him about her plans for the future.

She was horrified after her very first conversation with him. Alexander had no wish to rule. He claimed to hate despotism, violence and court intrigue. He said that his gentle and conciliating nature made him love tranquillity, simple life, and solid family virtues. A house in the country, a warm hearth, a good wife, good children – all the domestic cares and joys of the ordinary mortal. Catherine found her grandson to be, not the future Tsar she had expected, but a Swiss *petit bourgeois*. So she summoned La Harpe, whose influence over his pupil she recognized, and ordered him to restore in Alexander a sense of his imperial duties. No only must the young Grand Duke accept his destiny, but he must also consider himself as the direct heir to the throne, once his father had been removed from the line of succession. La Harpe was disgusted by this last suggestion. He considered that he would be an accessory to a serious moral failure if he encouraged a son to usurp a position that belonged by right to his progenitor. As Alexander's educator he had not instilled in him respect for his parents and love for his fellow-men in order to now encourage him to commit such an infamy. In short, he refused to become the Tsarina's political agent. She did not insist, hoping that, failing La Harpe, she might win Alexander's naive wife round to her cause. But La Harpe now set about bringing father and son together. He even went so far as to betray to his pupil the secret of his conversation with the Empress. Alexander was shattered, and became doubly kind towards his father, never missing an opportunity to honour and flatter him. He even called him, in anticipation, 'Your Imperial Majesty', as if to underline his own acceptance of the order of succession. Catherine, hearing of this outbreak of filial piety, summoned La Harpe and dismissed him. When he returned to the Grand Dukes' schoolroom – although he was now married, Alexander continued to learn – La Harpe was pale: with tears in his eyes he repeated his interview with the Empress. Alexander burst into tears and hung round his master's neck. When he was alone again he wrote a heart-rending letter: 'Goodbye my dear friend! How painful it is for me to write that word! Never forget that you leave here a man devoted to you, who cannot adequately express his gratitude, who owes everything to you except his birth . . . Be happy, my dear friend, that is the wish of a man who loves you dearly, who honours and esteems you beyond all expression. Goodbye for the last time, my best friend. Do not forget me! Alexander.' Later, he was to say: 'Everything I am, I owe to a Swiss.'

Alexander was deprived of moral guidance by La Harpe's departure, and, feeling tragically abandoned, began to drift aimlessly. Although he continued to behave as a respectful son, he was horrified by his father's eccentricities, his stupidity and petty nastiness. When he looked at his grandmother, he was filled with admiration for her application, her intelligence, authority and kindness, but grieved by her senile weakness for her young lover Plato Zubov. 'I am unhappy at finding myself in the company of people I couldn't have as servants,' he confided to his friend Kotchubei. However, and this was a sign of the weakness of his character, he went whichever way the wind was blowing. Worse, he even allowed Zubov to surpass himself in arrogance by paying eager court to his young wife. How could he put down such an important man? And could he prevent a woman from winning hearts by her beauty alone? Elisabeth Alexeievna had nothing to reproach herself for. Indeed she was highly embarrassed by Zubov's public attentions towards her. The fellow, it appeared, was sincere. He was tired of the Empress and enamoured of the Grand Duchess. He was prepared to sacrifice everything to satisfy his passion. The situation bordered on scandal, and Alexander feared that more than anyone. He had always avoided clear-cut issues; he was a compromiser at heart. He said to his beloved Kotchubei: 'My wife is behaving like an angel. But you must admit the attitude one has to adopt towards Zubov is fearfully embarrassing... If one is polite to him, it is as if one approved of his passion, and if one treats him coldly to cure him of it, the Empress, who knows nothing, might think it bad that one is not polite to a man she is so fond of. It is very hard to keep to the middle ground, particularly before such a gossiping and trouble-making audience.'[1]

When Catherine heard about this lamentable affair, she swallowed the pill without wincing. Could she really hold it against Plato if he were to turn his glances occasionally towards some younger, fresher rival? By choosing someone so young she had taken the risk of being deceived sometimes, if only in imagination. But to turn his attentions towards the Grand Duchess! Really, Catherine would always be astonished by these Russians: illogicality was their element. Here was a man, Plato Zubov, whom she had raised to every honour and given the most delicate political responsibilities, about to sacrifice all this for the sake of a guilty and fruitless passion. There was another man, Alexander, who also had Russian blood in his veins, and who had been offered the most prestigious throne in the world, and drew back before this pinnacle, on the pretext that he wanted a quiet life, far from the eddies of public affairs. She thought, too, of Potemkin, at the height of his glory, dreaming of retirement to a monastery. These absurd Slavs needed a dose of Germanic good sense. Catherine reasoned with her lover and her grandson. The former finally agreed to stay out of the Grand Duchess's way, and the latter not to take offence over a futureless passion.

There remained the business of the succession. Catherine returned to

[1] Daria Olivier *Catherine the Great*.

the attack. She turned all her willpower and kindness onto Alexander's malleable character. She told him that if Paul took power, he would blindly oppose any liberal reforms, whilst if Alexander acceded directly to the throne, he would have plenty of time to apply La Harpe's wise precepts upon his people. Thus he would demonstrate, in opposition to the bloody French revolution, what the will of an enlightened monarch could achieve in a great country like Russia. He was destined by birth and by education to fulfil this admirable role and he had no right to avoid it for personal reasons. If he accepted, she would end her days at peace with herself. This time, Alexander was shaken. As usual, he did not give a definite reply. But Catherine instinctively knew that she was on the right path.

With Plato Zubov too, it was a case of calm after the storm. Once he had detached himself from the Grand Duchess, he was seized with a new idea: to revive, under a new form, Catherine's beloved Greek project. He wanted to follow Potemkin's example and enlarge the Empire by some valiant conquest that would be forever connected with his name. Why not Persia? And from there they could push on to India. The operation would be led by Valerian Zubov, who had been campaigning as a humble lieutenant in Poland, where he had lost a leg. Meanwhile Suvorov would march on Constantinople by way of the Balkans. The Russian fleet would enter the Bosphorus, hemming in the Turkish capital by sea. To inspire the sailors perhaps, Catherine could lead the squadron in person. There was consternation in the Empress's entourage. This type of expedition was seen by everybody as a dangerous fantasy. Alexander could hardly conceal his scepticism. Surely his grandmother would not be taken in once again by such a mirage! She was. Catherine was tired and her judgment had become clouded, and she could not refuse anything to her adorable Plato. Since he wanted a war, it would be too cruel to deny him one.

Valerian Zubov set off, at the end of February, 1796, with twenty thousand soldiers. He swore that he would be in Isfahan by September. But, after taking Derbent and Baku, which fell without a fight, he came to a halt. At the end of the summer there were still six hundred versts of desert between himself and the Persian frontier, and he did not dare embark on them. A surveyor was sent from St Petersburg with instructions and geographical documents. Poring over the maps, he began to realize the folly of the enterprise and decided not to move from Baku.

Once again, Catherine saw her dream of Eastern hegemony fading fast. But she still hoped to live long enough to witness the fall of Byzantium. She was sixty-seven and her strength was waning; her heart beat irregularly and her legs were so swollen that she could hardly walk up three steps: some courtiers had gentle ramps placed over their steps in order to deceive her. Her bloated face, according to observers, showed 'signs of dropsy and dissipation'. But she refused to regard herself as old and weak: 'I am as merry and as active as a lark,' she wrote to Grimm. When she had a pain, she would analyse it and treat it in her own way: 'I think the gout has lodged itself in my stomach,' she said to one of her friends, 'I am getting rid of it with pepper and a glass of Malaga wine which I drink every day.'

As in the past, her days were run with rigid discipline. She worked relentlessly. But Plato Zubov was always at her side. No decision could be taken without him. And he still joined her at night in her bedroom. She knew that he would be the last of her lovers, and was all the more grateful for his efforts to satisfy her. The Swedish ambassador, Stedingk, gives us in his despatches a few glimpses of this political and sexual collaboration. 'What raises the favourite's stock,' he wrote, 'is the fact that the Empress must be sure that she will never change again... Zubov comes and goes to the Empress at all hours. All discussions take place with him. Most business is conducted from his ministry. The Empress now no longer holds councils in her quarters... Zubov's power grows and increases in the same measure as the esteem in which he is held diminishes.' On the lover's saint's day, the poet Derzhavin composed an ode in which he compared Plato Zubov with Aristotle, and the young inmates of the Smolny Institute presented him with a sampler embroidered by their hands, with this inscription: 'Lord, joy of our nation, our hearts long for your prosperity.'

The year 1796 was distinguished too for Catherine by an important family event. In the month of June, the elder Grand Duchess, Maria Feodorovna, Paul's wife, gave birth to her ninth child, a son, Nicolas. He was the prolific mother's third son. Catherine affected grandmotherly delight, but in fact she was annoyed. This baby had arrived too late for her to hope to bring him up as she had done Alexander and Constantine. He would be entirely under his father's pernicious influence. Who could tell what catastrophes could be predicted for Russia, at the sight of this madman in Prussian uniform, bent over yet another cradle?[1]

---

[1] Nicolas I (1796-1855) took the throne in 1825 after his brother Alexander's death, having quelled the Decembrist revolt.

CHAPTER XXVI

The End

If only she could be sure that the revolutionary epidemic would remain confined within the frontiers of France! As old age approached Catherine feared nothing more than the spread into Russia of those liberal ideas which she claimed had inspired her in the past. The terrible Pugachev rebellion had shown her that the Russian people were every bit as capable of violence as their French counterparts, and so she could not allow any movement in the country which might disrupt the social – or even just the spiritual – stability of her subjects. As the guardian of law and order she pursued with an iron hand those of them whom she judged guilty of 'Jacobinism'. Even her former friends lost favour if they tended at all towards 'the left'. She had been very close in the past to the journalist, publisher and editor Novikov – to the point of contributing anonymously to his magazine *The Painter;* now she held against him his energetic defence of the serfs' cause, and even reproached him for being a freemason. When it started in Russia the Masonic movement had been totally loyal to the government, but it had soon become imbued with visionary theories; and this tendency towards mysticism had struck Catherine as an attack upon her sovereignty. She decided that a proliferation of sects on the fringes of the Church could only lead to trouble in an untutored and easily influenced population: it was said that Novikov and his followers were planning to exploit Paul's taste for 'Martinist' theories; the Grand Duke had even been asked to be Grand Master of the Order of Freemasons in Moscow. Well, this could not be allowed. The correct formula was one country, one faith, one monarch. They had all seen only too well where the French philosophers had dragged their wretched country. As long as Catherine was alive, no Russian philosopher would be allowed to pontificate, whether in the streets, the drawing-rooms or the Masonic lodges. Novikov was arrested in 1792 and prosecuted with particular severity. Catherine personally dictated the questions she wanted the judges to put to the accused, and the sentence was a harsh one – fifteen years in the Schlüsselberg Fortress. All subversive books were suppressed and all Masonic lodges in Russia closed. Many years before the Empress had written in her journal, *All Sorts and Sundries:*[1] 'We want to walk on the earth, not float in the air – still less climb to the sky.' 'Moreover,' she added, 'we do not like gloomy writings.'

She showed the same severity towards humanitarian dreams when Radishchev published his *Journey from St Petersburg to Moscow.* This work which was both documentary and polemical, combining descriptions and opinions, denounced serfdom and advocated the immediate emancipation of the peasants by a generous gesture of the government. God knew how much Catherine had dreamt of this in the past; but she had come to realize in the course of her reign what risks there would be in suddenly throwing a population, accustomed to slavery, into the bright glare of freedom. For centuries the serf had been free of responsibility and the need for initiative: would he not go mad when told he was free? Would he not miss the security of subjection to an all-powerful master? In any case both the master and the slave had to be prepared gradually for the future upheaval in their relationship to one another. Radischev's book had come too soon. Feeble minds, of which there were so many in Russia, might become over-excited by reading it. All things considered, Catherine thought that this writer, because of his talent, was 'more dangerous than Pugachev'. Radischev was condemned to death but, benefiting from imperial clemency, was deported for ten years to Siberia instead.

Knyazhnin, who wrote two successful comedies, *The Braggart* and *The Eccentrics,* suffered from the Empress's fury only after his death. Princess Dashkova, who was president of the Russian Academy, had had a posthumous tragedy of his published, *Vadim of Novgorod;* Catherine saw it, decided that it had republican leanings, and ordered all copies to be seized and destroyed. When Princess Dashkova heard of this decision she cried to the Tsarina: 'What does it matter to me, Your Majesty, if this work is burnt at the hands of the executioner? I will not need to blush.'[2] This warning did not in any way shake Catherine's will. The execution took place. The ashes of *Vadim of Novgorod* were scattered to the winds. After this insult, Princess Dashkova publicly resigned from her position at the Academy and decided to leave St Petersburg and retire to Moscow. But before leaving she asked Catherine for a farewell audience. Were they not, after all, the oldest of friends? Her Majesty made the Princess wait for an hour in the antechamber before receiving her. Finally the two women came face to face. Catherine stood stony-faced. When the Princess Dashkova bowed

---

[1] Vsiakaya Vsiatchina.
[2] Princess Dashkova *Memoirs.*

silently before her, she said drily: 'I wish you a good journey, Madam.' Not another single word was spoken to the ex-President of the Academy. However Catherine explained to others why she was so severe in matters of censorship. 'The theatre is the nation's school,' she said. 'It must remain completely under my guidance; I am the chief teacher in that school, because my first duty before God is to be responsible for my people's morals.'[1]

On the whole, although she was interested both out of taste and out of a sense of duty in the rise of Russian Literature, her attitude towards the little world of Russian writers was one of authority mingled with contempt. She was a fervent admirer of French and German culture, and she thought that salvation for that of her own country lay in imitating Western examples. Few great names were added, during her reign, to those of Elisabeth's, such as Lomonossov, the founder of the Russian language, who died in 1765, or Sumarokov, who died in 1777, the author of fables, satires and plays inspired by Racine and Voltaire. There was of course the official poet Derzhavin, with his flashing lyricism, but his long poem *Felitsa* was no more than a piece made to order, combining praise for the Empress with criticism of the courtiers surrounding her. He even sank, with time, to singing the praises of Plato Zubov. Kheraskov, for his part, continued to ape the French, particularly Voltaire, putting his *Russiad* into verse, and Bogdanovich tried to adorn his *Doushenka* with graces borrowed from La Fontaine's *Loves of Psyche*. Fonvizin, who was far more original, was known as the Russian Molière, and in his comedy *The Brigadier*, mocked the Muscovite Trissotins' Gallomania; in *The Booby* (or *The Adolescent*) he satirized the idle and coarse life of the country squires. The general theme running through the latter was the idea that Russian society would perish if it proved unable to elevate its soul and educate its mind. A very 'Catherinian' concept. All the same, Fonvizin still had to struggle against the censorship policies which at first forbade any performance of this comedy. Grand Duke Paul intervened. *The Adolescent* appeared, and was an enormous success. But Fonvizin never wrote anything again – he became seriously ill and died at the age of forty-eight. Catherine was far less affected by this than she had been at the death of Voltaire or Diderot. As far as she was concerned all these Russian writers were mere apprentices. She appeared quite unaware of the growing genius of Karamzin whose romantic stories and *Letters from a Russian Traveller* were already enchanting many readers, or of the enormous promise shown by Krylov, who had already published his

---

[1] Ettore le Gatto *History of Russian Literature*.

first satirical essays, but had yet to show his full talents in his fables.

The Empress had no more faith in Russian architects than she had in Russian writers. She had 'building mania' and declared that no earthquake could destroy any monument built by her. She continued her impassioned embellishment of St Petersburg and its surroundings. In the capital itself she built the little Hermitage, the Smolny Institute, the superb façade of the Academy of Fine Arts, the Marble Palace and the Taurida Palace (for Potemkin), and transformed the old Trinity Cathedral; at Gatchina she erected the Great Castle; at Peterhof she enlarged Peter I's palace, whilst retaining its Versailles-like aspect; at Tsarskoe Selo, she made thousands of improvements and built the new Alexander Palace. Most of this work was done by French or Italian artists. On the Russian side, one could name only Starov, Bajenov, Kasakov... In any case the style of building was in no way Russian, and was completely inspired by the French and Italian schools, with no modifications for climate or setting. While Ivan III in the sixteenth century had got his architects, who were brought to Moscow from Milan and Bologna, to produce original conceptions which accorded with Russian traditions, Catherine followed Peter the Great's example and transplanted structures to the banks of the Neva which were certainly admirable but which were made for a different region.

Russian painters, sculptors and scientists were also in a minority around the throne. Catherine did not encourage them and showed towards them condescension verging on contempt. During his stay in Russia, Falconet became extremely indignant over the Tsarina's harshness towards the excellent painter Lossienko. 'The poor honest boy, reviled and penniless and wishing to live elsewhere than in St Petersburg, used to come and tell me his sorrows,' he wrote. One traveller (Fortia de Piles) was surprised that Her Majesty should allow a sculptor of Chubin's talent to moulder in a small room without models or pupils or offers of official work. Throughout her reign she very rarely commissioned work from Russian artists, saving her largesse for the purchase of foreign works.

The scientists who benefited from her attention also came from abroad. They had names like Euler, Pallas, Boehmer, Storch, Kraft, Muller, Backmeister, Georgi, Klinger... But if one excludes the famous journeys of the naturalist Pallas, Muller's historical researches and a few works of biology, it does not appear that these scientists' visits to the St Petersburg Academy of Science did much to enrich the sum of human knowledge. Catherine's main achievement in retrospect appears to have been her encouragement of the publication of a large number of old chronicles relating to the country's past, such as the famous *Sayings*

from Igor's country. The earliest *Bylines* (epic songs), which had hitherto
been transmitted orally from one generation to the next, were also
gathered together and published under her aegis. To demonstrate her
interest in history, she went as far as to write some *Memoirs Relative to
the Russian Empire.* In these hastily jotted down notes, she piled up
mistakes, inventing kings of Finland, marrying them to imaginary
princesses from Novgorod, had Rurik intervening in extraordinary
circumstances, trying all the time to demonstrate the all-importance of
ancient Muscovy. She was to write, describing her historical and
linguistic investigations: 'I have accumulated an enormous amount of
knowledge about the ancient Slavs, and I could easily show that they
gave their names to most of the rivers, mountains, valleys and provinces
in France, Spain, Scotland and elsewhere.'

However she soon became bored with these researches and handed
over to professionals such as Shcherbatov and Golikov the job of
producing a serious and lasting piece of erudition. Later, under the
influence of old age and the French Revolution, she began to regard all
scientists with suspicion. In the past she had dreamt of a circle of
academicians amiably and harmlessly discussing abstractions. Now she
saw them as incendiaries. The ex-disciple of the encyclopaedists was
now terrified of all new ideas. In 1795 she realized that she was paying
the Economic Society of St Petersburg four thousand roubles a year for
publications 'each one stupider than the last'. She jibbed at this, treated
the members of the learned assembly as 'rascals', and cut off their
funds.

By this time she had already dismissed La Harpe, and was turning all
her efforts towards persuading Alexander to take the Russian crown.
The Grand Duke, who had for a long time dreamt of passing his days
happily in the country – possibly beside the Rhine – now gradually
began to give way, little by little to his intractable grandmother. He
examined his conscience during the summer of 1796 and wrote to his
old tutor: 'You know well of my desire to expatriate myself. For the
moment I see no possibility of fulfilling it. The unhappy condition of
my country has turned my thoughts in quite another direction.' This
'other direction' was evidently that of the throne. However, with his
brother Constantine, Alexander had gradually become a regular guest at
Gatchina, where Grand Duke Paul initiated him into the military
profession. In a Prussian uniform with high boots, the young man
enthusiastically drilled the recruits, marched, counter-marched,
organized artillery exercises, and taught the handling of the sword and
musket. He was seduced by the martial atmosphere of the little
garrison, but was nonetheless horrified to see that the master of the

place had demolished houses, cut down forests and levelled the gound
in a large area around the castle, to enable the guards to watch the
surrounding countryside more efficiently. The house was ringed with
cordons of police. To get past them you had to be on the list of the
Grand Duke's friends. He saw spies behind every door. The Empress
was right to regard him as a madman. But the madman had his
attractions. Alexander hovered between the pleasure of playing soldiers
with his father and the no less great pleasure of playing at being heir to
the throne with his grandmother. But he did not in the least approve of
her political views. All his views were coloured by the memory of La
Harpe. He dared to confess his tormented conscience to his new friend,
the young Pole Adam Czartoryski, during a walk one day. 'The Grand
Duke said to me,' Czartoryski wrote in his *Memoirs,* 'that he did not in
any way share the views and doctrines held by the cabinet and the
Court; that he was far from approving his grandmother's behaviour,
that he condemned her beliefs ... He confessed to me that he loathed
despotism everywhere, whatever form it might take; that he loved
liberty; that all men had an equal right to it; that he had taken a very
lively interest in the French Revolution; that, whilst disapproving of its
terrible errors, he wished all success to the Republic and rejoiced in its
existence ... I went away, I confess, quite overcome and deeply moved,
not knowing if I was waking or dreaming. What? A Prince of Russia,
Catherine's successor, her beloved grandson and pupil, whom she
wanted to succeed her at the expense of her son – this Prince denied and
detested his grandmother's principles, rejected Russia's odious policies,
passionately loved justice and liberty, pitied Poland and wanted to see
her happy! Was it not miraculous?'

Catherine was perfectly well aware of Alexander's republican dreams.
She had been the same at his age. It was a youthful fever. He would
recover from it, as she had done. She felt instinctively that he had in
him the makings of a true monarch. Then of course she had no choice.
Anything was preferable to the ghastly Paul, with his Russianism and
other aberrations. She must move quickly otherwise she would be
overtaken by events. Nothing must be left to chance. There must be a
written act, in black and white, irrefutable. With Bezborodko's help,
she secretly prepared a proclamation removing Paul from the line of
succession, for the benefit of her grandson Alexander. She locked it up
among her private papers, planning to release it at the beginning of the
following year. First, on Plato Zubov's suggestion, she wanted to
betroth her eldest grand-daughter Alexandra Pavlovna to the very
young king of Sweden, Gustavus IV. 'Brother Gu,' Gustavus III, had
been assassinated four years earlier, and since then, despite the

diplomats' efforts, relations between Stockholm and St Petersburg had not improved. By uniting the new King, who was eighteen, with Alexandra, who was thirteen, many a political problem would be solved in the family. The idea was all the more appealing as Gustavus had, it was said, 'a charming physiognomy, which showed both spirit and good nature', and Alexandra was the prettiest, most candid and gentle of the available European princesses. As she was still too young to be properly married, the wedding would be delayed for two years. But the engagement could be announced immediately. Plato Zubov, in his position of Foreign Minister, conducted the negotiations. They were tricky, to say the least. The Swedish court considered it crucial that the young princess should convert to the Protestant faith; Catherine, on the other hand, considered that her grand-daughter was too high-ranking to submit to such a condition. As she was of imperial blood, Alexandra must keep her religion and have an Orthodox chapel and Orthodox priests in Stockholm. By being intransigent on the subject of religion, the Tsarina showed how far she had gone since the days when, as a little German princess, she had renounced the Lutheran faith in order to marry the Russian heir. What a revenge on her own past! Plato Zubov and his adviser Markov tried to bargain with the Swedes. The discussions became embittered, then calm, then embroiled, and ended with half-promises on both sides which did not clarify the situation. Both sides counted on last-minute confusion to break down the adversary's resistance and 'block' the engagement ceremony, as Markov put it.

The young King of Sweden, and his uncle, the Duke of Södermanland, who was Regent, arrived in Russia in August 1796. The negotiators were still on their guard but, between Gustavus and Alexandra, it was love at first sight. The young girl saw Gustavus as the Prince Charming of her childhood fairy tales. Countess Golovin confirmed this impression: 'The King's black Swedish outfit, his hair falling onto his shoulders, added a romantic touch to his air of nobility...' Catherine agreed, in a letter to Grimm: 'He is a most valuable young man and, truly, in Europe at present no other throne can boast of having anyone like him.' And, a few days later: 'Everybody, young and old, is mad about the young King. He is extremely polite, speaks very well, tells tales delightfully. He is charming to look at; his features are handsome and regular, his eyes large and bright; his bearing is dignified; he is quite tall, but slender and lively; he enjoys jumping and dancing and all forms of physical exercise, all of which he excels at. He appears to like it here... It appears also that the young lady does not find the aforementioned gentleman totally repulsive: she has lost the embarrassment she showed at the beginning, and appears quite at ease with her lover. One must admit that they form a rare couple.'

Watched by the whole Court, the young couple gazed at one another, spoke to each other hurredly and sought every possible occasion to be together. Catherine rubbed her hands. 'The course of love,' she said, 'is running smoothly.' A few more days and the whole business would be settled. After a ball at the Austrian embassy she wrote again to Grimm: 'The ball was extremely merry, as the rumour was flying that everything had been definitely settled in conversation. I do not know how it was but out of merriment or otherwise, our lover pressed his intended's hand a little when they were dancing. She turned as pale as death and said to her governess: "Imagine, I beg you, what he has just done? He pressed my hand when we were dancing. I did not know what would become of me." The other lady said to her: "What did you do then?" She replied: "I was so terrified that I nearly fell over!"

Gustavus was enchanted by such innocence, and without even consulting the Regent, went straight to the Empress and declared impetuously that he loved Alexandra and wanted her hand. The grandmother exploded with joy: obviously love was stronger than all the diplomats in the world. The idyll flourished all the more now that it had been officially sanctioned. The dowager Grand Duchess wrote note after note to her husband Grand Duke Paul, who had remained at Gatchina, informing him about the dear little things' behaviour: 'Our young couple are sitting side by side talking in low tones, and it is always his voice that I hear.' The King of Sweden was so much in love that he wanted to bring forward the marriage date. The dowager Grand Duchess assured him of her support. 'Trust in me, Monsieur Gustave. Do you wish me to speak to the Empress?' He assented to this and at supper 'carressed the little one in front of everybody'. The next day, renewed satisfaction and another note from the mother to the father: 'My dear and good friend, let us bless God: the betrothal is fixed for Monday evening. It will be celebrated by the archbishop . . . There will be a ball in the throne room.'

On the evening of Monday the 11th September at seven o'clock, the great chamber was filled with courtiers. There were the principal dignitaries of the Empire, the entire diplomatic corps, representatives of the higher clergy and distinguished foreign visitors. All the constellations of the heavens seemed to have gathered on these illustrious chests: there were crosses, medals, medallions and diamond monograms everywhere. The Empress sat imperturbably on her throne, beneath a canopy bearing the two-headed eagle, with her sceptre and crown and an ermine cloak over her shoulders. On her right, Grand Duke Paul, the official heir. On her left, her favourite Alexander. On a stool at her feet the pale fiancée bundled up in a white ceremonial dress with silver embroidery. The orchestra on the platform was ready to strike up a joyful fanfare as soon as the signal was given. Everybody was waiting for the young King. He was in a neighbouring room with Plato Zubov examining the marriage contract. This contract contained, of course, a little clause stating that Alexandra would retain her religion once she was married. Catherine considered that this had been implicitly understood by Gustavus during her intimate conversations with the young girl. This was a mere formality – just the signature was needed. So what was going on in there? Had Plato Zubov come up against some unforeseen obstacle?

Well, there was an obstacle, and a major one at that. The King of Sweden, when he read the contract, exploded with rage, saying that he had been tricked, swearing that he would never give his people an Orthodox queen; he threw the document to the ground in disgust. The panic-stricken Zubov explained that the Empress could not give way on this and that anyway it was too late to turn back, that not only was the charming Princess waiting on the other side of the door, but the whole Court, the whole of Russia, the whole of Europe, breathlessly awaited the fiancé's agreement. What an affront it would be to Her Majesty if he were to persist in his obstinacy!

While Plato Zubov was trying to rectify the blunder he had committed by not making the conditions clear from the start, in the throne room puzzlement was turning into apprehension. The fiancée kept turning her eyes up to the Empress as if to implore help – Catherine remained like marble, but those who knew her well could see the imperial temper rising behind the apparent calm. The long minutes ticked by. It seemed as though the world had frozen to a standstill. At last the two doors opened. There were a hundred sighs of relief. The party could begin. The conductor raised his baton. But alas – Plato Zubov appeared without the King and his pale, horrified face was that of a bearer of ill tidings. He advanced between the ranks of appalled courtiers, climbed the steps of the throne, and whispered in the Empress's ear. Catherine's heavy and faded face did not move an inch. Only her eyes froze. She moved her lips. They heard her murmur: 'I'll teach that brat!' Alexandra gazed at her with supplication. A deathly hush fell on the assembly. Catherine absorbed the shock. This drawing-room humiliation was worse than any defeat on the battle-field. Her valet, Zotov, handed her a glass of water. She swallowed it. After a long pause, she said in an unrecognizable flat voice: 'His Majesty King Gustavus IV has suffered a sudden illness; the engagement ceremony is postponed.'

Then she rose painfully and left the room with dragging footsteps, leaning on Alexander's arm. Behind her the young fiancée fell unconscious, and was carried away. The crowd dispersed, whispering.

During the night Catherine suffered from giddiness, possibly a mild stroke. She recovered immediately, and the next day determined to resume the talks and reach some sort of compromise. She had never enjoyed admitting defeat. No mere whipper-snapper would make her relinquish the prize. She would give a ball. Gustavus would attend and when he saw the pretty Alexandra, love would make him abandon his ridiculous Protestant monarch's pretensions. But the young girl was ill with grief and begged her grandmother to spare her the ordeal of meeting again the man who had publicly humiliated her. Catherine immediately scrawled a furious note: 'Why do you cry? What has been merely deferred is not lost. Wash your eyes with ice and your ears as well... I was ill yesterday. You are angry about the delay, that's all.'

After this lecture Alexandra appeared at the ball, drooping and with red eyes. Gustavus was there too, showing all possible courtesy. But the relationship between the two young people had deteriorated. From the first glance Catherine saw that no reconciliation was possible. The man standing beside Alexandra was no longer a loving suitor but an intransigent Lutheran, full of royal arrogance. A Swede making difficulties about a Russian Grand Duchess indeed! But he would not change his mind. And Catherine could not give way without losing face. She had not ruled with such splendour for thirty-four years to end now by bending her knee. Too bad for the 'little one'.[1] The person to be pitied in this business was not this child whose pride, and possibly love, had been wounded, but herself, the Empress, whose prestige had been muddied and authority successfully defied for the first time in her life. It sometimes seemed to her that her deepest springs of energy had been sapped by the political and romantic defeat of the 11th September. The affair had to be brought to a speedy conclusion. The Russo-Swedish alliance was over. The engagement was not mentioned again. After excuses, bows and compliments, the Regent and the King of Sweden set off back to Stockholm.

Alexandra fell ill, exhausted by her weeping. Catherine surrounded her with anxious care. But she too was suffering from frequent maladies. The colic she often suffered from after a violent emotion now never left her. Her legs were covered with suppurating sores. A doctor she chanced to meet recommended footbaths in ice-cold sea-water. One

[1] Alexandra married Archduke Joseph of Austria three years later and died in childbirth.

evening, when she was walking with Madame Naryshkin in the park at Tsarkoe Selo she saw a shooting star and said with a sigh: 'That is an omen of my death.' Her friend pointed out that in the past Her Majesty had refused to believe in omens and had condemned superstition. 'Yes, in the past,' she replied sadly. And she added that she felt herself 'sinking visibly'. She had sworn to herself that she would live until she was eighty; she was now sixty-seven and at the end of her strength. 'Catherine the Second came after Peter the First,' Diderot had written to her in 1774, 'but who will replace Catherine the Second? Such an extraordinary person could either succeed her immediately, or delay their appearance for centuries.' More than ever she worried about assuring the imperial succession. Paul, in her mind, had been definitively cast aside. The shining, noble Alexander would take the throne instead of him, and without abandoning his ideal of justice, would resist the revolutionary storms coming from France. The proclamation altering the order in succession had originally been intended for public release at the beginning of 1797. Why wait so long? Seized with a sudden haste, Catherine decided to proclaim her intentions on the 24th November, 1796 – her name-day.

She gathered her strength in preparation for this great event and did not appear before the Court except on Sundays in church, and at dinner. She walked with more and more difficulty, leaning on a stick. On the 4th/15th November, Sir Charles Whitworth found her 'gayer and more affectionate than ever'. But Rostopchin, who was better informed, wrote: 'Her health is bad. She was most upset by a storm, unusual at this time and in this area, such as had not been seen since Empress Elisabeth's death. She does not go out any longer.' However she continued to follow European affairs very closely, and was delighted to hear the news of General Moreau's retreat, when he was forced back across the Rhine. She found the Directoire just as odious as the Convention. She longed for the annihilation of regicide France. With a shaking pen she wrote a few lines to the Austrian diplomat, Cobenzl: 'I hasten to announce to Your Excellent Excellency that the excellent troops of his excellent court have completely defeated the French.' The same evening, she gathered her friends around her at the Hermitage, and laughed at the antics of the incorrigible clown, Leo Naryshkin. Dressed up as a travelling salesman, he offered her, with gypsy patter, seas, mountains, rivers, crowns, peoples. She laughed so much that she said she had colic and retired to her private apartments.

The next morning, she rose very early, as usual, chatted amiably with her maid, declared that she had passed a very good night, rubbed her face with an ice-cube, drank her boiling hot black coffee, received Plato

Zubov, who informed her of everything that was going on, summoned her secretaries, worked with them without showing the smallest sign of fatigue, and sent them away at last in order to be alone in her water-closet. After some time, as she did not return, they began to worry. Her valet Zotov and her maid Perekusikhina went into her bedroom, then into her dressing-room. They knocked on the door of the water-closet. No reply. With almost religious respect they pushed open the door. Horror! The Empress was there, inert, half slumped on the carpet against the closet. The door had prevented her from stretching out her legs. Her eyes were closed, her face dark red, her mouth was foaming and her throat rattled feebly. Zotov's cries alerted the other servants. They rushed to help, and, with a joint effort, managed to lift the heavy body. Staggering awkwardly, they first laid the patient at the foot of her bed, on a leather mattress from a sofa. She remained there, stretched out on her back, with her jaw dislocated. She had had a stroke. Plato Zubov, the first to be told, arrived on the scene in despair, and ordered the servants to call Her Majesty's official doctor, the Englishman, Rogerson. The latter observed the paralysis and, without much conviction, bled her and placed mustard plasters on her feet. Other doctors, who had come as reinforcements, backed him up. Although they considered that the Empress was dying they nonetheless persisted on trying out 'all the methods known to the art of medicine'.

Outside the window, snow fell on St Petersburg. Catherine was now stretched out on her great canopied bed. The powerless doctors gave way to the priests. The dying woman was surrounded by a murmur of prayer. She had not reopened her eyes. Oblivious to the agitation around her, she continued to breathe noisily, with a sinister gurgle from the back of her throat. The rattle grew louder. It could be heard even in the antechamber. Plato Zubov sobbed convulsively at the head of the bed. What would become of him after the Empress's death? All the hatred he had aroused in his position as favourite, that had been lying dormant, would now explode in his face. From one day to the next, he would be shunned, mocked, kicked out. If only he knew which branch to try and hang on to! But nobody even knew who would inherit the throne! How was it that Alexander had not appeared? They searched for him everywhere. He had gone off on a sledging expedition with his brother Constantine. At last they brought him in. He looked shattered. All the same, Countess Golovin claimed that he was very happy 'not to have to obey an old woman any more'.

What a strange character Alexander was! There is no doubt whatsoever that he knew about the act locked away in the imperial writing-box. He need only have produced it to be proclaimed Emperor of all the Russias. But he did not do it, although the Empress wished him to with all her dying strength. Only a few more days until the 24th November, St Catherine's day, when she herself would have officially designated him as her successor. All he would have had to do was to bow down to her wishes. He would have been spared the agonies of decision. But the Tsarina had fallen, just short of her goal. Now, if he waved the document, he would wound his father. He could not bring himself to do so. In order to act he had always needed a strong personality behind him: La Harpe, his grandmother ... Left to himself he preferred equivocation, twilight, short cuts, hiding behind bushes. Since the circumstances were against him, let it be so. After all, he was not that keen on becoming Emperor anyway!

All around him the Winter Palace buzzed like a beehive. The courtiers busied themselves around the place with terrified expressions. Some shook feverishly. They were worried, not about Catherine's fate, but about their own after she had gone. As they waited for her to breathe her last, they made hasty calculations, posited new alliances, dreaded old enmities, and, in their minds, juggled between favour and disgrace. At the Court, each change of ruler was the equivalent of a new deck of cards all round. Pulling himself out of his stupor, Plato Zubov sent his brother Valerian, 'The Persian', who had recently returned, crestfallen, from Baku, to alert Grand Duke Paul. He hoped, by this move, to gain the goodwill of the future sovereign. Rostopchin also set off, considering that it was up to him to bring the news to the heir to the throne, whose friend and confidant he was.

Paul and his wife were lunching with some friends at the mill of Gatchina, a few versts away from the castle. The couple were saying that they had been most upset by a dream they had both had simultaneously the previous night: a powerful hand was drawing them irresistibly towards the sky. Paul had hardly finished his account of the dream when a messenger was announced from St Petersburg with disturbing news of Her Majesty. He immediately ordered a sledge to be harnessed, and set off on the white road to the capital. What was he running towards in this way? He could not tell. There was so much intrigue around him! Half his family had turned against him. Perhaps it was an ambush? He would be arrested and thrown in a dungeon! In the Empress's name! Or Alexander's! Paul had heard rumours of his possible destitution whispered around him a hundred times. It was heads or tails, and everything was at stake, between his son and himself. At one moment, he thought of turning back. But he met other courtiers on the way who reassured him: The Empress really had had an attack. Finally he met Rostopchin with fresh news. Paul hugged him. What

was going on? The newcomer replied that the son could go without fear
to his mother's bedside. The whole Court awaited him. Paul made
Rostopchin climb into the sledge, installed him opposite the Grand
Duchess Maria Feodorovna, and ordered the coachman to force the
pace. The bells jingled. The Grand Duke appeared to be in ecstasy. At
the top of a hill not far from St Petersburg he had the horses stopped,
got out of the sledge and with his face contorted and his cheeks soaked
with tears, he gazed at the snowy landscape, frozen in the unreal
moonlight. 'My Lord, what a moment for you!' murmured Rostopchin.
'Wait, my dear fellow, wait,' said Paul, squeezing his hand. 'I have
lived for forty-two years. God has sustained me. Perhaps he will give me
the strength and the sanity to bear my appointed destiny. Let us hope
for the best from his goodness!'

They set off again. As they approached St Petersburg Paul persuaded
himself more and more that the hour for his revenge had struck. He had
lived for so long as the despised son and humiliated prince, now at last
he would know the glory of power. As long as no last-minute incident
were to inhibit the march of events. Anything was possible with a
mother as authoritarian as Catherine. Even though she was moribund,
she was still to be feared. Straight to the Winter Palace.

When Paul made his entry, at about eight thirty in the evening,
things appeared to present themselves well, in his view. All the
important dignitaries who were gathered there bowed down to
the ground when they saw him appearing. Plato Zubov, now reduced to the
state of a puppet, and Vice-Chancellor Bezborodko, who feared for his
position, fell to their knees before him. He made them stand, embraced
them, walked though the crowd of courtiers, who murmured blessings
as he passed, into the dying woman's room, where he glanced coldly at
the heavy-jowled bruised and rigid face, knelt at the end of the bed,
stood up and questioned the doctors. According to them, the end was
near. Metropolitan Gabriel must be called for to administer the last
sacraments.

Paul withdrew into a neighbouring office, where visitors came one
after the other. The future was being prepared. Vice-Chancellor
Bezborodko begged Rostopchin to intercede in his favour with the
future master of Russia. Grand Dukes Constantine and Alexander greeted
their father with a deference that delighted him. They had both, in
order to please him, put on the Prussian-style uniform of the
Gatchina battalions. They would never have dared come to the Palace
in this outfit in the Empress's time. It was certain now that Alexander
had renounced any thought of the throne. He would not call on the
guard to support his rights. This rough green cloth outfit was a better

token of his submission than any verbal declaration. Meanwhile, on the other side of the wall, Catherine still struggled against death. She still hung on to Russia. The echoes of the harsh and jerky death-rattle mingled with the conversation of those who stood, two paces away from her, planning the future. The night passed in an atmosphere of panicked uncertainty and morbid impatience.

On the morning of the 6th/17th November, 1796, the Empress was still there. Her face, Rostopchin noted, often changed colour, going from white to red or purple: 'The blood rushed to her head, disfiguring her features, then it withdrew, returning them to their normal aspect.' From time to time, doctor Rogerson, or the valet, Zotov, or the maid, Perekusikhina, would approach the patient to rearrange her pillows or wipe away the pink froth which oozed from her lips. Plato Zubov watched their movements with a glazed eye. According to eye-witnesses, he appeared to be a man 'whose despair had no parallel'. They feared that he might go mad. Perekusikhina sobbed noisily, going to and fro around her mistress's bed 'as if she expected her to wake up'.

Paul, insensible to these lamentations, hurried along. He ordered Bezborodko and Samoylov, the Attorney General, to sort out and seal all the papers in the Empress's and Plato Zubov's offices. Drawers were emptied, packets of letters and reports tied up, the imperial seal was pressed on warm wax. Did the proclamation about the succession appear amongst these papers? Yes, according to contemporary witnesses. Bezborodko drew Paul's attention to a folded paper tied with a black ribbon bearing the inscription: 'To be opened after my death, in the Council.' Without saying a word the heir to the throne took the paper and, as Bezborodko pointed out with his eyes a fireplace with a log fire burning in it, he threw the document into the flames. There was now no proof of what Catherine's wishes had been.[1]

At nine o'clock, doctor Rogerson came into Paul's room to announce that the last moments were approaching. Accompanied by his wife, Alexander, Constantine and several dignitaries, the Grand Duke went to the bedside of the woman who was still, for a few minutes more, the Empress of Russia. The breast of the dying woman bellowed in and out, with a hideous sound; her white face was contorted; her curved tongue swung to and fro in her half-open mouth.

'That moment will remain in my mind until the end of my days,' wrote Rostopchin. 'On the right stood the Grand Duke, the Grand

---

[1] Amongst the papers seized in Catherine's office, was, according to some, the famous letter in which Alexis Orlov confessed to the murder of Peter III.

Duchess and their children; at the head, myself and Plestcheiev; on the left the doctors and all the Empress's personal servants... The silence of all those present, their fixed stare, all towards the same object, the semi-darkness of the room, all inspired fear, and foretold the approach of death. A quarter to ten struck on the clock and Catherine the Great, having breathed her last like any other mortal, now appeared before God's tribunal.'

Hardly had Catherine died than her face returned to an expression of majestic serenity. Paul knelt, made the sign of the cross and stood up. Behind the doors swarmed a crowd of courtiers. The Attorney General Samoylov advanced towards them and announced: 'Gentlemen, the Empress Catherine is dead and her son, the Emperor Paul, has mounted the throne.' All adopted suitable expressions. 'It seemed,' Rostopchin continued, 'that they were all in the position of a traveller who has lost his way; but all expected to find it again soon.' Solemn joy reigned. Everybody embraced each other, sobbing. Russia continued. The order went out to immediately adjourn to the palace chapel for the swearing-in. It was midday. There was a general rush and scurry. A throne had been hastily brought to the chapel. Paul, drunk with the luck he had ceased to hope for, sat heavily down in his mother's place. Arrogant satisfaction was written all over his simian face with its pug nose, flabby lips and bulging eyes. The file-past began. First, the Empress kissed the Cross and the Bible, then she approached the Emperor and three times kissed his mouth and his eyes. Then came the turn of Grand Duke Alexander and his wife, followed by the Grand Duke and Grand Duchess Constantine,[1] and the Grand Duchesses Helena, Maria and Catherine, Paul's daughters. As they read the words of the oath, all knelt down before His Majesty and brushed his right hand with their lips. After the imperial family, Metropolitan Gabriel, the clergy, and the high court dignitaries swore their allegiance to the new Tsar. He never tired of savouring his triumph. After the ceremony was over, he went to give a last look at the Empress's remains, now dressed all in white; he then reviewed one of the guards regiments, showed his discontent at the state of their uniforms by blowing and stamping his feet, then withdrew into his office to confer with his cronies. Now that he was master of Russia he had one idea: to abolish all that his mother had established and take up the thread of history at the point where his father had been assassinated in 1762.

When he heard of the Empress's death, the Prince de Ligne cried 'Catherine the Great (I hope that Europe will confirm the name I have

---

[1] Constantine had finally married a princess of Saxe Cobourg.

given her), Catherine the Great is no more. These words are terrible to say!... The most brilliant star to illuminate our hemisphere has just gone out!' This funeral oration added nothing to the dead woman's prestige. When alive she had enjoyed the wildest praise. And the worst insults – 'Semiramis', and 'Messalina'. Throughout her life she had worked at enhancing her own glory. Certainly she had loved the Russian people sincerely and passionately, but was it not possible that her main concern when signing a treaty or declaring a war, had been for her personal prestige? The aims had, undeniably, been achieved: Turkish power had been wiped out, the Crimea and the Black Sea ports had been annexed, Poland had been carved up... All in the name of justice, international balance, or the holy interests of the Empire. In fact it was Catherine herself who had grown from one conquest to the next. This rock of will-power had a complex structure. Her fine philosophical ideas had not prevented her from increasing the numbers of serfs, in Russia, by the distribution of land and peasants to those who had served her throne or her bed. She had a hundred times proclaimed herself a liberal, she had made the 'Jacobin' La Harpe tutor to her grandsons, but she had always behaved as an autocrat, frowning at the slightest tremor in the fabric of society. The insurrection, the Revolution and the Convention were *bêtes noires* to this sovereign with a so-called republican heart. She had openly protected foreign writers and painters, but really more out of friendship for them than concern for European propaganda. She had read a great deal, but haphazardly 'in fits and starts' as she said herself, and the culture she accumulated was a hotchpotch of currently fashionable ideas. She had been the head of the Orthodox church, while professing Voltairian scepticism. She had claimed to govern alone, but had always leant on the nobility, which, thanks to her, became the ruling class, both economically and politically. In her amorous relationships, she was prudish in conversation, and unbridled in deeds. With her sanguine and impetuous temperament, she had never been tempted by vicious motives, only by her natural appetites. Men, to her, were instruments of pleasure. She chose them young, beautiful, strong and, if possible, not too stupid. Some had even become friends and advisers. But she very rarely allowed them to will the hand. Life, for her, always came back to a power-struggle between individuals. The weak must perish. The future was for the ambitious, the spirited, the obstinate and the masculine. These masculine characters could, moreover, possess seductive female exteriors. Was she not the proof of this? At moments she could be gentle and good, and as sentimental as moonlight on a German painting. But she would soon vigorously pull herself together. She had appreciated so much in life –

laughter, books, men, animals, trees, children! But none of these had ever turned her aside from politics. She was a demon worker. And, at the same time, a seductress, combining the attractions of her sex with virile authority. Everything she had ever wanted she had obtained through patience, intelligence, toughness and courage, taking incredible risks when necessary, suddenly changing direction to reach her goal more quickly. The little German princess had not been satisfied with learning Russian and changing her faith to be worthy of governing her adopted country. She had espoused the very soul of this strange nation. She had wanted to be the incarnation of Russia, without having a single drop of Russian blood in her veins. And this transformation remained perhaps her most stunning success. Her fiercest critics could not deny it. As soon as her death was announced the people gathered beneath the windows of the Winter Palace. Hundreds of humble people knelt in the snow. After all, life had not been so bad under 'the little mother Catherine'! What would the future bring, with this Paul I who was said to be more Teutonic than Russian?

Already the troops from Gatchina, in their Prussian uniforms, were entering the capital. Less than twenty-four hours after Catherine's death, the Court, previously so gay and refined, had turned into a guards corps. 'All one heard was the sound of spurs, hard boots and flint and steel; and, as in a conquered town, all the dwelling quarters were invaded by military men who made a stunning racket,' wrote Derzhavin. 'Little people, previously ignored, were strutting around pushing people about, and arrogantly giving orders,' wrote another contemporary Chichkov. And Prince Golitsin agreed: 'The Palace has become a barrack... As soon as one enters, one is made aware of the Emperor's exaggerated predilection for the military, and in particular for precision and regularity in all movements, inspired by Frederick, King of Prussia, whose attitudes the Emperor tries to copy.'

Everything had to be Prussian-style. War to the death was declared on round hats, turned-down collars, jackets, French costumes and turned-down boots. The glorious standards of the Ekaterinoslav Dragoon Regiment were treated by the new major-general Araktcheiev as 'Catherine's old skirts'. The Tsarina's memory was reviled and ridiculed at every step.

Plato Zubov, who had taken refuge with his sister Madame Gerebtsov, pretended to be ill and anxiously awaited the Emperor's decision about his fate. Suddenly there was a *coup de théâtre:* just as he was flinching from the approaching storm he heard that Paul I had given him a luxuriously furnished house with crockery, horses, carriages and footmen. An even greater honour – the imperial couple came to visit him the day after he had moved into his new house. When he threw himself at the monarch's feet, the latter comforted him, quoting the Russian proverb: 'Whoever remembers past injuries deserves to lose an eye.' After which, taking a glass of champagne, the Tsar added: 'I wish you as much prosperity as there are drops in this glass.' Plato Zubov floated in this unreal happiness; but it did not last long. Paul had only raised him up in order to better dash him to the ground. A few days after this meeting, all the ex-favourite's positions were removed from him, his land was sequestrated, and he received permission – in other words an order – to travel abroad. Nice punishment, but it gave Paul pleasure. As if to annoy the dead Empress even in her grave he released the Freemason Novikov, whose incarceration she had ordered, from the fortress at Schlüsselburg, and recalled the famous writer Radishchev, author of *Journey from St Petersburg to Moscow*. Better still, he went to the Marble Palace, where the Polish patriot Kosciuszko was under heavy guard, and showering him with gifts, authorized him to depart for America. He said to another Polish prisoner Potocki, before releasing him: 'I know that you have suffered a great deal, and that you have been ill-treated for a long time, but in the last reign all honest folk were persecuted, including myself.' Stanislaus Poniatowski was also removed, thanks to him, from his retreat at Grodno and superbly installed in St Petersburg.

His urge to redress past injustices was still not satisfied. He felt that he had been called upon by the Almighty to put right all his mother's mistakes and crimes. Having rehabilitated the living, he set about bringing justice even to the dead. On his orders, his father's coffin was removed from the cellars of the Alexander Nevsky Convent, adorned with imperial insignia, brought in great splendour to the Winter Palace, and laid in the Hall of Pillars next to Catherine's coffin. A gruesome conjugal meeting thus took place between the body of an old lady who had only died a few days earlier and the skeleton of her young husband who had died thirty-four years earlier. Above the lying-in-state bed there was a streamer with this inscription in Russian: 'Divided in life, united in death.' The inhabitants of St Petersburg were invited together with the courtiers, diplomats and dignitaries to file past these two corpses brought together by a son who wished to deny the past. 'What can one say,' wrote Baron Stedingk, 'about this proud woman who imposed her will on sovereigns, and who now finds herself exposed to the eyes and the judgment of the public, beside a husband whose death she caused. What a terrible lesson of Providence for the wicked.' Paul, as he contemplated the double catafalque, felt in a sort of morbid delirium that he was correcting the course of history. The ceremonies of atonement, which he supervised down to the smallest detail, continued with the transfer of the bodies of Peter III and Catherine II to the Cathedral of St Peter and St Paul, where the funeral was to take place. The procession moved through the snow-bound city, in a temperature of minus 18°C. The passing-bells tolled. To honour the assassinated Tsar, Paul with demonic irony had summoned the few survivors of the 1762 plot. This would be their punishment. Alexis Orlov, 'the Scarface', the man principally responsible for the murder, walked at the head of the procession, bearing his victim's crown on a cushion; Passek and Baryatinsky, his erstwhile accomplices, were pall-bearers. All three had aged a lot since the event. Very few amongst the crowd that had gathered to watch the procession go by had heard of this Peter III who was being buried for the second time. The people were not mourning him but Catherine, the 'little mother'. Sobs were heard all around Paul. He scorned this foolishness and walked, with his head raised high, behind the two coffins, followed by Empress Maria Feodorovna, the Grand Dukes, and the whole court. He felt that he was fulfilling a sacred duty by reuniting in death a father whom he admired but had hardly known, and a mother whom he hated for having known her too well.

In the cathedral the priests, in their black cassocks spangled with silver, celebrated the double funeral with all possible solemnity. For hours the same clouds of incense, the same seraphic chants honoured both parts of the reconstituted imperial couple. It was like a wedding of ghosts. The Church commended to the mercy of the Lord the souls of the two Russian sovereigns, cousins as they were, who had come as children, one from Kiel and the other from Zerbst, to rule a country whose language they could not, at first, speak, and whose religion they did not profess. The first had reigned for six months and the second for thirty-four years. But, for their son, the second was far less important than the first. He denied and rejected her; he wanted to live long enough to destroy everything she had built.

At the end of the religious ceremony he withdrew his mourning robe, and reviewed the troops massed on the Millionaya. But military exercises could only temporarily calm his boiling brain. He continued to be haunted by the thought of Catherine and Peter. His mother's lovers passed through his mind in one long cohort. He was seized with rage again: he must wipe it all out! Suddenly he remembered that the ostentatious Potemkin was buried in St Catherine's Church at Kherson. He had not only been his mother's lover but also, they said, her husband. It was an inadmissible situation, an insult to the memory of Peter III, Catherine's only true husband. The 'Serenissimo's' mausoleum must be opened and his cursed bones dispersed! The order was hurriedly carried out by trembling grave-diggers. Now that he had installed his parents in their burial-place, and hounded the Prince of Taurida out of his, Paul I felt better. He had tidied up the past, now he could turn to the future.

Four and a half years later, after terrorizing the country with his follies, he died, assassinated like his father, Peter III. Plato Zubov was one of the main conspirators involved in the murder, having returned just in time from his travels. Paul I's son, the indecisive, mysterious Alexander, who had been in tacit connivance with the conspirators, mounted the Russian throne. And thus, once again, against the wind and the tide, Catherine the Great's will was accomplished.

Chronology

Chronology

1729

Life of Catherine II *21 April/2 May:* Birth at Stettin of Sophia Frederica Augusta of Anhalt-Zerbst, the future Catherine II.

Events in Russia Oukase worsening the conditions of serfs.

Events in the World Natchez revolt in Louisiana/Treaty of Seville/First cabaret opens in Paris/Fashion for English gardens/Death of Law.

Intellectual Life Bach: *St Matthew's Passion*/Montesquieu in England/Goldoni: *The Venetian Gondolier*/Gray: transmission of electricity/Bouguer: photometry/Haller: *The Alps*/Death of Congreve/Birth of Lessing, Echouard-Lebrun, Monsigny/Voltaire: *History of Charles XII, 'Brutus', Philosophical Letters*.

1730

Events in Russia *29th January:* Death of Tsar Peter II, advent of Anna Ivanovna/Sino-Russian treaty of Kiakhta/Peace between Russia and Persia.

Events in the World Abdication of Victor Amedeus of Savoy/Walpole in government/Death of Benedict XIII/Beginning of papacy of Clement XII/Achmet III deposed/Death of Frederick IV/Advent of Christian VI of Denmark/Orry, controller-general.

Intellectual Life Mme du Deffand's famous salon/Hamilton: *Tales*/Rollin: *Ancient History*/Marivaux: *Le Jeu de l'amour et du hasard*/Buffon in England/Goldoni: *Don Juan*/Metastase: *Alexander*/First use of sextant/Birth of Gessner.

1731

Events in Russia Suppression of protectionist tariff/Replacement of High Council by Cabinet of three, creation of secret Chancellery.

Events in the World Dupleix at Chandernagore/English language replaces Latin in English courts/Dispersal of the Club de l'Entresol/La Cadière affair/Foundation of Academy of Medicine in France.

Intellectual Life Holberg: *Danish theatre*/Marivaux: *La Vie de Marianne*/Abbé Prévost: *Manon Lescaut*/Fielding: *Tragedy of tragedies*/Tull: theory of enclosures/Death of Defoe, Houdard de la Motte/Birth of Cowper.

1732

Events in Russia Austro-Prusso-Russian agreement at Loewenwolde/Russians give up Peter I's conquests on the Caspian.

Events in the World Foundation of English colony of Georgia/Treaty of Warsaw/Birth of Washington and Necker/Closure of Saint-Médard cemetery.

Intellectual Life Berkeley: *Alcyphron*/Metastase: *Demetrius*/Destouches: *Le Glorieux*/Montesquieu initiated a freemason in England/Voltaire: *Eriphile, Zaire*/Foundation of *London Magazine*/Lesage: *Don Guzman d'Alfarache*/Marivaux: *Les Serments indiscrets*/Boerhaave: *Elements of chemistry*/Maupertuis: *Discourse on the figuration of the stars*/Bach: *Coffee cantata*/Death of Boulle/Birth of Fragonard, Lalande, Haydn, Beaumarchais.

1733

Events in Russia *September:* Russo-Saxon invasion of Poland and installation of Augustus III in Warsaw.

Events in the World Beginning of war of Polish succession/Establishment of conscription in Prussia/Villars' campaign in Italy/Treaty of Turin/Foundation of Spanish colony in Philippines/In France: Introduction of tithe/Mme de Mailly becomes Louis XV's mistress/Franco-Bavarian and Franco-Dutch treaties/Death of Forbin.

Intellectual Life Beginning of publication of *Literary History of France* by Benedictines of Saint-Maur/Rameau: *Hippolyte et Aricie*/Bach: *Mass in B minor*/Pope: *Essay on Man*/Marivaux: *L'Heureux Stratagème*/Voltaire: *Temple du Gout*/Franklin: *Poor Richard's Almanac*/Pergoleso: *La Serva Padrone*/Kay invents the flying shuttle/Death of Couperin/Birth of Priestley, Wieland, Mesmer, Ducis, Malfilâtre, Zoffany, Borda, H. Robert.

1734

Events in Russia Danzig besieged and captured by the Russians/Anglo-Russian commercial treaty/Ukraine passes into Russian control/Creation of ballet school.

Events in the World The Emperor declares war on France/Battle of Parma/Zinzendorf: unification of Moravian brothers/Foundation of university of Gottingen/Order against Voltaire who hides at Mme du Châtelet's at Cirey; the Duke of Holstein, Russia's heir presumptive offers to take him into his service/Death of Berwick, Villars.

Intellectual Life Montesquieu: *Considerations... on the rise and fall of the Romans*/Hogarth: *Life of a courtesan*/Bach: *Christmas Oratorio*/Reamur: *History of insects*/Gresset: *Vert-Vert*/Goldoni: *Belisario*/Tartini: *Violin Sonatas*/Death of S. Ricci/Birth of Restif de la Bretonne, Dorat Ruhlière, Romney.

1735

Events in Russia Oukase creating people's schools/Russo-Turkish war.

Events in the World Armistice between France and Austria/La Bourdonnais, governor of the Ile-de-France/Ruling on wills in France.

Intellectual Life Dom Calmet: *History of the world*/Marivaux: *Le paysan parvenu*/Nivelle de la Chaussée: *Le Préjugé à la Mode*/Hogarth: *The Rake's Progress*/Salvi:

Trevi fountain in Rome/La Condamine and Maupertius measure the earth's circumference/Mme de Tencin: *Mémoires de Comte de Comminges*/Du Halde: *Description of the Chinese Empire*/Voltaire: First performance of *La Mort de Jules César*/Lemoyne decorates the hotel Soubise/Rameau: *Les Indes galantes*/Bach: *Italian concerto*/Death of Stradivarius/Birth of the Prince de Ligne, Lépicié.

1736

Events in Russia Russians invade the Crimea and take Azov.

Events in the World Indian revolt in Louisiana/Foundation of the Bank of Copenhagen/Construction of Summer Palace in Peking/Beginnings of Italian opera in St Petersburg/Franco-Austrian agreement.

Intellectual Life Marivaux: *Le Legs*/Lesage: *Le Bachelier de Salamanque*/Voltaire: First performances of *Alzire* and *l'Enfant Prodigue*, Epistle to Madame du Châtelet on Calumny/Chardin: *Le Chateau de cartes*/Pergolesi: *Stabat Mater*/Creation of glass-works at Murano/Hull takes out patent on steamship/Death of Pergolesi, Pater/Birth of Lagrange, Watt.

1737

Events in Russia Russia forced to evacuate the Crimea/Vain peace-talks. Russians establish outpost in Astrakhan. The German, Biron, the Empress's favourite, made Duke of Courland/Fire in St Petersburg.

Events in the World First theatres in Prague and Stockholm/Chauvelin's disgrace in France.

Intellectual Life Salon at the Louvre/Linné: classification of plants/Marivaux: *Les Fausses Confidences*/Goldoni: *l'Homme accompli*/Rameau: *Castor et Pollux*/Gluck in Italy/Walpole in France/Death of Lemoyne/Birth of Bernadin de Saint-Pierre, Parmentier.

1738

Events in Russia Appearance of false tsarevitch Alexis Petrovitch.

Events in the World Treaty of Vienna: end of war of Polish succession/Stanislaus Leczinsky, Duke of Loraine/England adheres to the treaty of Vienna/Franco-Swedish treaty/Workers' revolts in England/Whitefield's sermon. In France: ruling on forced labour/Mlle de Nesle, Louis XV's mistress/Crozat canal (in Picardy) completed.

Intellectual Life Piron: *La Métromanie*/Salon at the Louvre/Paul invents spinning-frame/Handel: *Israel in Egypt*/Rollin: *Roman History*/Crébillon: *Les Egarements du coeur et de l'esprit*/Bernouilli: *Hydrodynamics*/Cassini, Thury, Maraldy and La Caille measure the speed of sound/Creation of porcelain works at Vincennes (later moved to Sèvres)/Lancret: *The Four Seasons* (Mmes de France)/Voltaire: Death of Boerhaave/Birth of Beccaria, Hirschel, Boufflers, Delille.

1739

Life of Catherine II Princess Sophia (later Catherine II) meets Peter Ulrich of Holstein-Gottorp at Kiel.

Events in Russia Turkish victory at Krotzka/Russians recapture Jassy/Treaty of Belgrade: Russians keep the fortress of Azov/*December:* arrival in St Petersburg of French Ambassador La Chétardie.

Events in the World Opening of French bank of Karikal/Philip V signs the treaty of Vienna/Walpole declares war on Spain/Foundation of Stockholm Academy of Science/In France, Buffon made administrator of the King's gardens.

Intellectual Life Mme de Tencin: *Le Siège de Calais*/Salon at the Louvre/Hume: *Treatise on human nature*/Bouchardon: *Fountain* in the rue de Grenelle in Paris/Tocque: *Portrait of the Dauphin*/Deluze prints on material/De Brosses: *Intimate letters from Italy*/Voltaire: *Life of Molière, Light pieces of poetry and prose*/Clairaut's researches into integral calculus/Handel: *Susanna*/Birth of La Harpe.

1740

Events in Russia *17/28 October:* Death of Empress Anna Ivanovna, accession of Ivan VI, only a few months old, under the regency first of the minister Biron, then of Anna Leopoldovna, mother of the little tsar.

Events in the World *31st May:* Death of the Sergeant King/Accession of Frederick II; he invades Silesia/Death of Clement XII/beginning of papacy of Benedict XIV/Death of Charles VI/Accession of Maria-Theresa of Austria: beginning of War of Austrian succession/First Greek newspaper/Louis XV sends ultimatum to England; breakdown of relations/Voltaire visits Frederick II for the first time at Cleves.

Intellectual Life Foundation of Pellerin printing works at Epinal/Salon at the Louvre/Coustou: *Les Chevaux de Marly*/Chardin: *The Grace*/Richardson: *Pamela*/Crebillon: *Le Sopha*/Voltaire: *Zulime*/Marivaux: *l'Epreuve*/Abbé Goujet: *French Library*/Birth of Sade, Oberlin.

1741

Events in Russia *August:* Sweden declares war on Russia/*25th November/6th December:* Elisabeth, daughter of Peter the Great, overthrows little Ivan and mounts the throne.

Events in the World Franco-Prussian alliance/Walpole's defeat at the elections/Franco-Hanoverian agreement/Secret Austro-Prussian armistice/Charles-Albert of Bavaria has himself proclaimed King of Bohemia/More debate on the *Unigenitus* bill in France.

Intellectual Life Handel: *The Messiah*/Destruction of windows of Notre Dame in Paris/Gabriel, King's main architect/Salon at the Louvre/La Tour: *Portrait of the President of Rieux*/Hume: *Moral and political essays*/Goldoni: *The Capable Woman*/Favart: *La Chercheuse d'Esprit*/Abbé Prévost: *Histoire d'une Grecque moderne*/Voltaire: *Mahomet*/Death of J.B. Rousseau, Vivaldi, Rollin/Birth of Lavater, Laclos, Houdon, Chamfort, Füssli.

1742

Life of Catherine II *July:* Sophia's (the future Catherine II's) father made *field-marshal* by Frederick II of Prussia.

Events in Russia *February:* Arrival in Moscow of Peter of Holstein-Gottorp, summoned by Tsarina Elisabeth/*7th November:* Peter declared heir to the throne/*22 December:*

Defence treaty between Russia and England/Secret marriage between Elisabeth and Alexis Razumovsky.

Events in the World Benedict XIV condemns Jesuit policies in China/Austrians recapture Linz/Charles-Albert of Bavaria, King of Bohemia elected Emperor under the name of Charles VII/Walpole resigns/Franco-Danish treaty/Treaty of Berlin/Fall of Prague/Beginning of 'Reign' of Louis XV's mistresses.

Intellectual Life Salon at the Louvre/L. Racine: *La Religion*/Fielding: *Joseph Andrews*/Young: *The Nights*/Piranesi: *Prisons*/Tresaguet perfects tarmacadam/Death of Massillon.

1743

Events in Russia *17th August:* Russo-Swedish treaty of Abo: Russia keeps part of Finland/Alexis Razumovsky made Count and Chief Huntsman.

Events in the World Franco-Sardinian war/Second family pact/Frederick II re-opens the Berlin Academy, which was to publish his works in French/Foundation of Danish Academy/The La Verendryes discover the Rocky Mountains/Death of Fleury/D'Argenson, Voltaire's friend, made Secretary of State for War/Marquise de Tournelle is Louis XV's mistress/Birth of Jeanne Bécu (future Mme du Barry).

Intellectual Life Mlle Clairon's debut at the Comédie Française/Handel: *Joseph and his brethren*/Salon at the Louvre/Fielding: *Jonathan Wilde*/D'Alembert: *Treatise on dynamics*/Death of Vivaldi, Crécourt, Faa Ghislandi, H. Rigand, Desportes, Lancret, Lorrain/Birth of Cagliostro, Lavoisier, Condorcet, Jacobi.

1744

Life of Catherine II *10th January:* Departure of Sophia and her mother for Russia, via Berlin/*3rd/14th February:* Sophia's arrival in St Petersburg/*9th/20th February:* Sophia's arrival in Moscow/*28th June:* Sophia embraces Orthodox faith and becomes Grand Duchess Catherine Alexeievna/*29th June:* official engagement to Grand Duke Peter.

Events in Russia *June:* French ambassador La Chétardie has to leave Russia.

Events in the World First Methodist general conference/Frederick II takes Prague/Construction of Schoenbrunn Castle/*28th November:* D'Argenson minister of Foreign Affairs/Louis XV declares war on England and Austria, invades Piedmont and the Netherlands, takes Freiburg/Law giving underground property to the State.

Intellectual Life Albinoni: *Symphonies*/Pigalle: *Mercury*/Hogarth: *Marriage à la Mode*/Gluck: *Sophonisbe*/Frederick II: *La Miroir des Princes*/Hénault: *Chronological resumé of French History*/Métastase: *Antigone*/Death of Vico, Pope, Campra/Birth of Herder, Lamarck.

1745

Life of Catherine II *21st August:* Catherine's marriage to Grand Duke Peter/*28th September:* Departure of Catherine's mother, the Princess of Anhalt. Lestocq, the doctors disgrace.

Events in the World Convention of Aranjuez/Charles Stuart lands in Scotland/Death of the Emperor/Frances III of Lorraine (François I), husband of Maria-Theresa, elected

Emperor/*11th May:* battle of Fontenoy/Beginning of la Pompadour's period in favour/Machaut, general controller of finances.

Intellectual Life Morelly: *Essay on the Human Heart*/Swedenborg: *On the Worship and Love of God*/Voltaire: *Bataille de Fontenoy*/Servandoni: *Door of Saint-Sulpice*/Tiepolo: *Frescoes in Cornano Palace*/Salon at the Louvre/Gluck: *Hippolytus*/Destouches: *Works*/Rameau: *Pygmalion*/Death of Swift, Guarnerius, J.B. Vanloo/Birth of Volta, Goya, Huet.

1746

Events in Russia Death in prison of Anna Leopoldovna, mother of Ivan VI/*22nd May:* Treaty between Russia and Austria/Oukase ordering commoners to sell their estates, forbidding them to buy serfs.

Events in the World Brussels taken by the French/Battle of Plaisance/Death of Philip V/Accession of Ferdinand VI/Surrender of Genoa/Battle of Racoux/Foundation of Princeton University/Christophe de Beaumont, archbishop of Paris/Death of Torey/*25th April:* Voltaire member of the St Petersburg Academy/*November:* Voltaire gentleman of the King's Bedchamber.

Intellectual Life Salon at the Louvre/Rousseau gives away his first child to orphanage/Diderot: *Pensées philosophiques*/Vauvenargues: *Reflections et Maximes*/Abbé Prévost: *Histoire générale des voyages*/Handel: *Judas Maccabeus*/Death of R. Walpole, Largillière, Coustou/Birth of Monge, Pestalozzi.

1747

Life of Catherine II Death of Catherine's father, Prince Christian Augustus of Anhalt-Zerbst.

Events in Russia *June:* Anglo-Russian alliance.

Events in the World Orange revolt in Zetland/Franco-Dutch war/French take Berg-op-Zoom/Argenson's disgrace/Birth of Louis-Philippe of Orléans (later Philippe Egalité).

Intellectual Life Librarian Le Breton puts Diderot and d'Alembert in charge of the *Encyclopedie*/Bach: *Musical offering*/Salon at the Louvre/Franklin: Lightning conductor/Trudaine founds the *école des mines* in Paris/Gresset: *Le Méchant*/La Tour: *Portrait of M. de Saxe*/Johnson: *Dictionery of the English Language*/Gluck: *Marriage of Hebe and Hercules*/Nivelle de la Chausée: *l'Amour castillan*/Death of Vauvenargues, Lesage, Solimena/Birth of Galvani.

1748

Events in Russia Treaty of permanent neutrality between Turkey and Russia.

Events in the World Treaty of Aix-la-Chapelle: end of war of Austrian Succession/'Reign' of Madame Henriette of France.

Intellectual Life Crébillon: *Catilina*/Handel: *Samson*/Vestris' debut at the Opéra/Construction of Opera at Bayreuth/Salon at the Louvre/Grimm arrives in Paris/Diderot: *Les Bijoux indiscrets*/Montesquieu: *l'Esprit des Louis*/Hume: *Philosophical essays*/Richardson: *Clarissa Harlowe*/Klopstock: *La Messiad*/Voltaire: First performances of *Semiramis, Panégyrique de Louis XV*/Euler: Works on mathematical analysis/Needham: theory of spontaneous generation/Discovery of ruins at Pompei/Pigalle: *Venus*/La Tour:

Portrait of Louis XV/La Mettrie: *l'hommemachine*/Birth of Berthollet, David, Jussieu, Bentham, Corais.

1749

Events in the World Italian league against the North African pirates/Fight about *vingtième* tax in France/Maurepas' disgrace.

Intellectual Life Huntsmann casts steel/Mme Geoffrin's famous *salon*/Bach: *The Art of the fugue*/Salon at the Louvre/Buffon: *Natural History*/Fielding: *Tom Jones*/Swedenborg: *Les Arcanes célestes*/Tournefort: *Studies in comparative anatomy*/Diderot: *Letter on the blind;* he is imprisoned at Vincennes/Death of Magnasco, J. van Huysum, Clérambault/Birth of Goethe, Alfieri, Mirabeau (son), Subleyras.

1750

Events in the World Death of John V/Accession of José I of Portugal/Pombal's ministry/Dissolution of Languedoc États/Riot in Paris/Machault, Keeper of the Seals.

Intellectual Life Goldoni: *Le Café*/Rousseau: *Discourse on sciences and arts*/Distribution of *The Prospectus for the Encyclopedia*/Pigalle: *L'Enfant à la cage*/Marmontel: *Cléopâtre*/Death of Bach, Muratori, Oudry/Birth of Berquin, Valenciennes.

1751

Events in Russia Bestuzhev's disgrace. Rise of Peter Shuvalov.

Events in the World Portuguese government forbids autodafés/'Reign' of Mme Adelaide in France.

Intellectual Life Salon at the Louvre/Diderot: *Letter on the deaf and the dumb*/Burlamaqui: *Principles of political law*/Handel: *Jephta*/Gozzi: *Burlesque verses*/Fielding: *Amelia*/Hume: *Inquiry into moral principles*/Duclos: *Considerations on the customs of this century*/Voltaire: *The Century of Louis XIV*/Publication of first volume of *Encyclopedie* (d'Alembert's preliminary discourse)/Death of La Mettrie/Birth of Sheridan, Gilbert, Jouffroy d'Abbans.

1752

Life of Catherine II Catherine's liaison with Serge Saltykov.

Events in the World Stanislaus Leczinski begins to build the square in Nancy bearing his name/Construction of palace at Caserta/Confession notes affair in France/Last prosecution of Protestants.

Intellectual Life Réaumur: experiments on digestion/Hume: *Political essays*/Rousseau: *Le Devin du Village*/First condemnation of the *Encyclopedie*/Maupertuis: *Complete Works*/Wieland: *On Nature*/Gainsborough: *Portrait of Mr and Mrs Sandby*/Death of J-F. de Troy, Ch. A. Coypel/Birth of Filangieri.

1753

Events in Russia Suppression of internal customs.

Events in the World War between America and Canada/Conference in London on the Indian question/Great remonstrances from French parliament/Parliament recalled.

Intellectual Life Favart: *Bastien et Bastienne*/Holberg: *The Haunted House*/Salon at the Louvre/La Tour: *Portrait of Rousseau and d'Alembert*/Beginning of *Grimm's Literary Correspondence*/Buffon at the Academy: *Discourse on Style*/Gabriel begins the construction of the opera at Versailles/Richardson: *Sir Charles Grandison*/Liguori: *Moral theology*/Publication of 3rd volume of the *Encyclopedie* with preface by d'Alembert/Death of Berkeley/Birth of J. de Maistre, Outamaro, Parny, Rivarol.

1754

Life of Catherine II *20th September:* Birth of Paul Petrovich, son of Catherine, future Paul I.

Events in Russia Creation in Russia of credit houses. Land registry project and new code.

Events in the World Dupleix leaves India/Foundation of King's College in New York/Jesuits expelled from Brazil/*23rd August:* Birth of Dauphin (future Louis XVI)/Machault at the navy.

Intellectual Life Rousseau: *Discourse on inequality*/First publication of *l'Année Littéraire* by Fréron/Condillac: *Treatise on sensations*/Diderot: *Thoughts on the interpretation of nature*/Gabriel undertakes the construction of Place Louis XV (Place de la Concorde) in Paris/Hume: *History of England*/Goldoni: *The philosopher in the country*/Winchelmann in Italy/Boucher: *Mlle O'Murphy*/Falconet: *Milon de Crotone*/Death of Holberg, Fielding, Piazetta/Birth of Bonald.

1755

Life of Catherine II Catherine's liaison with Stanislaus Poniatowski.

Events in Russia Foundation of Moscow University/Anglo-Russian convention.

Events in the World Diplomatic break between England and France/*1st November:* Earthquake in Lisbon/Jesuits expelled from Paraguay/Construction of Château de Compiègne/Mandrin executed.

Intellectual Life Salon at the Louvre/Publication of Volume V of *Encyclopedie*/Black invents carbonic gas/Morelly: *Code de la nature*/Lessing: *Miss Sarah Sampson*/Greuze: *Le père de famille*/La Tour: *Portrait of Mme de Pompadour*/Death of Montesquieu, Saint-Simon, Gentil-Bernard, Maffei/Birth of Fourcroy, Corvisart, Florian, Quatremère de Quincy, Collin d'Harleville, Fabre d'Eglantine, Debucourt, E. Vigée-Lebrun, Prony.

1756

Events in Russia Ivan VI in Schlusselburg fortress/Oukase establishing a theatre in St Petersburg.

Events in the World Beginning of Seven Years War/Montcalm in Canada/First Pitt ministry/Troubles in Dauphiné.

Intellectual Life Rousseau: *Letter on providence*/Voltaire: *Essay on customs*/Birth of Lacépède, Mozart, Raeburn.

1757

Life of Catherine II *9th December:* Birth of Anne, Catherine's daughter.

Events in Russia *2nd February:* Austro-Russian alliance/*15th July:* Russians take Memel/*August:* Russian victory over Prussians at Gross Jaegersdorff/Foundation of Fine Arts Academy

Events in the World *5th November:* Frederick II demolishes French army at Rossbach/*4th January:* Damiens assassination attempt.

Intellectual Life Salon at the Louvre/Diderot: *The natural son*/Helvétius: *On the Soul*/Mme Leprince de Beaumont: *Le magasin des enfants*/Rameau: *Les Surprises de l'Amour*/Burke: *European establishments in America*/Death of Fontanelle, Réamur, Vadé, R. Carriera/Birth of W. Blake.

1758

Events in Russia Apraxin conspiracy, Bestuzhev arrested/Russians take Konigsberg/*25th August:* Bloody battle between Russians and Prussians at Zorndorf.

Events in the World Death of Benedict XIV/Beginning of papacy of Clement XIII/English take Frontenac, Gorea, and St Louis in Senegal/Lally-Tollendal in India/Choiseul, Secretary of State for foreign affairs.

Intellectual Life Rousseau: Letter to d'Alembert/d'Alembert leaves *Encyclopedie*/Diderot: *The father of the family*/Voltaire: *History of Russia*/Quesnay: *Economic picture*/Swedenborg: *Heaven and Hell*/Birth of Prudhon, C. Vernet.

1759

Life of Catherine II *March:* death of little Grand Duchess Anne.

Events in Russia Russian victories at Zullichau and Kunersdorf. Russians take Frankfurt in the Oder.

Events in the World Jesuits expelled from Portugal/Battle of Minden/Quebec falls/English in Guadeloupe/M. de Silhouette reforms administration of leases in France.

Intellectual Life Salon at the Louvre (Diderot)/Parliament burns *Encyclopedie*/Wieland: *Cyrus*/Sterne: *Tristram Shandy*/Gossec: *Symphonies*/Foundation of British Museum/Death of Handel, Montcalm/Birth of Schiller, Burns, Wilberforce.

1760

Life of Catherine II Beginning of liaison between Catherine and Gregory Orlov/*16th May:* Death of Catherine's mother, Princess of Anhalt-Zerbst.

Events in Russia Russians occupy Romerania/*October:* Austrians and Russians sack Berlin.

Events in the World Death of GeorgeII/Accession of George III in England/Capitulation of Montreal/Siege of Pondicherry/Small post in Paris/Taxes rise in France.

Intellectual Life D'Alembert: differential equations/Macpherson: *Ossian*/Voltaire: first performances of *Tancrède and L'Ecossaise* in Paris/Spallanzani: *New physiological researches*/Gainsborough: *Portrait of Admiral Hawkins*/Palissot: *The Philosophers*/Birth of Cherubini (Count), Saint-Simon, Hokusai.

1761

Events in Russia *December:* Russians take Kolberg.

Events in the World Fall of Pondicherry/*18th February:* Pastor Rochette executed/*13th October:* Suicide of Marc-Antoine Calas/Choiseul, Secretary of State for War and the Navy/Negotiations at Versailles: family pact.

Intellectual Life Salon at the Louvre (Diderot)/Rousseau: *La Nouvelle Héloise*/Gozzi: *The Crow*/Greuze: *The Village meeting*/Death of Richardson/Birth of Boilly.

1762

Life of Catherine II *25th December 1761/5th January 1762:* Death of Elisabeth, accession of Peter III, Catherine's husband/*11th April,* birth of Alexis Bobrinski, son of Catherine and Orlov/*28th June/9th July:* Peter overthrown by Orlov, Catherine proclaimed Empress/*6th/17th July:* Peter III assassinated on Orlov's orders/*22nd September:* Catherine II crowned in Moscow.

Events in Russia Abolition of secret chancellery, secularization of Church wealth, replacement of senatorial conference by Secret High Council/Peace with Prussia. *July:* Oukase protecting 'landowning gentlemen'/*October-November:* military plot against Orlov: three officers arrested and executed.

Events in the World *10th March:* Jean Calas executed in Toulouse/Parliament orders suppression of Jesuits/J.J. Rousseau's *Emile* condemned by parliament/English in Manila and Havana/Preliminaries for peace between England, France and Spain.

Intellectual Life Rousseau: *Emile, The Social Contract*/Curé Meslier: *My Testament*/Lord Chesterfield: *Letters*/Gluck: *Orpheus*/Pigalle: *Louis XV*/Gabriel: *Le Petit Trianon*/Birth of Fichte, A Chénier.

1763

Events in Russia Catherine confirms nobles' privileges/Oukase dividing Senate into six departments/German settlers brought to the Ukraine and the Volga/*September:* Russians invade Lithuania.

Events in the World Treaties of Paris and Hubertsbourg.

Intellectual Life Salon at the Louvre (Diderot)/Voltaire: *Volume II History of Russia, Treatise on Tolerance*/Beccaria: *Treatise on Crime and Punishment*/Reynolds: *Portrait of Miss O'Brien*/Death of Marivaux, l'abbé Prévost, L. Racine.

1764

Life of Catherine II *October:* Catherine vaccinated against smallpox.

Events in Russia *26th February/8th March:* Confiscation of Church wealth/*March:* Defence treaty with Frederick II/*4th/15th July:* Assassination of Ivan VI/Foundation of Smolny Institute for the education of 'noble young ladies'.

Events in the World Wilkes affair/Archduke Joseph elected King of Romans/*18th May:* Death of Marshal of Luxembourg/Trial and condemnation of Sirven/Death of Mme de Pompadour/Stanislaus Poniatowski elected King of Poland.

Intellectual Life Rousseau: *Letters from the mountains*/Voltaire: *Dictionary of* *philosophy*/Soufflot: *Le Panthéon*/Winchelmann: *History of Ancient Art*/Houdon: *St Bruno*/Walpole: *The Castle of Otranto*/First Almanack of Gotha/Death of Hogarth, Rameau/Birth of M.J. Chénier, A. Radcliffe.

1765

Events in Russia Catherine orders survey of all estates/Confirmation of social privileges of nobility/Death of poet and thinker, Michael Lomonossov.

Events in the World Frederick II creates Bank of Berlin/Free trade for all subjects of the King of France/Calas rehabilitated.

Intellectual Life Salon at the Louvre (Diderot)/*Encyclopedie* completed/Greuze: *The paternal curse*/Sedaine: *Le philosophe sans le savoir*/Voltaire: *The philosophy of history*/Russian ambassador visits Ferney/Turgot: *Origin and distribution of wealth*/Cavendish: study of hydrogen/Death of Comte de Caylus, Pannini, C. Vanloo.

1766

Events in Russia Catherine produces her Nakaz (Instruction towards the elaboration of a code of law)/*22nd June:* Treaty of commerce and friendship with England/Death of Bestuzhev.

Events in the World Jesuits condemned in Spain/Lorraine joined to the French crown/Chevalier de la Barre executed.

Intellectual Life Rousseau visits Hume in London/Veterinary school founded at (Maisons) Alfort/St Lambert: *The Seasons*/Goldsmith: *The Vicar of Wakefield*/La Tour: *Portrait of Belle de Zuylen*/Bougainville starts his journey/Death of Nattier, Aved/Birth of Germaine Necker(future Mme de Staël), Malthus, Maine de Biran.

1767

Events in Russia 'Grand Commission' assembled to study reform plans.

Events in the World Denmark acquires Schleswig and Holstein/Revision of Sirven trial in France.

Intellectual Life Salon at the Louvre (Diderot)/Watt: Steam engine/Rousseau: *Dictionary of Music*/Priestley: *Story of Electricity*/Lessing: *Minna von Barnhelm*/Holbach: *Christianity unveiled*/Voltaire: *L'Ingénu*/Death of Malfilâtre/Birth of B. Constant, Schlegel, G. de Humboldt, Girodet, Isabey.

1768

Events in Russia Creation of Council of Empire/*December:* 'Grand Commission' dissolved/*December:* Declaration of war on Turkey.

Events in the World Boston assembly/Maupeou, French Chancellor/Beginning of Mme du Barry's period in favour/France acquires Corsica.

Intellectual Life Cook's first voyage/Quesnay: *La Physiocratie*/Carmontelle: *Dramatic proverbs*/Sedaine: *La Gageure imprévue*/Voltaire: *L'Homme aux quarante écus, Précis of the Century of Louis XV, La Princesse de Babylone*/Diderot and Mme d' Epinay relieve Grimm of the *Literary Correspondance*/Euler: *Studies in integral calculus*/Monge: *Descriptive Geometry*/Gainsborough: *Portrait of Elisa Linley*/Death of Winchelmann, Canaletto, Sterne/Birth of Chateaubriand, J. Crome.

1769

Events in Russia Beginning of Russo-Turkish war/Rumyantsov's victory at Khotin. The Russians occupy Danube principalities. Creation of paper money in Russia/*April:* Russian fleet leaves Kronstadt, and reaches the Aegean via Gibraltar.

Events in the World Death of Clement XIII/Beginning of Papacy of Clement XIV/Suppression of privileges of French East India Company.

Intellectual Life Salon at the Louvre (Diderot)/Voltaire: *History of Paris Parliament*/Birth of Cuvier, A. de Humboldt, N. Bonaparte, Lawrence.

1770

Events in Russia Rumyantsov's victory at Kagul/*5th July:* Naval victory over Turks at Chesme in the bay of Khios.
Events in the World Dumouriez' mission in Poland/Marriage of Dauphin and Marie-Antoinette/Conflict between Louis XV and Parliament/*24th December:* fall of Choiseul.

Intellectual Life Rousseau finishes his *Confessions*/Saint-Lambert at the Academy/Holbach: *The System of Nature*/Raynal: *History of European establishments in England*/Goldsmith: *The Deserted Village*/Gainsborough: *The Boy in Blue*/Death of G.B. Tiepolo, Boucher, Moncrif, Hénault/Birth of Beethoven, Holderlin, Wordsworth, Gérard, Hegel.

1771

Events in Russia Russians conquer the Crimea/Plague in Moscow.

Events in the World Abolition of servage in Savoy/Gustavus III King of Sweden/duc d'Aiguillon Secretary for foreign affairs.

Intellectual Life Salon at the Louvre (Diderot)/Poinsinet: *Le Cercle*/Bougainville: *Journey around the world*/Lavoisier analyses the composition of air/Houdon: *Diderot*/Goya decorates the cathedral at Saragossa/Death of Helvetius, L.M. Vanloo/Birth of Bichat, W. Scott, Gros.

1772

Events in Russia *January/February:* Signature of agreements with Prussia and Austria on partition of Poland/*30th May:* Armistice at Fokchany with Turks/*25th July/5th August:* First partition of Poland.

Events in the World Warren Hastings, governor of India/France partially bankrupt.

Intellectual Life Lagrange: *Postscript to Euler's algebra*/Priestley: *Observations on air*/Goldsmith: *She stoops to conquer*/Cazotte: *The Devil in Love*/Weiland: *The Gold Mirror*/Diderot finishes *Jacques the Fatalist*/Voltaire: *Ode* (on the 2nd centenary of the massacre of St Bartholomew)/Cook's second voyage/Death of Swedenborg, Duclos, Tocqué/Birth of Novalis, Coleridge, Broussais, Ricardo, Geoffroy-Saint-Hilaire, Fourier.

1773

Life of Catherine II Vasilchikov in favour, Orlov dropped/*29th September/10th October:* Marriage of Grand Duke Paul and Wilhelmina of Hess, who becomes Grand Duchess Natalia.

Events in Russia *June:* War again with Turkey/Rumyantsov victory at Choumla/Beginning of Pugachev revolt/Russian setback in Roumania/*October:* Diderot arrives in Russia.

Events in the World Clement XIV dissolves Society of Jesus/Diderot in Russia/First iron bridge at Coalbrookdale/Foundation of Grand Orient in France/Beaumarchais-Goezman affair.

Intellectual Life Salon at the Louvre/B. de St-Pierre: *Journey to the Ile de France*/Goethe: *Goetz von Berlinchingen*/Diderot replaced by Meister on the *Literary Correspondence*/Death of Piron/Birth of J. Mill.

1774

Life of Catherine II Potemkin in favour.

Events in Russia *March:* Pugachev besieges Orenburg/New Russian offensive in the Balkans/*21st July:* Treaty of Kitchuk-Kainadi with Turks/*24th August/4th September:* Pugachev defeated.

Events in the World Death of Clement XIV/*10th May:* Death of Louis XV/Accession of Louis XVI/Maurepas his close adviser/Vergeness, secretary for foreign affairs/Turgot, navy and finance: free circulation of grain, reduction of contributions to the Ferme Générale, re-establishment of Parliament.

Intellectual Life Wieland: *The Abderitans*/Goethe: *Werther*/Voltaire: *The One-Eyed Thief*/Priestley's studies on oxygen/Scheele discovers chlorine/Herschel builds his great telescope/Death of Goldsmith, Quesnay, La Condamine/Birth of Southey, C.-D. Friedrich.

1775

Events in Russia *10th/21st January:* Pugachev tortured and put to death. Order modifying the districts of the Empire/Russia cedes Bukovinia to Austria/*May:* incarceration of fake daughter of Empress Elisabeth, Princess Tarakanova.

Events in the World Beginning of American War of Independence: Washington Commander in Chief/Beginning of papacy of Pius VI/Famine in Paris: Flour war.

Intellectual Life Salon at the Louvre (Diderot)/Gentil-Bernard: *The Art of Loving*/Beaumarchais: *The Barber of Seville*/Diderot: *d'Alembert's Dream*/Sheridan: *The Rivals*/Death of Voisenon, F.-H. Drouais/Birth of Ampère, Turner, C. Mayer, Boieldieu, Schelling.

1776

Life of Catherine II Zavadovsky in favour, end of liaison with Potemkin/*15th May:* Death of Grand Duchess Natalia, Catherine's daughter-in-law, after birth of still-born child/*26th September:* Grand Duke Paul's second marriage to Sophia Dorothea of Württemburg, who becomes Grand Duchess Maria Feodorovna.

Events in the World *4th July:* American Declaration of Independence/First trade union in England/Temporary suppression of forced labour and guilds/Malesherbes resigns/Fall of Turgot/Necker attached to controller-general of Finances/Franklin in Paris.

Intellectual Life Jouffroy sails a steam-boat on the Doubs/Cook's third voyage/Beginning of publication of 4 volumes of *Supplément* to the *Encyclopedie*/Restif de la Bretonne: *The corrupted peasant and his wife*/Gibbon: *The Decline and Fall of the Roman Empire*/Halbach: *Universal Morality*/Mably: *Principles of law*/A. smith: *The Wealth of Nations*/Death of Hume, Fréron/Birth of Constable, Avogadro.

1777

Life of Catherine II The Serb, Simon Zorich in favour/*12th/23rd December:* Birth of Catherine's grandson Alexander Pavlovich, the future Alexander I.

Events in Russia *2nd April:* Alliance with Prussia/Russian difficulties in the Crimea.

Events in the World Lafayette in America/Vote on the articles of the Swiss federal constitution/Necker director general of finances/Creation of War Academy/Franco-Swiss alliance.

Intellectual Life Salon at the Louvre/*Journal de Paris,* first French daily/Lavoisier: theory of combustion/Sheridan: *School for Scandal*/Houdon: *Diana*/Pigalle: *Monument to the Maréchal de Saxe*/Death of Gresset, Natoire/Birth of Gauss, Kleist, Dupuytren.

1778

Life of Catherine II Rimsky-Korsakov in favour.

Events in the World Cook in Hawaii/Frederick II invades Bohemia/Creation of Paris Discount Bank.

Intellectual Life Rousseau finishes *Daydreams of a solitary wanderer*/Parny: *Erotic poems*/Buffon: *The Stages of Nature*/Mozart: *Divertimenti*/Lamarck: *French Flora*/Houdon: *Molière*/Death of Piranesi, Linné, Pitt, Voltaire/Birth of Foscolo, Gay-Lussan, Bretonneau.

1779

Life of Catherine II *8th May:* Birth of Catherine's second grandson, Grand Duke Constantine Pavlovich.

Events in Russia Catherine II establishes freedom of enterprise in Russia/*31st March:* New Russo-Turk agreement.

Events in the World Franco-Spanish alliance of Aranjuez/Teschen Treaty between Prussia and Austria, thanks to Catherine's mediation. Provincial assembly in Guyenne/Suppression of servage on royal estates.

Intellectual Life Goethe: *Iphigenia*/Lessing: *Nathan the Wise*/Reynolds: *Portrait of the Duchess of Devonshire*/Gluck: *Iphigenia*/Falconet: *Statue of Peter the Great*/Death of Chardin/Birth of Berzelius.

1780

Life of Catherine II Break with Rimsky-Korsakov, Lanskoy in favour/*September:* Prince de Ligne at the Russian court.

Events in Russia *June:* First meeting at Mohilev between Catherine and Joseph II/The Crown Prince of Prussia at St Petersburg/Panin dismissed.

Events in the World Rochambeau in America/Battle of Camden/End of siege of Gibraltar/Abolition in France of preparatory question.

Intellectual Life Burke: *Discourse on economic reform*/Wieland: *Oberon.*

1781

Life of Catherine II Grand Duke Paul and Grand Duchess Maria Feodorovna, Catherine's son and daughter-in-law, travel to Europe.

Events in Russia Alliance pact between Russia and Austria.

Events in the World Edict of toleration in England/De Grasse in Martinique/Tupac's revolt in Peru/Abolition of peasant hard labour in Austria/Necker resigns/Edict reserving high military rank for the nobility/Maurepas dies/Foundation of factory of the Creusot.

Intellectual Life Herschel discovers the planet Uranus/Kant: *Critique of Pure Logic*/Publication of Rousseau's *Confessions*/Schiller: *The Brigands*/Mozart: *The Abduction from the Seraglio*/Death of Lessing, Turgot, Soufflot/Birth of Laënnec.

1782

Events in the World Joseph II establishes freedom of labour and secularizes the convents. Franco-Spanish setback before Gibraltar/Peace talks between England and America/Suffren in India/Re-establishment of third twentieth tax in France.

Intellectual Life Laclos: *Les Liaisons Dangereuses*/Death of A.J. Gabriel, Metastase/Birth of Paganini, Lamennais.

1783

Life of Catherine II *12th April:* Death of Gregory Orlov/La Harpe arrives in St Petersburg/Birth of Grand Duchess Alexandra, Catherine's granddaughter.

Events in Russia Russians occupy the Crimea/Death of Panin.

Events in the World Second Pitt ministry/Peasant revolt in Bohemia/Calonne, controller general of Finances in France/Treaty of Versailles.

Intellectual Life Lavoisier: analysis of water/Cort and Onions invent puddling/Balloon flight by Montgolfier and Pilâtre de Rozier/Kant: *Prolégomènes*/Mably: *On the way to write history*/David: *Andromache*/Beaumarchais: *The Marriage of Figaro*/Gainsborough: *The Bailey Family*/Death of D'Alembert, Euler/Birth of Stendhal, W. Irving.

1784

Life of Catherine II *June:* Lanskoy's death from dysentery/Birth of Grand Duchess Helena, Catherine's granddaughter/Ermolov in favour.

Events in Russia *January:* Crimea annexed by Russia/Bill allowing private printing presses.

Events in the World Foundation of Spanish colony in Philippines/Foundation of the Bank of New York.

Intellectual Life Haüy: structure of crystals/B. de Saint-Pierre: *Studies of nature*/Herder: *Ideas on the philosophy of history*/Schiller: *Love and Intrigue*/Death of Diderot, S. Johnson/Birth of Rude.

1785

Life of Catherine II Ermolov disgraced, Mamonov in favour.

Events in Russia Statutes on the nobility and the towns.

Events in the World Peasant revolt in Hungary/Order on the sale of land in the American west/W. Hastings recalled/La Perouse expedition and disaster/Affair of the Queen's necklace/Calonne re-forms the French East India Company/Treaties of Fountainebleau/Cagliostro in Paris.

Intellectual Life Berthollet: analysis of ammonia/Cartwright invents mechanical loom/First steam cotton-mill in Nottingham/Blanchart crosses the Channel by balloon/Larmarck: *Botanical dictionary*/Mozart: *The Marriage of Figaro*/David: *The Horatian Oath*/Kant: *Foundation of Metaphysics*/Necker: *Treatise on the administration of finances*/Death of Pigalle, Mably/Birth of J. Grimm, Boechk, Manzoni.

1786

Life of Catherine II Birth of Grand Duchess Maria, Catherine's granddaughter.

Events in Russia Statute on working men's schools.

Events in the World Tax strike in Belgium/Death of Frederick II/Mexico open to international trade/Calonne's financial reforms/Mirabeau's secret mission to Berlin/First ascension of Mont Blanc.

Intellectual Life Birth of Arago, W. Grimm.

1787

Events in Russia Catherine's journey to the Crimea/*11th January:* Franco-Russian commercial treaty/Last meeting between Catherine and Stanislaus Poniatowski/Meeting between Catherine and Joseph II at Kherson.

Events in the World American parliament and vote on constitution/Warren Hastings indicted/Re-establishment of stathouderate in the Netherlands/English in Australia/In France: Death of Vergennes/Assembly of Notables/Calonne falls/Loménie de Brienne/Notables disbanded/Parliament exiled/Riots in Paris/Parliament recalled/Law giving civil rights to Protestants/Establishment of rural municipalities.

Intellectual Life Lagrange: *Analytical mechanics*/Bernardin de Saint-Pierre: *Paul et Virginie*/Schiller: *Don Carlos*/David: *The Death of Socrates*/Mozart: *Don Juan*/Death of Gluck/Birth of Ohm, Uhland.

1788

Life of Catherine II Birth of Grand Duchess Catherine, the Empress's granddaughter.

Events in Russia *May:* Russia imposes its protectorate on Poland/war between Sweden and Russia: Swedes threaten St Petersburg/*December:* siege and capture of Otchakov.

Events in the World American constitution takes effect/Trial of W. Hastings/George III's madness/Prince of Wales becomes Regent/Polish Diet/Austro-Turkish war/Treaties of Berlin and The Hague/Foundation of Sydney/In France: abolition of interrogation by torture/Esprémesnil affair/Riots in the provinces/Vizille assembly/Gathering of the States General/Bankruptcy/Brienne's disgrace/Necker recalled/Lamoignon's disgrace/Parliament recalled/Second assembly of notables.

Intellectual Life Creation of *The Times*/Kant: *Critique of practical reason*/Bentham: *Moral Principles*/Monge: *Treatise on statistics*/Goethe: *Egmont*/Houdon: *Washington*/Cherubini: *Iphigenia in Aulis*/Death of Gainsborough, Quentin de la Tour/Birth of Byron, Fresnel, Schopenhauer.

1789

Life of Catherine II Mamonov's infidelity. Plato Zubov in favour.

Events in Russia *July:* Suvorov's victory over the Turks at Fokchany/Potemkin seizes Bender Akkerman and Kilia/*14th July:* Inconclusive naval battle between the Russian and Swedish fleets before Bornholm.

Events in the world The Abbé de Fontbrune's mission to Madrid/Revolt in Belgium/Accession of Selim III/Washington president of USA/In France: Famine/Riots/Opening up of the States General/The Tennis Court Oath/Necker dismissed/Bastille stormed/Necker recalled/Comte D'Artois emigrates/The Great Terror/Abolition of privileges/Declaration of the Rights of Man/Days of October/Martial law/Wealth of clergy placed at nation's disposal/Foundation of Jacobin Club/Collapse of lending bank/Creation of assignats.

Intellectual Life Jussieu: *On the generation of Plants*/Lavoisier: *Treatise on chemistry*/David: *The Tennis Court Oath*/Death of Holbach, J.Vernet/Birth of F. Cooper, S. Pellico, Cauchy.

1790

Events in Russia *March:* Defence pact with Poland/*June:* Defeat of Russian fleet at Svenskund/*14th August:* Peace treaty of Varela between Russia and Sweden/*December:* Suvorov takes Ismail.

Events in the World Rupture of family pact/Death of Charles III: accession of Charles IV/Belgium proclaims its independence/Death of Joseph II: accession of Leopold II/In France: Foundation of Cordeliers' Club/Mirabeau sells his services to the Court/Creation of weights and measures commission/Counter-revolutionary riots/Sale of Clergy wealth/Election of departmental assemblies/Vote on the civil constitution of the clergy/Reorganization of the law/New fiscal system.

Intellectual Life Jussieu organizes the Botanical Gardens in Paris/Priestley: work on air/Kant: *Critique of judgment*/Burke: *Reflections on the French Revolution*/Goethe: *Torquato Tasso*/Mozart: *Cosi fan Tuttel*/Death of A. Smith, Ch.-N. Chochin/Birth of Lamartine.

1791

Events in Russia *August:* Start of negotiations with Turkey/Plan for expedition against India/*October:* Death of Potemkin.

Events in the World Pope condemns civil constitution of clergy/Declaration of Pillnitz/New Polish constitution/First amendments to the American Constitution/Kentucky joins Union/Autonomy for French Canadians/In France: corporations abolished/Death of Mirabeau/Depreciation of assignats/Le Chapelier Law/Louis XVI's flight and arrest at Varennes/The Assembly suspends the King/Foundation of Feuillant Club/Champ-de-Mars massacre/Tax assessment increase/Louis XVI swears to uphold the constitution/separation of the Assembly/Joining of the Legislature/Decrees against émigrés, princes and dissidents/Narbonne minister of war/Avignon rejoined to France.

Intellectual Life Lenoir creates French Museum of Monuments/Volney: *Les Ruines*/Mozart: *The Magic Flute*/Paine: *The Rights of Man*/Death of Mozart/Birth of Meyerbeer, Faraday, Grillparzer.

1792

Events in Russia *29th December 1791/9th January 1792:* Peace between Russia and Turkey at Jassy/*May:* Russians enter Poland/*July:* Envoy Genet sent back.

Events in the World French ultimatum to Austria and declaration of war/Brunswick manifesto/Battle of Valmy/French take Chambéry, Nice, Spire and Mayence/Battle of Jemmapes/Dumouriez conquers Belgium/Annexation of Savoy/Riots in England/Godoy prime minister of Spain/Gustavus III assassinated; Gustavus IV succeeds/Riots in France/Girondin ministry: Dumouriez/Rouget de Lisle: *The Marseillaise*/Decree against refractionaries/Girondin ministry deposed/*20th June:* Nation in danger/*10th August:* Louis XVI deposed. Measures against the suspects/Desertion of Lafayette/Abolition of feudal rights/September massacres/Conscription for the army/Assembly of the Convention/Secularization of the civil status/Institution of divorce/Abolition of royalty/Proceedings against Louis XVI instituted.

Intellectual Life Galvain's works on electricity/Fichte: *Critique of all revelation*/Goethe: *Roman elegies*/Schiller: *History of the Thirty Years War*/Death of Reynolds/Birth of Shelley, Pradier, V. Cousin, Rossini.

1793

Life of Catherine II *28th September:* Marriage of Grand Duke Alexander Pavovitch, Catherine's grandson, to Princess Louise of Baden.

Events in Russia *23rd January:* Second partition of Poland/*February:* Break with France/Foundation of Odessa.

Events in the World War declared on England, Holland and Spain/First coalition/Belgium and Rhineland taken/Battle of Nerwinden/Cobourg takes Condé and Valenciennes/Fall of Mayence/Siege of Landau and Perpignan/Victory of Hondschoote/Siege of Maubeuge/Victory of Wattignies/In France: the King condemned and executed/The Amalgame/Revolutionary Tribunal created/Vendée rises/Dumouriez betrayal/Public Safety Committee created/Failure of assignats/Trial and acquittal of Marat/Law of maximum/Arrest of Girondins/Vote on Constitution/Robespierre's fight with the Enragés/Marat assassinated/Embargo on exports/Suppression of universities/Mass levies/Forced borrowing/People's days/Creation of revolutionary army/Law on suspects/Trial and execution of Marie-Antoinette/Execution of Girondins/Dechristianization/Vendéans quelled/Churches closed/Free and obligatory primary education/Toulon recaptured from the English/Nice annexed.

Intellectual Life Creation of Natural History Museum/Adoption of metric system/Whitney invents cotton carding machine/Fichte: *Rectification of public judgments*/Herder: *Letters towards the progress of humanism*/Death of Goldoni, Guardi/Birth of Chasles, Lobachevsky.

1794

Events in Russia *March:* Polish insurrection, Russians driven from Warsaw and Krakow/*October:* Polish leader Kosciuszko defeated and captured/Insurrection quashed.

Events in the World Scandinavian armed neutality/Treaty of The Hague/French in Catalonia/Victory of Fleurus/Fuentarabia, Antwerp, Cologne and Coblenz captured/Franco-Prussian peace negotiations/French in Holland/Suspension of *Habeas corpus* in Scotland/Praga massacre/English annex Lahore/In France: Ventôse decrees/Cordeliers in state of insurrection/Arrest and execution of Dantonists and Hébertists/Creation of École Polytechnique/Revolution as religion/Attempts on Robespierre's life/Festival of Supreme Being/Reorganization of revolutionary tribunal/Creation of national archive/Fall of Robespierre/Separation of State and Churches/Creation of Arts and Crafts Conservatory and the Ecole Normale Supérieure/Closure of Jacobin Club/Trial and execution of Carrier/Abolition of maximum.

Intellectual Life Fichte: *Foundations of general scientific doctrines*/Condorcet: *Historical sketch of the progress of the human spirit*/Dupuis: *On the origin of all religions*/Death of Beccaria, Lavoisier, Chenier, Condorcet/Birth of Raspail.

1795

Life of Catherine II Birth of Grand Duchess Anne, Catherine's granddaughter.

Events in Russia *January:* Austro-Russian treaty/*October:* Third partition of Russia.

Events in the World Pichegru captures Dutch fleet/Treaties of Basel and The Hague/Franco-Austrian armistice/Riots in Dublin and London/Revolt in Hungary/In France: negotiations with the Chouans/Constitutional Church abandoned/Girondins recalled/Creation of School of Oriental Languages/Faubourg St Antoine disarmed/Suppression of revolutionary tribunal/White Terror/Churches reopen/Charette's revolt in Vendée. Depreciation of assignats/Vote on the Year III Constitution/Bonaparte defeats the royalists/Lakanel law on education/Creation of the Institute/Separation of convention/Installation of Directoire.

Intellectual Life J. de Maistre: *Considerations on France*/Turner: *Tintern Abbey*/Death of Cagliostro/Birth of Keats, A. Thierry, Carlyle, Barye, Ranke.

1796

Life of Catherine II Engagement broken off between Grand Duchess Alexandra, Catherine's granddaughter, and Gustavus IV of Sweden/*June:* Birth of Grand Duke Nicholas, grandson of Catherine and future Nicholas I/*16th/17th November:* death of Catherine II, accession of Paul I.

Events in Russia Russian campaign along the Caspian, Baku taken.

Events in the World Italian campaign/Treaty of Paris/Moreau and Jourdan invade Germany/Convention of Boulogne with Pope/Hoche tries to land in Ireland/Foundation of Cispaduan republic/Montenegro independence/Tennessee joins the Union/In France: Ramel Finance minister/Destruction of assignat press/Chouans repressed/Creation of land vouchers/Babeuf plot, his arrest/Law on civil rights/Bonaparte commander in chief of Italian army/Directoire rejects English peace proposals.

Intellectual Life Jenner's work on vaccine/Senefelder invents lithography/Laplace: *Exposition of system of the Universe*/Bonald: *Theory of power*/Fichte: *Principles on natural law*/Goethe: *Wilhelm Meister*/Death of Burns, Raynal/Birth of Corot.

Bibliography

Bibliography

There are hundreds of books about Catherine II and her period. I have confined myself to listing here the major works I have consulted.

I

SOURCES

CATHERINE II—*Oeuvres de l'imperatrice Catherine II* (in Russian and in French), compiled by Pypine, 12 vols. 1907.

— *Mémoires* (in French), published in 1857 by Herzen then by the Academy of Sciences in St Petersburg, and finally, in 1953, in a text edited and produced by Dominique Maroger and Pierre Audiat (Hachette).

— *Lettres d'amour de Catherine II à Potemkine,* published by Georges Oudard, Paris, Calmann-Levy, 1934.

— *Catherine II's Letters to Grimm,* edited by Grot, St Petersburg, 1878.

— *Lettres de Catherine II à Stanislas-Auguste Poniatowski, roi de Pologne. (1762-1764).* Paris, 1914.

— *Lettres de Catherine II à Voltaire et à Diderot,* quoted in the publication 'Russian Antiquity'.

— *Lettres de Catherine II au prince de Ligne.*

Foreign Office Archives in Paris. Correspondance politique de Russie, vols. LXVIII a CXXXIX.

Prince M.L. Vorontzov's Archives, Moscow, 1870–1895 (in Russian).

Collection of Works by the Imperial Society of Russian History (in Russian), vols. I a LXXII.

A Hundred Years of the Russian Court, collected letters and despatches, Berlin 1864.

ALLONVILLE, le Comte d': *Mémoires secrets,* Paris, 1838.

CASTÉRA, J. *Vie de Catherine II,* 3 vols. Paris, 1797.

CHOISEUL, Duc de: *Mémoires,* Paris, Buisson, 1790.

CORBERON, le Chevalier de: *Un diplomate français a la cour de Catherine II*, Paris, Plon, 1901.

DASHKOVA, Princesse Catherine: *Mémoires*, Paris, Mercure de France, 1966.

ENGELHARDT, L.N.: *Mémoires*, Moscow, 1863.

ESTERHAZY, Comte Valentin: *Mémoires*, Paris, Plon, 1905.

— *Lettres*, Plon, 1907.

— *Nouvelles Lettres*, Plon, 1909.

FALCONET: *Correspondance avec Catherine II*, Paris, Champion, 1921.

FREDERIC II: *Mémoires*, 2 vols. Paris, Plon, 1866.

GOLOVIN, Comtesse, née Golitsin: *Souvenirs*, Paris, Plon, 1910.

KHRAPOVITSKY: Diary (in Russian), St Petersburg, 1874.

LIGNE, Prince de: *Mémoires*, Paris, 1860.

MASSON: *Mémoires secrets sur la Russie*, 3 vols. Paris, 1802.

OBERKIRCH, Baronne d': *Mémoires*, 2 vols. Paris, 1853.

PONIATOWSKI, Stanislaus-Augustus: *Secret and Unedited Memories* Leipzig, 1862.

RADISHCHEV: *Journey from St Petersburg to Moscow* (in Russian), 1790

RIBEAUPIERRE, Comte de: *Mémoires*, in 'Archives russes', 1877.

RULHIÈRE, C. de: *Histoire ou anecdotes sur la Revolution de Russie en 1762*, Paris, 1797.

SABATIER DE CABRE: *Catherine II, her Court and Russia in 1772*, Berlin, 1861.

SÉGUR, Comte de: *Mémoires*, Paris, 1859.

SCHERER, Jean-Benoit: *Anecdotes interessantes et secretes sur la cour de Russie*, Paris, 1792.

TCHITCHAGOV, Paul: *Mémoires*, 2 vols. Paris, 1862.

TOOKE, Reverend Father M.: *Secret Mémoires*, 3 vols. Amsterdam, 1800.

VIGÉE-LEBRUN, Mme: *Souvenirs*, 3 vols. Paris, 1835–1837.

II

WORKS ON CATHERINE AND HER PERIOD

BILBASSOV, V.A.: *Story of Catherine II* (in Russian), 3 vols., Berlin, 1900.

BRIAN-CHANINOV, Nicholas: *Catherine II, Empress of Russia*, Paris, Pavot, 1932.

— *Alexandre Ier*, Paris, Bernard Grasset, 1934.

— *Histoire de Russie*, Paris, Fayard, 1929.

BRUCKNER, A.: *Story of Catherine II* (In Russian), 3 vols. St Petersburg, 1885.

—*Russian Culture in France*, 'Literary Heritage' edition (in Russian), 3 vols. Moscow, 1937.

DOUBROVIN: *Pugachev and his accomplices*, 3 vols.

GAISSINOVITCH, A.: *La Revolte de Pougatchev*, Paris, Payot, 1938.

GAXOTTE, Pierre: *Le Siecle de Louis XV*, Paris, Fayard, 1933.

— *Frederic II*, Paris, Fayard, 1938.

GREY, Ian: *The Great Catherine*.

GRUNWALD, Constantin de: *L'Assassinat de Paul Ier, tsar de Russie*, Paris, Hachette, 1960.

— *Alexandre Ier, le tsar mystique*, Paris, Amiot-Dumont, 1955.

— *Trois siecles de diplomatie russe*, Paris, Calmann-Levy, 1945.

HASLIP, JOAN: *Catherine the Great*, 1977.

HENRI-ROBERT: *Les Grands Proces de l'histoire*, IIIe, serie, Paris, Payot, 1924.

KAUS, Gina: *Catherine la Grande*, Paris, Grasset, 1934.

KOBEKO, Dimitre: *Prince Paul Petrovitch*.

KRAKOWSKI, Edouard: *Histoire de Russie*, Paris, Edition des Deux Rives, 1954.

LARIVIÈRE, Charles de: *Catherine II et la Revolution Française*, Paris, 1895.

LAVATER-SLOMAN, M.: *Catherine II et son temps*, Paris, Payot, 1952.

LEROY-BEAULIEU, A.: *L'Empire des tsars et les Russes*, Paris, 1883–1889.

LORTHOLARY: *Le Mirage russe en France au XVIIIe siecle*, Paris, Boivin, 1951.

MELGOUNOVA: *Russian Customs in the time of Catherine II, from contemporary recollections* (in Russian), Moscow, 1922.

MICHEL, R.: *Potemkine*, Paris, Payot, 1936.

MILIOUKOV, SEIGNOBOS ET EISENMANN: *Histoire de Russie*, 3 vols. Paris, Leroux, 1932–1933.

MORANE: *Paul Ier de Russie*, Paris, Plon, 1907.

OLDENBOURG, Zoe: *Catherine de Russie*, Paris, Gallimard, 1966.

OLIVIER, Daria: *Catherine la Grande*, Paris, Librairie Academique Perrin, 1965.

ORIEUX, Jean: *Voltaire*, Paris, Flammarion, 1966.

PASCAL, Pierre: *Histoire de la Russie*, Paris, 1961.

— *La Revolte de Pougatchev*, Paris, Julliard, 1971.

PINGAUD, Leonce: *Les Français en Russie et les Russes en France,* Paris, 1889.

PLATONOV, S.F.: *Histoire de Russie,* Payot, 1929.

POLOVTSOFF, A.: *Les Favoris de Catherine la Grande,* Paris, Plon, 1939.

RAMBAUD, A.: *Histoire de Russie,* 6ᵉ edition, 1913.

SAINT-PIERRE, Michel de: *Le Drame des Romanov,* Paris, Robert Laffont, 1967.

SCHIDLER, N.: *Histoire anecdotique de Paul Iᵉʳ,* paris, Calmann-Levy, 1899.

SÉGUR, Comte A. de: *Vie du Comte Rostopchine,* Paris, 1871.

SOLOVEITCHIK, G.: *Potemkine,* Paris, Gallimard, 1940.

SOLOVIOV: *History of Russia* (in Russian), St Petersburg.

TCHOULKOV, G.: *Les Derniers Tsars autocrates,* Paris, Payot, 1928.

TEGNY, Edmond: *Catherine II et la princesse Dachkov,* Paris, 1860.

VALLOTTON, Henry: *Catherine II,* Paris, Fayard, 1955.

WALISZEWSKI, K.: *Le Roman d'une impératrice,* Paris, Plon, 1893.
— *Autour d'un trone,* Paris, Plon, 1894.

WORMSEV, Olga: *Catherine II,* Paris, le Seuil, 1962.
— *Catherine II,* Club français du Livre, 1957.

Index

THE BEST IN BIOGRAPHY FROM GRANADA PAPERBACKS

Maurice Ashley
Charles II   £1.25 ☐

John Brooke
King George III   £1.95 ☐

Margaret Forster
The Rash Adventurer   £1.25 ☐

Antonia Fraser
Mary Queen of Scots   £3.95 ☐
Cromwell: Our Chief of Men   £2.50 ☐

Elizabeth Jenkins
Elizabeth the Great   95p ☐

Eric Linklater
The Prince in the Heather   £1.50 ☐

Douglas Liversidge
Prince Philip   £1.00 ☐
The Queen Mother   £1.95 ☐
Prince Charles   £1.50 ☐

Peter Townsend
The Last Emperor   £1.95 ☐

P23481

THE BEST IN BIOGRAPHY FROM GRANADA PAPERBACKS

Dirk Bogarde

A Postillion Struck by Lightning	£1.50	☐
Snakes and Ladders	£1.25	☐

Elizabeth Longford

Winston Churchill	£2.50	☐
Wellington: Pillar of State	£1.95	☐
Wellington: The Years of the Sword	£1.25	☐

Jasper Ridley

Lord Palmerston	£1.50	☐

Han Suyin

The Morning Deluge *(Volume I)*	£1.75	☐
The Morning Deluge *(Volume II)*	£1.25	☐
Wind in the Tower	£1.75	☐
The Crippled Tree	95p	☐
A Mortal Flower	£1.50	☐
Birdless Summer	£1.25	☐

Kim Philby

My Silent War	£1.50	☐

Dusko Popov

Spy/Counter Spy	£1.25	☐

P22481

THE BEST IN BIOGRAPHY FROM GRANADA PAPERBACKS

David Cairns
The Memoirs of Berlioz   £3.95 ☐

John Chancellor
Wagner   £1.95 ☐

Max Jones & John Chilton
Louis   95p ☐

Alfred Einstein
Schubert   £1.50 ☐
Mozart   £1.95 ☐

Newman Flower
Handel   £1.25 ☐

F E Halliday
Thomas Hardy   £1.50 ☐

Alan Kendal
Vivaldi   £1.50 ☐

Jack Lindsay
Turner   90p ☐

Bryan Magee
Aspects of Wagner   95p ☐

Graham Reynolds
Constable: The Natural Painter   90p ☐

P21481

HISTORY – NOW AVAILABLE IN GRANADA PAPERBACKS

Ronald Auguet
The Roman Games   £1.00 ☐

N Branson & M Heinemann
Britain in the 1930s   £1.25 ☐

Angus Calder
The People's War   £1.50 ☐

Frederick Engels
The Condition of the Working Class in England   £1.95 ☐

Christopher Farman
The General Strike   £1.95 ☐

Joyce Marlow
The Tolpuddle Martyrs   £1.25 ☐

Thomas Packenham
The Year of Liberty   £1.75 ☐

Christopher Sinclair-Stevenson
Inglorious Rebellion   £1.25 ☐

P27481

THE BEST IN BIOGRAPHY FROM GRANADA PAPERBACKS

Ernle Bradford
Nelson: The Essential Hero   £1.95   ☐

James Cameron
Point of Departure   £1.50   ☐

Larry Collins & Dominique Lapierre
Or I'll Dress You in Mourning   £1.25   ☐

Ladislas Farago
Patton: Ordeal and Triumph   £1.50   ☐

F E Halliday
Thomas Hardy   £1.50   ☐

Hermann Hesse
A Pictorial Biography   £1.50   ☐

A E Hotchner
Papa Hemingway   £1.25   ☐

All these books are available to your local bookshop or newsagent, or can be ordered direct from the publisher. Just tick the titles you want and fill in the form below.

Name ....

Address ....

....

Write to Granada Cash Sales, PO Box 11, Falmouth, Cornwall TR10 9EN
Please enclose remittance to the value of the cover price plus:
UK: 40p for the first book, 18p for the second book plus 13p per copy for each additional book ordered to a maximum charge of £1.49.
BFPO and EIRE: 40p for the first book, 18p for the second book plus 13p per copy for the next 7 books, thereafter 7p per book.
OVERSEAS: 60p for the first book and 18p for each additional book.
Granada Publishing reserve the right to show new retail prices on covers, which may differ from those previously advertised in the text or elsewhere.